The Personal History of
Samuel Johnson

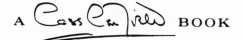 A **BOOK**

The Personal History of
Samuel Johnson

Christopher Hibbert

HARPER & ROW, PUBLISHERS
New York   Evanston   San Francisco   London

FIRST U.S. EDITION

STANDARD BOOK NUMBER: 06-011879-2

LIBRARY OF CONGRESS CATALOG CARD NUMBER: 70-138734

Author's Note

This narrative of the personal life of Dr Johnson is based entirely on published material, or, in the case of the eleven volumes of Aleyn Lyell Reade's *Johnsonian Gleanings* and the nineteen volumes of *The Private Papers of James Boswell from Malahide Castle* (now gradually being superseded by *The Yale Editions of The Private Papers of James Boswell*), on privately printed material. Since these and all the most recent editions of the principal sources for Johnson's life and work have detailed indexes, it has not been considered worthwhile to burden a book of this nature with references. The only important source which has not so far been printed is Mrs Thrale's 'Children's Book or rather Family Book' which I have been allowed to consult and to quote from with the kind consent of its owners, Donald and Mary Hyde of New York.

I am in no sense a Johnsonian scholar, and my debt to those scholars upon whose work and generous advice I have been able to rely is naturally very great. I am particularly indebted to Professor James L. Clifford, Dr L. F. Powell, the late Professor Joseph Wood Krutch and to Dr J. D. Fleeman of Pembroke College, Oxford. I am most grateful to Mr George Walker and to Mr Hamish Francis for having read the book in proof and for having given me much useful advice for its improvement.

For their great help in a variety of ways I want also to thank Mr K. K. Yung of the Johnson Birthplace Museum, Lichfield, Miss Margaret Eliot of Dr Johnson's House, Gough Square, Mrs John Rae, Mrs Sheila Kidd, and, finally, my wife for having compiled the comprehensive index.

C. H.

To Phyllis Auty

Contents

List of Illustrations

Acknowledgements

The author and publishers wish to acknowledge the following for permission to reproduce photographs: Radio Times Hulton Picture Library for Nos 1, 2, 10, 13, 22, 34; National Portrait Gallery for Nos 5, 11, 19, 20, 21, 23, 27, 31, 32, 35, 37, 38, 39; Dr Johnson's House Trust for Nos 14, 17, 18, 25, 26, 30; British Museum for Nos 28, 33; Hyde Collection, New Jersey, for No 7; Beaverbrook Art Gallery Collection, Fredericton, N.B., Canada, for No 24. Nos 3, 4, 6, 7, 8,9, 12, 15, 16, 29, 36 are from an early edition of Boswell's *Life of Johnson*

Part I

1709—1755

I

The Bookseller's Son

'He was then lean and lank so that his immense structure of bones was hideously striking to the eye, and the scars of the scrofula were deeply visible.'
                                                    Lucy Porter

Early one afternoon in 1764 Ozias Humphry, a young portrait painter, was taken by a friend to visit 'the most famous author in England'. He was conducted down the Strand, into Inner Temple Lane, up some narrow stairs, through 'three very dirty rooms and into a little one that looked like an old counting-house'. In this last room were five ragged chairs of four different sets, a very large deal writing-desk, an old walnut table, and Dr Johnson rolling about in one of the chairs as he ate his breakfast.

Humphry was astonished by the spectacle. The great author was a huge, scarred man dressed in 'a dirty brown coat and waistcoat, with breeches that were brown also (though they had been crimson), and an old black wig. His shirt collar and sleeves were unbuttoned; his stockings were down about his feet which had on them, by way of slippers, an old pair of shoes.' He did not speak for some time, concentrating on his tea and his bread and butter, and Humphry could 'hardly help thinking him a madman for some time as he sat waving over his breakfast like a lunatic'. But then, at last, he began to talk; and his visitor sat enthralled. It was as though he were reading from a book. Everything, Humphry said, was 'as *correct* as a *second edition*'.

3

Samuel Johnson was born in the little cathedral town of Lichfield in Staffordshire on 18 September 1709 at about four o'clock in the afternoon. His mother was over forty and this was her first child; it was a long and difficult labour. 'Here is a brave boy!' announced the man-midwife comfortingly when at last he had the baby in his hands; but he could not have felt other than concerned, for the child was almost dead and could not at first be made to cry. It was decided that the christening must take place without delay.

The poor weak little creature that survived was put out to a wet-nurse. His eyes were infected; an inflamed swelling rose and broke on his back; and, through his wet-nurse's milk it was supposed, he contracted scrofula, a tubercular disease that necessitated an operation on the glands of his neck and left him scarred for life. Later he developed smallpox and this, too, left permanent scars. His aunt Jane confessed that 'she would not have picked such a poor creature up in the street'.

As soon as his mother was well enough, she went to visit him. The wet-nurse, a former maidservant married to a bricklayer, lived in George Street which was only a few minutes' walk from the Johnson house; so Mrs Johnson was able to go there frequently. Anxious not to be thought fussy by the people of the town she took a different route each time; and to make sure that the wet-nurse was taking every possible care of her little baby she often left a fan or a glove behind so that she would have an excuse to go back when least expected.

Sarah Johnson was a well-intentioned woman, practical, sensible, domestic and unintellectual, with little charm and less beauty. She was very proud of her family connections, of her father, Cornelius Ford, who had owned land and had a private library, of her great-uncle, Henry, who was a barrister, of her uncle Joseph, a well-known physician, and of her rich cousin, Mrs Elizabeth Harriotts, who lived in a manor house in Warwickshire. She spoke of them all, and of her other well-to-do relations so often, contrasting them with the far humbler origins of the family into which she had married, that her husband was exasperated.

Michael Johnson's family was certainly obscure and he did not choose to talk about it. His father, who had worked on the land, had moved to Lichfield in 1664 and had died eight years later, leaving an impoverished widow and four young children. Michael, the eldest child, had been educated by a local charity which had paid for him to be apprenticed to a London stationer. Thereafter he had done well for himself; he had opened a shop of his own in Lichfield's main street in 1681, and had eventually become one of the leading citizens of the town, prominent in its local affairs, a respected member of the Corporation. He had built himself a substantial, four-storeyed house with eleven bedrooms on the corner of Sadler Street and Breadmarket Street facing the cobbled market-place and St Mary's parish church. In the shop, which was on the ground floor of the house, he sold prints and wallpaper, patent medicines and books, as well as stationery. He also had a small but successful parchment factory on the outskirts of the town to the east of the Cathedral, and branches of his shop—or at least stalls in the markets—at Uttoxeter and Ashby-de-la-Zouch. Although, therefore, Sarah 'had no value for his relations', as her son was later to put it, she could not but respect the position Michael Johnson had made for himself, nor but consider him, when at the age of forty-nine he asked her to marry him, an agreeable, reliable, sober bachelor, a satisfactory match for a spinster already middle-aged herself.

They did not get on very well together, though. It was not just that Sarah would talk so much about her family; she would also try to talk to him as often as she could about his business; and since she did not understand the trade and never read books, he found her suggestions, enquiries and complaints so irritating that he could scarcely bring himself to reply to them. Also, Sarah soon discovered that her husband's finances were far from being as stable as his position in the town and his large house led people to believe; he was in debt, and his reluctance to talk about his affairs stemmed as much from his incapacity to set them right as from her own nagging interference.[1] Being constantly in debt, he endeavoured to impose a strict economy in the household expenses. He forbade her, for instance, to receive visits from her neighbours when he was out, for this would mean giving them tea, and tea was outrageously expensive. 'My father and mother,' their son was later to comment sadly, 'had not much happiness from each other.'

Soon after his second birthday Sam was taken to London by his mother to be touched by Queen Anne and thus, it was hoped, to be cured of his scrofula. For Sir John Floyer, Lichfield's distinguished doctor who had once been one of Charles II's physicians, was a confirmed believer in the miraculous properties of the monarch's hands. So, daring to hope for a speedy cure, and with a doctor's note, a certificate from the parson to the effect that her son had not been touched before, and with two guineas sewn inside the lining of her petticoat for fear lest the stage-coach should be stopped by highwaymen, Mrs Johnson left Lichfield for London via Birmingham towards the end of March 1712.

In later life Johnson could remember little of this journey, though he had some recollection of being sick in the coach, and of two women

5

passengers, one of them fondling him, the other being 'disgusted'. He and his mother stayed with one of his father's bookseller friends over a shop off Aldersgate Street, but he could not recall much about this either. In a 'little dark room behind the kitchen, where the jack weight fell through a hole in the floor', he played with a bit of string and a ball, and he seemed to think there was a dog, called Chops, that jumped over a stick. But perhaps, he had to admit, he did not really remember these things, just the talk about them afterwards. Nor could he say that he really remembered Queen Anne, to whom he was presented at St James's Palace on 30 March, though he had a 'confused but somehow a sort of solemn recollection of a lady in diamonds, and a long black hood'. But he greatly prized the golden touchpiece she gave him, a thin medallion on a white ribbon; and he wore it round his neck until he died. He also prized a speckled linen frock which his mother bought him, known grandly as his 'London frock', and a small silver cup and spoon marked not merely with the initials '*S. J.*' which were the same as hers, but more specifically '*Sam. J.*' so that there would be no mistake about their ownership when she died. Apparently she spent more money than she should have done, as on the homeward journey they travelled in the rough and rattling stage wagon, an economy which Mrs Johnson justified by saying that Sam's incessant cough would disturb the other passengers if they went by coach.

Six months after their return to Lichfield, Mrs Johnson gave birth to another son, Nathaniel; and Sam did not take kindly to this rival for his mother's affections. Often he felt that his mother loved the new baby better than himself; he was jealous, naughty and unhappy. And his mother, a woman of narrow intellect and rather blunted sensibilities, exacerbated his emotional sufferings. Sometimes she would indulge him by letting him have his own way, by giving him things that would normally be denied to children in homes such as his; at other times she would lecture him crossly about his bad behaviour without giving him any guidance as to what good behaviour was and why it was to be desired. Occasionally, it seems, she beat him. He could not bring himself to respect her, although he afterwards claimed that he loved her and perhaps, indeed, he really did love her. But as he grew older his outbursts of irritation with her became both more violent and more frequent. 'And one day,' so he recorded, 'when in anger she called me a puppy, I asked her if she knew what they called a puppy's mother.'

To escape such quarrels his father would leave the house and ride off, with the excuse that he had business to attend to. Often enough he did have business to attend to, for as well as the parchment factory and the branches or stalls at Uttoxeter and Ashby-de-la-Zouch, on market days he had stalls at various other towns, including Birmingham which at that time had no permanent book-shop. He also travelled long distances to the houses of valued customers with books in his saddlebags, had to attend all the local auction sales, conducted regular sales himself, and went as far as Scotland and Ireland to buy skins for the parchment factory. So Sam did not see much of a father who was 'little at home'.

What he did see of him he did not much like; certainly he did not carry any happy memories of him into his adult life. For Michael seems to have been a dour father, remote and reserved, preoccupied with his affairs, which his unmethodical methods made far more troublesome and far less remunerative than they should have been. He was also morbidly afraid that he might suffer from a mental breakdown. He was, in the son's opinion, 'a foolish old man' in that whenever they visited relatives or relatives came to see them, he would boast about his elder son's precocious accomplishments, and make him repeat the verses he had recently learned or the knowledge he had acquired. Sam, indeed, grew so to dread these injunctions 'to exhibit his knowledge' to his relations, or to the few friends his parents had, that he 'used to run up a tree when company was expected, that [he] might escape the plague of being showed off to them'. He remembered with particular displeasure the evening of Nathaniel's christening when he was made to repeat the words 'Lit-tle Nat-ty', syllable by syllable, to the assembled godparents and guests.

Certainly Sam was precocious and had a remarkably retentive memory. He quickly learned to read and what he read was soon stored up in his mind word for word. One morning, as part of his religious instruction, he was required by his mother to get the collect for the day by heart. Having given the little boy this duty she began to climb the stairs, but before she had reached the second-floor landing, she heard her son walking up behind her. 'What's the matter?' she asked him. 'I can say it,' he said, and he did say it without a mistake.

Most of the instruction he received from his mother was of this nature. In her bed of a morning she would tell him of Heaven and Hell and the everlasting punishment that awaited the transgressor; and to fix the lesson in his memory she made him repeat what she had told him to the manservant.

From the maidservant, Sam learned less disturbing things, in particular the heroic tale of St George and the Dragon, which she recounted to him as he sat on her knee. *That* was the sort of story that babies liked to hear, he used to say, a story about giants and castles; they did not want to be told about other babies or to read moralising homilies. Of course, he agreed, books like *Tommy Prudent* and *Goody Two-Shoes* were sold in large numbers; but 'remember always that the parents buy the books, and that the children never read them'.

As soon as he was old enough, Sam was sent to a nearby dame's school kept by a widow who also had a sweet shop. He was taken and brought back by the maid, not so much because he was so young—the school was less than a hundred and fifty yards away across the market-place—but because his eyesight was so bad that his mother feared he would fall into the street drain or even into the market-place sewer. One day the maid did not come to fetch him and, refusing to be accompanied by the dame, he determined to find his own way home, getting down on all fours when he came to the street drain to make sure he did not stumble into it. As he approached his house he became aware that the dame was following him to see that he came to no harm. Immediately he flew at her in a fury of resentment, punching and kicking her as hard as he could.

As well as being extremely short-sighted he was also almost deaf in his left ear; and an incision which had been made in his left arm to drain an infection had not yet been allowed to heal. At the age of seven and a half, however, he was deemed strong enough to go to Lichfield Grammar School, a quarter of a mile away across the footpaths through the fields.

There was just one large schoolroom in the Grammar School with rows of desks from wall to oak-panelled wall, and a single, taller desk for the masters at each end. The master in charge of the lower school was a kind-hearted, over-worked man named Humphrey Hawkins who was obliged to take on other jobs such as washing the choirboys' surplices, to supplement his meagre income of £10 a year. He had come to the school as a junior usher thirty-two years before, was still an usher when Sam came in 1717, and remained an usher for the remaining twenty-four years of his life.

Yet Hawkins was a first-rate teacher, his pupils thought, patient, concerned and kind; and he contrived to make the relentlessly tedious curriculum—devoted almost exclusively to Latin—as interesting as possible. Sam had no difficulty with his lessons, and he actually looked forward to the examinations on Thursdays and Saturdays, and to the days when he had to recite the Catechism which he had already been taught by his mother.

His defective eyesight prevented him from joining in the other boys' games, but his already strong will and increasingly strong body ensured that he was not teased or bullied for his infirmities, and he made friends easily enough. His particular friends, now and later, were Edmund Hector, a nephew of the man-midwife who had delivered him, and John Taylor, a boarder, the son of a Derbyshire lawyer.

He enjoyed these days, the walks home from school, jumping over the fence rails, vaulting over the stiles and climbing trees in the fields. He enjoyed the holidays, too—the annual fairs, the crowds that came to Lichfield races, the pageants and processions, the summer afternoons swimming in the fast-flowing stream that ran through the green meadows and into the Trent, eating apples and plums in the orchard behind his wet-nurse's house, the winter mornings when 'he took a pleasure in being drawn upon the ice by a boy barefooted, who pulled him along by a garter fixed round him'. He did not much like Sundays, though, gloomy days when there were family readings from the Bible, when his mother shut him up in his room to read *The Whole Duty of Man,* and when he had to go to church and sit in the family pew beside his tall, devout father who was a magistrate now as well as a Brother of the Corporation and thus required to wear a gown—which would not have been at all displeasing to Michael Johnson, for, in his son's opinion, he was a man of 'much vanity'.

Then one day some stones from the steeple fell on to the church roof, and it was decided that the steeple would have to be pulled down and rebuilt and the building closed until the repairs were finished. His mother and father and Nathaniel thereafter went to services in the chapel of St John's Hospital to which the church pews were removed. Sam, however, refused to go there with them, using as an excuse his bad eyes and the scars on his neck and the lower part of his face which strangers stared at; and he was allowed to walk in the fields instead and, if it was warm enough, to read there.

One summer when he was nine and his brother six, they were sent for a fortnight on their own to Birmingham where they stayed at first with their uncle, Nathaniel Ford, a clothier, and then with another uncle, John Harrison, a saddler, who had married their mother's elder sister, now dead, and was looked after by his niece Sally. Sam liked Sally and he liked uncle Harrison's daughter, Phoebe, who was about his own age; but he did not care for the uncle himself: 'He was a very mean and vulgar man, drunk every night, but drunk with little drink, very peevish, very proud, very ostentatious, but, luckily, not rich.'

He thought his aunt Ford vulgar, too, but she was good-natured as well as vulgar, and she made a fuss of the boys, who were consequently happy there. In later years memories of his visit to Birmingham came back to Sam with a strange clarity: his eating so much of a boiled leg of lamb that aunt Ford marvelled at his appetite; Sally dancing in the kitchen while he wrote a letter by the window; a whip with a rattle on it; a new watch which his father had in his pocket when he came to take them home, a watch that was not paid for and had to be sent back when the time allowed for approval had expired; his father demeaning him by telling the ostler that he had 'two *boys* under his care'.

In the new term Sam found himself in the upper part of the school. He cried at having to leave kind Mr Hawkins and to come before a 'peevish and ill-tempered' young usher, the Rev Edward Holbroke. This Cambridge graduate appeared to think he was cast for a more important role in life and took little interest in his duties which he, therefore, performed in the most perfunctory manner. Far more intimidating than Holbroke, however, was the formidable headmaster, the Rev John Hunter, to whom the boys had to recite their lessons on Friday afternoons. Hunter was 'very severe, and wrongheadedly severe'; he beat the boys 'unmercifully', making no distinction between idleness and ignorance. He would ask a boy a question and if he could not answer it, 'without considering whether he had an opportunity of knowing how to answer it', he would have his victim held down by two other boys over a three-legged stool—always kept in a permanent position in the schoolroom for the purpose—and then, announcing, 'This I do to save you from the gallows', he would flog him savagely, sometimes with the victim's trousers pulled down as an additional humiliation.

In later life Johnson was to express his approval of beating in schools in the most categorical terms, since he felt convinced that what boys might 'gain at one end' by its abolition they would 'lose at the other'.[2] But Hunter was not merely severe; 'a master ought to be severe. He was cruel.' Whenever he entered the schoolroom, dressed as always in his gown and cassock 'with his wig full dressed', the boys gazed in universal trepidation upon his stern, relentless face. The only way to please him that the boys were able to discover was to pander to his sportsman's instincts by telling him where a covey of partridges might be found. According to one of his contemporaries, Sam, perhaps 'from being a boy of genius', was treated less roughly than his fellow-pupils; but he was nevertheless as frightened of Hunter as they were and 'whenever in a state of delinquency, from whatever cause, he used to enter the school with his back to his master, and to sneak along to his seat in that direction'. He confessed that the very sight of Hunter's granddaughter made him tremble, so strong was the family resemblance. All the same, Sam recognised Hunter's competence. He was a genuine scholar, which his assistant Holbroke so evidently was not, and he did succeed, for all the violence of his methods, in turning out knowledgeable pupils. He did not actually teach them, Johnson had to admit; but 'he *whipped* and they learned'. Certainly Hunter's list of old boys was uncommonly distinguished for so small a school, and included from Samuel Johnson's years of attendance, a bishop, an archdeacon, a chief justice, a poet and a celebrated doctor. The doctor, Robert James, who, although said to have been drunk every day for twenty years, compiled a medical dictionary in three stout volumes and invented a famous fever powder which was prescribed for George III.

Of all Hunter's pupils Sam Johnson stood out as the most remarkable scholar. 'They never thought to raise me by comparing me to anyone,' he proudly recalled; 'they never said, Johnson is as good a scholar as such a one; but such a one is as good a scholar as Johnson; and this was said but of one, of [Theophilus] Lowe; and I do not think he *was* as good a scholar.' Certainly Sam's reliable knowledge was much called upon by the other boys, who, as one of them recorded, 'endeavoured by every boyish piece of flattery to gain his assistance' by calling for him at his house every morning, three at a time. When Sam had finished his breakfast of oatmeal porridge, which was eaten in the basement kitchen where the family spent most of their time—it being the only room in the house where there was a fire, except on Sundays—the three boys would give him a triumphant ride to school on their backs.

Sam's knowledge was not gained easily, for he was incorrigibly, constitutionally lazy. Already he found it a dreadful effort to get out of bed in the morning; and, as his friend Edmund Hector said, he could never settle down to his homework until the very last minute. He still did not play games, but, as he later remarked to a friend, it was extraordinary 'how wonderfully well he had contrived to be idle without them'. Once he had started work, however, he could get through it with remarkable speed and accuracy. Yet while he took pride in this speed and his remarkable memory, he was anxious that the other boys should not consider him a swot: he took trouble to ensure that they did not see him studying, encouraged them to believe that he gained his knowledge by a kind of intuitive perception. Once when he found that he had completed almost twice as many exercises as the rest of the class, he declined to show them all to the master, keeping some of them hidden in a drawer in his father's shop.

So the 'long, lank, lounging' boy with the scars on his neck and his ungainly walk and his bad eyes and deaf ear was popular with his fellow pupils. He was rather peculiar, they had to agree, sometimes moody, already an eccentric: occasionally on walks he would talk to himself rather than to his companions; and it seems that two brothers who once invited him to their house were reprimanded by their father for bringing home so 'disagreeable a driveller' whose appearance was one of 'idiocy'.

The impression of idiocy he made upon some strangers was emphasised by his convulsive restlessness. He evidently found it difficult if not impossible to sit still. Although in later life one friend said of him that he 'could sit motionless, when he was told so to do, as well as any other man', most people agreed that the infirmity was 'of the convulsive kind, and of the nature of the distemper called St Vitus's dance', described by the seventeenth-century medical authority, Thomas Sydenham, as manifesting itself 'by halting or unsteadiness of one of the legs, which the patient draws after him like an ideot. If the hand of the same side be applied to the breast, or any other part of the body, he cannot keep it a moment in the same posture, but it will be drawn into a different one by a convulsion, notwithstanding all his efforts to the contrary.' Even when he was reading, with the book held close to his face to enable him to distinguish the type, Sam constantly rolled his big body about from side to side, adopting the most awkward-looking postures and rocking his head spasmodically.

He read a great deal. He was fond of romances of chivalry and of the plays of Shakespeare, and he was profoundly affected by what he read. He was so shocked by Cordelia's death in *King Lear* that he could scarcely bear to look at the closing scenes of the play again until he was obliged to do so as its editor. The first time he read the ghost scene in *Hamlet* he was so frightened he ran out of the basement kitchen and up the stairs to the street to have people of flesh and blood about him. And once when he was searching the shelves of his father's shop for some apples he thought his brother had hidden there, he became so absorbed in a volume of Petrarch that he quite forgot his hunger. Yet he rarely finished a book; he hardly ever got to the end of a poem. His eye skimmed over the lines, the pages were turned with astonishing speed, his capacious memory retained the substance of what he had read. But before the end was reached he would put the book aside and pick up another, or go out to walk in the fields or compose something of his own.[3]

He could not bring himself to write many of these compositions down; he was content to recite them to his school friends. The poems he did write down—some stanzas, for example, 'On a Daffodill, the First Flower the Author Had Seen that Year', written in the manner of Herrick when Sam was fourteen or fifteen, and an ode on 'Friendship' composed at about the same time—were of unusual promise, but there were very few of them. He remained constitutionally incapable of much sustained effort; he was in need of stimulation; he was bored.

At last stimulation was provided for him from an unexpected source. When he was sixteen he met, evidently for the first time, his cousin Cornelius Ford, son of his uncle Joseph, the well-to-do physician.

Cornelius Ford, who was later to achieve notoriety as the convivial pipe-smoking parson who presides over the punch bowl at the drunken party in Hogarth's *A Modern Midnight Conversation*, was at this time thirty-one. After a distinguished career at Cambridge, where he was elected to a fellowship at Peterhouse, he had fallen a delighted victim to the expensive pleasures of London society. In order to pay off his debts he had married the daughter of a rich Quaker ironmaster, thirteen years older than himself; and in order at the same time to retrieve his character, he had taken holy orders. While waiting for some patron to offer him a desirable benefice, he was living at Pedmore, near Stourbridge in Worcestershire, in a house that had belonged to his father. Here Sam was invited to stay in the autumn of 1725.

He found Cornelius so witty, so worldly, so different from his parents' staid acquaintances in Lichfield, so marvellously invigorating a companion, so exciting an informant about London literary society, so knowledgeable a guide to the classics, that he was immediately captivated by him. And Cornelius in his turn found his young, clumsy unprepossessing cousin as gifted a conversationalist as men twice his age, a companion whose presence at the dinner table provided a pleasant relief from the rather tedious society of his worthy wife. So taken with each other were they, indeed, that Sam stayed on at Pedmore week after week, hearing about Philip Stanhope and Alexander Pope, of the London theatres and the London taverns, improving his Latin and Greek, talking about Congreve and Addison and Prior, receiving sound advice to seek general knowledge, to 'study the principles of everything'.

There was 'no need perhaps to turn over leaf by leaf', he was told, 'but grasp the trunk hard and you will shake all the branches'. He was also advised 'to dispute no man's claim to conversational excellence', not to be over-determined to win every argument—advice of which Sam was no doubt already in need and was certainly unable afterwards always to follow. Perhaps, also, Ford was able to allay some of Sam's religious doubts which had assailed him since the age of ten. For wanton as his behaviour had been in the past, and was to be in the future, Ford was sincere in his own religion. The conversation might become wild at his table when his guests had drunk as heavily as it was his own habit to do, but he never condoned any sort of profanity. At the first hint of it he would protest resignedly: 'So you are resolved, I see, to send the poor parson to bed.' Whether or not they discussed his religious doubts, Sam seems to have resolved the most troublesome of them while at Pedmore. At Lichfield he had come to be 'a sort of lax talker' about religion, and had said silly or outrageous things to his mother for which he later thought he ought to have been whipped. After his visit to Pedmore he wrote a long poem about St Simon and St Jude which displays a depth of religious feeling remarkable in a boy of his age.

The visit extended beyond the holidays and into the school term, through the winter and into the spring of 1726, and still Sam did not go home to Lichfield. When he did return in June, John Hunter was so displeased by his lengthy absence that he refused to have him back at the grammar school. Less than perturbed by this, Sam gladly accepted a place at the King Edward VI School, Stourbridge, a school which had benefited from the generosity of the family of Cornelius Ford's half-brother, Gregory Hickman, a leading citizen of the town.

The headmaster of this new school, the Rev John Wentworth, was an Oxford graduate and a sound classical scholar, though not unduly devoted to the task of imparting his knowledge to the pupils: he was eventually dismissed by the governors for taking too many holidays. Discipline in the school, where lessons began at six o'clock in the morning, was nevertheless strict, the boys being required to speak to each other in Latin when walking in the streets of the town and being flogged for failing to do so.

Sam seems to have helped in the teaching of the younger boys in return for his own education by Wentworth and his keep with the other boarders in the headmaster's house. He was, as at Lichfield, the best scholar in the school, so gifted, indeed, that the headmaster thought some of his best exercises—translations from Virgil, Horace and the *Iliad*—worth preserving. But Sam was unhappy at Stourbridge; he did not get on well with the headmaster, and after six months he left.

He was seventeen now, and forced to accept the fact that his formal education was over. His father had recently been elected senior bailiff, an office roughly equivalent to that of mayor. But his financial affairs were in a worse state than ever; he was over four years in arrears with his taxes, and he was reduced to borrowing from friends. There could therefore be no question of a university education for Sam, who had to go into his father's business.

Sam did not take kindly to bookselling. He learned how to bind books, an essential craft in days when books were normally issued in sheets and bound according to the customer's requirements; but he was not a success as a salesman, for his manner in the shop was far from gracious and he was often so absorbed in reading the stock himself that he did not even notice the people waiting to be served. He read widely, in Latin as easily as in English, and in all manner and variety of books, or rather, as he put it himself, he 'looked into' them, particularly those 'which were not commonly known at the universities, where they seldom read any books but which are put into their hands by their tutors'.

There were some customers, however, who recognised in the uncouth figure of the big youth with the scarred face, with the rambling gait, the clumsy gestures and the pronounced Staffordshire accent, a remarkable personality. At Stourbridge he had been asked out to dinner by Cornelius Ford's wealthy relations and well-to-do friends, and although he 'had never sought to please', as he afterwards protested, his intellect and gifts had soon been recognised. So were they, too, at Lichfield. He was entertained by the town clerk, Theophilus Levett, by the family of Peter Garrick, a retired army officer who had married the daughter of one of the Cathedral clergy, and by the rich bachelor, Gilbert Walmesley, who lived in a handsome house in the Cathedral Close. At the tables of these and other of Lichfield's more prominent citizens, Sam was a welcome guest, a little inclined to be overbearing in conversation, it was allowed, but, when not in one of those dark and gloomy moods that occasionally overwhelmed him, the most amusing company. He liked to laugh and to make others laugh; he was a skilful mimic; and his turns of phrase, carefully ordered and orotund without being unduly grandiloquent, were considered remarkable coming from one so young. He was attentive to ladies whom he obviously liked, and to whom he himself was not unattractive, for all his physical peculiarities. He already seemed perfectly at his ease in the best and most polite society.

The house where he felt most at home and most happy was that of Gilbert Walmesley, son of a former Member of Parliament for Lichfield and himself the registrar of the ecclesiastical court. He was forty-seven at the time of Sam's first visit—he did not marry until he was fifty-six—but he delighted in the company of bright young men such as Robert James, now studying medicine at Cambridge, and Samuel Johnson. Both were regular guests at his beautiful house where David Garrick, the gay, exuberant, intelligent ten-year-old son of Captain Peter Garrick, who lived nearby, was also a welcome visitor.

Walmesley was a scholar whose studies had been so various that Sam could not 'name a man of equal knowledge. His acquaintance with books was great'—he was one of Michael Johnson's best customers. At the same time, in the opinion of John Hunter's granddaughter, he was 'the finest gentleman in Lichfield'. But he was also what Sam described as a 'violent Whig', almost fanatical in his political opinions; and although Sam's own political views were not yet as firmly fixed as they were later to become, he argued the Tory case with 'great eagerness'. His eagerness, as he himself admitted, was not always due to his own convictions as to his delight in argument for argument's sake. 'When I was a boy,' he later confessed, 'I used always to choose the wrong side of a debate, because most ingenious things (that is to say, most new things) could be advanced upon it.' Sometimes Sam's arguments, his categoric contradictions of all that his host quite as dogmatically asserted, made Walmesley 'irritable', even 'violent'; but he soon calmed down. There was a true friendship between the two of them, a friendship strengthened rather than undermined by their heated disputations. 'Difference of opinion did not keep us apart,' Sam wrote feelingly of their relationship. 'I honoured him and he endured me. . . . He was of an advanced age and I was only a boy; yet he never received my notions with contempt. . . . I hope that at least my gratitude made me worthy of his notice.' Johnson recognised that his own views had been much overstated owing to Walmesley's opposition. 'After his death,' he said, 'I felt my Toryism much abated.'

Walmesley had been at Oxford; and it was to Oxford—or to Cambridge where Cornelius Ford had been—that Sam longed to escape from the restrictions and limitations of his present life. Dinner at the Garricks', visits to the Levetts, discussions and arguments with Gilbert Walmesley were all very well in their way; but his days were occupied in what he had come to think of as drudgery: binding books, selling books, buying books, carting books about on long boring rides which sent him to sleep in the saddle. Yet unless he could get to Oxford or Cambridge, or perhaps to one of the Inns of Court, he might well have to remain a bookseller for the rest of his life.

Then, in the autumn of 1728, his mother's rich cousin Mrs Harriotts died and left her forty pounds for her 'own separate use'; and Sarah could not think to what better use she could put her legacy than to give Sam a start at Oxford. Forty pounds would barely cover his bills for a year; but one of Sam's friends at the grammar school, Andrew Corbet, who had come into a sizeable fortune by the death of his parents and who was now at Pembroke College, offered to help: he would pay part of Sam's expenses for the sake of his companionship. The offer was eagerly accepted, and at the end of October, it became known in Lichfield that Sam Johnson was going up to Oxford. The old woman who kept the dame's school came round with a present of gingerbread and the compliment that Sam was the best scholar she had ever had. Soon afterwards Sam and his father rode south for Oxford.

On arrival at Oxford, Sam wished that his father had not come; for at their first meeting with the fellows and tutors of the college, Michael Johnson assured them all, in that excessive paternal pride which his son found so exasperating, that Sam was a most clever lad, the best scholar at his school, the author of some remarkable Latin verses. Sam sat silent and despondent until some remark gave him the opportunity of quoting Macrobius, a fifth-century Roman philosopher of whom most nineteen-year-old boys could not be expected even to have heard.

It was not long before Sam gave further evidence of his wide reading and quick mind, and of his indolence. As at school he could not bring himself to do any work until the last minute, and sometimes failed to produce the required tasks at all. Nor did he attend lectures with any regularity. On the first day he went to a lecture by his tutor, William Jorden, but he 'did not profit much from his instructions' and did not trouble to go to the next four. He remembered afterwards with shame how rude he had been when Jorden—'a worthy man' and a kind one for all his faults as a teacher—asked him why he had missed his lectures on logic. Sam replied, with 'as much nonchalance' as he later retold the story, that he had spent the time sliding about on the ice on Christ Church meadow. When the friend to whom he related this said that his easy response displayed 'great fortitude', there came the sharp retort, 'No, sir, stark insensibility.'

'Ah, Sir, I was rude and violent,' he lamented on another occasion.[4] 'I disregarded all power and all authority.' He developed a perverse relish in 'vexing the tutors and fellows', in refusing to answer the knock of a servitor sent round the college rooms by the Master to make sure the undergraduates were studying; when it was discovered that he, for one, was not, he chased the unfortunate servitor round the quadrangle clattering a candlestick in a chamber pot. Once, apparently, when he had been fined for not attending a lecture, he tartly complained that he had been sconced twopence for something not worth a penny; and in response to a further reprimand, he 'replied with great rudeness and contempt for the lecturer'. He was quite as domineering with his fellow undergraduates, one of whom remembered that he 'would not let us say *prodigious* at college. For even then he was delicate in language, and we all feared him.'

They liked him, too, though. He made them laugh; he was derisively sardonic in the most admired undergraduate manner. Often he was to be found 'lounging' at the college gate entertaining a group of them, or declaiming in a tavern, trying out his hand at cricket—and failing, no doubt, to hit the ball—or playing draughts and drinking ale in the common-room with one of his special friends.

One of these friends was Philip Jones, a Scholar who 'loved beer and did not get much forward in the college', an 'affected fellow', according to various ribald entries in the buttery book, 'a foppish dog, alias Coxcomb, an ass and a foolish long guts'. An untidy, ill-shaven, convivial young man, 'Philip Jones without any stones' was to get on no better in the Church than he had done in the college. Another friend was John Fludger, also a Scholar, who, so Johnson declared, 'turned out a scoundrel, a Whig and said he was ashamed of having been bred at Oxford. . . . But he had been a scoundrel all along to be sure.' He, too, became a parson.

Johnson's best friend outside Pembroke College was John Taylor, the Derbyshire lawyer's son who had been at Lichfield Grammar School with him. Taylor had come to Oxford hoping to join his friend at Pembroke College. But the tutor under whom he would have been placed at Pembroke was in Johnson's dismissive opinion a 'blockhead', and Taylor was strongly advised to go to Christ Church, opposite Pembroke on the other side of St Aldates, where he would be able to study under the more reputable Edmund Bateman. Taylor accepted the advice; and Johnson went over to see him every day, to ask him how he was getting on with Bateman, and to learn what Bateman was teaching him.

Despite his determination to vex the tutors in his own college, however and to pay as scant regard to authority as possible, Johnson did not altogether neglect his studies. In his room at the top of the staircase above the main gateway, he had over a hundred volumes from his father's stock, mostly Greek and Roman classics, volumes of poetry, and religious books; and these he studied with as much diligence as he could muster, reading Homer and Euripides '*solidly*'. He also picked up William Law's *Serious Call to a Devout and Holy Life*, 'expecting to find it a dull book (as such books generally are) and perhaps to laugh at it'. But he was profoundly impressed by it; it made him think about religion 'in earnest', and from this time forward religion was 'the predominant object of his thoughts; though with the just sentiments of a conscientious Christian, he lamented that his practice of its duties fell far short of what it ought to be'.

He also lamented his inability at Oxford to study with more concentration and regularity. He prepared a detailed programme of work, calculating how much he would have to get through each day to read what he ought to read; yet he could never settle down to it. He was probably not so 'idle and neglectful' as in later, sternly self-critical moods he blamed himself for having been; but he certainly could not bring himself to be a conscientious student. He did manage to earn a name for himself as a poet, translating Pope's *Messiah* into Latin verse so well that it found its way into a published collection and reputedly moved Pope to remark that posterity would not be able to judge whether the English or the Latin version was the original. But this was a rare performance. When one of the junior fellows, William Adams, reproached him for missing so many lectures, though he was too proud to show his contrition, he admitted that he felt it. He had every confidence in the depth and breadth of his knowledge; already he had little to learn from lesser men. But he knew that there were other undergraduates as competent as he. There was, in particular, one John Meeke, later to be a fellow of the college, whose superiority so distressed him that at the classical lecture in the hall, Johnson purposely sat as far away from him as he could so that he would be unable to hear him construe.

As the months passed—he remained in residence all through the long vacation—he became increasingly unhappy. He did not know what he wanted to do with his life. Sometimes he thought he would like to be a lawyer, but one needed money for that; at other times he thought he would like to study abroad. One day the Master of the college heard him talking to himself in his room: 'Well,' he announced in his strong voice, 'I have a mind to see how they go on in other places of learning. I'll go see the universities abroad. I'll go to France and Italy. I'll go to Padua . . .' But, of course, one needed money for that, too. Money, indeed, was a constant worry to him after the first six months or so. The hopes he had entertained of being helped by the rich young Andrew Corbet came to nothing when Corbet went down from Oxford without mentioning the matter again. Nor did there now seem any possibility of his being recommended for a scholarship. He had to find about eight shillings a week for his board as a commoner, and another eight shillings or so for the rent of his room, for fuel and candles, his tutor's fees, the wages of the servitor and the bedmaker; and towards the end of 1729 the money that his mother had given him was all but exhausted. He could afford to spend nothing on clothes, and his friend Taylor said that his shoes were so worn that his naked toes stuck through the broken leather. When he went to see Taylor one day he felt that the other Christ Church men, standing upon the pavement of Peckwater Quad, were laughing at his broken-down appearance, and he refused ever to set foot in the college again. A sympathetic undergraduate, William Vyse, took pity on him, bought a new pair of shoes for him, and asked his servitor to put them outside Johnson's door. When he found them there Johnson angrily threw them away.

As Christmas approached, Johnson decided that he had no alternative but to go home to Lichfield to see what he could do to raise some more money. He left Oxford early on the morning of 12 December. Taylor, who accompanied him as far as Banbury, was relieved to notice that his toes were hidden in a 'large pair of boots'.

Johnson, having no money to pay for their cartage home, left his books with Taylor. He hoped, he said, to return to Oxford in the new year. But he never did return.

Soon after his arrival back in Lichfield, Johnson walked the fifteen miles to Birmingham. He wanted to consult his godfather, Dr Samuel Swynfen, who as a young man practising in Lichfield had lived with Michael and Sarah Johnson and had moved to Birmingham in 1727. He was deeply concerned, he told the doctor, about the utter depression which had gradually grown deeper and deeper during the last weeks of his time at Oxford and was now overwhelming. He felt himself oppressed by a 'horrible hypochondria, with perpetual irritation, fretfulness, and impatience; and with a dejection, gloom, and despair, which made existence misery'. He had already confessed to Taylor that he 'strongly entertained thoughts of suicide'; and his other close friend, Edmund Hector, was so anxious about him that he feared for his reason and even for his life. Sometimes his mind was so disturbed that he could not tell the time upon the town clock.

Swynfen could do little to help him. Indeed, he so offended his godson by showing to others the patient's account, written in Latin, of his complaint—on the grounds that it described his symptoms and fears with 'extraordinary acuteness, research and eloquence'—that Johnson could never bring himself entirely to forgive him.

Johnson tried to throw off his depression—as his father attempted to treat his own similar complaint—by arduous physical exertion. His walk to Birmingham and back to see Dr Swynfen was only one of several he made at this time. He also tried to regain his spirits by discussions and arguments with Gilbert Walmesley and with others in Lichfield who could give his mind and imagination more stimulation than could be found at home. One entertaining and agreeable young companion was the Hon Henry Hervey, a younger son of the Earl of Bristol who, after a wild and brief career at Christ Church, had got his father to buy him a commission in the 11th Dragoons and was now stationed at Lichfield. A witty, prodigal, profligate libertine, he combined—like the Rev. Cornelius Ford —a delight in the ways and gossip of the social world with an interest in literature, a combination of pleasures that Johnson was always to find peculiarly alluring.

But even with Walmesley and Hervey and his other friends to divert him from his worries, Johnson found life in Lichfield stale and burdensome. Now that he had tasted Oxford life, he found bookselling more of a trial than ever. He helped his father and brother, Nathaniel, in the shop; but every day there was a misery to him; and once when his father, ill in bed, asked him to go to open the stall in Uttoxeter market for him, he refused. It was a refusal which troubled his conscience ever afterwards and was to lead to an extraordinary act of penance.[5]

Michael Johnson was in his seventies now, tired and ailing. He managed to keep the business going; but it was not making the money that it might have done, and the parchment factory was 'fallen half down for want of money to repair it'. He was forced, as in the past, to borrow. He received help from William Innys, a friendly London bookseller, and, as a 'decayed tradesman', he was granted ten guineas from a local trust of which he himself in the past had been one of the guardians. On his death in December 1731 he left no will, and when all the bills had been paid his elder son received no more than nineteen pounds from his estate.

Little as was this sum, compared with the £500 which the old man had hoped to leave both his sons, it was enough to encourage Sam to resign from a post which he was finding intolerable. This was an appointment as a schoolmaster at Market Bosworth Grammar School in Leicestershire which he had accepted to escape from the Lichfield shop.

He had become a teacher since that was all he seemed capable of doing or qualified to do. He had heard, during the early autumn, that both the headmaster, Wentworth, and a recently appointed usher were leaving the school at Stourbridge which he had attended some years before. After some hesitation he left for Stourbridge to apply for the post of usher and to see what Cornelius Ford's relations, the Hickmans, could do to influence the governors on his behalf. But, although Gregory Hickman agreed to support his application, his literary abilities were considered insufficient substitute for a university degree, and an Oxford graduate was appointed instead.

Johnson's second attempt to become a teacher was more successful. For appointments to the staff of Market Bosworth Grammar School in

Leicestershire were in the control of Sir Wolstan Dixie of Bosworth Hall, a descendant of the founder of the school. And Dixie, who in any case had no regard for intellectual attainments, agreed to overlook the fact that Johnson had no degree provided he consented to live at the Hall and to act as a kind of chaplain and secretary there. The arrangement proved disastrous. Sir Wolstan was aggressively Philistine, notoriously ignorant, an 'abandoned brutal rascal', in his employee's opinion, ill-mannered and ill-natured. As ready to knock a man down as look at him, Sir Wolstan's reputation for violence was by no means undeserved. He was said to have once attended a levee at one of the royal palaces where, upon hearing the announcement, 'Sir Wolstan Dixie of Bosworth Park', George II, dredging up some recollection of Bosworth Field from his muddled knowledge of English history, remarked, 'Bosworth—Bosworth! Big battle at Bosworth, wasn't it?' 'Yes, Sir,' replied Sir Wolstan. 'But I thrashed him.'

Johnson's work in the schoolroom—paid for at the rate of £20 a year—was no more congenial to him than his duties at the Hall. The headmaster was a dull old clergyman; the boys, required to communicate with each other only in Greek or Latin during school hours, were instructed by Johnson out of Lillie's Grammar; and it was hard to say 'whose difficulty was the greater', Johnson confessed to Edmund Hector, 'I to explain nonsense, or they to understand it'. Tired out by the 'dull sameness of his existence', quarrelling constantly with his dreadful employer, Johnson took advantage of a particularly virulent altercation to leave Bosworth Hall; he returned to Lichfield, trusting to his patrimony to keep him until some less irksome employment could be found.

His mother and brother were now running the bookshop on their own, and Sam lent them an unwilling and clumsy hand. In July he applied for an appointment as usher at the grammar school at Ashbourne where his friend, John Taylor, having left Christ Church without taking a degree, had now taken over his father's practice; but his application was turned down. And it was with a kind of despairing relief that he accepted an invitation from Edmund Hector to go and stay with him in Birmingham. Hector, like Taylor, indeed like most of Sam's contemporaries at Lichfield Grammar School, was now successfully established; he was a surgeon with comfortable rooms in the house of Thomas Warren, a bookseller in Birmingham's High Street near the Swan Inn.

Often in the evenings Johnson and Hector went out to the Swan where Johnson drank a good deal—sometimes a good deal too much—of a punch known as 'Bishop', made of port, sugar and roasted orange. On one occasion they agreed to meet there a relation of Johnson's from Stourbridge, one of the Fords, whose capacity for strong liquor was celebrated. Realising they could not keep up with him all evening, Johnson suggested that they should take him on in shifts. 'This fellow will make us both drunk,' he said. 'Let us take him by turns, and get rid of him.' Hector took the first shift and by the time Johnson arrived three bottles of port had already been disposed of. Ford was ready for more; but Hector, lurching precariously, was obliged to go upstairs to bed, the walk down the High Street being considered beyond the ability of his legs. Johnson himself was in a scarcely better state, having already been drinking at the house of one of Hector's friends, and by the time his shift was completed he, too, felt compelled to go upstairs at the Swan where he fell into Hector's bed, 'Very drunk'.

Hector had made several good friends in Birmingham, notably Monsieur Desmoulins—a Huguenot refugee who was writing-master at the Birmingham Free Grammar School and had married Dr Swynfen's daughter, Elizabeth—and the family of Harry Porter, an agreeable, uninspiring mercer whose forbears had been in the textiles trade—rather more successfully than he—for several generations. Harry and Elizabeth Porter had two sons, Jervis Henry aged fourteen in 1732 and Joseph, aged eight; there was also a daughter of sixteen, named Lucy.

Lucy Porter afterwards gave a description of Samuel Johnson's 'very forbidding' appearance at the time of this visit to Birmingham which was less than flattering. 'He was then lean and lank,' she remembered, 'so that his immense structure of bones was hideously striking to the eye, and the scars of the scrofula were deeply visible. [Instead of a wig he wore his own] hair, which was straight and stiff and separated behind; and he often had, seemingly, convulsive starts and odd gesticulations.'

A strange appearance and unsettling mannerisms were combined with disturbing eccentricities of behaviour. He was given to muttering to himself and to relapsing from outbursts of cheerful gregariousness into moods of gloomy despondency. Conversations with Edmund Hector would suddenly erupt into bitter quarrels and then he would lope off, his huge shoulders hunched under his stiff brown hair. For a time he left the Warrens' house, where Hector had been paying for his meals, to go to live by himself in another part of the town. But he could not bear to be by himself for long; and after each quarrel he would go back to Hector to make it up with him. Hector forgave him; but there were others who could not excuse his rudeness and moody brusqueness. As a whole, the people of Birmingham, Lucy Porter said, 'could not bear Mr Johnson'.

Once again, Hector feared that his friend might be going mad. If only,

Hector thought, he could settle down to some literary task all might be well. But he seemed as incapable as he had ever been at school of getting down to work. One day Hector persuaded him to write some verses for a friend who wished to impress a girl. At the end of a week he had done nothing; and when Hector asked him how he was getting on he lumbered up to his room as though he were going to get them. Within a matter of minutes he came down with the finished verses in his hand.

Perhaps he had already worked them out in his head, yet was unable to make the effort of putting them down on paper; or perhaps he had already put them down on paper, yet wanted to retain his reputation for being able to knock off such work in a trice. Certainly he was still always unwilling to be seen hard at work. Hector noticed this when he slipped away to read, and then tried to disguise the fact that he had been studying. It was as though he wanted his friends to think that all his illuminating and entertaining talk came out of his head without the benefit of any stimulus.

Even when he agreed, under strong persuasion from Hector and Thomas Warren, to undertake a literary task he repeatedly postponed beginning it. He said that he would like to make a translation into English of a book about the travels in Abyssinia of a Portuguese Jesuit which he had read, in French, at Oxford. Yet when he could not find a copy of the book in Birmingham he put the idea aside; and it was only after Hector had gone to the trouble of borrowing one for him from Oxford that he consented to reconsider the project. With the big quarto volume in his hands he set to work with a sudden access of energy, supplying several pages of copy for the printer to set up in type within a few days. But then what Hector called his 'constitutional indolence' overwhelmed him again, and thereafter he did no more than dally with the work until Hector persuaded him that the printer was waiting for the rest of the copy, could not get on with anything else in the meantime, and was consequently losing work. Even then Johnson could only arouse himself sufficiently to dictate the translation from his bed to Hector who wrote it down for him, copied it out, took it to the printer, and corrected most of the proofs.[6]

At the end of his labours, Johnson received five guineas and, eventually a not unkindly review in the *Literary Magazine*. But when he went back to Lichfield in February 1734 he was no more decided about his ultimate future than he was about his immediate plans. He considered writing a life of Angelo Poliziano, the fifteenth-century poet, together with an edition of his poems and an account of Latin poetry up to his time from that of Petrarch. He stirred himself sufficiently to send out printed proposals asking subscribers to put their names down for a copy of the book—price five shillings unbound—with Nathaniel Johnson, bookseller of Lichfield; he also wrote various letters to possible purchasers. But the idea of an edition of Poliziano by one Samuel Johnson was received with a blank indifference by the book-buying public of the Midlands, and the idea had to be abandoned.

It was during these days of bleak despondency that Edmund Hector's friend, Harry Porter, the mercer, died. Johnson, who had grown to know the family well while staying in Birmingham, went out of the way to comfort the widow, Elizabeth—Tetty to her friends. He had a high regard for Tetty, as she had for him; indeed, according to her daughter, Lucy, at one of his earliest visits to their house she had been so disarmed by his conversation as to overlook all his physical peculiarities, and to remark upon his departure that he was 'the most sensible man' she had ever seen in her life.

At the time of her husband's death she was forty-five—though she liked to pretend that she was no more than forty—rather stout, rather flushed, with an ample bosom and a face that did not seem quite big enough to contain so long a nose, such large wide-set eyes and so full a pair of red lips. Her hair was very fine and very blonde. To some of her acquaintances she seemed rather silly; to one, strongly prejudiced against her, she 'had an unbecoming excess of girlish levity, and disgusting affectation'; to another she was 'a little painted puppet of no value at all, quite disguised with affectation, full of odd airs and rural elegance . . . flaring and fantastic in her dress, and affected both in her speech and her general behaviour'.[7] There can be little doubt that she was, indeed, rather more coquettish than is considered seemly in a woman of her age, rather too given to striking attitudes, and assuming airs unbecoming in the daughter of a country squire. But she was certainly not stupid; nor was she physically unattractive. Johnson fell in love with her.

He was twenty-five now; and no one who knew him well had any doubt that he was a virgin. His celibacy was not due, as all his friends understood, to any distaste for women. Indeed, he felt strongly drawn to them, particularly to those of a sensual nature. A pretty face and shapely body were never by themselves enough, for his bad eyesight prevented his enjoying them to the full; but 'unless a woman had amorous heat', he once confided to a friend, he found her a 'dull companion'. Yet, until now, he had shrunk from making any advances to the girls he had known. He had conceived a youthful passion for Edmund Hector's pretty sister, Ann, when he was seventeen; while at Stourbridge School he 'was much enamoured of Olivia Lloyd, a young quaker', a niece of Mrs Cornelius

Ford; and after leaving Oxford he had been captivated on a visit to Stourbridge by Gregory Hickman's daughter, Dorothy, for whom he had composed a poem. But it was considered unlikely that he had even so much as kissed any of them, however much he may have wanted to. It was not only that his moral scruples were already unusually strong, but that he was at the same time painfully aware that he was not a man whose physical presence had much to recommend it: in fact, who was to say that a young girl might not find his advances repellent?

With Tetty there was no such problem. She was a mature, experienced woman, fully-blown yet flirtatious, welcoming, sensual and understanding. He would be able to make love to her with all the passion that lay stifled within him. And she longed for him to do so, fascinated by his strength, his ugliness, his clumsy eagerness. 'Sir, it was a love marriage upon both sides,' Johnson later announced to a friend with appealing satisfaction and 'much gravity'. And so it was. But it was more than that; for Tetty was 'a lady of great sensibility and worth . . . shrewd and cultivated'. They could be happy together, he was sure, even when passion was spent. He asked her to marry him and she accepted.

Her family were appalled. How could she consent to marry a man young enough to be her son, a man without work, without money, and she so recently a widow? Her brother-in-law, Joseph Porter, offered her an annuity to give the man up; her elder son, then at a naval college and one day to be a captain in the Royal Navy, 'much disgusted' by his mother's behaviour, threatened never to see her again; her younger son went to live with his uncle. Only her daughter, Lucy, acquiesced.

Sarah Johnson seems to have accepted her son's decision without enthusiasm. 'Mother, I have not deceived Mrs Porter,' he is reported to have said when informing her of his forthcoming marriage. 'I have told her the worst of me; that I am of mean extraction; that I have no money; and that I have had an uncle hanged. She replied, that she valued no one more or less for his descent; that she had no more money than myself; and that, though she had not had a relation hanged, she had fifty who deserved hanging.'[8]

But if his mother, however reluctantly, accepted the match, he knew that the people of Lichfield would not; and, rather than face the ridicule of his more ribald friends and acquaintances, he decided to get married in Derby where no one knew him well. So, at St Werburgh's Church in Derby, on 9 July 1735, the quiet wedding took place.

Some time before the wedding, Johnson determined that, although he was so much younger than his bride, he would have to show her that he meant to be her master, that he would have to get out of her head the 'fantastical notion', derived from 'old romances', that 'a woman of spirit should use her lover like a dog'. One day when riding together—it was the summer day that they rode to Derby for their wedding—Tetty told him that he was going too fast and that she could not keep up with him; then, when he rode a little slower, she passed him, complaining that he lagged behind. 'I was not to be made the slave of caprice,' he commented, as he recounted the story to a friend, 'and I resolved to begin as I meant to end. I therefore pushed on briskly, till I was fairly out of her sight. The road lay between two hedges, so I was sure she could not miss it; and I contrived that she should soon come up with me. When she did, I observed her to be in tears.'

At the time of his marriage, Johnson was still out of work. In the spring he had had a job as a tutor in a village near Lichfield where he had taught five children from the ages of thirteen to nineteen, accompanying them to church on Sundays and astonishing them on the walk back by 'repeating the greatest part of the sermon, with criticisms, additions and improvements'. But this job had been a temporary one, suitable only for a bachelor, and he must now find something else.

Fortunately Tetty had a little money. Harry Porter had died almost penniless with his affairs in as confused a muddle as Michael Johnson's; but she still had the bulk of a £600 dowry which her father had settled on her at the time of her marriage; and with this she and her husband decided to open a school of their own.

In preparation for this, with a businesslike resolution he would have been quite unable to muster before he had fallen in love with Tetty, he sent to Oxford for the books he had left there five and a half years before. He wrote to a Christ Church undergraduate of his acquaintance, telling him of his intention 'to furnish a house in the country and to keep a private boarding school for young gentlemen who would be instructed in a method somewhat more rational than those commonly practised. . . . Before I draw up my plan of education,' he went on, 'I shall attempt to procure an account of the different ways of teaching in use at the most celebrated schools, and shall therefore hope that you will favour me with the method of the Charterhouse, and procure me that of Westminster. It may be written in a few lines by only mentioning under each class their exercise and authors.'

Before suitable premises had been found, however, Johnson heard that the headmaster of the village school at Solihull was leaving, and he asked Gilbert Walmesley to recommend him as the successor. Walmesley obligingly did so; but the governors were not responsive. They all agreed he was an 'excellent scholar' and upon that account deserved much better than to be schoolmaster of Solihull. 'But then,' the reply to Walmesley went on, 'he has the character of being a very haughty, ill-natured gent., and that he has such a way of distorting his face (Wh though he can't help it) ye gents. think it may affect some young lads; for these two reasons he is not approved on.'

Walmesley, however, had something exciting to suggest which would make up for any disappointment the Johnsons might feel about Sam being turned down at Solihull. There was, he said, a large house just outside Lichfield at Edial, a house built in Charles II's time, which would be ideal for their purposes. It was a strange-looking building with a sharply-sloping pantiled roof surmounted by a structure which looked like a miniature light-house and was, in fact, an observatory. Because of its appearance no tenant could be found; but it had a good garden, commodious outbuildings surrounded by high and solid walls, and plenty of accommodation. It would not cost much to convert it for use as a boarding school; and it was available at a reasonable rent. He would do his best to find some pupils.

Walmesley did, in fact, find three pupils: David Garrick, now nineteen, his younger brother, George, and Lawrence Offley, a relative of his wife. But few, if any, others could be found. An advertisement in the *Gentleman's Magazine* announcing, 'At Edial, near Lichfield, in Staffordshire, young gentlemen are boarded, and taught Latin and Greek languages by Samuel Johnson', apparently aroused no interest. 'We can scarce wonder the notification failed of its end,' observed one of Johnson's friends in later years, 'if we reflect that he was little more than twenty-seven years of age [in fact twenty-six] when he published it, and that he had not the vanity to profess teaching all the sciences, nor the effrontery of those, who, in these more modern times [1787], undertake, in private boarding schools, to qualify young men for holy orders.' Moreover, Johnson had no degree, had published nothing but his translation of Lobo's *Voyage to Abyssinia* and that anonymously, and was generally considered far too peculiar in his appearance and manner to become a respected teacher. Nor was the proposed curriculum of the school likely to impress an enlightened parent. For, despite his promise of a 'more rational' method of instruction, his lessons were to be limited to Eutropius and Justin, Terence and Sallust, Ovid's *Metamorphoses* and Caesar's *Commentaries*, and just such other Greek and Latin classics as were taught in any other school.

'The first class,' the headmaster proposed, 'are to repeat by memory, in the morning, the rules they had learned before; and, in the afternoon, the Latin rules of the nouns and verbs. They are also, on Thursdays and Saturdays [precisely as at Lichfield Grammar School] to be examined in the rules they have learned. The second class does the same . . . Afterwards, they are to get and repeat the irregular nouns.'

It was clear that Johnson's heart was not really in his new school, that his forlorn enterprise was likely to succeed no better than was that school opened in Gower Street North in 1823 by Mrs John Dickens, and derided by her son as 'Mrs Micawber's Boarding Establishment for Young Ladies'. Undoubtedly David Garrick derived little or nothing from his short residence there, settling down no better to Greek and Latin under Samuel Johnson than he had done under John Hunter, spending most of the time that he should have spent on classical exercises in writing comedies and dramatic poetry, lightening the tedium of evening study by peering through the keyhole of his schoolmaster's bedroom to watch the wild, chaotic love-making that went on inside.

When he was famous, Garrick delighted his friends by enacting the turbulent scenes he claimed to have witnessed—Johnson stumbling round the bed, calling 'I'm coming, my Tetsie! I'm coming!', falling upon his ample bride, getting out of bed again and, mistaking the sheets for his shirt-tails, depriving Tetty of all covering by stuffing the bedclothes into his breeches. Sometimes, in Garrick's outrageous and hilarious imitations of the bridegroom's 'tumultuous and awkward fondness' for his bride, Johnson was portrayed writing a tragedy beside the bed, or oratorically reciting to Tetty what he had written, while his wife, impatient of the delay, implored him to get into bed with her.

The tragedy that Johnson was writing was that of *Irene*, the Greek slave slain by the Sultan Mahomet I. He was taking an unwonted amount of trouble over it, spending hour upon hour upon it, rewriting it and reshaping it; for upon it, he felt, depended his future success, his salvation from the failure of Edial which was rapidly swallowing up all Tetty's money.

Towards the end of 1736 he made one last effort to obtain paid employment as a schoolmaster. He applied for the vacant post of assistant master at the grammar school at Brewood. But back came the sadly familiar reply from his sponsors: it was feared that Mr Johnson's 'paralytic affection might become the object of imitation or of ridicule, among his pupils'. His present pupils were leaving one by one. Lawrence Offley went on to Cambridge in November; George Garrick later left to go to Appleby Latin School; arrangements were made for David Garrick to go to a school at Rochester where he might enjoy the benefits of a wider curriculum than was available at Edial and prepare himself for a career in the law. So Edial was closed; and had it not been for the future fame of its headmaster and his eldest pupil, it would long since have been forgotten. Indeed, a man who had worked there as a boy confessed, in his old age, that he had all but forgotten it; the only two things that he could remember about it, he said, pronouncing a not unworthy epitaph, was that Mr Johnson 'was not much of a scholar to look at, but that Master Garrick was a strange one for leaping over a stile'.

There seemed to Johnson, then, nothing left but to try out his fortune in London. David Garrick was due to go there, on his way to Rochester, in February or March; and Johnson decided to go with him. Leaving Tetty in the care of her daughter, Lucy, he prepared himself for the long journey.

2

Grub Street

'His practice was to shut himself up in a room assigned to him at St John's Gate, to which he would not suffer any one to approach, except the compositor or Cave's boy for matter, which, as fast as he composed it, he tumbled out at the door.'   John Hawkins

Johnson and Garrick left Lichfield together on the morning of 2 March 1737. To save money, Garrick said, they 'rode and tied', sharing a horse between them, one of the travellers going on ahead for a mile or two then tying up the horse for the other to use when he came up with it. According to Johnson, who chose always to exaggerate his early poverty, they certainly had need to save money, for when they arrived in London he had only twopence halfpenny in his pocket and Garrick had but three halfpence in his.

Soon after their arrival they called upon an acquaintance of the Garrick family, a bookseller in the Strand, and prevailed upon him to lend them five pounds. The bookseller asked Johnson how he intended to make his living in London. Johnson replied, 'By my literary labours.' Looking him up and down, as though measuring his obvious strength, the bookseller commented, 'Young man, you had better buy a porter's knot.' Johnson afterwards remembered the comment with evident satisfaction, referring to Wilcox as 'one of my best friends', gratified not so much by the knowledge that he had been able to make his living by his pen as by the compliment to his physical strength which he very much liked people to notice and to talk about.

Both Garrick and Johnson were in sore need of the bookseller's loan.

Garrick's father died very soon after they had left Lichfield, and although he was still able to attend the school at Rochester for a time with the help of a small legacy from an uncle, he soon had to abandon all idea of the law as a career and started a wine-merchant's business with his eldest brother, Peter, while awaiting his opportunity to go on the stage.

Johnson, in even worse financial straits, took pride in his ability to get along on very little. He lived in what must have been extremely cheap lodgings with a Mr Norris, a staymaker in Exeter Street, a narrow, noisy and undesirable cul-de-sac between the Strand and the river. He had already been told by an Irish painter he had met in Birmingham that it was quite possible for a man to live in London on thirty pounds a year 'without being contemptible'. No more than ten pounds need be spent on clothes and linen; 1s 6d a week would procure the rent of a garret. 'Few people would enquire where he lodged,' the painter had told him, 'and if they did, it was easy to say, "Sir, I am to be found at such a place"', giving the name of a respectable coffee-house. In the coffee-house, he had no need to spend more than threepence a day, and for that could enjoy the pleasure 'of very good company'. 'He might dine for sixpence,' the painter had continued, 'breakfast on bread and milk for a penny, and do without supper. On *clean-shirt* day he went abroad, and paid visits.'

Johnson himself dined 'very well for eightpence, with very good company, at the Pine Apple' in New Street, not far from Exeter Street. Others of the 'very good company' there paid a shilling for their dinner for they had wine with it. 'But I,' he said, 'had a cut of meat for sixpence, and bread for a penny, and gave the waiter a penny; so that I was quite well served, nay, better than the rest, for they gave the waiter nothing.'

It was obvious that he was beginning to develop that love—though not an uncritical love—of London and London life that was to become a passion with him. Never a fastidious man, he could overlook its frequent glimpses of filth and squalor; never particularly sensitive to smells he could walk its back streets without undue distaste; and although cruelty never failed to anger him—as a boy he had grown into the habit of tugging furiously at the iron ring, fixed into the cobbles of the market-place at Lichfield, to which bulls were tied for baiting—he found that the cruelty and suffering to be witnessed in London had necessarily to be endured and were, in any case, outweighed by the happiness to be enjoyed there. 'The happiness in London is not to be conceived but by those who have been in it,' he was later to observe. 'I will venture to say, there is more learning and science within the circumference of where we now sit [in the Mitre tavern] than in all the rest of the kingdom. . . . Why, sir, you find no man at all intellectual, who is willing to leave London. . . . To a man whose pleasure is intellectual, London is the place. . . . No, sir, when a man is tired of London, he is tired of life; for there is in London all that life can afford . . . the full tide of existence is at Charing Cross.' Having seen London he was content that he had seen 'as much of life as the world could show'. As a friend was to say of him 'such was his love of London, so high a relish had he of its magnificent extent, and variety of intellectual entertainment, that he languished when absent from it. . . . He was at all times sensible of its being, comparatively speaking, a heaven upon earth.'

Even in these early days with few friends, scarcely any money, no work, no recognition of his talents, he seems to have been—if on occasions admittedly frustrated—not unduly discontented and he sat in coffee-houses and taverns and wandered about in the 'great streets and squares', those 'innumerable little lanes and courts', amongst that 'multiplicity of human habitations' that comprised the 'wonderful immensity', the 'wonderful extent and variety' of London.

Particularly enjoyable at this time were the evenings he spent at the house of his old friend the Hon Henry Hervey, now promoted captain and married to Catherine Aston, a sister of Gilbert Walmesley's young wife, Magdalen. Hervey, extravagant and hospitable, was still a delightful companion, often drunk, invariably cheerful and friendly; and Johnson never forgot his kindness. It mattered nothing to Hervey that Johnson was poverty-stricken and humbly born, that his Staffordshire accent was so pronounced that, even at a time when provincial accents had not acquired their later social significance, it was remarked upon, and Garrick, at least, took pleasure in imitating it, 'squeezing a lemon into a punch-bowl, with uncouth gesticulations, looking round the company, and calling out, "Who's for *poonsh*?" ' To Hervey it was of no consequence that Johnson said 'poonsh' for 'punch', 'woonse' for 'once', 'shuperstition' for 'super-stition', that he pronounced 'there' as though it rhymed with 'mere'. John-son was a welcome guest at his table whatever his idiosyncrasies; and he was ever afterwards grateful. Oh, yes, he knew all about Hervey's vices, he said, 'but he was very kind to me. If you call a dog Hervey, I shall love him.'

Yet although he discussed poetry and literary gossip for hours on end with Hervey and his other friends, he found it impossible to sit down to any prolonged writing himself.

In the summer he left his noisy lodgings in Exeter Street for the peace and quiet of a room next door to the Golden Heart, Church Street, Greenwich, intending to settle down to work on *Irene* of which the last two acts were still to be finished. But he did not manage to add to it more than a few lines which he composed in his head, walking up and down in the park. Hoping in the meantime to earn some immediate money as a translator, he wrote to Edward Cave, owner of the *Gentleman's Magazine* which had published its first issue a few years before. He had already written to Cave while he was staying in Birmingham, offering to supply criticism, poems, inscriptions and Latin dissertations. This first letter can scarcely have recommended itself to Cave as an example of ingratiating tact, for he had added that he had 'other designs to impart' if he could be secure from 'having others reap the advantage' of his suggestions, and that he had observed that the magazine's offer of a prize of fifty pounds in a poem competition led him to expect generous payment. He had also proposed various ways in which the magazine's pages might be 'better recommended to the public, than by low jests, awkward buffoonery, or the dull scurrilities of either party'. There is no record of his letter ever having received a reply.

In his second letter Johnson was more circumspect. He had a definite proposition to put forward: a new edition of Paolo Sarpi's *History of the Council of Trent* first printed in London in 1619 and recently translated and annotated by the French theological writer Pierre François le Courayer. If the idea appealed to Mr Cave, Sam Johnson would submit for examination a specimen of his new translation.

Apparently Johnson received an encouraging reply to his letter, and he returned to Lichfield to fetch Tetty with hopeful expectations that he might be able to earn their living in London by his 'literary labours'. There was, however, an objection to this scheme: his mother was now alone in the business in Lichfield, for in his absence in London, his brother had died.

Nathaniel Johnson is an enigma. Sam almost never referred to him, or even to the fact that he had had a brother at all. When he did refer to him, he seemed to imply that Nathaniel was an insensitive fellow, rowdy, unimaginative and immature; on writing for some information about his last days, Sam described him as a 'lively, noisy man, that loved company. His memory might continue for some time in some favourite alehouse.' It seems that in 1736 Nathaniel left Lichfield to work in Burton-on-Trent and that while in Burton, where he got into some sort of trouble, he made an offer for a shop at Stourbridge. On his brother's advice his mother forbade Nathaniel to go to Stourbridge, perhaps because it was feared that he would try to borrow money from his rich, respectable relations, the Hickmans, who had been so kind to Sam in the past.

In a sad letter to his mother, written shortly before his death, Nathaniel repented of 'some Crimes' which had been committed at Burton and which would not have been committed had he been allowed to go to Stourbridge where he 'might have lived happily'. 'As to My Brother's assisting me,' he went on, 'I had but little Reason to expect it when he would scarce ever use me with common civility and to whose Advice was owing that un-willingness you showed to my going to Stourbridge. . . . I know not nor do I much care in What way of life I shall hereafter live, but this I know that it shall be an honest one and that it can't be more unpleasant than some part of my Life Past. I believe I shall go to Georgia in about a fortnight. . . . I thank you heartily for your generous forgiveness and your Prayers which pray continue. Have Courage my dear Mother God will bear you through all your troubles. If my brother did design doing anything for me I am much obliged to him and thank him. . . . I am Dear Mother your Affectionate and obedient Son Nath Johnson.'

Instead of emigrating to America as he suggested he was about to do in this letter, Nathaniel appears to have gone to work in the West Country. He died, at the age of twenty-five, the cause unknown, a few days after his brother arrived in London. That Johnson's behaviour towards Nathaniel troubled his conscience thereafter, cannot very well be doubted. He did not speak of him, but he could never forget him. On the very day that his mother was buried in Lichfield, on 23 January 1759, more than twenty years after Nathaniel's death, he entered in his diary—after prayers for his mother's soul, thanks for her example, and a plea for pardon for neglecting it—this bleak sentence: 'The dream of my brother I shall remember.'

Before his return to London—having disposed of his responsibilities at Edial and at last finished his tragedy, *Irene*—Johnson was, at least, able to leave his mother more contentedly settled in the shop. For his step-daughter, Lucy, kindly agreed to stay behind with her to take turns behind the counter with the maid, Catherine Chambers, a trusted servant who had been with the Johnson family since she was fifteen and who was to remain with Sarah until her death.

In London Johnson and his wife took lodgings in Woodstock Street, which led into the Oxford road to the west of Hanover Square, and then moved to 6 Castle Street, on the other side of the Oxford road not far from Cavendish Square. They had not managed to salvage much of Tetty's money from the misfortune of the Edial school, and it was essential that Johnson should earn some money soon. First of all he tried to do so with *Irene*, which he read one evening, in the Fountain Tavern in the Strand, to Peter Garrick who shared his brother's interest in the stage and who had friends who worked at the Drury Lane Theatre. But the manager of the Drury Lane did not take much interest in five-act tragedies on such solemn themes as *Irene* and declined even to read it. So Johnson felt obliged to turn once more to Edward Cave and the *Gentleman's Magazine.*

He did so with some foreboding, for he had heard what a hard task-master Cave was, keeping his staff working 'from twenty-four to fifty hours at a stretch, and even on Sundays to get copy ready'. He was also known to be far from generous in his payments for contributions, contracting to pay for material by the hundred printed lines and expecting, as Johnson discovered, 'the long hundred' before he would pay for them.

A slow-thinking, slow-moving man, big and ponderous, 'with no great relish for mirth', he worked hard himself, having, apparently, no interest in anything other than his magazine, never even looking out of the window, Johnson thought, without an eye to finding something that might be worked up into an article. A stranger going into his office would always find him sitting down, one of his other contributors observed, and he would remain seated and silent, in the loose horseman's coat and the great, bushy, uncombed wig that he constantly wore. 'If at any time he was inclined to begin the discourse, it was generally by putting a leaf of the magazine, then in the press, into the hand of his visitor, and asking his opinion of it.'

Deliberate, phlegmatic, often dogmatic and sometimes obtuse, he was also extraordinarily tactless. He was capable of supposing he had settled the complaint of a man, whose name was given on an illustration without the prefix Mr, by asking the engraver to add the missing title above a caret; and remarking to one of his authors, 'I hear you have just published a pamphlet, and am told there is a very good paragraph in it, upon the subject of music. Did you write that yourself?'

Yet, for all his apparent insensitivity, Cave was a shrewd man and a highly successful editor. Forty-six years old at the time Johnson first went to work for him, he had had a chequered career. The son of a cobbler, he had been expelled from Rugby Grammar School for robbing the head-master's wife's hen-roost. Thereafter he had held a variety of jobs from clerk to printer before starting the *Gentleman's Magazine* in premises inside St John's Gate, Clerkenwell. Within six years he had built up the magazine, the first of its kind, into one of the most important periodicals of the day with a circulation of about ten thousand copies a month. He had done so with the help of an assembly of highly gifted colleagues, assistants and contributors, most of them working part-time. His principal adviser was the Rev Thomas Birch, a lively, bustling Fellow of the Royal Society, a prolific—and appallingly dull—writer on all manner of historical subjects. He was 'as brisk as a bee in conversation', so Johnson said, having 'more anecdotes than any man living . . . but no sooner did he take a pen in his hand' than it numbed 'all his faculties'. He was an amusing companion, Horace Walpole concurred, 'a worthy, good-natured soul, full of industry and activity, and running about like a young setting-dog in quest of anything new or old, and with no parts, taste or judgement'.

A faithful supporter of the Whig doctrines both in Church and State, Birch enjoyed the patronage of the Hardwicke family who ensured that he was never in want of ecclesiastical preferment. Nor, as a regular contributor of biographical sketches since 1734 to the *General Dictionary, Historical and Critical*, was he ever in want of literary commissions. He lived in comfort.

Most of Cave's contributors, however, lived on the verge of penury. One of them, John Duick, who provided the magazine with much of its verse, lived with his large family in the most abject poverty in a squalid house in Clerkenwell which contained only two books, one a Bible, the other a copy of the hymns of Isaac Watts.

Johnson's own first contribution to the *Gentleman's Magazine* was a poem. It was a poem in Latin defending the 'indefatigable' Cave—whom Johnson genuinely liked in spite of all his foibles—against attacks from the 'servile imitating crew' who were his competitors. The verses so pleased Cave that Johnson thereafter became one of the magazine's most regular contributors.

Soon after these verses appeared, in the March issue of 1738, Johnson finished a longer and far more effective poem, *London*, modelled on Juvenal's third satire on the corruption and follies of life in Rome. Written, as David Garrick said, when Johnson 'lived much with the Herveys and saw a good deal of what was passing in life', *London* was an indictment of the malice, the shocking degradation, the recurrent dangers, of all that was worst in the city that he was so passionately to love, and, at the same time a fierce political attack on the administration of Robert Walpole. The political aspects of the poem could not have failed to give pleasure to Johnson's friends, the Herveys. For Harry and Kitty Hervey were on bad and worsening terms with Hervey's father, the Earl of Bristol, and with his elder brother, John, Lord Hervey of Ickworth, who, as an intimate friend of the Queen, gave invaluable help to Walpole in the administration's control of the Court and the King. Both Hervey and his wife were as full of sympathy for the Opposition as Johnson himself, who felt that Walpole's venal government was undermining the morality of the entire country and endangering all the ideals that the Tories held dear.

It is an angry, recriminative, emphatically polemical poem, a 'juvenile poem naturally impregnated with the fire of opposition', clearly the work of that young 'truculent, raw-boned figure', later to be described by Thomas Carlyle as 'coarse, irascible, imperious . . . proud as the proudest, poor as the poorest; stoically shut up, silently enduring the incurable'. In it London is seen as a capital suitably barbaric for the 'cheated nation', the 'sinking land' that England had become. Just as Juvenal's hero looks eagerly for some country retreat where the evils of Rome will seem remote, so Johnson's hero, Thales, resolves 'to breathe in distant fields a purer air' and to escape from London, where

> . . . malice, rapine, accident, conspire,
> And now a rabble rages, now a fire;
> Their ambush here relentless ruffians lay,
> And here the fell attorney prowls for prey;
> Here falling houses thunder on your head,
> And here a female atheist talks you dead . . .
> Prepare for death if here at night you roam,
> And sign your will before you sup from home.

It was all much overdone, of course; and the exaggeration is implicitly admitted. Only its most prejudiced critics pretended to find London as bad as that, and Johnson was certainly not one of them even at this early and frustrating stage in his career. Indeed, most of the sentiments expressed in the poem are not his sentiments at all: and as for the hero's much-praised resolve to leave the vicious city and seek purer air as a hermit 'in distant fields', Johnson himself was later to deride such preference for pastoral peace as arrant idiocy. But then Johnson was imitating Juvenal, and the contemporary taste for neoclassical poetry insisted on close, not to say strained, parallels. However, in the passages that dwell upon the miseries of poverty and the slow rise of worth 'by poverty depress'd', he was clearly writing from the heart.

When he sent the poem to Cave, Johnson presented it as the work of some other author of whose abilities he would say nothing, suggesting—'it is a matter of curiosity to observe the diffidence', as a friend of Johnson's said later—that Cave should feel free to alter 'any stroke of satire' which he disliked. Cave felt the poem should be printed but proposed Robert Dodsley as a more suitable publisher for it than himself. Dodsley readily agreed, acknowledged that he found it 'a creditable thing to be concerned in', and offered ten guineas for it, which was accepted. It was published in

May 1738, on the same day as Pope's *One Thousand Seven Hundred and Thirty-Eight*.

London, which appeared anonymously, was immediately successful. The first edition was sold out within a week, the third edition before the end of the year. It was highly praised both for its literary excellence and for its effectiveness as a political broadside and social satire. Pope himself 'commended it highly, and was very importunate with Dodsley to know the author's name'. George Lyttelton believed that it was actually *by* Pope; while Pope's numerous enemies declared that it was too good to be written by him.

Gratified by the success of *London,* Johnson renewed his efforts to get *Irene* performed; but there was still no enthusiasm for it, and he had to be content with further work for the *Gentleman's Magazine,* on which he now became a kind of assistant editor, making selections from new books, choosing verses for publication, answering correspondents' letters, correcting and rewriting contributions, and eventually writing accounts of parliamentary debates.

Previously the debates had been reported factually, but, after a serious breach of privilege, this had been forbidden by the House in April 1738. Imitating the *London Magazine,* which continued to provide accounts of the proceedings of Parliament under the pretence that it was reporting the meetings of a 'Political Club', the *Gentleman's Magazine* resorted to a similar device. Giving the members' pseudonyms which were scarcely difficult to decipher—'Walelop' for Walpole, for example, 'Haxilaf' for Halifax— parliamentary debates were described as though conducted in the 'Senate of Lilliput', a legislative assembly discovered on a voyage by Captain Lemuel Gulliver's grandson. At first these thinly disguised accounts of debates in Parliament were written by one of Cave's other contributors, William Guthrie, a 'man of parts' in Johnson's description, if possessing 'no great regular fund of knowledge'; but in later numbers they were written by Johnson. He did not attend the debates himself. 'I never had been in the gallery of the House of Commons but once,' he later explained. 'Cave and the persons employed under him, gained admittance: they brought away the subject of discussion, the names of the speakers, the side they took, the order in which they rose, together with notes of the arguments advanced in the course of the debate. The whole was afterwards communicated to me, and I composed the speeches. . . .'

Although he liked to pretend in later years that he had taken good care to doctor his reports so as to ensure that the 'WHIG DOGS should not have the best of it', he was proud of the apparent authenticity of the reporting.

One evening a dinner guest at the house of Samuel Foote, the actor, remarked that a certain speech by Pitt was the best he had ever read, and that there was nothing in Demosthenes to equal it. Johnson, who was also of the company, waited until the praise had subsided. Then he said with some complacency, 'That speech I wrote in a garret in Exeter Street.'

By the summer of 1738, Johnson was also at work on his translation of Paolo Sarpi's *History of the Council of Trent,* which Cave was paying for 'in sums of one, two, three and sometimes four guineas at a time, most frequently two', as copy was supplied. Always careful to pay as little as possible for work in advance, Cave was particularly cautious in the case of Johnson, whom he knew to be extremely haphazard in his working hours, not yet reliable in meeting his deadlines. When work was not produced on time, Cave had to prod him; Johnson replied that he would endeavour to keep up to time in future; but it required an enormous effort of will, which was sometimes beyond him. He asked God for help, entering in his journal long prayers to his merciful Father to enable him by His grace to 'redeem the time' which he had spent in sloth, to lead a new life in his Faith.

In fact, the translation of Sarpi's work never was finished. Advertisements appeared in the Press, announcing that the work was being 'diligently prosecuted by S. Johnson' and calling for subscribers. But the advertisements led to a peeved announcement in the *Daily Advertiser* that the Keeper of the Tenison library in Castle Street, Leicester Square, was already at work on the same or rather a 'more extensive' project; and although Cave and Johnson protested that they would nevertheless proceed with their own design, they decided in the end not to do so. Instead Johnson undertook to make a translation of a commentary on Pope by the Swiss theologian, Jean Pierre de Crousaz; and this, although there was again the threat of competition, was eventually completed, the work being done in those sudden bursts of activity between bouts of indolence to which Cave had long since grown accustomed.

Meanwhile work for the *Gentleman's Magazine* went on, poems and extracts and prefaces, epigrams in Greek and Latin, 'An Address to the Reader', 'An Appeal to the Publick', a life of the Dutch physician, Herman Boerhaave, which was printed in four instalments. Also Johnson produced two political pamphlets directed against the government, *Marmor Norfolciense* and *A Compleat Vindication of the Licensers of the Stage,* both in the manner of Swift and neither financially rewarding. Indeed, in these days, he later estimated, he was earning no more than fourpence halfpenny a day; sometimes he could not afford the price of a candle and so was unable to write at night, even when he felt up to it. 'When I was running about this town a very poor fellow,' he said, remembering these days, 'I was a great arguer for the advantages of poverty; but I was, at the same time, very sorry to be poor.'

All Tetty's money had gone and she had been forced to sell most of their few valuable possessions, including the little silver cup which his mother had bought for him on his first visit to London when he was a child. Then there was a quarrel, it seems, and he took lodgings by himself in Fleet Street while she went to live with a friend near the Tower.

So Johnson reverted to the life of a bachelor, walking about in the streets by himself at night, changing his lodgings often, moving from street to street, and sometimes out of the town altogether, taking prostitutes to taverns 'to hear them relate their history', listening attentively as he rolled about in his chair, giving them advice that might persuade them to lead a different life. One day he asked a pretty prostitute to whom he was talking in the street what she thought she was made for. She supposed 'to please the gentlemen'. It was a reply, innocent, touching and pathetic, that he long remembered. He remembered, too, with some pride, that he had once been acquainted with Bet Flint, 'generally slut and drunkard, occasionally whore and thief. She had, however, genteel lodgings, a spinnet on which she played, and a boy that walked before her chair. Poor Bet was taken up on a charge of stealing a counterpane, and tried at the Old Bailey. Chief Justice [John Willes], who loved a wench, summed up favourably and she was acquitted. After which Bet said, with a gay and satisfied air, "Now that the counterpane is *my own*, I shall make a petticoat of it." '

Sometimes Johnson would be asked out to dinner by the cheerful Thomas Birch whose stream of anecdotes 'flowed on like the River Thames'. Birch's young wife had died of puerperal fever ten years before and he was now taking an interest in Elizabeth Carter, the daughter of a clergyman who was an old friend of Cave's. Johnson, making a third at Birch's dining-table, found Miss Carter's company as highly congenial as his host's. She was an attractive girl in her early twenties, a gifted poet and prose writer, whose pieces had appeared regularly in the *Gentleman's Magazine* since she was seventeen. Johnson still did not much care for the company of women whose cleverness was all they had to recommend them. 'A man is in general better pleased,' he thought, 'when he has a good dinner on his table than when his wife talks Greek.' But Elizabeth Carter, of whom Johnson remained fond for the rest of his life, could put a good dinner on a table as well as talk Greek. She 'could make a pudding as well as translate Epictetus', he said of her affectionately, 'and work a handkerchief as well as compose a poem'.

Another of Johnson's favourite companions during these years was the extraordinary Richard Savage, also a contributor to the *Gentleman's Magazine*. Savage, who was a few years older than Johnson, claimed to be the illegitimate son of Richard Savage, fourth Earl Rivers, and the Countess of Macclesfield. According to his own story, he had been put out to the care of a baker's wife in Covent Garden by his mother, who detested him. His mother had then attempted to have him kidnapped and shipped to the West Indies and, when that scheme failed, had had him apprenticed to a cobbler so that he might grow up in obscurity and be forgotten. Had he not discovered some papers about himself on the death of his erstwhile foster-mother, he would forever have remained in ignorance of his true identity.

This identity, however, his mother absolutely refused to admit. He was an impostor, she insisted, and she would have nothing to do with him. He, in return, plagued her life with his claims and insults, publishing attacks on her and dramatising his rejection in such works as his poem *The Bastard*.

He made a meagre and erratic living by both poetry and drama, and once tried out his talents as an actor by taking the name part in his tragedy *Sir Thomas Overbury* at Drury Lane; but most of the time he contrived to make ends meet by the acceptance of charity and loans from friends which he made no pretence of attempting to repay. For some years he was supported by the actress Anne Oldfield; and Lady Macclesfield's nephew, Lord Tyrconnel, agreed to grant him a pension if he would desist from further attacks. Once he received twenty guineas from Sir Robert Walpole for praising his gifts fulsomely in a panegyric; and Queen Caroline was so delighted with a poem written in honour of her birthday that she settled £50 a year on him on condition that he celebrated her birthday annually. But he quarrelled with one benefactor after another until he had no patrons left. He quarrelled with Tyrconnel whom he castigated as a '*Right Honourable Brute and Booby*', and paranoically accused him of hiring bullies to beat him up at a coffee-house; he never forgave Sir Robert Walpole for refusing to continue his royal pension after the Queen's death, although he had written a poem in her memory; he denounced the Prince of Wales for failing to reward him for a eulogy on the Prince's public spirit. In 1727, having been drinking all evening with two friends, he became involved in a brawl near Charing Cross; he stabbed a man to death with his sword and wounded a maid who tried to prevent his escape. He was condemned to death, and saved from execution only by the intercession of the Countess of Hertford who obtained his pardon the following year.

When Johnson first met him his wild career was almost over. Unbridled, unbalanced and quarrelsome, he had offended all his benefactors and lost nearly all his friends. Yet Johnson was captivated by his wayward charm, his fascinating conversation, his astonishing resilience, his extraordinary capacity for survival. He contrived to keep himself fed by dining out at tables where his discreditable reputation, his sudden outburst of quarrelsome invective would be overlooked for the sake of his effervescent talk, his brilliantly related anecdotes, and that infectious gaiety which demanded that 'if he was entertained in a family, nothing was any longer regarded there but amusements and jollity; wherever Savage entered, he immediately expected that order and business should fly before him'. Savage contrived also to keep himself in drink by frequenting taverns, 'for his conversation was so entertaining, and his address so pleasing that few thought the pleasure which they received from him dearly purchased, by paying for his wine'. He did not manage so successfully, however, to keep himself well dressed, since, although he expected all his friends and benefactors to support him as a matter of right, they were required to do so with true delicacy. Once when a friend, anxious to help him, left a message that he desired to see him 'about nine in the morning', Savage, very much disgusted that he should presume to describe the hour of his attendance, refused to have anything to do with him. On another occasion, when he 'received notice that at a coffee-house some clothes and linen were left for him', he disdainfully refused the offer because it was made with 'some neglect of ceremonies', and 'declined to enter the house till the clothes that had been designed for him were taken away'. Even when some of his friends 'proposed to send a tailor to him to take his measure and then to consult among themselves how best to equip him', he flew into 'the most violent agonies of rage; and, being asked what it could be that gave him such disturbance, he replied with the utmost vehemence of indignation, "that they had sent for a tailor to measure him!"' He would choose his own clothes or he would have no clothes at all. Once Johnson came across him wearing a gorgeous cloak of scarlet trimmed with gold lace, which he had bought with a recently raised loan, regardless of the fact that his naked feet could be seen through the gaping holes in his shoes.

As Johnson well knew, Savage did not always contrive to find for himself a room to sleep in, and on occasions he had to stay out in the streets all night, in winter lying down on the ashes by the walls of a glass factory, 'with his associates in poverty'.

Sometimes he and Johnson would leave a tavern together and they would spend the night walking about in each other's company. Johnson was 'often to relate,' said Arthur Murphy, the actor and writer whom Johnson 'very much loved', 'that he and Savage walked round Grosvenor Square till four in the morning; in the course of their conversation reforming the world, dethroning princes, establishing new forms of government, and giving laws to the several states of Europe, till, fatigued at length with their legislative office, they began to feel the want of refreshment; but could not muster up more than fourpence halfpenny'. Johnson said himself that 'one night in particular, when Savage and he walked round St James's Square for want of a lodging, they were not at all depressed by their situation; but in high spirits and brimful of patriotism, traversed the Square for several hours, inveighed against the minister, and "resolved they would stand *by their country*"'.

For all his faults, there was something irresistibly appealing, even lovable, about Savage. He was, his tavern acquaintances would say, repeating the age-old *cliché*, his own worst enemy. Johnson, who published a short life of him in 1744, the year after his death, was alive to many of his faults. He allowed that in his arguments he 'returned reproach for reproach, and insult for insult', that in his quarrel with Tyrconnel he 'wrote to him, not in a style of supplication or respect, but of reproach, menace and contempt; and appeared determined, if he ever regained his allowance, to hold it only by the right of conquest'. It was 'always dangerous to trust him, because he considered himself as discharged by the first quarrel from all ties of honour or gratitude; and would betray those secrets, which in the warmth of confidences, had been imparted to him. . . . It was his peculiar happiness, that he scarcely ever found a stranger, whom he did not leave a friend; but it must likewise be added, that he had not often a friend long without obliging him to become a stranger.'

Yet Savage, his friend insisted, was guilty more of 'negligence than ingratitude', for 'a little knowledge of the world is sufficient to discover that there are few who do not sometimes, in the wantonness of thoughtless mirth, or the heat of transient resentment, speak of their friends and benefactors with levity and contempt, though in their cooler moments they want neither sense of their kindness, nor reverence for their virtue'. Savage himself 'was compassionate both by nature and by principle, and always ready to perform offices of humanity. . . . His distresses, however afflictive, never dejected him: in his lowest state he wanted not spirit to assert the natural dignity of wit. . . . His mind was in an uncommon degree vigorous and active. His judgement was accurate, his apprehension quick, and his memory tenacious. His veracity was questioned, but with little reason; his accounts, though not always the same, were generally consistent. When he loved any man, he suppressed all his faults . . .'

He loved Johnson. And when he said goodbye to him to go and live in Wales—as Thales does in *London*—there were tears in his eyes. Although those who provided the pension of £50 a year on which he was to live in Wales hoped that he would remain in exile for ever, Savage himself intended to write such work in those 'scenes of flowery felicity' as would enable him to return to London and 'live upon the profits of his labour'. But he never did return. He died a debtor in Bristol, having alienated by petulant letters and haughty demands all those who had continued to support him.

Johnson felt a compassionate sympathy for Savage; he understood him as well as any man could; he believed his story of his birth without question, and censured his mother, who was still alive at the time the *Account . . . of Mr Richard Savage* was published, with as much bitter severity as Savage in his lifetime had done himself. Johnson understood Savage so well and sympathised with him so deeply because there was so much in his friend's character, misfortunes and limitations, that were in his own. They both 'willingly practised' the 'arts of conversation' in which they 'excelled'; they both had 'a sturdy confidence' in their own capacity; they both dreaded being left alone, abandoned to their own 'gloomy reflections'; they had both acquired a breadth of knowledge seemingly inconsistent with the 'small time spent in visible endeavours to acquire it'. Indeed, on occasions, it almost seems that Johnson is not writing about Savage but about himself. 'For his life, or for his writings,' Johnson wrote towards the end of the *Account*, 'none who candidly consider his fortune, will think an apology either necessary or difficult. If he was not always sufficiently instructed in his subject, his knowledge was at least greater than could have been attained by others in the same state. If his works were sometimes unfinished, accuracy cannot reasonably be exacted from a man oppressed with want, which he has no hope of relieving but by speedy publication. The insolence and resentment of which he is accused, were not easily to be avoided by a great mind, irritated by perpetual hardships, and constrained hourly to return the spurns of contempt, and repress the insolence of prosperity; and vanity surely may be pardoned in him, to whom life afforded no other comforts than barren praises, and the consciousness of deserving them. Those are no proper judges of his conduct, who have slumbered away their time on the down of plenty.'

Deprived of Savage's comforting and exhilarating company, Johnson became more and more depressed. He had shared Savage's political opinions, his contempt for the government, his prejudices and ideals; he had delighted in talking rebellion with him, fascinated by the talk, withdrawing from the thought of action. But Johnson was aware that even in those few political tracts he had so far written, no coherent, consistent policies had been expressed. Sometimes Johnson had written as an old-fashioned Tory, sometimes as a progressive Whig or as an anti-Hanoverian Jacobite; at one moment attacking the King's mistress or Robert Walpole, the next supporting various discontented London merchants in calling for war with Spain, then joining that section of the Whig opposition known as the Young Patriots in attacking the theatrical licensing act which, for over two hundred years to come, required all stage plays to be licensed by the Lord Chamberlain.

If his political writings had not been coherent, and had also lacked that Swiftian brilliance he had been at pains to emulate, his other work had been scarcely more successful. *London* had sold quite well and had received some heartening praise; several notes in his translation of de Crousaz's *Commentaire* had been marked by that downright, honest and robust good sense that was to distinguish his future criticism, but most of his work for the *Gentleman's Magazine* had been neither memorable nor profitable; his other writings were fundamentally hack-work; his tragedy still remained unproduced. There seemed the real possibility that if he were to remain in London trying to gain his living by writing, he might end his days like poor John Duick with nothing to show for it but a miserable house in Clerkenwell, a Bible and a book of old hymns. He had only once, as he later admitted, ever gone to bed hungry; but who could tell what might happen in the future?

He decided to go back to the country, as Savage had done.

Johnson's opportunity to return to the Midlands came when he was recommended once more for an appointment as a schoolmaster. This time the vacancy which he hoped to fill was at the grammar school at Appleby in Leicestershire. Johnson made the journey to Leicestershire to present his application in person. But although several of his influential friends supported the application, it was unsuccessful. He still had no degree; he was still afflicted with what Pope described as 'an Infirmity of the convulsive kind, that attacks him sometimes, so as to make Him a sad Spectacle'; it was still feared that he would consequently be unable to gain the boys' respect. As a last resort a letter was written on his behalf to Dean Swift to inquire as to the possibility of his gaining a Master of Arts degree at Trinity College, Dublin, by submitting to the 'strictest examination'; but Swift would do nothing to help. The appointment at Appleby went to an Oxford graduate who was related to the school's founder.

Disappointed in this final attempt to obtain regular employment as a schoolmaster—which would have brought him sixty pounds a year—Johnson was disappointed too by the sad decline in the family business which, no longer dealing much in books, was being overtaken by all its competitors. Lucy Porter was proving a great help to Sarah Johnson, whom she called 'Granny', serving uncomplainingly behind the counter, thinking it 'no disgrace', as John Hunter's granddaughter, Anna Seward, put it, 'to thank a poor person who purchased from her a penny battle-dore'. But there was little money to be made from selling cheap toys and stationery in Sadler Street; and her step-father was sadly depressed by the family's endeavours.

Relief from this dispiriting aspect of affairs could, however, still be enjoyed in the Cathedral Close in the house of Gilbert Walmesley. Here, even more than that of Walmesley himself, Johnson could enjoy the company of Mrs Walmesley's young sister, Molly Aston.

Molly was not in the least good-looking: her nose was long and pro-tuberant, her upper lip overhung the lower like a frill of pastry over the rim of a pie-dish, her jaw was slightly undershot. Yet she was always lively, sympathetic, responsive, and wonderfully intelligent, being able to talk with as much sense and erudition about the problems of economics as about literature. She wrote poetry herself; and Johnson once confessed that the letters he had had from her would be the last papers he would ever destroy. He also once said with characteristic exaggeration but deep sincerity of feeling that the only time in his life that he had experienced 'measureless delight' was an evening which had been spent entirely in talking to Molly Aston.

Women did not usually take to Molly Aston as quickly as Johnson did: her tongue was too sharp, they thought, her wit too caustic; Anna Seward found her haughty. But to Johnson it seemed that she could do no wrong. Even her blatant Whiggery was readily forgivable. He had never liked vapid women with no opinions of their own; they had softness, he agreed, but so had pillows. Being married to such a sleepy-souled woman would be just like playing at cards for nothing. Honeysuckle wives were, after all, creepers at best, and commonly destroyed the trees they so tenderly clung to.

Molly Aston was not the only young woman in whose company Johnson delighted during this visit to the Midlands from London. He was asked to stay in Ashbourne by his old school friend, John Taylor, who was now extremely comfortably—if somewhat discontentedly—established with a wife in a big, well-ordered house. Taylor took Johnson out to other comfortable and even bigger houses in the district, and in one of these, three miles from Ashbourne at Bradley, he met the entrancing Mary Meynell.

Mary's parents were an oddly assorted couple. Her mother, the daughter of a man who had made a fortune from his sugar plantations in the West Indies, was a profoundly religious, kindly, understanding woman; her father a gruff, down-to-earth country squire who lived for his hunting, professed himself a free-thinker—he forbade his children to be given any religious training, an injunction his wife quietly ignored—and was possessed of so violent a temper that in his most savagely malignant moods, 'he really wished evil to others', Johnson said, 'and rejoiced at it'. But Johnson nurtured, in retrospect, a kind of affection for 'Old Meynell'. He remembered—and repeated without disapprobatory comment—his categoric statement on the merits of foreigners: 'For anything I see, foreigners are fools.' Meynell was also the author of a remark with which Johnson was equally satisfied: 'The chief advantage of London is, that a man is always so near his burrow.'

Of all the Meynell family, however, it was the daughter, Mary, with whom Johnson expressed himself as being the most taken. 'She had,' he said, temporarily forgetting in his enthusiasm Molly Aston and all those others whom he had formerly praised in similar terms, 'She had the best understanding' he had ever met with 'in any human being'.

She was only seventeen at the time of Johnson's first visit to Bradley; and in later years, after her marriage to a near neighbour, William Fitzherbert of Tissington, it had to be admitted that she became rather managing. Her husband was a 'good-humoured fellow,' Johnson said, 'generous of his money and of his meat, and desirous of nothing but cheerful society'. One evening, in his 'happy discriminative manner', Johnson gave his companions a portrait of this Mr Fitzherbert of Derbyshire. 'There was (said he) no sparkle, no brilliancy in Fitzherbert; but I never knew a man who was so generally acceptable. He made everybody quite easy, overpowered nobody by the superiority of his talents, made no man think worse of himself by being his rival, seemed always to listen, did not oblige you to hear much from him, and'—a crowning virtue, Johnson's listeners could not but feel inclined to suppose—'did not oppose what you said. . . . People were willing to think well of everything about him. . . . He was an instance of the truth of the observation, that a man will please more by negative qualities than by positive; by never offending, than by giving a great deal of delight. In the first place, men hate more steadily than they love; and if I have said anything to hurt a man once, I shall not get the better of this, by saying many things to please him.'

No doubt it was these rather negative qualities in the generally acceptable, easy-going Fitzherbert that made his wife so managing, so anxious to keep his soul from corruption, to 'keep his estate entire for their children'. 'He felt her influence too powerfully,' Johnson was forced to admit. 'She stood at the door of her Paradise in Derbyshire, like the angel with the flaming sword, to keep the devil at a distance. But she was not immortal, poor dear! She died, and her husband felt at once afflicted and released.'

With such pleasant companions as Fitzherbert, Gilbert Walmesley and Molly Aston, Mr and Mrs Meynell and their as yet unmarried daughter, Mary, Johnson let the weeks go by in the Midlands without making any arrangements to go back to work in London. John Taylor's house with its regular, ample, well-cooked meals, its attentive servants, was so very agreeable, so very different from the discomforts and privations of his London lodgings. The summer passed and the autumn; the new year, 1740, began; and Johnson remained in the country. At the end of January he was still there when a letter came from Tetty. She was in great pain, even 'danger', from a badly injured leg which was keeping her confined to bed.

Although Johnson, in his reply on 31 January, assured her that he would be 'very uneasy' until he knew that she had recovered, that he hoped she did not think so unkindly of him as to imagine he could be at rest while he believed his 'dear Tetty' in pain, the letter appears to have been the first he had written to her in the six months that they had been separated. 'You have already suffered more than I can bear to reflect upon,' he continued, 'and I hope more than either of us shall suffer again. . . . Our troubles will surely never separate us more. . . . I beg therefore that You will more regard my happiness, than to expose Yourself to any hazards. I still promise myself many happy years from your tenderness and affection, which I sometimes hope our misfortunes have not yet deprived me of . . .

'Be assured, my dear Girl, that I have seen nobody in these rambles upon which I have been forced, that has not contributed to confirm my esteem and affection for thee, though that esteem and affection only contributed to increase my unhappiness when I reflected that the most amiable woman in the world was exposed by my means to miseries which I could not relieve. I am my charming Love Yours *Sam: Johnson.*'

He told her not to hesitate to call in another surgeon, if her present doctor did not 'succeed in his endeavours'. For two or three visits she would have to pay a guinea which she must not scruple to part with. He would send her 'twenty pouns more on Monday'.

He was able to afford the money as that very day his mother and he, as 'son and heir', had mortgaged the Lichfield house. Theophilus Levett, the town clerk, had advanced them £80 at 4½ per cent interest.

Yet, despite his being in funds again, despite the affectionate tone of his letter to Tetty, he did not immediately set off for London to be with her. He stayed on in Lichfield for at least another month, the coldest time that he or anyone else in Lichfield could remember; and when he did go back to London it seems that he was drawn as much by *Irene* as by Tetty.

He had heard that *Irene* had 'at last become a kind of favourite among the players' at Drury Lane. Fleetwood, the patentee, had said that he would try to put the tragedy on either that season or the next; an offer of fifty guineas for the right to print the text once it had been performed had been made by William Chetwood, who was also himself a dramatist as well as a bookseller.

But when he got back to London, Johnson found that plans for the production of *Irene* had not progressed as far as he had hoped. Fleetwood was noncommittal: he might put the play on soon; but then again he might not; he was not sure that he could fit it in this season; perhaps he might do something about it next. Nor could Johnson get any money by selling the copyright. For Chetwood, 'a blockhead and a measureless and bungling liar' according to his contemporary, the critic George Steevens, was not interested in publishing the play until it had been acted by the Drury Lane Company. So, instead of seeing *Irene* performed, Johnson had to be content with listening to an actor recite a prologue which he wrote for a short comic piece entitled *Lethe* by David Garrick who, though still in the wine trade with his brother, spent far more time at Drury Lane and in those coffee-houses around Covent Garden frequented by actors than in his business premises at Durham Yard.

Disappointed at Drury Lane, Johnson was compelled to return to St John's Gate. Cave was glad to have him back and provided him with more and more work until he was writing over half the contents of the *Gentleman's Magazine* single-handed. He contributed book reviews, further parliamentary debates, condensations of reports, occasional poems—usually refinements of verses recited impromptu after a few moments' pause, as he stirred his drink in a tavern the night before—and more short biographies in the style of his life of Boerhaave. He wrote of scholars and physicians, Robert Blake and Francis Drake, using any reliable printed materials to hand, condensing them and rewriting them with what he considered to be appropriate critical comments and asides, taking the opportunity to knock down blockheads, and the ideas of blockheads, as when, on encountering cant about the noble savage in accounts of Drake's voyages, he characteristically interpolated the observation: 'The question is not, whether a good Indian or bad Englishman be most happy; but which state is most desirable, supposing virtue and reason the same in both. . . . He that never saw, or heard, or thought of strong liquors, cannot be proposed as a pattern of sobriety.'

He worked at great speed, when he could be brought to work at all, locking himself in a room assigned to him at St John's Gate so that nobody could get in to disturb him or tempt him to go out. The only exceptions, a fellow-contributor recalled, were the compositor or Cave's boy, who was sent up for more matter, which, as fast as Johnson composed it, 'he tumbled out at the door'.

The magazine prospered, its circulation rose from ten to fifteen thousand copies a month, and Cave, who prospered with it, manifested his good fortune by buying 'an old coach and a pair of older horses; and, that he might not incur the suspicion of pride in setting up an equipage, he disclosed to the world the source of his affluence, by a representation of St John's Gate, instead of his arms, on the door panel'.

Johnson, on the other hand, though less poverty-stricken than he had been the previous year, enjoyed but little share of the magazine's prosperity. He and Tetty moved their lodgings constantly, up and down the Strand, then to Bow Street, then to Fetter Lane, then to Holborn. Few of Johnson's friends ever saw these lodgings, for he could not afford to entertain, and, in any case, spent much if not most of his time, when not working in his St John's Gate room, at the coffee-houses and taverns where his fellow writers met to talk, to read the newspapers by the fire, to eat and to drink.

Johnson himself did not drink alcohol any more. He had discovered, while living with Edmund Hector in Birmingham, how difficult it was for him to stop drinking wine or punch once he had had one glass; so he had made up his mind he must never have even one glass, otherwise he might become a drunkard, as many of his friends already were.

One of the most frequently drunk of these friends was Tom Cumming, a merchant engaged in the African trade who was known as the 'fighting Quaker'. It was said to be his peculiar distinction that in one of his belligerent moods he had overborne Johnson in argument. But this, so Johnson objected when asked about so remarkable an occasion, was not quite the case: Cumming had been drunk, had attacked him with rudeness, and Johnson had not answered him 'because he was in such a situation'. Later he had walked home with him.

Another friend—'intoxicated whenever he had the means to avoid starving'—was the extraordinary Samuel Boyse, poet, translator, and, when pressed, contributor to the *Gentleman's Magazine*. Boyse, son of a Presbyterian minister, was a year older than Johnson, but although he could write verse 'as fast as most men wrote prose', he had produced no more than his debts demanded. Whenever he could he contrived to live on borrowed credit, by raising subscriptions for books he had not the least intention of writing, by persuading his wife that he was dying and that she must solicit loans for his medical expenses or even for his funeral. He had absolutely no pride when it came to borrowing or begging money. 'You were pleased to give my wife the enclosed shilling last night,' he once wrote to Sir Hans Sloane, the rich physician and collector; 'I doubt not but you thought it a good one, but as it happened otherwise you will forgive the trouble occasioned by the mistake.'

When appeals to friends, acquaintances, editors and patrons all failed, Boyse would resort to the pawnbroker. First his shirt went, and he made do with strips of white paper round his wrists and neck; then his breeches and waistcoat went, and he was obliged to appear without them in his editor's office where, on one occasion at least, several ladies who were present were necessarily 'obliged immediately to retire'. Finally all his clothes would be pawned; and Colley Cibber, the actor and dramatist who to Richard Savage's disgust had become Poet Laureate in 1730, related that once in the winter of 1740, Boyse, having pawned all his clothes, was obliged to dispose of his sheets as well. 'During this time he had some employment in writing verses for the magazines, and whoever had seen him must have thought the object singular enough. He sat up in bed with a blanket wrapped about him, through which he had cut a hole large enough to admit his arm, and placing the paper upon his knee, scribbled, in the best manner he could, the verses he was obliged to make.'

Needless to say, Boyse's books went the same way as his clothes and sheets. Even the foreign books supplied to him by booksellers for translation were pawned immediately the first instalment was supplied for the

printer. The bookseller had to redeem the pledge to obtain another instalment, and, when that was produced, back to the pawnbroker the book
would go.

Cave was indulgent towards his difficult contributor. Once he was
faced by a long and urgent letter in which Boyse, writing from a coffee-
house, pleaded for 'half a guinea for support'. 'I humbly entreat your
answer,' Boyse went on imploringly, 'having not tasted anything since
Tuesday evening I came in here, and my coat will be taken off my back,
for the charge of the bed. So that I must go into prison naked, which is
too shocking for me to think of.' At the bottom of the letter Cave wrote the
single word 'Sent', adding at the top a resigned note: 'Mr S. Boyse
poetical writer. A singular character.'

Johnson, who also thought him a singular character, loved him in the
way that he had loved the equally importunate, equally improvident,
more quarrelsome and far more gifted Savage. In his life of Savage,
Johnson described how his friend, no 'exact economist', would immediately go off and spend the pension he was granted by the Queen as soon as
he received it, returning afterwards to his favourite coffee-house once more
penniless. Boyse also behaved in this way, and wholeheartedly sympathised
with the idiosyncrasies of a man who would buy himself a costly coat
although he had no stockings. When Boyse, pitiably hungry, was given the
price of a dinner or two, he sent out for a piece of roast beef but then
declined to eat it without ketchup, truffles and mushrooms, a meal that
cost him the last half-guinea he possessed.

Cave's difficulty in getting Boyse to produce his material on time was
matched by the problems he encountered with one of Johnson's other
friends, the young poet, William Collins. Collins, the son of a mayor of
Chichester, was eighteen when Johnson returned to London from Lichfield, and had already published poetry in the *Gentleman's Magazine* while
still a schoolboy at Winchester. But it was with the utmost difficulty that
he could be persuaded to write anything after he had come down from
Oxford, although the little he inherited from his parents was soon spent
and he was obliged to earn his own living somehow. An uncle, a colonel in
the 8th Foot, concluding that he was 'too indolent even for the army',
decided that he ought to go into the church. The church, however, did not
appeal to Collins and he had come to London to write.

Yet he found it as difficult to settle down to write as ever Johnson did.
He was full of ideas and projects about which he would talk with great
intelligence and enthusiasm; but when it came to setting them down on
paper, he often quailed at the attempt and abandoned it.

From the several odes he did publish, however, Johnson was well aware of his remarkable gifts, and was anxious to do all he could to help him. He visited him one day at his lodgings, outside which a bailiff was 'prowling in the street'; and proposed that he make a translation of Aristotle's *Poetics*. Collins agreed; and when Johnson had found a bookseller willing to publish the work and obtained an advance for it, Collins 'escaped into the country' to write it. He never did write it, though. An inheritance from his uncle, mortally wounded with his regiment in Flanders, enabled him to pay back the advance. Soon after he lost his reason.

Another highly eccentric member of Johnson's circle at this time was the celebrated George Psalmanazar. Introduced into the company of Cave's assistants and hacks by Thomas Birch, who employed him as an indexer for some of his books, Psalmanazar was a most mysterious figure. No one knew his real name—he took the one by which he was known from Shalmaneser, the Assyrian prince mentioned in the second book of Kings. No one knew exactly how old he was—he seems to have been about sixty-two when Johnson first met him. No one knew exactly where he had come from—he said himself that he was born somewhere on the road between Avignon and Rome. Johnson confirmed that he spoke French with 'a spice of the Gascoin accent' and English with a cockney accent.

Psalmanazar spoke many other languages, too, including Latin in which he was fluent; and at an early stage in his career he had invented an elaborate language of his own. This language he had first represented as being that of a remote region of Japan but afterwards as that of the island of Formosa.

Describing himself as a native of Formosa, who had been abducted from his homeland by Jesuits intent on converting him to Roman Catholicism, Psalmanazar had come to England from the Continent in the company of a Scottish army chaplain, William Innes, at the invitation of the Bishop of London. In England his extraordinary self-possession, and his apparent fluency in a language which was 'sufficiently original, copious, and regular to impose on men of very extensive learning', persuaded most people to believe his story. He was a welcome guest at 'every great table in the kingdom' where his fascinating stories of life and customs in Formosa delighted his hosts and fellow-guests. He spoke of human sacrifices and cannibalism, maintaining that it was no sin to eat human flesh, even if it was, perhaps, a trifle unmannerly.

The Bishop of London and others had paid for him to spend six months at Christ Church in order 'to teach the Formosan language to a set of gentlemen, who were afterwards to go with him to convert the people to

Christianity'; and he had left behind him at Oxford a manuscript describing in detail the coinage of Formosa. He later published in Latin, *An Historical and Geographic Description of Formosa . . . Illustrated with several Cuts*, based to some extent upon a Dutch account of Japan but to a considerably larger extent upon his own imagination. The first edition of this book had soon been sold; French and German translations appeared. But its very success marked the beginning of Psalmanazar's downfall, for it had come into the hands of people qualified to deny its accuracy. His position as a Formosan scholar became less and less secure; and when his accomplice and mentor, William Innes, was appointed chaplain-general to the British forces in Portugal—as a reward for having converted his charge to Protestantism—Psalmanazar decided that the time had come to retreat into obscurity.

Since then he had supported himself precariously by working as a tutor and a clerk, by painting fans and later by hack-writing. He had confessed his past deceits and now lived a life of the utmost virtue. He worked extremely hard, writing from seven in the morning until seven at night and teaching himself Hebrew which he learned to speak with as much fluency as he spoke Latin. Everyone who knew him in Clerkenwell where he came to live in Ironmonger Row, Old Street, revered him; and as one of Cave's writers said, 'scarce any person, even children, passed him without showing him the usual signs of respect'. To Johnson who used to sit and talk with him in an alehouse in Old Street, he seemed positively saintly. When asked in later life who was the best man he had ever known, Johnson replied without hesitation, 'Psalmanazar'. He had never seen 'the close of the life of any one that he wished so much his own to resemble for its purity and devotion. . . . Psalmanazar's piety, penitence and virtue exceeded almost what we read as wonderful in the lives of the saints.' His single indulgence was in laudanum, of which he took an enormous quantity, at one time drinking 'ten or twelve spoonsfuls every night, and very often more', though in later years he succeeded in reducing the dose to the ten or twelve drops he consumed in the pint of punch he drank every evening after work.

Although Johnson and he talked of all manner of things, they never once spoke of Formosa. Indeed, when he was asked whether or not he had ever felt inclined to refer to it, Johnson replied that he had not dared even to mention *China*. Nor had he ever contradicted Psalmanazar. Why, he would 'as soon have thought of contradicting a bishop'.

With other of his fellow-customers at the ale-houses, taverns and coffee-houses of Clerkenwell, Johnson was not, of course, so restrained. He argued with them and contended with them with all that determination for victory which had characterised his discussions with Gilbert Walmesley in Lichfield. Amongst the best remembered of these customers was an eccentric tailor, known to his companions as 'the metaphysical tailor', a man far too interested in intellectual problems, in drawing 'squares and triangles on his shop board . . . to excel in the cut of a coat'. There was also John Hawkins, a hard-working, serious, strait-laced attorney's articled clerk who was also a contributor of essays and poems to the *Gentleman's Magazine*. And there was Lewis Paul, an ingenious if disingenuous inventor from Birmingham who had devised a machine for pinking shrouds, and in 1738 had taken out a patent for an 'engine for spinning of wool and cotton in a manner entirely new'.

Johnson, intrigued by machinery and always willing to help a friend, took a great interest in this invention, as did his old Lichfield acquaintance, the hard-drinking Robert James, now practising as a physician in London, and Edward Cave, both of whom invested money in it. But although the invention was highly original it did not become a commercial success until taken up by Richard Arkwright later on in the century; and there were endless disputes between Paul and his backers which Johnson, their mutual friend, made strenuous though vain efforts to resolve.

In the summer of 1741 Johnson and Robert James became involved in a more successful project, a medical dictionary. Having conceived the plan, James approached Johnson who prepared a big and imposing four-page sheet explaining the purpose and scope of the dictionary, and calling for subscribers. The response was favourable; and the dictionary began to appear in February 1742, at first in fortnightly, and then in weekly instalments, until the five sheets of each issue, interspersed with copperplate illustrations, had built up into its three large folio volumes. As well as helping with the proposals, Johnson wrote the elegant dedication and contributed various entries, mainly short biographies of medical men, for the main body of James's text.

This work brought him into contact with Thomas Osborne, the publisher of the *Medicinal Dictionary*, who now asked Johnson to assist in preparing the catalogue of the huge library of Edward Harley, second Earl of Oxford, which Osborne had recently bought for resale for £13,000, an enormous sum, but one 'not more than the binding of the books had cost'. Johnson was also to write 'A General Account of the Harleian Library' as a prelude to the forthcoming sale; and later on was to help Osborne with the publication of a series of extracts from books in the library which, like the *Medicinal Dictionary*, were to be issued in instalments under the title of *The Harleian Miscellany*.

This commission occupied Johnson for the last few months of 1742 and for the whole of 1743. The cataloguing, in particular, was an arduous task. Only one other person, William Oldys, who had been Lord Oxford's secretary, was engaged upon it, and there were almost forty thousand volumes to list. All the volumes had to be 'digested under distinct heads, and very frequently accompanied with curious notes, relating either to the history of the book, the life of the author, the peculiarity of the edition, or the excellence of the particular copy exposed to sale.'

Then, following the death of Richard Savage in Bristol, in August 1743, came the idea to publish his life which Johnson, encouraged and prodded by Cave, wrote at such a rate that it was finished in December, though not published until February 1744. So great was Johnson's anxiety to get it completed, indeed, that he sacrificed accuracy for speed, sending sheets to the press as soon as they were written, dashing off forty-eight of the printed pages at one single all-night sitting, checking few facts or references.

Nor was Johnson able to write the book free from the disturbance of other work. There were still the parliamentary debates and his other contributions for the *Gentleman's Magazine*; there was the cataloguing for Osborne; there were reviews, proposals, advertisements, dedications, a Shakespearean commentary entitled *Miscellaneous Observations on the Tragedy of Macbeth*. And as soon as these were finished more work piled up, little of it remunerative, all of it burdensome.

Occasionally there was a pleasant surprise. One day in 1745 he was asked to prune a long poem written by an Irish clergyman in memory of the late Primate of Ireland. He struck out many lines, 'and might have blotted out many more,' he afterwards decided, 'without making the poem worse'. 'However, the doctor was very thankful, and very generous, for he gave me ten guineas, *which was to me at that time a great sum.*'

At about the time he received this welcome and generous sum he was approached by his old friend Harry Hervey, who had entirely changed his way of life and even his name. On the death of his brother-in-law, Sir Thomas Aston, his wife had come into part of the family fortune; and, in consequence of this, Hervey had decided to cut himself still further loose from his family and to call himself Aston. He had also decided to end his career in the Army and he had entered the Church.

As the Hon and Rev Henry Hervey Aston, he had been invited to preach a sermon at St Paul's Cathedral on 2 May 1745 at the annual service held for the Sons of the Clergy. He would have a distinguished congregation; as well as the Lord Chief Justice and the City Aldermen, eight bishops would be there together with the Archbishop of Canterbury himself. He appealed to Johnson to help him; and Johnson readily agreed. He enjoyed writing sermons—in so far as he enjoyed writing at all—and he eventually became so adept at producing them for his clerical friends and acquaintances that he could sit down after dinner to write a long one and get it into the post that night. The one he wrote for Harry Hervey Aston in 1745 was highly effective. It was later published, and favourably received.

It was published, of course, under Hervey Aston's name. Indeed Johnson's name, for all the work he had produced, was still not widely known. *An Account of the Life of Mr Richard Savage*, like his *London* was published anonymously as was nearly all his journalism though he sometimes used a pseudonym such as 'Probus Britannicus' or 'An Impartial Hand'. Nor had he yet succeeded, after five years of hard writing, in making anything more than a bare subsistence. Sometimes, in fact, he was as close to penury as he had ever been in his life, quite unable to pay the few pounds a year interest on the mortgage of the Lichfield house until, when three years interest was due and Theophilus Levett was becoming rather pressing, Harry Hervey Aston came to his help and paid the arrears off for him. He was forced to complain of the necessity of working 'almost in the dark' for lack of candles, of writing with worn-out pens, and he was often obliged to write to Cave for a little more money to see him through a particularly difficult time: 'If you could spare me another guinea I should take it very kindly tonight, but if you do not I shall not think it an injury.— I am almost well again—'

Although compelled to write to him in these terms, he remained on good terms with Cave who, while never paying more than he could possibly avoid, always helped his writers in times of real distress. Johnson was frequently a guest at his dinner table, though once there he was expected to do more than 'eat and drink and talk', for Cave could think of nothing other than the *Gentleman's Magazine* even over his meals. One afternoon Johnson was dining at St John's Gate with Cave and a young curate, the Rev Stephen Barrett, a classical scholar just down from Oxford. After the cloth had been removed and they were drinking their wine, Cave opened his bag of papers and took out some Latin verses, announcing, 'Here is, gentlemen, a very indifferent performance, but it is just an exact length for my purpose; and yet, if ye will not brush it up for me, it cannot appear.'

'Give it to Barrett,' said Johnson immediately, true to his rule of doing no more work than was strictly necessary and hoping to persuade the younger man to do it by flattery. 'He'll correct it for you, in a minute.'

'Why, no,' said Barrett and, 'in return for the manœuvre of throwing it all' upon him, he insisted that Johnson share the task with him, couplet by couplet.

'Very well,' said Johnson, 'do you begin.'

'By no means! *Seniores priores,*' replied Barrett, throwing the paper across the table. Johnson 'returned it in a moment,' Barrett recalled; 'and so it passed from the one to the other, like a shuttle cock; Cave chuckling all the while to see it pass and repass so rapidly.'

Sometimes, when other, more distinguished contributors to the *Gentleman's Magazine* came to dinner at St John's Gate, Johnson himself chose not to appear at the table because of his shabby clothes. One day Walter Harte, the Vice-Principal of St Mary Hall, Oxford, who had accompanied Lord Chesterfield's natural son on the Grand Tour, came to dine with Cave. Johnson also was invited; but he did not come. Cave, suspecting the reason, filled 'a plate of victuals' at the table and sent it out for him.

Forty years later Johnson was still talking of Cave with great affection. He was a 'penurious paymaster'; that could never be denied. 'But he was a good man.'

No such praise could possibly be bestowed upon Thomas Osborne, the Gray's Inn bookseller for whom Johnson did the Harley cataloguing. Osborne was a 'blockhead' who had inherited his business from his father. He was also 'entirely destitute of shame, without sense of any disgrace but that of poverty'. Rude, rich and mean, he was as much disliked by those who worked for him as by his customers to whom he was notoriously insolent if they declined to buy books that he himself had published. A short, thickset man, he stared at them with a kind of 'impassive dulness', and then made some arrogant or offensive remark. 'Of booksellers he was one of the most ignorant,' confirmed another acquaintance. 'Of title pages or editions he had no knowledge or remembrance, but in all the tricks and arts of his trade he was most expert. . . . He used to boast that he was worth forty thousand pounds.'

One day, when he was working on the *Catalogus Bibliothecae Harleianae,* Johnson received an unwelcome call from him. Evidently he accused Johnson of idling, of spending far too much time reading the books instead of listing them, ignoring the fact that in order to describe a volume the cataloguer must of necessity look into it. In the course of the argument, he called Johnson a liar. That was too much: Johnson picked up the heaviest book to hand, hit Osborne across the side of the head with it and knocked him to the floor.

'I have beat many a fellow,' Johnson remarked complacently when reminded of this incident in his old age, 'but the rest had the wit to hold their tongues.' Osborne apparently had not; and his numerous enemies delighted in embellishing the story he told with details to his further shame. The most pleasing version had Johnson with his foot on Osborne's neck warning him that 'he need not be in a hurry to rise; for if he did he would have the further trouble of kicking him downstairs'.

Johnson had every reason to burst out in anger and resentment. Well aware of his peculiar talents, he had yet to work as a hack and a drudge to make such men as Osborne rich. He had no money; he had no reputation after five years' grinding labour. Often he thought he would give up trying to make his living as an author. But he had had no success in teaching and, without a degree, could not get into the law, except as an attorney; and he did not think highly of attorneys. Speaking of one of them, he said that he did not care to speak ill of any man behind his back, but he 'believed the gentleman was an *attorney*'. He caused enquiries to be made of Richard Smalbroke, Chancellor of the diocese of Lichfield, 'as to whether a person might be permitted to practise as an advocate in Doctors' Commons without a doctor's degree in civil law'. And he added with characteristic self-confidence, that, although he was 'a total stranger to these studies', that should be no stumbling block as 'whatever is a profession, and maintains numbers, must be within the reach of common abilities, and some degree of industry'. He did not believe, and always refused to believe, that there were any particular mysteries in any profession or craft.[1] A man of talent could do well at anything he set his mind to. 'I am persuaded that had Sir Isaac Newton applied to poetry he would have made a very fine epick poem,' he said. 'I could as easily apply to law as to tragick poetry. . . . Sir, the man who has vigour, may walk to the east, just as well as to west, if he happens to turn his head that way.' But this was a belief not generally shared; certainly not by lawyers, and a career in Doctors' Commons was not open to him.

Resigned to authorship, he considered all sorts of ideas that might set him on the road to success. He issued proposals for a 'New Edition of the Plays of William Shakespeare, with Notes Critical and Explanatory, in Which the Text Will be Corrected'. But then the celebrated Strand bookseller, Jacob Tonson, claimed the right to control the copyright of Shakespeare and threatened to defend it by a Chancery suit. Johnson thought of a life of Dryden, a biography of Alfred the Great, new translations of Aristotle and Cicero, of Machiavelli and Herodian, new editions of Chaucer and of the seventeenth-century poets, John Oldham and Wentworth Dillon, Earl of Roscommon; he planned essays and poems, histories and treatises, but none of the works was undertaken. He had the instincts of a scholar, but neither the patience nor the application.

He long considered compiling a dictionary; and one day when he was sitting in Robert Dodsley's shop, and the bookseller remarked to him that a dictionary of the English Language would be well received by the public, 'Johnson seemed to catch at the proposition'. There was a pause. But then he said, 'in his abrupt decisive manner, ' "I believe I shall not undertake it." '

3
'Poor Dear Tetty'

'A suspicion of his conjugal infelicity certainly went abroad and procured him much commiseration among his friends.'

William Shaw

By the early spring of 1746 Johnson had changed his mind about the dictionary. He needed no persuasion that such a work was badly needed. It was said that Addison had been offered £3,000 'to make an English dictionary and to put it out under his name'. Later Pope had been approached and had got as far as making a list of suitable authorities; Pope's enemy, the poet Ambrose Philips, had gone even further and brought out proposals for a dictionary in two folio volumes. But none of these writers had progressed beyond the planning stage, and it was left to a Stepney schoolmaster, Nathan Bailey, to compile the one reputable dictionary in the language. This was the *Universal Etymological English Dictionary*. It had been published in 1721, and since then several new editions had appeared—there were to be no less than thirty editions in all. An expanded folio edition of 1736 contained about 60,000 words; and a revision made after Bailey's death in 1742 contained some 5,000 more; whereas Johnson's dictionary was to list only 40,000. But there were serious objections to Bailey's dictionary, particularly in the matter of definitions: his definition of a mouse as 'an animal well known' was notoriously reticent; and, although he altered this in later editions the new definition was scarcely more explicit: 'a small Creature infesting Houses.'

Johnson was determined that *his* dictionary should contain no such weaknesses. On the contrary it was to 'rival the academies' of France and Italy whose *Dictionnaire* and *Vocabolario* were models for the conscientious lexicographer. It was to contain illustrations of the meanings of the words, taken from those 'English writers who were most correct in their language', as well as etymological derivations. He had no reservations about his fitness to undertake the task; he was even confident that he could complete it within three years. When William Adams, the junior fellow of Pembroke who had advised him not to miss so many lectures, called to see him on a visit to London and heard of his proposed undertaking, he was appalled. 'But, Sir,' Adams protested, 'How can you do this in three years?'

'Sir, I have no doubt that I can do it in three years.'

'But the French Academy, which consists of forty members, took forty years to compile their dictionary.'

'Sir, thus it is. This is the proportion. Let me see; forty times forty is sixteen hundred. As is three to sixteen hundred, so is the proportion of an Englishman to a Frenchman.'

When the immense work was at last finished—though certainly not in three years—another friend suggested that perhaps he had not fully comprehended what he was undertaking. 'Yes, Sir,' he retorted with pride, 'I knew very well what I was undertaking—and very well how to do it—and have done it very well.'

Robert Dodsley also had confidence that Johnson could do it well, if he would do it at all; but his own bookselling business did not have the resources to finance the undertaking without the help of others. So a combination of six booksellers was formed, including, besides Dodsley himself, Thomas Longman, formerly apprenticed to Thomas Osborne's father—whose daughter he had married—and now in business on his own account with his nephew at the Sign of the Ship in Paternoster Row, and Andrew Millar, Henry Fielding's Scottish publisher, a man much respected by Johnson for his generosity to authors, for having 'raised the price of literature', yet a man 'so habitually and equably drunk' that his printer 'never perceived that he was more sober at one time than another'.

These booksellers and their colleagues offered Johnson the sum of £1,575 for the dictionary. Out of this sum he was to meet all his expenses during the three years the work was expected to take. During the first year or so he was to be given periodical payments on account, though once the work was well under way he seems to have been paid an agreed sum for each printed sheet. As soon as the contract was engrossed, Johnson invited all the booksellers to have breakfast with him at the Golden Anchor near

Holborn Bar so that the document could be signed. This was done on 18 June 1746.

The printer chosen was William Strahan, a Scotsman like Millar, and in Johnson's opinion the proprietor of the best printing-house in London. His premises were in New Street, off Fleet Street; and it was in order to be near them that Johnson moved into a house in Gough Square.

It was a handsome house of three storeys, a basement and a garret; and it was in the garret, 'fitted up like a counting-house', that work on the dictionary eventually began. The furniture consisted of desks and stools for his six assistants, though Johnson himself was content with what a visitor described as an 'old crazy deal table', and an even older wooden arm-chair which eventually lost one of its legs and an arm. By this time, however, its owner was used to it and perfectly accustomed to its defects. Despite the convulsive movements of his body he managed to sit in it without falling over, and when he raised his great bulk out of it he would balance it with his hand or 'place it with great composure against some support'.

The assistants were paid twenty-three shillings a week between them. There were six of them, five of them Scottish, recommended to him perhaps by their fellow-countrymen, Millar and Strahan.

'In truth' he did not get 'much assistance from them', Johnson complained to Strahan; but they had their uses. One of the Scotsmen had an unusual knowledge of 'low cant phrases' and the language of gambling; another was an able linguist; a third, Robert Shiels, was 'a man of very acute understanding, though with little scholastic education'. They at least ensured that Johnson had company during his hours of tedious reading, hands capable of performing the drudgery of copying and clipping and pasting, and people to talk to when he was tired of work. Once a discussion began about the poetry of James Thomson which Shiels, in his loyalty to a fellow Scotsman, uncritically praised but to which Johnson, while allowing great merit, raised the objection that the meaning did not always 'peep through' the welter of words. Since Shiels refused to admit the objection Johnson took down a volume of Thomson's poetry from a shelf and began to read some verses aloud.

What did Shiels think of them? He thought them very fine. 'Well,' Johnson announced, snapping the book shut triumphantly, we may be sure. 'Well, Sir, I have omitted every other line.'

Thomson, nevertheless, 'had as much of the poet about him as most writers' and was as worthy of being quoted as several others whose works Johnson consulted to discover examples of the good usage of words to be included in his dictionary. For this, he had decided, was to be his method of approach. Instead of using another dictionary as a basis for his own, he first of all went through the works of a vast array of English writers, marking passages which he considered worthy of quotation by strokes at the beginning and end, and underlining the word the meaning of which the passage was intended to illustrate. Then he would write the first letter of the word in the margin of the book. When the entire book had been read and marked in this way, he handed it to one of his assistants who copied out each passage on a slip of paper with the appropriate word underlined. The slips were then arranged in alphabetical order. Finally, Johnson wrote out each word, with its etymology and definition, on to big sheets of paper, and the assistants pasted the slips underneath.

Johnson used as many suitable books as he could lay his hands on, borrowing a great number of them from friends and acquaintances who received them back with underlinings and pencil markings on almost every page, 'so defaced as to be scarce worth owning, and yet, some of his friends were glad to receive and entertain them as curiosities'. Whenever he could, he selected a passage which not only illustrated the meaning of the key word exactly but which was also, as he put it himself, 'useful to some other end'. He therefore 'extracted from his philosophers principles of science; from historians remarkable facts; from chemists complete processes; from divines striking exhortations; and from poets beautiful descriptions'. He also endeavoured to choose quotations that seemed to him to express a just and sensible opinion, citing 'no author whose writings had a tendency to hurt sound religion and morality'.

What he did not attempt to do was to give any guidance as to how words should be pronounced, for he could not himself find any common ground of agreement. To indicate the difficulty he cited to a friend conflicting opinions as to the pronunciation of the word 'great'. A peer of the realm born in London of ancient lineage, educated by accomplished tutors and at Cambridge, one of His Majesty's principal Ministers in the House of Lords, insisted that the word 'should be pronounced so as to rhyme to *state*', whereas a baronet born in Devonshire of equally ancient lineage, a Fellow of the Royal Society, and one of the most distinguished members of the House of Commons, was of the firm opinion that 'it should be pronounced so as to rhyme to *seat*, and that none but an Irishman would pronounce it *grait*. Now here were two men of the highest rank, the one, the best speaker in the House of Lords, the other, the best speaker in the House of Commons, differing entirely.'

After nine months' work in the garret at 17 Gough Square, Johnson and his backers decided that the time had come to make an announcement in the Press that an English dictionary 'etymological, analogical, syntactical, explanatory and critical' was being prepared by Samuel Johnson and that it was in a state of 'great forwardness'. Soon afterwards an explanation of his intentions which he had drafted in April was distributed under the title, *The Plan of a Dictionary*. At Dodsley's instigation this *Plan* was dedicated to Lord Chesterfield, courtier, essayist, Minister, one of the richest and most discerning literary patrons of the time.

In its early stages Lord Chesterfield took a real interest in the work. He received Johnson with his cool, reserved charm and his manner was 'exquisitely elegant'. He was the 'politest man' his visitor had ever met; he displayed more knowledge of philology and literature than Johnson had expected; he gave him £10. But Johnson felt that he was no more to Chesterfield than any other protégé, dependant, minion or parasite, who was kept waiting in the great man's ante-chamber. It was a humiliation that continually rankled, and perpetually irked him. He defined the word 'patron' in his dictionary as 'one who countenances, supports or protects. Commonly a wretch who supports with insolence, and is paid with flattery.' And although he had to admit Chesterfield's dignity, politeness and good taste, even these virtues 'were like certain species of fruit which is pleasant enough to the eye, but there is no tasting it without danger'. Chesterfield was the 'proudest man' in existence. As for his renowned wit, well, 'this man, I thought,' said Johnson, 'had been a Lord among wits; but I find he is only a wit among Lords.' Moreover, his published *Letters* were disgraceful: they 'taught the morals of a whore, and the manners of a dancing master'.

Disappointed in his patron, Johnson had other reasons for feeling dispirited during the first year or so of his life at Gough Square.

He always spoke kindly of Tetty; she was always a little jealous of his affection for Molly Aston and other young ladies, he had to admit. 'She was jealous to be sure,' he confided to a woman friend in his old age, remembering a time early in the marriage, 'and teased me sometimes when I would let her; and one day, as a fortune-telling gypsy passed us when we were walking out in company with two or three friends in the country, she made the wench look at my hand, but soon repented her curiosity; for (says the gypsy) your heart is divided, Sir, between a Betty and a Molly: Betty loves you best, but you take most delight in Molly's company: when I turned to laugh, I saw my wife was crying. Pretty charmer! She had no reason!'

The affection was genuine enough, and he never failed to respect her judgement. When she praised an essay that he wrote in the 1750s by saying to him, 'I thought very well of you before; but I did not consider you could have written anything equal to this', he valued the compliment highly, for he knew the piece to be a good one and her opinion of it well considered. She was as good at reading literature aloud as she was a judge of its quality. She 'always mouthed too much' when reading tragedy, but with comedy she was better than anyone he had ever heard. She had a ready wit, he insisted, and a sound intelligence.

She was, however, no more tactful than her husband was, quite as capable of lamenting the 'sorrows of celibacy to an old maid' as of informing a waterman that 'he was no happier than a galley-slave'—one was chained to the oar by authority, she said, and the other by want. Nor, despite her readiness to start crying when her husband teased her, was she a submissive and subservient wife. Johnson himself related that as he was about to say grace before a meal one day, Tetty stopped him. 'Nay hold,' said she, tired of his huffing about his meat, 'and do not make a farce of thanking God for a dinner which you will presently protest not eatable.'

If *she* was an indifferent cook, *he* was no easy man to housekeep for. In the days before they could afford servants—as they could do, and did do, at Gough Square—'she was extremely neat in her disposition', and always fretful that Johnson in his clumsy way made the house so dirty. 'My wife had a particular reverence for cleanliness,' he recalled after she was dead, 'and she desired the praise of neatness in her dress and furniture, as many ladies do till they become troublesome to their best friends, slaves to their own besoms, and only sigh for the hour of sweeping their husbands out of the house as dirt and useless lumber. . . . A clean floor is *so* comfortable, she would say by way of twitting,' he went on; 'till at last I told her, I thought we had had talk enough about the *floor*, we would now have a touch of the *ceiling*.' There were other differences, too. 'Women,' he said, condemning the entire sex in general, 'give great offence by a contemptuous spirit of non-compliance on petty occasions. The man calls his wife to walk with him in the shade, and she feels a strange desire just at that moment to sit in the sun. He offers to read her a play, or sing her a song and she . . . advises him to seize that opportunity of settling the family accounts.'

But although Johnson did have repeated domestic quarrels with his wife, he roundly condemned the view—then, and still, fashionable—that such disputes served a useful purpose in a marriage or a family. '*What* a pernicious maxim is this now!' he exclaimed. '*All* quarrels ought to be avoided studiously, particularly conjugal ones, as no one can possibly tell where they may end; besides that, lasting dislike is often the consequence of occasional disgust. . . . The cup of life is surely bitter enough, without squeezing in the hateful rind of resentment.'

So Johnson's petty quarrels with his wife were soon made up. What was difficult to overlook in Tetty was that the older she grew, the more she drank. Johnson never admitted this, though he did admit that the reason he himself did not drink alcohol was not only because he found moderation so difficult but also because he feared that excessive drinking might lead to insanity. This seems not to have troubled him unduly in the days at Birmingham before his wedding; but, whether or not Tetty was already a heavy drinker herself then, it is certain that the twenty-odd years of his total abstinence dated from about the time that he married her.

By the late 1740s Tetty appears to have become a confirmed drunkard. David Garrick, describing her as 'very fat, with a bosom of more than ordinary protuberance . . . flaring and fantastic in her dress', attributed her 'swelled cheeks of a florid red' not merely to the thick layer of paint she applied to them, but also to 'the liberal use of cordials'. John Taylor, Johnson's old friend at Lichfield and Oxford who had now given up the law for the Church and was rector of Market Bosworth in Leicestershire, was far more condemnatory, characterising Tetty as being 'abominably drunken and despicable'. Another of Johnson's friends said that she 'was always drunk and reading romances in her bed where she killed herself by taking opium'.

Taylor went on to say that Johnson 'had frequently complained to him of the wretchedness of his situation with such a wife'; and the Gaelic scholar, William Shaw—though he did not meet Johnson until after Tetty's death—affirmed that 'a suspicion of his conjugal infelicity certainly went abroad and procured him much commiseration among his friends'. Nor was it only her drunkenness, her nagging and the fact that she was, in the words of the precise John Hawkins, 'little disposed to parsimony', that Johnson had cause to complain of. She did not want him to make love to her any more. Insisting that her failing health made sexual intercourse an ordeal to her, she declined to sleep with him. To Johnson this was a cruel deprivation. According to Garrick—who related the story to Arthur Murphy without, apparently, telling him the date of the conversation—when asked what was the greatest pleasure in life Johnson 'answered fucking and the second was drinking. And therefore he wondered why there were not more drunkards, for all could drink tho' all could not fuck.'[1]

But even if these two were, in his opinion, the greatest pleasures, he denied himself the pleasures of them both. For although he once declared to a friend that a 'woman of a very cold constitution' had no right to complain of her husband's infidelity, he himself, it seems certain, was never unfaithful to Tetty. She had given him permission to be so, he said: 'My wife told me I might lie with as many women as I pleased, provided I *loved* her alone.'

'She was not in earnest!'

'But she was. Consider, Sir, how gross it is in a wife to complain of her husband's going to other women, merely as women; it is that she has not enough of what she would be ashamed to avow.'

If, for instance, 'from mere wantonness of appetite,' he said on another occasion, a man stole to the chambermaid, 'his wife ought not greatly to resent it'. 'A wife should study to reclaim her husband by more attention to please him. Sir, a man will not once in a hundred instances leave his wife and go to a harlot, if his wife has not been negligent of pleasing.'

Of course, 'between a man and his Maker' it was 'a different question'. And Johnson himself, all his friends agreed, was far too strict a moralist ever to take advantage of his wife's complaisance. Indeed, his insistent morality was already becoming proverbial. An Irish clergyman on a visit to England was told a story that was 'proof of' Johnson's being always 'very correct both in his conduct and language'. It was a story concerning Dr Robert James, whose *Medicinal Dictionary* Johnson had helped to compile; and all Johnson's friends who were present at the dinner agreed in the truth of it.

'Dr James, (who is it seems a very lewd fellow both *verbo* and *facto*),' the clergyman recorded in his diary, 'James, it seems, in a coach with his whoor, took up Johnson and set him down at a given place—Johnson hearing afterwards what the lady was, attacked James, when next he met him, for carrying him about in such company—James apologised by saying that he always took a swelling in his stones if he abstained a month etc.— Damn the rascal, says Johnson.'

Sometimes, however, Johnson did come very close to infidelity himself. The object of his suppressed passion was Mrs Elizabeth Desmoulins, the daughter of his god-father Samuel Swynfen.

Mrs Desmoulins's husband, the Huguenot writing-master at the Birmingham Free Grammar School, had died shortly after his wife had given birth to a daughter. Subsequently, she and the child had come to stay with the Johnsons. Mrs Johnson, for the sake of her health and disregarding the limitations of the household purse, used occasionally to leave London while work on the dictionary was slowly progressing and go to stay in the village of Hampstead in a house near the church known as Priory Lodge. Usually Elizabeth Desmoulins went with her.

Johnson would go over to Hampstead occasionally and sometimes arrive late at night after his wife, who went to bed early—with, as was suspected, her drink, her romances and her opium—was already asleep in her room. Mrs Desmoulins was left to wait up for him, to prepare him a drink if he wanted one, to remove the warming-pan from his bed. When he had undressed and got into bed, Johnson would call her back into the room and ask her to sit down and talk to him. He did not sleep well and could not bear to be alone. 'The great business of his life (he said) was to escape from himself; this disposition he considered as the disease of his mind, which nothing cured but company.' As he talked he would reach out his hands to the young woman, to touch her and stroke and fondle her; from time to time he would kiss her and she would, on occasions, put her head on his pillow. She never thought of him as other than a father, she insisted, and nothing improper ever took place, though, she had to admit that, such was her awe of him, she would have felt quite unable to resist him had he attempted to make love to her. But as soon as he became too excited, he would push her away from him with a sudden cry of lament and tell her sharply to leave him.

Whenever there was another visitor in the small house, Elizabeth Desmoulins, who normally slept in a small bed in the same room as Tetty, joined her in the bigger bed. But Tetty made her promise never to tell her husband what arrangements had been made: if he knew that Elizabeth had been allowed in with her, he might renew his demands to share her bed himself.

Despite this dark shadow across their marriage, despite her drunkenness and opium-taking, and the way in which she 'indulged herself' at 'unsuitable expense', Johnson always treated Tetty with great respect and even with affection and admiration, attentions which she received, so Arthur Murphy said, 'with the flutter of an antiquated coquette'. They seemed an odd, almost ludicrous couple to strangers who saw them walking together in the street, he, lumbering clumsily along, rolling his head, his shoulders shaking convulsively, sometimes murmuring to himself; she, fat and painted, gaudily dressed like an elderly actress, fretting about the colour of her hair which she would have dyed black had her husband not dissuaded her, an antiquated beauty who could never bring herself to step off the stage.

Johnson recognised that she had had much to endure, not merely as the

wife of an impoverished writer but as a mother. Her elder son, Jervis, only
once made an attempt to see her after her marriage to Johnson. It was
while she was living at Gough Square. He knocked at the door and asked
the maid if her mistress was at home. She answered, 'Yes, Sir; but she is
sick in bed.'

'Oh,' said he, 'if it's so, tell her that her son, Jervis, called to know how
she did.' And he turned to walk away. The maid begged she might run up
to tell her mistress and, without waiting for him to answer, left him. 'Mrs
Johnson enraptured to hear her son was below, desired the maid to tell
him she longed to embrace him. When the maid descended, the gentleman
was gone, and poor Mrs Johnson was much agitated by the adventure; it
was the only time he ever made to see her. Johnson did all he could to
console his wife.'

Hard as Johnson and his six assistants worked at the dictionary, after a
year's labour there was little to show for their efforts, apart from the ever
growing numbers of filed slips. There could be no question for several
months yet of passing even the A's to the printer.

Johnson's own work, interrupted by those bouts of unconquerable
lethargy that overwhelmed him, hampered by an increasing inability to
get out of bed much before the middle of the morning, was also slowed
down by an unwillingness to refuse help to those who asked for it. When
the *Gentleman's Magazine* was in urgent need of extra copy, he roused himself to supply it; when Dodsley began a new magazine *The Preceptor* and
was short of material, he sat up most of the night to provide it. There was
also the need to get down on paper a poem that he had been turning over
in his mind for several weeks. It was *The Vanity of Human Wishes*, a solemn,
even gloomy poem inspired by the tenth satire of Juvenal but reflecting
Johnson's own dejected view of the world in which he lived, far more
faithfully than ever *London* had done. The poem had been forming for a
long time in his mind and was almost complete by the time that he came to
write it down, so that once he could bring himself to put pen to paper the
lines flowed across the page with wonderful speed. The first seventy lines
were written during the course of a single morning at Hampstead, and a
further hundred lines in a single day. It is a beautiful and deeply moving
poem, containing lines that T. S. Eliot has described as being 'the finest
that have ever been written in that particular idiom', and Johnson himself
could not recite it without emotion, so profoundly personal was it, reflecting, as much of his poetry does, sentiments that he would not have cared to

set down in prose.[2] Once in his old age he repeated part of it aloud to a dear friend and when he came to the lines about the poor scholar's life:

> There mark what ills the scholar's life assail;
> Toil, envy, want, the patron, and the jail.
> See nations slowly wise, and meanly just,
> To buried merit raise the tardy bust[3] . . .

he burst into tears.

The poem, published under his own name as a little book of twenty-eight pages, was sold to Robert Dodsley for fifteen guineas.

For Johnson the days of pitiable want were now for the moment over. But the expenses of his commodious house in Gough Square and the tastes of his by no means thrifty wife were barely covered by the payments for the dictionary, intermittently made to him by the drunken Andrew Millar. Accordingly, when David Garrick, having become joint manager of Drury Lane, told him that arrangements had at last been made for the production of *Irene* in February 1749, Johnson was highly gratified.

It was not that he had any very great interest either in the theatre or in the art of acting. Indeed, his opinion of actors, expressed upon every available opportunity, appeared to be one of utter contempt: 'Players, Sir, I look upon them as no better than creatures set upon tables and joint-stools to make faces and produce laughter like dancing dogs.' Very well, he would allow that some actors gave better performances than others, but then so did 'some dogs dance better than others'. Charles Burney told the story that Johnson and Robert Sumner were once 'talking and laughing loud' in the wings of the theatre while Garrick was performing *King Lear*. When Garrick came off the stage, he said, 'You two talk so loud you destroy all my feelings.' 'No, no Davy,' replied Johnson dismissively, 'Punch never feels.'[4]

The further David Garrick advanced in his profession, the more did Johnson decry it, the more readily did he rise into warmth to condemn these players, these showmen, these fellows who exhibited themselves for a shilling. They had 'a kind of rant' with which they ran on, 'without regard to either accent or emphasis'; and when Johnson succeeded, to his own satisfaction at least, in putting Garrick right as to where the emphasis should fall in a given phrase, he 'enjoyed his victory with great glee'. On another occasion, he objected so 'very freely to certain passages' in one of

Colley Cibber's birthday odes, which the proud author was reading aloud to him, that the declamation was abandoned in exasperation. It later being suggested to him that he ought to have treated Cibber with more respect, Johnson, smiling disdainfully, exclaimed, 'Now, Sir, to talk of *respect* for a player!'

'There, Sir,' objected one of the company, 'You are always heretical: you will never allow merit to a player.'

'Merit, Sir, what merit? Do you respect a rope-dancer, or a ballad singer?'

'No, Sir, but we respect a great player, as a man who can conceive lofty sentiments, and can express them gracefully.'

'What, Sir, a fellow who claps a hump on his back, and a lump on his leg, and cries, *"I am Richard the Third"*? Nay, Sir, a ballad-singer is a higher man, for he does two things; he repeats and he sings: there is both recitation and musick in his performance: the player only recites.'

'My dear Sir! You may turn anything into ridicule. . . . A great player does what a very few are capable to do: his art is a very rare faculty. *Who* can respect Hamlet's soliloquy. "To be, or not to be," as Garrick does it?'

'Anybody may. Jemmy there' [pointing to a boy about eight years old who happened to be in the room], 'Jemmy will do it as well in a week.'

'No, no, Sir: and as a proof of the merit of great acting, and of the value which mankind set upon it, Garrick has got a hundred thousand pounds.'

'Is getting a hundred thousand pounds a proof of excellence? That has been done by a scoundrel commissary.'

All his life he was to carry on in this prejudiced, unreasonable way, as though Garrick's apparently effortless success, contrasted with his own hard-won reputation at a craft so infinitely more difficult and worthy, was an affront he found insupportable. Yet he enjoyed visiting the green-room at Drury Lane, and talking to the actresses there. He was 'very easy and facetious with them', and he was particularly taken with Kitty Clive, the down-to-earth Irish actress who was described by a contemporary critic as 'peculiarly happy in low humour, with a most disagreeable face and person, always the joy of her audience when she kept clear of anything serious and genteel'. Johnson also had a 'very high opinion of her comick powers'; in the 'sprightliness of humour he had never seen her equalled'; she was 'a better romp' than any he had seen in nature. All in all, she was the best player he ever saw. He conversed more with her in the green-room than with any of the other actresses. 'Clive, Sir,' he used to say, 'is a very good thing to sit by; she always understands what you say.'

Mrs Clive, whose sound sense made up for the scantiest of educations, returned the compliment: she loved to sit by Johnson; he 'always' entertained her. There came a day, however, when he thought that he had better not go behind the scenes any more since, as he confessed to Garrick, 'the white bubbies and silk stockings of your actresses excite my genitals'.

Affecting to despise Garrick's gifts as profoundly as he did, Johnson found it all the more intolerable when his former pupil suggested that one or two alterations ought to be made to *Irene* to make it suitable for the stage. Johnson flew into a rage; he would have no mere player interfering with his work just so that he could get a better part out of it for himself. 'Sir,' he protested angrily to a friend, 'the fellow wants me to make Mahomet run mad, so that he may have the opportunity of tossing his hands and kicking his heels!'

In the end, however, Johnson's obstinancy was overcome; and on 6 February 1749 under the title of *Mahomet and Irene*, Johnson's tragedy was at last performed, Garrick having given up the part of Mahomet to Spranger Barry and playing instead Demetrius.

'Thinking his character of an author required upon the occasion some distinction of dress', Johnson appeared in one of the side boxes—to the astonishment of everyone in the audience who was familiar with his usual garb—in a brilliant scarlet waistcoat, richly embroidered with gold lace, and a gold-laced hat.[5]

Before the curtain went up there were shouts, whistling and catcalls from the restive audience, which Dr Adams, who was present, described as alarming. But the piece was received well enough, except towards the end when Hannah Pritchard, in the character of Irene, appeared with a bow-string around her delicate neck. There were loud protests at such cruelty. Cries of 'Murder! Murder!' filled the theatre; and Mrs Pritchard, having failed to make herself heard above the uproar, was obliged to leave the stage and be done to death behind the scenes.[6]

Nevertheless, the performance was politely applauded. It was repeated the following night and thereafter for a week, supported at the end of the run by curtain raisers and Savoyard dances. Yet the nine days run—not an unduly short one for the time—was due more to the popularity of Garrick, Barry, Hannah Pritchard and Susannah Cibber than to any particular virtue in the play itself. It had one or two favourable reviews; but it was a 'laboured piece', in the opinion of its author's friend, John Hawkins, 'a tragedy which excited no passion. . . . However excellent its precepts, and however correct its language, it lacks those indispensable qualities in the drama, interest and pathos. We read it, admit every proposition it advances, commend it, lay it by, and forget it.'

Johnson himself was prepared to accept the public's verdict. Indeed, it was his firm opinion that every author ought to do so. An author might think himself 'wiser or wittier than the rest of mankind', he might suppose that he could 'instruct or amuse them'; but the public to whom he appealed 'must, after all, be the judge of his pretensions'. It was not an admission of defeat. He remained as confident in his ability as he had always been; without doubt he could write a good tragedy if he set his mind to it. But he did not care to set his mind to it again. His plans for writing a play about Charles XII of Sweden were never revived.[7]

He did not blame Garrick or his fellow players for the failure. To be sure, Mrs Pritchard was 'a mechanical player', a 'vulgar idiot' with 'something affected in her manner'; it was 'wonderful how little mind she had'. 'She no more thought of the play out of which her part was taken than a shoemaker thinks of the skin out of which the piece of leather out of which he is making a pair of shoes is cut.' But her portrayal of Irene was not responsible for the tragedy's failure.

He never afterwards looked upon *Irene* with favour. He affected not to care that it had been ill received. When asked how he felt about its reception, he replied phlegmatically, 'Like the Monument'. When it was later suggested at some social gathering that one of the guests should read parts of it aloud, he immediately left the room; and when one Mr Pot, to whom he had just been introduced, was reported to have expressed the view that it was the finest tragedy of modern times, he delivered himself of the terse comment, 'If Pot says so, Pot lies.'

Irene was, however, financially profitable. Including the £100 that Robert Dodsley gave him for the right to publish an edition of it, he received in all nearly £300. This was a highly satisfactory sum, more than he had ever been paid for his work before; yet before the end of the year he was in financial difficulties again despite his payments for the dictionary, and was driven to consider new means of making money. He hit upon the idea of a magazine containing a series of essays to be issued at regular intervals, somewhat on the lines of the *Tatler* and the *Spectator*, two periodicals which had enjoyed a shortlived success under Steele and Addison in the early years of the century. He decided to call it *The Rambler*. It was not a very suitable title for the kind of publication he had in mind; but he

75

grew so tired of thinking of names for it, that one night he sat down on his bed 'and resolved that I would not go to sleep till I had fixed its title. *The Rambler* seemed the best that occurred, and I took it.'

He found a publisher, Edward Cave, who promised him two guineas a paper, and so he set to work, having the first number ready for publication, price two pence, on Tuesday, 20 March 1750. Thereafter every Tuesday and Saturday without intermission until Saturday 14 March 1752, *The Rambler* appeared, favouring its readers with all manner of advice and information, with instruction in piety and wisdom, with allegories and criticism, with character studies, with discourses on practical religion and moral duty, with homilies and sermons on penitence, self-examination and patience.

With the exception of five numbers—two of which were by Elizabeth Carter and one by Samuel Richardson—all of them were entirely written by Johnson himself. He wrote them at extraordinary speed in the intervals left between work on the dictionary, eating and conversation, sending them off to the printer without bothering to read them through. Sometimes, according to a visitor from Lichfield, he would write them in a room full of company with the printer's boy waiting at the door. He could not have written nearly so much had he not been obliged to get the material off to the press on time. The necessity of meeting his dead-line enabled him to overcome his natural indolence and concentrated his mind wonderfully. 'A man may write at any time,' he said, 'if he will set himself doggedly to it.'

In Johnson's own opinion these essays were better than anything he had written or was yet to write. 'My other works are wine and water,' he told an acquaintance of Samuel Rogers's, 'but my *Rambler* is pure wine.' For *The Rambler* contained the essence of Johnson's views on the principles of human behaviour. Here he set out his belief in the frail impermanence of worldly pleasures and success, the supreme importance of man's 'futurity' —'the great incentive to virtue is the reflection that we must die'—the insignificance of power and position in the world, even of politics and economic change, when set beside man's duty to cultivate virtue and wisdom. Whether the essays are about fortune-hunters or prostitution, fashionable dissipations or the problems to be encountered in choosing a wife, the vanity of human wishes is never allowed to stray far from the reader's mind.

Johnson's professed intention, indeed, was to 'inculcate wisdom or piety' while 'refining our language to grammatical purity'; and he reveals himself in these essays not merely as a solemn moralist but as a man of sympathy and understanding, of humour and sound common sense. When he writes about the life of Lady Bustle, a country lady who has 'contracted her cares into a narrow space', his indulgent affection and tender compassion for such women is unmistakable and infectious.

Ladies such as Bustle set themselves 'free from many perplexities with which other minds are disturbed'; but they are no more free from disquiets 'than those whose understandings take a wider range'. Lady Bustle's marigolds, for instance, 'when they are almost cured, are often scattered by the wind, and the rain sometimes falls upon fruit when it ought to be gathered dry. While her artificial wines are fermenting, her whole life is restlessness and anxiety. Her sweetmeats are not always bright, and the maid sometimes forgets the just proportions of salt and pepper, when venison is to be baked. Her conserves mould, her wines sour, and pickles mother; and, like all the rest of mankind, she is every day mortified with the defeat of her schemes, and the disappointment of her hopes. With regard to vice and virtue she seems a kind of neutral being. She has no crime but luxury, nor any virtue but chastity; she has no desire to be praised but for her cookery, nor wishes any ill to the rest of mankind, but that whenever they aspire to a feast, their custards may be wheyish, and their pye-crusts tough.'

What might be indulged in a Lady Bustle, however, could not so readily be excused in others. And in an essay on the 'narrowness of fame' he castigated such a blinkered outlook on life: 'The naturalist has no desire to know the opinions or conjectures of the philologer: the botanist looks upon the astonomer as a being unworthy of his regard: the lawyer scarcely hears the name of a physician without contempt: and he that is growing great and happy by electrifying a bottle, wonders how the world can be engaged by trifling prattle about war or peace.'

For all the breadth of Johnson's own knowledge and curiosity, however, and for all the wide range of subjects which came under his notice, *The Rambler* did not achieve a wide circulation. A few discerning readers acknowledged 'its uncommon excellence', but the numbers of copies sold rarely exceeded five hundred, and it cannot have been a very profitable undertaking for its publisher.

Johnson himself touched upon one of the reasons for this when, reading through one of the essays in later life, he pronounced his verdict upon it in a brief phrase: 'Too wordy.' And a devoted admirer of Johnson, who 'ever entertained a profound veneration for the astonishing force and vivacity of mind which the Rambler exhibits', had to allow 'that the structure of his sentences is expanded, and often has somewhat of the inversion of Latin, and that he delighted to express familiar thoughts in philosophical language'. It also had to be admitted that he delighted in the use of difficult or antiquated words—acidulous, alexipharmic, internerate, fugacity, oraculous may, for example, be found without any undue effort.[8] These and other formidable words he used, so people said, 'to render his dictionary indispensably necessary'.

A critic of a later generation, Lord Macaulay, characterised the style as 'Johnsonese', 'pompous and unbending'; and certainly there are times when the slow, measured, majestic roll of the language becomes tedious. In a later essay Johnson ridicules the sort of writer who is no more than a 'ponderous dictator of sentences', who 'proves with mathematical formality what no man has yet pretended to doubt', who employs 'a mode of style—by which the most evident truths are so obscured that they can no longer be perceived'.[9] If applied to certain long passages in *The Rambler* this might well be taken for self-criticism.

While making no alterations to his themes, conclusions or arguments, Johnson repeatedly pruned and polished the language of the essays for the subsequent collected editions, ten of which were to appear in London alone during his lifetime and were eventually to acquire 'high favour among persons of learning and good taste'. But all the time *The Rambler* was appearing as a bi-weekly paper it failed to attract the kind of readership that the *Tatler* and the *Spectator* had enjoyed. Johnson was forced sadly to conclude in the final number, 'I have never been much of a favourite of the public'.

4
'The Giant in his Den'

*'Down from his bed-chamber, about noon, came, as newly risen,
a huge, uncouth figure, with a little dark wig which scarcely
covered his head, and his clothes hanging loosely about him.'*—
Bennet Langton

Although he kept hard and resolutely at work on *The Rambler* and the dictionary, Johnson found time enough for those excursions out of the house and into the tavern without which he could not well have survived. 'As soon as I enter the door of a tavern,' he used to say, 'I experience an oblivion of care, and a freedom from solicitude: when I am seated, I find the master courteous, and the servants obsequious to my call; anxious to know and ready to supply my wants. . . . I dogmatise and am contradicted, and in this conflict of opinions and sentiments I find delight.' There was nothing, he considered, 'which has yet been contrived by man, by which so much happiness is produced as by a good tavern or inn'. A tavern chair was 'the throne of human felicity'. He loved to fold his legs under it, he said, and have his talk out. Whoever thought of leaving him and going to bed before midnight was a scoundrel.

He would sit contentedly for hours on end, drinking lemonade or tea, and talking, or awaiting his opportunity to talk, appearing to muse as he mumbled and rolled in his chair, then bursting in upon the conversation as though the flood gates of his mind had been suddenly thrown open. Already his reputation as a talker was renowned, and his observations on life and art—forthright, sharp, quick and pungent—were cast to memory and repeated by his friends and acquaintances. Francis Hayman, the

79

painter, for instance, vividly recalled and retailed a conversation about Bishop William Warburton's edition of Shakespeare and Thomas Edwards's sardonic 'supplement' to it. Someone had suggested that Edwards's criticisms were so telling that he must be considered as great an authority as the victim of his attack. 'Nay, Sir,' objected Johnson, 'he has given him some smart hits to be sure; but there is no proportion between the two men, they must not be named together. A fly, Sir, may sting a stately horse and make him wince; but one is but an insect and the other is a horse still.'

He would talk on far into the night, so long as company would sit up with him, speaking as fluently as he wrote, Sir Brooke Boothby said, 'like a number of the *Rambler*'. He was 'as correct and elegant in his common conversation as in his writings,' Edmond Malone, the critic, confirmed; he never seemed 'to study either for thoughts or words, and [was] on all occasions so fluent, so well-informed, so accurate.' He did not care much to whom he talked so long as the person had a bottom of sound sense. He remembered many a pleasant evening spent at the table of Jack Ellis, a money-scrivener behind the Royal Exchange, with whom he had dinner once a week. But so as to provide himself with a group of rewarding companions upon whom he could regularly rely, he founded a little club whose meetings were held weekly at a well-known beefsteak house, the King's Head, Ivy Lane, near St Paul's.

One of the members of this club was John Hawkins, the attorney, whom Johnson met when they were both contributors to the *Gentleman's Magazine*. Hawkins described what 'a great relief' it was to Johnson to resort to this club after the fatigue of study. 'He generally came to it,' Hawkins said, 'with both a corporal and mental appetite; for our conversation seldom began till after a supper, so very solid and substantial, as led us think that with him it was a dinner. By the help of this refection, and no other incentive to hilarity than lemonade, Johnson was, in a short-time after our assembling, transformed into a new creature: his habitual melancholy and lassitude of spirit gave way; his countenance brightened; his mind was made to expand, and his wit to sparkle: he told excellent stories; and in his didactic style of conversation, both instructed and delighted us.'

'He had a heavy look,' another admirer of his style, John Coakley Lettsom, confirmed, 'but when he spoke it was like lightening out of a dark cloud.' Although, as a woman friend said, 'he always wished to retain authority, and leave his company impressed with the idea that it was his to teach in this world and theirs to learn', so great were his powers that this was rarely resented. As William Cooke wrote of him, 'his friends generally flattered him with the most profound attention—yet surely it was well bestowed; for in those moments, the great variety of his reading broke in upon his mind, like mountain floods, which he poured out upon his audience in all the fulness of information'.

It was not all delight, Hawkins had to confess. Johnson was not uniform in his opinions, contending as often for victory as for truth. At one time he would insist that good was predominant in the moral constitution of the world, at another evil; one day he would maintain that there was no decline in public worship, the next deplore the prevailing non-observance of Good Friday. Also, most of the other members of the club were Whigs, so politics were best not mentioned, and great care had to be taken to avoid referring in his formidable presence to the Jacobites 'by those names which others hesitated not to give them'. 'But the greatest of all our difficulties,' Hawkins decided, 'was to keep alive in Johnson's mind a sense of the decorum due to the age, character, and profession of Dr Salter, whom he took delight in contradicting and bringing his learning, his judgment, and sometimes his veracity to the test.'

This Dr Salter was Samuel Salter, Archdeacon of Norfolk, an extremely ancient and extremely tall divine who had been admitted to Corpus Christi College, Cambridge, long before Johnson was born. He was, said Hawkins, 'well bred, courteous and affable', a man of general reading, if no deep scholar; but neither his cloth nor his great age, nor his quiet courtesy protected him from the scornful outbursts of Johnson. Johnson, a devoted High Churchman, was 'more than sufficiently respectful' to bishops, provided that they showed no inclination to degrade the dignity of their order. Bishops, he contended, had 'nothing to do at a tippling-house' and if one of their number were to be found whipping a top in Grosvenor Square he hoped that the boys would fall upon him and whip *him*. All suitably decorous bishops, however, were treated with the utmost reverence. William Seward who saw him presented to the Archbishop of York described his bow 'as such a studied elaboration of homage, such an extension of limb, such a flexion of body, as have seldom or ever been equalled'. Lesser church dignitaries were treated with scant respect, as though he considered they occupied positions to which he had a better title. He was, in fact, offered several country livings but he refused them all, partly because he could not bear the idea of leaving London but also because he did not consider himself suited for the 'assiduous and familiar instruction of the vulgar and ignorant'. Of one conscientious country parson in Lincolnshire he said, 'This man, Sir, fills up the duties of his life well. I approve of him, but could not imitate him.' Of unduly convivial clergymen his scorn was complete; and once finding himself in the company of several, who assumed the 'lax jollity' of men of the world which they carried to 'noisy excess', he remarked to his lay companion, by no means in a whisper, 'This merriment of parsons is mighty offensive.' If the parsons were Whigs, so much, of course, the worse. He did not much like to see a Whig in any dress, but he *hated* to see a Whig in a parson's gown. Archdeacon Salter's political opinions were not above reproach, which lent additional heat to Johnson's outbursts.

With other members of the club Johnson was less cantankerous. Indeed, to one of the younger members, Richard Bathurst, he was deeply attached, and remained so all his life. Bathurst, a young physician born in Jamaica, was 'a fine fellow, a man to my heart's content,' Johnson said of him; 'he hated a fool, and he hated a rogue, and he hated a Whig: he was a very good hater'. Having failed to make a decent living out of medicine in London, never having opened his hand, so he said, to more than a guinea, Bathurst became an army surgeon and died of fever in the expedition against Havannah; and after his death, Johnson remembered him more often than any other man in his prayers and could scarcely talk about him without tears starting to his eyes. The conquest of Havannah had been too dearly obtained, Johnson insisted, for Bathurst had died before it; he had loved him 'above all living creatures'.

Two other leading members of the Ivy Lane Club, as it was called, were John Hawkesworth, a writer, who, like Hawkins, had been one of Cave's contributors at St John's Gate, and Samuel Dyer, a quiet and unassuming young gentleman of no occupation and modest means, who 'had improved his relish for meats and drinks up to such a degree of refinement' that he was once found in a fit of the deepest melancholy 'occasioned by a discovery that he had lost his taste for olives'. An indolent sensualist, Dyer was at the same time a man of deep reflection, 'an excellent classical scholar, a great mathematician and natural philosopher. . . . In all questions of science Johnson looked up to him', listening to him with close attention whenever he talked about chemistry which fascinated Johnson and which Dyer had studied for a time under Dr Henry Pemberton at Gresham College.

A bookseller, John Payne, a merchant, John Ryland, and two doctors, Edmond Barker, a slovenly fellow whom Johnson so frequently snubbed for being a Unitarian that he did not often attend the meetings, and William M'Ghie, a Scotchman, 'one of those few of his countrymen whom Johnson could endure', completed the membership of the club.

Another medical practitioner whom Johnson came to know at this time was the strange Robert Levett who was later to come to live in his house. Levett, born near Hull, Yorkshire, in about 1702, was the son of poor parents with whom he lived till he was about twenty when he went to work for a woollen draper. Not caring for the life of a shopman he had left Hull where he became an upper servant in the household of Lord Cadogan. Having saved some money, he decided to travel; and while working as a waiter in a coffee-house in Paris he had met some French surgeons who took an interest in him and helped him to gain admission to lectures on pharmacy and anatomy, subjects in which he had long been interested. On his return to London he had taken lodgings with an attorney in Northumberland Court near Charing Cross, had set himself up as 'a practiser of physic', and had become a habitual customer of Old Slaughter's coffee-house in St Martin's Lane. Old Slaughter's was the resort of 'many respectable literary characters, and of artists of the first eminence'; it was also a well-known rendezvous for French émigrés in London, and Johnson visited it on occasions for the purpose of improving his knowledge of the language. It was probably there that he met Levett.

Levett was a silent, even surly man of uncouth appearance and manners. 'His person was middle-sized and thin,' according to an obituarist in the *Gentleman's Magazine*; 'his visage swarthy, adult and corrugated. His conversation, except on professional subjects, barren. When in deshabille, he might have been taken for an alchemist, whose complexion had been hurt by the fumes of the crucible, and whose clothes had suffered from the sparks of the furnace.' He was not infrequently drunk as the poor people whose unlicensed doctor he was could rarely afford his modest fees and he would accept their offer of a drink instead. 'He would swallow what he did not like, nay what he knew would injure him, rather than go home with an idea that his skill had been exerted without recompense,' Johnson said. 'Had all his patients maliciously continued to reward him with meat and strong liquors instead of money, he would either have burst like the dragon in the Apocrypha, through repletion, or been scorched up, like Portia, by swallowing fire.'

Despite Levett's strange habits, grotesque appearance and unattractive manners, Johnson recognised his worth, his honesty and the conscientiousness with which he ministered to the impecunious patients of an extensive practice that called him as far afield as Houndsditch and Marylebone at all hours of the day and night. Johnson professed to hold his abilities as a doctor in high regard, far higher regard, in fact, than anyone else seems to have done; and he once said that if he were ill he would not be satisfied, 'though attended by all the College of Physicians', until the opinion of

Mr Levett was called upon. All Levett's medical knowledge, 'and it is not inconsiderable,' he added, 'was obtained through the ear. Though he buys books, he seldom looks into them.'

To most of Johnson's friends his affection for this odd, ill-favoured, often ill-tempered man appeared inexplicable, for few of them could see any virtue in the fellow at all. To be sure, one of them described him as 'a modest, reserved man; humble and unaffected; ready to execute any commission for Johnson; and grateful for his patronage'. But although all agreed that he was loyal to Johnson, not many could find much else to recommend him. To Hawkins he was 'one of the lowest practitioners in the art of healing that ever sought a livelihood by it. . . . He had no learning, and consequently was an unfit companion for a learned man; and though it may be said, that living some years abroad, he must have seen and remarked many things that would have afforded entertainment in the relation, this advantage was counterbalanced by an utter inability for continued conversation, taciturnity being one of the most obvious features of his character; the consideration of all which particulars almost impels me to say, that Levett admired Johnson because others admired him, and that Johnson in pity loved Levett, because few others could find anything in him to love.' Johnson would have strongly denied that there was little in Levett to love. Certainly his 'external appearance and behaviour were such that he disgusted the rich and terrified the poor'; certainly, too, he was a 'brutal fellow'; but he had a 'good regard for him', for his brutality was 'in his manners, not in his mind'.[1]

More easily understood by Johnson's friends was his affection for another person who was later to share his home, Miss Anna Williams. She was the daughter of Zachariah Williams, an apothecary who had persuaded himself that he had discovered the means of ascertaining longitude at sea by magnetism. Hoping to make his name by his discovery, he had come with his daughter to London where, finding that no one was much interested in it and falling ill, he had been obliged to seek shelter as 'a poor brother pensioner' in the Charterhouse. In contravention of the rules of the charity, his daughter had moved into the Charterhouse to look after him, and the governors, taking exception to this and to the letters of complaint with which he regularly assailed them, expelled them. He had appealed to Johnson for help.

Both Johnson and his wife were touched by this sad story, in particular because his daughter, Anna, a well-educated woman 'of more than ordinary talents', had lost her sight some time before. In spite of her defect she contrived to support herself by needlework and by what literary work she could obtain through her expert knowledge of French and Italian. The Johnsons determined to do all they could to help her. Samuel undertook to write for her father *An Account of an Attempt to Ascertain the Longitude at Sea by an Exact Theory of the Magnetical Needle* in the hope that this would lead to an acceptance of Mr Williams's theories; and this treatise was eventually published, under Williams's name, in 1755. Tetty undertook to do her best to care for Anna who thereafter was regularly seen by visitors in the house in Gough Square.

At the time her father was expelled from the Charterhouse, Anna Williams was forty-two; Elizabeth Johnson was fifty-nine and in increasingly poor health. She was a confirmed hypochondriac now and, according to Robert Levett, 'always drunk' and 'perpetually' doped with opium. Undoubtedly her husband found her a difficult wife.

Yet, for all their petty bickering Johnson was fond of Tetty to the end, and became so accustomed, perhaps, to her complaints that he did not even notice them any more. 'He does not know that she whimpers,' he said himself of a man who had a 'whining wife that found everything painful to her', 'when a door has creaked for a fortnight together, you may observe the master will scarcely give sixpence to get it oiled.'

During Tetty's last illness her husband nursed her tenderly; but it was not until she died, on 17 March 1752, that he realised just how much she had meant to him.

His grief was overwhelming. He wrote to his old friend John Taylor to come to comfort him; but he felt beyond the reach of comfort. Over a month later he was ardently praying to God that he might 'not languish in fruitless and unavailing sorrow'. 'Grant me the assistance and the comfort of thy Holy Spirit,' he wrote as a prayer on 25 April, 'that I may remember with thankfulness the blessings so long enjoyed by me in the society of my departed wife. . . . Forgive me, O merciful Lord, all my sins, and enable me to begin and perfect that reformation that I promised her . . .' For the rest of his life he remembered her constantly. 'Poor Tetty,' he wrote twenty-five years after her death, 'whatever were our faults and failings, we loved each other.' She was never far from his mind. He could not bring himself to read any more in the rooms at Gough Square which she had sat in; and he took his books up into the garret. Someone asked him why he always studied up there. 'Because in that room only,' he explained sadly, 'I never saw Mrs Johnson.'

More than two years later he wrote to a friend upon the death of Mrs

Robert Dodsley, the bookseller's wife: 'You know poor Dodsley has lost his wife. . . . I do hope he will not suffer so much as I yet suffer for the loss of mine. . . . I have ever since seemed to myself broken off from mankind; a kind of solitary wanderer in the wild of life, without any direction, or fixed point of view: a gloomy gazer on a world to which I have little relation.'

'He that outlives a wife he has long loved,' he wrote in a subsequent letter of condolence, 'sees himself disjoined from the only mind that has the same hopes, and fears, and interest; from the only companion with whom he has shared much good or evil; and with whom he could set his mind at liberty to retrace the past, or anticipate the future.'

'Sir,' he replied to a man who had been married twice and supposed that Johnson had not been married at all, 'I have known what it was to have a wife, and (in a solemn, tender, faltering tone) I have known what it was to *lose a wife.*—It had almost broke my heart.'

John Hawkins, while admitting that 'the melancholy which seized Johnson', on the death of his wife, was of the 'blackest and deepest kind', thought that this was due to a fear that she might not have passed on to 'a state of happiness'. 'That these gloomy conceptions were in part owing to the books he had been accustomed to read,' Hawkins had little doubt. 'Sundry passages occur in his writings, which induce a suspicion, that his notions of the state of departed spirits were such as are now deemed superstitious.'

Hawkins, indeed, went so far as to suggest that Johnson had not really loved his wife nearly as much as he afterwards pretended he had done. To be sure, he inserted in many of her books of devotion such 'endearing memorials' as 'This was dear Tetty's book', or 'This was a prayer which dear Tetty was accustomed to say'. Also, he called the blue and white saucer on which his bread roll was placed for breakfast each morning 'Tetty' because it had belonged to her; and he carefully preserved her wedding ring in a little wooden box inside which he pasted a slip of paper with the date of their marriage—incorrectly assigned to 1736 instead of 1735—upon it. But Hawkins, who had never met her because 'during her lifetime Johnson invited but few of his friends to his house', was 'inclined to think that if this fondness of Johnson for his wife was not dissembled, it was a lesson that he had learned by rote, and, that when he practised it, he knew not when to stop till he became ridiculous'.

Perhaps remorse that he had not cared for her as devotedly as he ought to have done, that with more patience he might have been able to make their marriage more tranquil, did lead Johnson to imagine that he had loved his Tetty with a deeper devotion than in truth he had done. But of the sincerity of his grief at losing her there can be no doubt. His prayers are full of references to her. On the first anniversary of her death he remembered her 'with prayers and tears in the morning', and again in the evening, though he was worried, as an Anglican, about the propriety of saying prayers for departed souls. A few days later he prayed that by true contrition he might 'obtain forgiveness of all the Sins committed and also of all duties neglected in my union with the Wife whom thou has taken from me, for the neglect of joint devotion, patient exhortation, and mild instruction'. The next day he went to Bromley where she lay buried, and received the Sacrament in the church there.[2] 'I repeated mentally the commendation of her with the utmost fervour larme a l'œil before the reception of each element at the altar', he recorded in his diary. 'I repeated it again in the pew, in the garden before dinner, at home at night. I hope I did not sin. Fluunt lacrymae. I likewise ardently applied to her the prayer for the Church militant where the dead are mentioned and commended her again to eternal mercy, as in coming out I approached her grave.'

The next year on the anniversary of her death, he cried again when he remembered her and prayed for her. 'The melancholy of this day,' he recorded, 'hung upon me.' And so, throughout the years to come, as his diaries and prayers reveal, his thoughts constantly returned to her in desolation: 'I prayed for Tett . . . I recommended Tetty in a prayer by herself. I did it only once, so far as it might be lawful for me . . . I pray for Tetty . . . *Tetty* . . . This was the day on which Tetty died. . . . I commended (so far as it was lawful) Tetty, dear Tetty, in a prayer by herself, then my other friends. . . . I recommended my wife again. . . . I thought on poor dear Tetty. . . . I commended Tetty, and my other friends. I was for some time much distressed. . . . This is the day on which in 1752 dear Tetty died. On what we did amiss, and our faults were great, I have thought of late with more regret than at any other time. She was I think very penitent. May God have accepted her repentance: may He accept mine. Perhaps Tetty knows that I prayed for her. Thou, God, art merciful, hear my prayers, and enable me to trust in thee. Perhaps Tetty is now praying for me. God help me. We were married almost seventeen years, and have now been parted thirty. . . . This is the day on which my poor Tetty was taken from me. My thoughts were disturbed in bed. I remembered that it was my wife's dying day, and begged pardon for all our sins, and commended her. . . . God have mercy upon my poor dear Tetty. . . . Poor Tetty . . . I did not forget thee yesterday. . .'

Every Good Friday he fasted in remembrance of her; and every Easter after her death he received the Sacrament and said a prayer for her. Whenever he recollected the time in which they lived together, his grief, he confessed, was not abated. 'I have less pleasures in any good that befals me, because she does not partake it. On many occasions I think what she would have said or done. When I saw the sea at Brighthelmston I wished for her to have seen it with me.' Similarly, when he saw the Palais Bourbon in Paris, he wished that she had been with him for she would have been pleased; but having by then nobody to please, he was 'little pleased' himself.

The early days of Johnson's affliction were made rather less intolerable for him not only by the presence in his house of Miss Williams, who came to stay with him while an operation on her eyes, which proved unsuccessful, was performed, but also by that of a Negro boy, Francis Barber, who entered his employment about a fortnight after Tetty's death when he was about ten years old.

Francis Barber was the son of a slave and had himself been bought as a slave by Richard Bathurst's father, a planter and colonel in the Jamaican militia. When Colonel Bathurst returned to England from Jamaica in the early 1750s to spend his last years at home in retirement, he had brought Barber with him and had sent him to a village school in Yorkshire.[3] Upon the Colonel's death he had received his freedom and a bequest of £12 and had gone to live with Dr Bathurst in London. Bathurst could not afford to keep him; nor could Johnson have done so while his wife was alive, since her extravagances at Hampstead made additional expenses unthinkable; but now that he was released from the necessity of supporting her, he agreed to take the boy into his service. He was to grow very fond of him.

In later life Francis Barber recalled how many people came to visit his master during the first few months of his service at Gough Square. They helped him, Barber thought, to overcome the lonely miseries of his 'great affliction'. Among these visitors there were Dr Bathurst, of course, and Dr Hawkesworth, Edward Cave and Elizabeth Carter. There were also Strahan the printer, Dodsley the bookseller, the Earl of Orrery, whose *Remarks on the Life and Writings of Dr. Jonathan Swift* had just been published, the tall young bluestocking Catharine Sawbridge, who was soon to achieve fame as Mrs Macaulay, Mary Masters, the poet, and David Garrick. Other visitors, Barber continued, 'were Mr Diamond, an apothecary in Cork Street, Burlington Gardens, with whom [Mr Johnson] and

Mrs Williams generally dined every Sunday. There was talk of his going to Iceland with him, which would probably have happened, had he lived. There was also Mr Ryland, merchant on Tower Hill . . . also Mrs Gardiner, wife of a tallow chandler on Snow Hill, not in the learned way, but a worthy good woman, and Mr (now Sir Joshua) Reynolds.'

Johnson had recently met Reynolds, who had just returned—at the age of twenty-nine—from a tour of Italy. Johnson had immediately taken to him as a man who 'had the habit of thinking for himself'. He had first made his acquaintance in the house of the daughters of Admiral Cotterell, who lived opposite the Johnsons' former lodgings in Castle Street, Cavendish Square; and Reynolds enjoyed telling the story of how they were talking there one evening when the Duchess of Argyll and another lady of high rank came in. Charlotte and Frances Cotterell immediately became so attentive to the distinguished new arrivals that they quite neglected the two men as though they were 'low company of whom they were somewhat ashamed'. Much put out by this treatment, and by not being properly introduced to the Duchess, Johnson and Reynolds decided to pretend to her and her friend that they were very low company indeed and began talking to each other as 'common mechanicks'. 'I wonder which of us two could get most money by his trade in one week,' Johnson asked Reynolds with a strong Cockney accent, 'if we were to work as hard as we could from morning till night?'

Perhaps the genteel Misses Cotterell, fond of Johnson though they undoubtedly were, had been a little ashamed of him, for the 'sordidness of his apparel and the complexion of his linen', marked enough in his wife's lifetime, had certainly not changed for the better now that he shared his home with a blind lady and a little black boy. On one well-remembered occasion he was following some other visitors upstairs to the drawing-room of a lady of fashion when a housemaid, who saw the huge, shambling figure lumbering after them and 'mistook him for an intruder', suddenly seized him by the shoulder, exclaiming 'Where are you going?' and striving at the same time to drag him back. 'Mr Johnson,' Reynolds's sister recorded, 'growled all the way upstairs.'

Moreover, his convulsions were as startling to strangers as they had ever been. When William Hogarth first saw him at the house of Samuel Richardson in 1753, he thought that he was an imbecile whom the novelist had taken under his protection. He was 'standing at a window in the room, shaking his head, and rolling himself about in a strange ridiculous manner'. When this extraordinary creature began to talk with authority and fluent power, Hogarth 'looked at him with astonishment and actually imagined that this idiot had been at the moment inspired'.

His first sight of Johnson came as much of a surprise to Bennet Langton, a young gentleman not long out of school, whose admiration for *The Rambler* was so great that he had come to London from his family home at Langton in Lincolnshire, 'chiefly with a view of endeavouring to be introduced to its author'. By a fortunate chance he had taken lodgings in a house where one of the other lodgers was attended by Robert Levett. His landlady introduced him to Levett who had taken him to Gough Square to meet his hero. Langton had not received 'the smallest intimation' of Johnson's figure, dress or manner, but supposed from his writings that he would be presented to 'a decent well-drest, in short, a remarkably decorous philosopher. Instead of which, down from his bed-chamber, about noon, came, as newly risen, a huge, uncouth figure, with a little dark wig which scarcely covered his head, and his clothes hanging loosely about him.'

As soon as he began to talk, however, Johnson's conversation, 'so rich, so animated and so forcible', completely disarmed his young visitor who, finding his 'religious and political notions so congenial', 'conceived for him that veneration and attachment which he ever preserved'. Johnson, for his part, was immediately attracted to the tall, thin, long-faced young man—who, according to Richard Paget, strongly resembled the stork standing on one leg in Raphael's cartoon of the miraculous draught of fishes—and was especially pleased to have gained his friendship when he learned how ancient was the family from which he came. 'Langton, Sir,' he announced with evident satisfaction, 'has a grant of free warren from Henry the Second; and Cardinal Stephen Langton, in King John's reign, was of this family.' The one trouble with Langton was that on occasions he was inclined to be rather too intense. 'His mind is as exalted as his stature,' Johnson wrote to the Rev Thomas Warton, Langton's tutor at Trinity College, Oxford, 'I am half afraid of him.' When he was in one of his unduly serious moods he 'had a style of conversing so peculiarly eloquent and verbose, as to be sometimes unintelligible. Johnson had a mind one day to give [Hawkins] a specimen of it, and assuming his manner, he, in a connected speech on a familiar subject, uttered a succession of sentences, in language resembling the style of metaphysics, but, though fluent, so obscured by parentheses and other involutions that [Hawkins] was unable to collect from it a single idea.'

It was nothing unusual for Johnson to remain in bed until noon, as he did on the occasion of Langton's first visit to Gough Square. He confessed in his diary in 1753, 'I do not remember that since I left Oxford I ever rose early by mere choice, but once or twice at Edial, and two or three times for the *Rambler*.' Years later he told a friend that Burton's *Anatomy of Melancholy*, with which he had tried to solace his depression at the time the school at Edial was proving so unprofitable an undertaking, 'was the only book that ever took [him] out of bed two hours sooner than [he] wished to rise'.

'To rise early', 'to rise early as I can', 'to rise at eight every morning. . . . I hope to rise yet earlier', 'to rise at eight if I well can', 'to try to rise more early', 'to rise early in the morning, at eight, and by degrees at six', 'to rise by degrees more early in the morning', 'to rise in the morning by eight', 'to rise at eight or as soon as I can', 'to rise at eight or sooner', are resolutions which appear in his diary time and time again, year after year, with pathetic regularity. He was quite unable, however, to follow his precept for more than a few days at a stretch, and then he would lapse into his old habits again and lie in bed, sometimes until two o'clock in the afternoon. 'The other day, looking over old papers,' he was to write in the summer of 1773, 'I perceived a resolution to rise early always occurring. I think I was ashamed or grieved to find how long and how often I had resolved, what yet except for about one half year I have never done. My Nights are now such as give me no quiet rest; whether I have not lived resolving till the possibility of performance is past, I know not. God help me, I will try.' Yet he could not do it. Two years later he recorded, 'As my life has from my earliest years been wasted in a morning in bed my purpose is from Easter day to rise early, not later than eight.' He did manage to rise early that Easter Day, but it was an effort he could not bring himself to repeat with any sort of constancy.

Slowly and laboriously, month after month, the work on the dictionary went on, occasionally interrupted by pieces of journalism—for the *Gentleman's Magazine*, an extended obituary of Edward Cave who died in January 1754 at the age of sixty-two, for his friend, Charlotte Lennox, a dedication to the Earl of Orrery of her *Shakespeare Illustrated*, and for the *Adventurer*, a magazine started by John Hawkesworth and Richard Bathurst, several short anonymous essays. It was the dictionary, however, which occupied most of Johnson's working day, and which he sometimes thought would never be completed.

At last towards the end of 1754, however, after eight years of wearying labour, the tedious work was finished, and the final sheets were despatched by messenger to Andrew Millar who had almost despaired of ever getting them. 'Well,' asked Johnson of the messenger the next time he saw him, 'what did he say?'

'Sir,' answered the messenger, 'he said, thank God I have done with him.'

'I am glad,' replied Johnson with a smile, 'that he thanks God for anything.'

Chesterfield, who had neglected to show the interest in the undertaking which had earlier been expected of him, now made amends for this negligence by recommending the forthcoming volumes by writing two papers in praise of them for the *World*. Had these compliments not come so late, Johnson would no doubt have accepted them with pleasure; 'praise, in general, was pleasing to him, but by praise from a man of rank and elegant accomplishments, he was peculiarly gratified'.

Yet praise at this stage, after what he took to be years of indifference, Johnson refused to accept. It was 'all false and hollow'; for years Chesterfield, 'after making great professions', had taken no notice of him until the dictionary was almost out, and then 'he fell to scribbling in the *World* about it'. Johnson determined to write him a letter to show he 'did not mind what Chesterfield said or wrote', and that he had 'done with him'. The letter was dated 7 February 1755:

My Lord

I have been lately informed by the proprietor of The World that two Papers in which my Dictionary is recommended to the Public were written by your Lordship. To be so distinguished is an honour which, being very little accustomed to favours from the Great, I know not well how to receive, or in what terms to acknowledge.

When upon some slight encouragement I first visited your Lordship I was overpowered like the rest of Mankind by the enchantment of your address . . . but I found my attendance so little encouraged, that neither pride nor modesty would suffer me to continue it. When I had once addressed your Lordship in public, I had exhausted all the art of pleasing which a retired and uncourtly Scholar can possess. I had done all that I could, and no Man is well pleased to have his all neglected, be it ever so little.

Seven years, My Lord, have now past since I waited in your outward Rooms or was repulsed from your Door, during which time I have been pushing on my work through difficulties of which it is useless to complain, and have brought it at last to the verge of Publication without one Act of assistance, one word of encouragement, or one smile of favour. Such treatment I did not expect, for I never had a Patron before. . . . The notice which you have been pleased to take of my Labours, had it been early, had been kind; but it has been delayed till I am indifferent and cannot enjoy it, till I am solitary and cannot impart it, till I am known and do not want it . . . I have been long wakened from that dream of hope, in which I once boasted myself with so much exultation.

> My Lord,
> Your Lordship's Most humble
> Most obedient Servant . . .

This letter soon became the talk of the town, and there was much argument about whether Johnson should be 'honoured for his manly behaviour in rejecting the condescensions of Lord Chesterfield' or condemned for his pride and resentment.

Robert Dodsley, naturally, was 'very sorry' that Johnson had written the letter, 'for he had a property in the Dictionary to which his Lordship's patronage might have been of consequence'. Dr Adams was sorry, too, and suggested to Johnson that his not being admitted when he called upon him was probably not Chesterfield's fault, since 'his Lordship had declared to Dodsley that "he would have turned off the best servant he ever had, if he had known that he denied to a man who would have been always more than welcome."' Johnson replied, 'Sir, that is not Lord Chesterfield; he is the proudest man that ever existed.'

'No, Sir,' said Dr Adams, 'I know a prouder man that exists now. And that is yourself.'

'But mine was *defensive* pride.'

Chesterfield himself appeared to be quite untroubled by the whole affair. He showed Johnson's letter to Dodsley, and when Dr Adams expressed surprise at this, saying he thought he would have chosen to conceal it, Dodsley exclaimed, 'Poh! Do you think a letter from Johnson could hurt Lord Chesterfield? Not at all, Sir! It lay upon his table, where anybody might see it. He read it me; said, "This man has great powers," pointed out the severest passages, and observed how well they were expressed.'

Two months after the letter was written, when Johnson was forty-six, the dictionary at last appeared in two big folio volumes at the comparatively high price of £4. 10s. Two thousand copies were printed and these sold well enough for the publishers to issue proposals for a reprinting in 165 weekly parts at sixpence a number and for the production of an abridgement the next year. In 1773 the original version, revised, was published in its fourth edition.

Johnson, profoundly relieved that the work was finished, was content that it had been well done. It had been written, he proudly claimed in the preface, 'with little assistance of the learned and without any patronage of the great; not in the soft obscurities of retirement, or under the shelter of academic bowers, but amidst inconvenience and distraction, in sickness and sorrow'. To Bennet Langton he wrote that the work had no patrons and had as yet 'no opponents, except the critics of the coffee-house, whose outcries are soon dispersed in the air, and are thought of no more'.

He was so confident of its merit that minor criticisms did not disturb him. To be sure he bridled when a man told him that a friend had failed to find the word 'ocean'. He marched from the room immediately, protesting, 'Sir, I doubt the veracity of your information.' He pulled down a copy from his library shelves, impatiently turned over the pages until he came to the word upon which he triumphantly placed a heavy finger. 'There, Sir; there is ocean!'

The visitor began to apologise for the mistake, but Johnson interrupted him. 'Never mind it, Sir, perhaps your friend spells *ocean* with an s.'

There were naturally some mistakes: *windward* and *leeward* were defined as though they meant the same thing; and *pastern* was defined as the knee of a horse rather than as part of the animal's foot. But when a lady, who had 'the most profound reverence for his character so as almost to suppose him endowed with infallibility', asked him the reason for this, expecting to hear an explanation 'drawn from some deep-learned source' with which she was unacquainted, he replied carelessly—though with forthright honesty—'Ignorance, Madam, pure ignorance.' There were omissions, too; and at least two virtuous ladies were thankful that there were, that rude words had been omitted. 'What, my dears!' Johnson cried when they praised him for his delicacy, 'then you have been looking for them.'

There were more serious faults. His conjectures on etymologies are far from learned by modern standards and several now seem actually ridiculous, while some of his definitions are more than a little laboured, as his contemporaries pointed out 'with sportive malignity' in citing the example of '*Net*: Anything reticulated or decussated at equal distances, with interstices between the intersections.'

Other contemporaries found fault with the insertion of personal references and political and social asides into what properly should have been an objective work. A *dedication*, for example, is 'a servile address to a patron', a *patriot*, 'one whose ruling passion is the love of his country . . . sometimes used for a factious disturber of the government',[4] a *patron* is 'commonly a wretch who supports with insolence and is paid with flattery', a *pension*, an 'allowance made to any one without an equivalent—in England generally understood to mean pay given to a state hireling for treason to his country'. A *stockjobber* is a 'low wretch who gets money by buying and selling shares in the funds', *excise* is 'a hateful tax levied upon commodities', *oats* are 'a grain which in England is generally given to horses, but in Scotland supports the people'. While a *Tory* is 'one who adheres to the ancient constitution of the state, and the apostolical hierarchy of the Church of England', a *Whig* is 'the name of a faction'.

Stages in the compiler's own career are marked with such entries as '*Lich:* A dead carcase; whence *lichwake*, the time or act of watching by the dead; *lichgate*, the gate through which the dead are carried to the grave; *Lichfield*, the field of the dead, a city in Staffordshire so named from martyred Christians. *Salve magna parens.*' The definition of *Grubstreet* is followed by a Greek quotation reminding the reader that Johnson himself had worked as a 'grubstreeter' once, before becoming a *lexicographer*, 'a harmless drudge'.

Less obtrusive, but no less pointed, are the personal opinions and prejudices included in the illustrative quotations. Over ten anti-Scottish jibes, for instance, are taken from John Cleveland's *The Rebel Scot*, and inserted as examples of the usage of such innocuous words as *twilight*. His dislike of Lord Bolingbroke, 'a scoundrel and a coward' who had left 'half a crown to a beggarly Scotchman' to publish some deistic essays after his death, is evidenced by his example of the meaning of *irony*: 'a mode of speech in which the meaning is contrary to the words as, *Bolingbroke was an holy man*', and by his quoting—extracted from its context—a phrase in a letter from Swift under '*Sophistically:* With fallacious subtility': 'Bolingbroke argues most sophistically'.

Again, in the quotations from his own works there are semi-private references to himself and to his past.

All this is delightful to most modern readers, but to some contemporary critics it was intolerable. Needless to say, the most antagonistic criticism came from Scotchmen whom Johnson admitted that he 'meant to vex'. Archibald Campbell, the classical scholar, who in 1767 published '*Lexiphanes, a Dialogue in imitation of Lucian*—which was intended to 'correct as well as expose the affected style of our English Lexiphanes, the Rambler' —condemned Johnson as 'the great corrupter of our taste of language'. His dictionary was 'very facetious', 'personal', 'political', 'national', 'patriotical', 'in a word, everything but what it ought to be'.

This, however, was a minority verdict. Johnson was now 'Dictionary Johnson', an important literary figure who had performed a remarkable feat. The French Academy acknowledged him as a worthy colleague by presenting him with their *Dictionnaire*, the Academia della Crusca sent him a copy of their *Vocabolario*. The University of Oxford had already been prevailed upon to confer upon him the degree of Master of Arts on the grounds that the letters M.A. on the title page of the work would reflect credit not only upon himself but upon the University which he had left without a degree.[5]

Part II

❧

1756–1764

5
'A New Wife'

'Mr Johnson was a very seducing man among the women when he chose it.'
Peter Garrick—on the evidence of 'a lady, a very fine woman'.

Johnson had finished his dictionary during a period of intense depression. At the end of his preface to it, in an outburst of unaccustomed self-pity, he had written, 'I may surely be contented without the praise of perfection, which if I could obtain in this gloom of solitude, what would it avail me? I have protracted my work till most of those whom I wished to please have sunk into the grave. . . . I therefore dismiss it with frigid tranquillity, having little to fear or lose from censure or praise.'

Towards the end of his task he had considered the possibility of rendering the solitude of which he complained less gloomy. On 22 April 1753, he had recorded in his diary his purpose to try on the following day, Easter Monday, 'to seek a new wife without any derogation from dear Tetty's memory'. Marriage, he believed, was 'the best state for a man in general'; even ill-assorted marriages were 'preferable to cheerless celibacy', provided they did not take place too late in the partners' lives. Also, in his opinion, by taking a second wife a man paid the highest compliment to the first by showing that she had made him so happy as a married man that he wished to be so again. Of course, a man who had been very unhappy in his first marriage yet re-married immediately after his wife died demonstrated 'the triumph of hope over experience'.

The selection of a suitable wife was a problem that much interested

Johnson. With or without thoughts of his own case in mind, he maintained that a man who married a widow when he might have had a maid did 'a very foolish thing', and that it was 'commonly a weak man' who married for love. Marriages would 'in general be as happy, and often more so, if they were all made by the Lord Chancellor, upon a due consideration of the characters and circumstances, without the parties having any choice in the matter'. There were fifty thousand women in the world with whom a man might be as happy as any one in particular. If he himself, he decided towards the end of his life, had married Edmund Hector's sister, Ann, instead of Tetty, it 'might have been as happy' for him. Naturally, the chosen wife ought to be 'a suitable companion'; it 'was a miserable thing when the conversation could only be such as whether the mutton should be boiled or roasted, and probably a dispute about that'. On the other hand, it would be very troublesome if she were of an over studious disposition and continually dwelled 'upon the subject of the Arian heresy'. 'No, Sir,' he said, 'I would prefer a pretty woman, unless there are objections to her. A pretty woman may be foolish; a pretty woman may be wicked; a pretty woman may not like me. But there is no such danger in marrying a pretty woman as is apprehended. . . . Beauty is of itself very estimable.'

On the day he had appointed to 'seek a new wife', Johnson had gone to Bromley to receive the Sacrament, and, as he put it, 'to take my leave of Tetty in a solemn commendation of her soul to God'. During the sermon, which as usual he 'could not perfectly hear', he had composed a prayer 'against unchastity, idleness and neglect of publick worship'; and 'during the whole service,' he recorded, 'I was never once distracted by any thoughts of any other woman or with my design of a new wife . . . God guide me'.

That he was often distracted by thoughts of other women, and that these thoughts deeply disturbed him is obvious enough from his journals. He prayed repeatedly for help to purify his 'thoughts from pollutions', to 'reject or expel sensual images', to be 'chaste in thoughts, words and actions', to extinguish 'all corrupt desires'. He frequently lamented his 'sensuality', his 'vain longings of affection'.

Knowing him to be so physically attracted to women, many of his contemporaries supposed that on occasions he had given way to his desires. It was common knowledge that after meetings of the Rambler Club in Ivy Lane, rather than go home, he would wander the streets of the town late at night and talk to 'those miserable females who were there to be met with', as he had done in earlier years. Peter Garrick averred that 'a lady, a very fine woman' had once told him that 'Mr Johnson was a very seducing man among the women when he chose it', and Garrick added that it was suspected that this woman had herself been seduced by him. John Hawkins, who looked into a diary that Johnson apparently burned shortly before his death, confessed in a 'grave and earnest' conversation that he wished that he 'had not read so much. [Johnson] had strong amorous passions.' When it was objected, 'But he did not indulge them?', Hawkins replied, 'I have said enough.'[1] Later Hawkins expressed the opinion that Johnson was 'a man too strict in his morals to give any reasonable cause of jealousy to a wife'. But there was a strong belief that before marriage, when he had roamed the town with the rakish Richard Savage, and soon after his wife's death, when his dread of solitude and his physical needs prompted him to consider a second wife, Johnson may well have succumbed to his passions.

In later conversations he strongly condemned the brothels of Rome, and avowed that he would punish, 'much more than it is done', 'irregular intercourse between the sexes'. But the sin was much greater in the woman than in the man. When he heard that an old clergyman had quoted the Bible in denunciation of whoremongers and had, upon that authority, condemned fornication as a heinous sin, he had exclaimed, 'Why, Sir, observe the word *whoremonger*. Every sin, if persisted in, will become heinous. Whoremonger is a dealer in whores, as ironmonger is a dealer in iron. But as you don't call a man an ironmonger for buying and selling a penknife; so you don't call a man a whoremonger for getting one wench with child.'

With women, however, the case was quite different, particularly with married women. Between a man and his wife, a husband's infidelity was 'nothing', wise married women didn't 'trouble themselves about infidelity in their husbands'. But the difference between the offence in the man and the woman was 'boundless': 'The man imposes no bastards upon the wife.'

Upon being asked if it were not hard that one deviation from chastity should 'absolutely ruin a young woman', he replied, 'Why no, Sir, it is the great principle she is taught. When she has given up that principle, she has given up every notion of female honour and virtue, which are all included in chastity.' On other occasions he maintained that it was right that women should do penance in church for fornication; he would not reveal her sin, if he alone knew of it, nor would he commend a parson who divulged a woman's first offence, but 'being once divulged it ought to be infamous . . . The chastity of women is of the utmost importance.' He would not even allow that the new wife of a friend of his, being treated disgracefully by her former husband who had divorced her, had had some excuse for being unfaithful to him. 'The woman's a whore,' he said, 'and there's an end on't.'[2]

Johnson's surviving diaries give no hint as to whether he would have liked to take as his second wife any of the women he knew. Ann Hector, Edmund's sister, the first girl with whom he had ever been in love, was now married; so were Olivia Lloyd, the girl to whom he had addressed affectionate verses at Stourbridge, and the delightful Molly Aston. Molly's sister, Elizabeth, had not married, but Johnson had never felt for her the same sort of affection that he had felt for Molly.

Of more recently acquired friends he was much attached to the American-born former actress Charlotte Lennox for whose *Shakespeare Illustrated* he had written the dedication and whose words on 'Talent' he had quoted in his *Dictionary*. In 1751, to celebrate the publication of her first novel, *Harriot Stuart*, he had given a party for her at the Devil Tavern. It was a very gay party which had gone on all night until eight o'clock the next morning, and during the course of it a huge apple pie had been placed upon the table. He had caused this pie to be stuck with bay leaves and he had made for her a crown of laurel with which he encircled her brow, his face shining with 'meridian splendour', a guest recalled, 'though his drink had only been lemonade'. But although he was much attracted by Charlotte Lennox, an entertaining and lively woman of thirty-three in 1753, he cannot have considered her as a wife; she had a husband already.

Another of his women friends, Elizabeth Carter, was still unmarried at thirty-six. She had the makings of a good wife, as Johnson admitted, for as well as being attractive and clever she was an excellent cook, an expert seamstress and needlewoman, and although she had at one time 'looked upon having a sweetheart with as much horror as if it had been one of the seven deadly sins', she had recently shown herself less timid in male company. She lived with her father in Kent, but she was staying in lodgings in London in the spring of 1753. From her correspondence it does not seem that Johnson made any advances to her, however; she died unmarried. So, too, did Frances Cotterell. But Johnson had never been as fond of this sister as of Charlotte whom, so he told her towards the end of her life when inviting her to dine with him, he had not forgotten, nor ever could forget. It does not appear, however, that he ever thought of Charlotte Cotterell as a wife; in 1756 she married the Dean of Ossory.

Of the women whom his servant, Francis Barber, remembers having been regular visitors at Gough Square after the death of his wife, there was one whom he might perhaps have considered, Catharine Sawbridge. She was twenty-two in 1753 and was not to marry George Macaulay, a Scottish physician, for another seven years; but even then her republican sympathies were pronounced and she was already beginning to display that argumentative manner which was later to ruffle Johnson's temper.

A woman far more attractive to Johnson than Miss Sawbridge was Hill Boothby, one year older than himself, a friend of Mary Meynell, the daughter of the bluff squire, Littleton Poyntz Meynell, whom he had met when staying with John Taylor at Ashbourne in 1739.

The daughter of Brooke Boothby of Ashbourne Hall, and granddaughter of Sir Brooke Boothby, Bt, Hill was a kind, religious, understanding woman, the only woman, so Johnson told Taylor, with whom he had ever regularly corresponded. The acidulous Anna Seward, granddaughter of Johnson's fierce schoolmaster, John Hunter, described her as 'the sub- limated methodistic Hill Boothby, who read her Bible in Hebrew'; but Johnson became increasingly devoted to her the longer he knew her. In March 1753, however, her dear friend Mary Meynell died naming her the sole executor, and out of love for her and a sense of duty to her husband and six young children, Hill undertook to look after them. If Johnson had ever hoped to marry her, he could not do so now.[3]

Not long after the dictionary was published, Hill Boothby fell ill; and Johnson was beside himself with anxiety less he should lose her. He wrote to her several times a week, begging her 'to endeavour to live', and giving her advice as to what medicines she ought to take. Ever since he had helped his old school friend, Robert James, with his *Medicinal Dictionary* he had prided himself on his knowledge of physic and did not hesitate to prescribe for his friends and acquaintances as soon as he had some knowledge of their symptoms. For Bennet Langton's rheumatism he prescribed 'equal quantities of flour of sulphur and flour of mustard seed, make them an electuary with honey or treacle; and take a bolus as big as a nutmeg several times a day, as you can bear it; drinking after it a quarter of a pint of the infusion of the root of Lovage'. For himself he prescribed all manner of medicines and drugs, writing out his own prescriptions with such mastery of the technical characters that apothecaries mistook him for a physician. Once when he was staying with friends in the country and, by mistake took tincture of antimony instead of emetic wine for a vomit, he directed his host and hostess what to do for him with 'as much coolness and deliberation' as if he had been a doctor prescribing for someone else. He was a firm believer in the benefits of purging, and he puffed and snorted in high derision when John Taylor confessed that he did not like taking emetics for fear of breaking some small vessels. 'Poh!' he cried. 'If you have so many things that will break, you had better break your neck at once, and there's an end on't. You will break no small vessels.'

For Hill Boothby he recommended—as one who had 'thought much in Medicine'—'a very probable remedy for indigestion and lubricity of the bowels':

Take an ounce of dried orange peel finely powdered, divide it into scruples [⅓ dram], and take one Scruple at a time in any manner; the best way is perhaps to drink it in a glass of hot red port, or to eat it first and drink the wine after it. If you mix cinnamon or nutmeg with the powder it were not worse, but it will be more bulky and so more troublesome. This is a medicine not disgusting, not costly, easily tried, and if not found useful easily left off.
I would not have you offer it to the Doctor as mine. Physicians do not love intruders, yet do not take it without his leave, but do not be easily put off, for it is in my opinion very likely to help you, and not likely to do you harm, do not take too much in haste, a scruple one in three hours or about five scruples a day will be sufficient to begin or less if you find any aversion. I think using sugar with it might be bad, if Syrup, use old Syrup of Quinces, but even that I do not like. I should think better of conserve of Sloes. Has the Doctor mentioned the bark [quinine]? In powder you could hardly take it, perhaps you might bear the infusion?
Do not think me troublesome, I am full of care. I love you and honour you, and am very unwilling to lose you . . .

But she did not improve, and Johnson became increasingly concerned. Addressing her as 'my dearest' and 'my Sweet Angel', he assured her repeatedly of his love. 'Do not forget me, my heart is full of tenderness,' he wrote. 'I have none but you on whom my heart reposes . . . I beg of you to endeavour to live. . . . I am in great trouble, if you can write three words to me, be pleased to do it. I am afraid to say much, and cannot say nothing when my dearest is in danger.

The all merciful God have Mercy upon You.
I am Madam Your
Sam: Johnson.'

This letter was written on 8 January 1756. A week later Hill Boothby died; and Johnson, so a friend said, was 'almost distracted with his grief'.

For some time he had been in very poor health as well as being unhappy. At Christmas he had been suffering from hoarseness and so violent a cough that he once fainted from its convulsions; and on 30 December, when he was, at midnight, writing to the dying Hill Boothby of his 'weakness and misery', a rumour was circulating in London that he had actually died himself. His illness, from which he had 'suffered something and feared much', had depressed his 'confidence and elation', he complained, and made him consider all that he had promised himself 'as less certain to be attained or enjoyed'. To add to all his other troubles, after Hill Boothby's death he suffered for several weeks from a most painful inflammation of his good eye.

Contributing to the weight of his unhappiness was his continuing poverty. His dictionary, so he told Charles Burney, then a little-known organist at Lynn Regis in Norfolk who had written to congratulate him upon it, had not been praised much by his friends. 'Your praise was welcome,' he wrote to Burney, 'not only because I believe it was sincere, but because praise has been very scarce. A man of your candour will be surprised when I tell you, that among all my acquaintances there were only two, who upon the publication of my book did not endeavour to depress me with threats of censure from the publick, or with objections learned from those who had learned them from my own preface. Yours is the only letter of goodwill that I have received.'

If the dictionary had not brought him much praise from his acquaintances it had not brought him much money either. When all his expenses had been paid, his profits were 'very inconsiderable'. He did not blame the booksellers; they were 'generous liberal minded men' who had, after all, taken the risk of commissioning a work which they did not know would be profitable, or even completed. But it was distressing that now he had finished it he was no better off than he had been when he had started it. He had hoped that a large sum might still be due to him on the conclusion of the work; but he was 'no very accurate accountant', and it was discovered by the booksellers that, instead of this, he had actually been paid more than was due to him. The booksellers, however, agreed not only to forget the difference but to pay for his meal at a tavern to which *he* had invited *them* for the purposes of settling accounts with them.

In March 1756 he was actually under arrest for a debt of £5. 18s, and was obliged to appeal for help to Samuel Richardson, the success of whose novels, *Pamela* and *Clarissa Harlowe*, had made him relatively rich. Richardson had lent him money in the past and readily agreed to do so again, sending six guineas immediately. But the respite was a temporary one. Frank Barber later said that he 'used to be disturbed by people calling frequently for money which he could not pay'.

So, unable to support himself in any other way, Johnson had to return once more to the hack work which he found so tedious and so burdensome,

Unwillingly, but from necessity, he wrote articles for the monthly magazine, *The Universal Visitor*, and undertook to assist in the editing of a new periodical, *The Literary Magazine*, or *Universal Review*, and to contribute both essays and reviews to it. Most of his contributions were run-of-the-mill journalism into which he put no more effort than was necessary, though an occasional piece, such as his demolishing review of Soame Jenyns's ill-argued and complacent *Free Enquiry into the Origin and Nature of Evil*, displayed both his supreme talents as a dialectician and his characteristic style at its most majestic and anfractuous. Also, in his defence of tea against Jonas Hanway's attack upon that 'elegant and popular beverage', he was writing from the heart; his relish for the 'infusion of that fragrant leaf' was already legendary.

The range of the subjects that fell under his notice was, indeed, extraordinary. One day he pleaded the cause of Admiral Byng, the next he reviewed a natural history of Aleppo, on a third he wrote a preface and a dedication to *An Introduction to the Game of Draughts*, on a fourth he provided Robert Dodsley with an introduction to a new evening newspaper, *The London Chronicle*, which he thereafter took regularly himself.

In April 1758 he began a series of weekly essays known as *The Idler* which appeared every Saturday for two years, in the newspaper, the *Universal Chronicle or Weekly Gazette*. They were rather lighter than most of the *Ramblers*, but were no more popular with the public for that. As with his work for the *Literary Magazine* he did not take much trouble with most of these pieces, writing them as quickly as he would write a letter. His young friend Bennet Langton recalled being with him once when he asked how long it was before the post went; and, on being told half an hour, he sat down with the comment, 'Then we shall do very well.' Before the half hour was over he had finished the piece. Langton asked if he might read it as there was still time before it was posted. But no, said Johnson, his friend should do no more than he had done himself, and he folded it up and sent it off.[4]

Such speedy composition was indeed essential, for, as Arthur Murphy, the dramatist, said, his way of life left him very little time for writing. 'He took no exercise, rose about two, and then received the visits of his friends. Authors, long since forgotten, waited on him as their oracle, and gave responses in the chair of criticism. He listened to the complaints, the schemes and the hopes and fears of a crowd of inferior writers. . . . He believed that he could give a better history of Grub-Street than any man living. His house was filled with a succession of visitors till four or five in the evening. During the whole time he presided at the tea-table.'

'A New Wife'

Arthur Murphy, so Johnson told Bennet Langton at the beginning of 1758, 'is to have his *Orphan of China* acted next month [it was actually produced at Drury Lane in April 1759 and played, like *Irene*, nine times] and is therefore, I suppose, happy. I wish I could tell you of any great good to which I was approaching, but at present my prospects do not much delight me. . . . I am not much richer than when you left me; and, what is worse, my omission of an answer to your first letter will prove that I am not much wiser. But I go on as I formerly did, designing to be some time or other both rich and wise, and yet cultivate neither mind nor fortune. Do you take notice of my example, and learn the danger of delay. When I was as You are now, towering in the confidence of twenty-one, little did I suspect that I should be at forty-nine what I now am.'

What he considered himself to be is pathetically revealed in the pages of his diary where he continued to upbraid himself for his faults, to magnify his sins, to lament his recurrent religious doubts, his 'idleness, intemperate sleep, dilatoriness, immethodical life. Lust. Neglect of Worship.' On Easter Day 1758 he prayed that after all his past lapses he might 'now continue steadfast in obedience, that after long habits of negligence and sin', he might 'at last work out his salvation with diligence and constancy'. 'Purify my thoughts from pollutions', he pleaded, 'and fix my affections on things eternal. . . . O God enable me to avoid sloth, and to attend heedfully and constantly to thy word and worship. Whatever was good in the example of my departed wife, teach me to follow, and whatever was amiss give me grace to shun, that my affliction may be sanctified and that remembering how much every day brings me nearer to the grave, I may every day purify my mind, and amend my life, by the assistance of thy Holy Spirit, till at last I shall be accepted by thee, for Jesus Christ's sake. Amen.'

In January 1759 he learned that his old mother, aged eighty-nine now, was seriously ill; and he was given further cause for self-condemnation. For he had not been once to see her during all the years that he had been living in London since his return there from Lichfield in 1740. He had often intended to go; earlier he had written to Bennet Langton, telling him that he was resolved to go, that he had an old mother 'more than eighty years old' who had 'counted the days' to the publication of his dictionary in hopes of seeing him. It was his 'duty' to go, he admitted; but he had recoiled from fulfilling that duty. Even now, when he felt more strongly still that he ought to go, that if he did not make the effort he might never see his mother again, he hesitated, writing to Lucy Porter that he would come down to them 'if it were possible', letting the days slip by, staying in London. To his mother, he wrote:

Honoured Madam,

The account which Miss [Lucy Porter] gives me of your health pierces my heart. God comfort and preserve you and save you, for the sake of Jesus Christ.

I would have Miss read to you from time to time the Passion of our Saviour, and sometimes the sentences in the Communion Service, beginning *'Come unto me, all ye that travail and are heavy laden, and I will give you rest.'*

I have just now read a physical book, which inclines me to think that a strong infusion of the bark would do you good. Do, dear mother, try it.

Pray, send me your blessing, and forgive all that I have done amiss to you. And whatever you would have done, and what debts you would have paid first, or anything else that you would direct, let Miss put it down; I shall endeavour to obey you.

I have got twelve guineas to send you, but unhappily am at a loss how to send it tonight. If I cannot send it tonight [he did send the money that night by the postmaster] it will come by the next post.

Pray, do not omit anything mentioned in this letter. God bless you for ever and ever.

I am your dutiful son
Sam: Johnson

Three days later he wrote again saying, 'Your weakness afflicts me beyond what I am willing to communicate to you. I do not think you unfit to face death, but I know not how to bear the thought of losing you. Endeavour to do all you can for yourself. Eat as much as you can. I pray often for you; do you pray for me. I have nothing to add to my last letter.'

By the same post he wrote to Lucy telling her that he was obliged to her 'beyond all expression of gratitude' for her care of his dear mother. She was to tell Kitty [his mother's maid, Catherine Chambers] that he would never forget her tenderness for her mistress. 'Whatever you can do,' he added, 'continue to do. My heart is very full.'

He wrote to his mother again on the 18th, saying that as he feared she was too ill for long letters he would only tell her that she had from him 'all the regard that can possibly subsist in the heart'; he prayed God to bless her 'for evermore, for Jesus Christ's sake. Amen.' Two days later he assured her that she had been the best mother and, he believed, the best woman in the world. He thanked her for her indulgence to him and begged her forgiveness for all that he had done ill and had omitted to do well. 'God grant you his Holy Spirit, and receive you to everlasting happiness, for Jesus Christ's sake. Amen. Lord Jesus receive your spirit. Amen.'

That same day he told Lucy that he would come to Lichfield if possible. 'God grant that I may yet find my dear mother breathing and sensible. Do not tell her lest I disappoint her. If I miss to write next post, I am on the road.' But he did not get on the road, and by the time this letter reached Lichfield his mother was dead. 'If she were to live again, surely I should behave better to her,' he wrote to Lucy Porter. 'But she is happy and what is past is nothing to her; and for me, since I cannot repair my faults to her, I hope repentance will efface them. . . . Write to me, and comfort me, dear child. I shall be glad likewise, if Kitty will write to me. I shall send a bill of twenty pounds in a few days, which I thought to have brought to my mother; but God suffered it not. I have not power or composure to say much more. God bless you, and bless us all . . .'

Ten years before when his mother had been ill he had confessed to Lucy Porter that her death was 'one of the few calamities' on which he thought with 'terror'. And terror was perhaps not too strong a word. To a man who so dreaded solitude that even the departure of casual visitors from his house was a disturbing deprivation, the death of a friend was more than a tragedy, it was a frightening, foreboding portent. The death of his mother, coming so soon after the death of his 'dearest angel, Hill Boothby', and of his 'darling, beloved Tetty', was a fearful warning as well as a cause of grief.

Grief for the death of his mother, however sharp it was at the time, was soon past. In the week of her funeral he wrote in *The Idler* of the fallacy of hoping that life may be extended beyond its allotted span: 'The last year, the last day must come. It has come, and is past. The life which made my own life pleasant is at an end, and the gates are shut upon my prospects.' Yet the prayer he offered for her on the night of her funeral—the night he had so vivid a dream of his brother—was the last time he mentioned her in the prayers that have survived. Fifteen years later, on Easter Sunday, he prayed for Tetty as usual and for Richard Bathurst, also as usual. He prayed, too, for Hill Boothby. But if he prayed for his mother, he did not record it.[5]

Unable to find the expenses of her funeral or the money to pay off some little debts which she had left, he went to William Strahan to ask him to pay him for a story which he was already, so he said, 'preparing for the press'. Strahan, in association with Robert Dodsley and William

Johnston, agreed to pay him a hundred pounds for it—he received a further twenty-five pounds for the second edition—and he set to work with a determination to get it finished as soon as he possibly could. He finished it, in fact, so he told Joshua Reynolds, in the evenings of a single week, writing it at the rate of about 3,000 words a sitting, and sending it off to the printer chapter by chapter.

It was published on 19 April at 4*s* a copy under the title of *The Prince of Abissinia* and was immediately successful. The second, revised, edition came out two months later, and four subsequent editions followed it. An American edition soon appeared, and it was translated into Dutch, French, German and Italian.[6]

The story concerns a Prince Rasselas who, growing tired of the joys of the 'happy valley' where he lives and where the inhabitants know only 'the soft vicissitudes of pleasure and repose', escapes to Egypt with his sister and an old philosopher, Imlac. Believing that 'surely happiness is somewhere to be found', complaining 'that I want nothing, or that I know not what I want is the cause of my complaint', he travels the world to discover how men lived and fared. But he finds that 'human life is everywhere a state in which much is to be endured, and little to be enjoyed'; and he returns to his valley convinced of the 'insufficiency of human enjoyments'. Only virtue can give a quiet conscience and the prospect of a happier state.

The appeal of this melancholy, didactic romance lies not in its story, however, but in what *The Gentleman's Magazine*, in a long and enthusiastic review, referred to as 'the most elegant and striking pictures of life and nature, the most acute disquisitions, and the happiest illustrations of the most important truths'.

It was naturally compared to Voltaire's *Candide* which had been published about two months before; and Johnson himself admitted that 'if they had not been published so closely one after the other that there was not time for imitation, it would have been in vain to deny that the scheme of that which came latest was taken from the other'. But although Voltaire and Johnson both proposed that there is more evil than good in life, Voltaire's intention in satirising the optimism of Leibnitz and Rousseau, was, as one contemporary critic put it, 'to discredit the belief of a superintending Providence', whereas Johnson meant, 'by shewing the unsatisfactory nature of things temporal, to direct the hopes of man to things eternal'.

Having finished *Rasselas*, and having disposed of the money he received for it as soon as it came into his hands, Johnson decided that the time had come to make radical economies in his way of life. The house in Gough Square had been all very well for a man who was married, assured of a regular income, and under the necessity of providing space for several assistants. But it was a much bigger house than he needed now, and the upkeep of it was more than he could afford. He decided, therefore, to move. By March 1759 he was living in lodgings in Staple Inn. From there he moved to Gray's Inn; and from there to rooms on the first floor at No. 1 Inner Temple Lane, a house two doors down the Lane, next door to a shop on the corner. Miss Williams moved into separate lodgings nearby; and so, until Robert Levett came to live with him, Johnson was now alone again, for the Negro boy, Frank Barber, had run away to sea.

Frank had not settled down very well in the Johnson household. He had run away for the first time upon some difference with his master soon after Mrs Johnson's death, and had gone to work for an apothecary in Cheapside. After a time he had returned to Gough Square; but he did not get on with Miss Williams and, 'being disgusted in the house', as Johnson put it, had run away again.

Johnson, who had grown fond of the boy, was very concerned about him. He had a horror of the navy: 'As to the sailor, when you look down from the quarter-deck to the space below, you see the utmost extremity of human misery: such crowding, such filth, such stench!' 'No man,' he thought, 'will be a sailor who has contrivance enough to get himself into a jail; for being in a ship is being in a jail, with the chance of being drowned.' In fact, 'a man in a jail has more room, better food, and commonly better company'.[7] He asked Tobias Smollett, who had been a ship's surgeon, if he could use his influence to get him released. Frank was 'a sickly lad of a delicate frame', Smollett was assured, 'and particularly subject to a malady in his throat' which made him 'very unfit for His Majesty's Service'. Smollett agreed to do what he could to help, saying that he would write to his friend John Wilkes who might be able to arrange the matter by application to *his* friend, Sir George Hay, one of the Lords Commissioners of the Admiralty.

Smollett approached Wilkes on behalf of 'that great Cham of literature . . . our lexicographer' with some diffidence, for he knew 'what matter of animosity the said Johnson' had against him. It was not just that Johnson disapproved of Wilkes's demagogic escapades and blasphemies; he had cause to be offended by an essay that Wilkes had written in the *Public Advertiser* on his dictionary. In a 'Grammar of the English Tongue', prefixed to the dictionary, Johnson had laid it down that 'H seldom, perhaps never, begins any but the first syllable'; and Wilkes had observed, 'the author of this observation must be a man of quick *apprehension* and a most *compre-hensive* genius'.

Wilkes, however, for all his public reputation, was a man of the kindest instincts. He well knew Johnson's attitude towards him but he readily agreed 'to ask Sir George Hay to procure the discharge of his lacquey'. So, after some delay, so Frank said, 'without any wish of his own', he was released. He returned to Johnson's service and never thereafter left it.

While awaiting Frank's return, Johnson decided 'to refresh himself' by a visit to Oxford. He had made a previous visit there at the beginning of the long vacation in 1754, the first since his undergraduate days, and had evidently enjoyed himself.[8] He had stayed about five weeks, lodging at a house called Kettel Hall near Trinity College and making friends with the Rev Thomas Warton, author of the recently published *Observations on the Faery Queen of Spenser*, whom he had persuaded to write occasional pieces for Hawkesworth's *Adventurer*. He had intended 'visiting the libraries of Oxford' so as to be able to put the finishing touches to his dictionary; but he apparently had done little work, spending most of his time visiting his old haunts, talking and walking with Warton and with the 'very ingenious poetess' Mary Jones, sister of the Rev Oliver Jones, Chanter of Christ Church, a 'most sensible, agreeable and amiable woman' whom he called the Chantress. 'Thee, Chantress,' he had said more than once, quoting a passage from *Il Penseroso*, 'oft the woods among I woo'.

On this visit to Oxford in 1754 he had gone to Pembroke, his old college, the morning after his arrival. 'I went with him,' Thomas Warton recalled. 'He was highly pleased to find all the College servants which he left there still remaining, particularly a very old butler [John Hopkins]; and expressed great satisfaction at being recognised by them, and conversed with them familiarly. . . . He much regretted that his first tutor [William Jorden] was dead; for whom he seems to retain the greatest regard. . . . He waited on the Master [Dr Ratcliff], who received him very coldly. Johnson at least expected that the master would order a copy of his Dictionary, now near publication; but the Master did not choose to talk on the subject, never asked Johnson to dine, nor even to visit him, while he stayed at Oxford. After we had left the lodgings, Johnson said to me, "There lives a man, who lives by the revenues of literature, and will not move a finger to support it. If I come to live at Oxford, I shall take up my abode at Trinity."'

Johnson met with a much more pleasant reception from John Meeke whose excellence as a classical scholar had so exasperated him when they were undergraduates together. Now, however, there was 'a most cordial greeting on both sides'. But when they were outside again, Johnson could not forbear to comment complacently, 'I used to think Meeke had excellent parts, when we were boys together at the college: but alas! "Lost in a convent's solitary gloom! . . ." About the same time of life, Meeke was left behind at Oxford to feed on a Fellowship, and I went to London to get my living: now, Sir, see the difference of our literary characters.'

In the course of this visit [Warton continued], Johnson and I walked three or four times to Ellsfield, a village beautifully situated about three miles from Oxford, to see Mr [Francis] Wise, Radclivian librarian, with whom Johnson was much pleased. . . . One day Mr Wise read to us a dissertation which he was preparing for the press, intitled, 'A History and Chronology of the fabulous Ages'. Some old divinities of Thrace, related to the Titans, and called the CABIRI made a very important part of the theory of this piece; and in conversation afterwards Mr Wise talked much of his CABIRI. As we returned to Oxford in the evening, I out-walked Johnson, and he cried out *Sufflamina*, a Latin word, which came from his mouth with peculiar grace, and was as much as to say, '*Put on your drag chain.*' Before we got home, I again walked too fast for him; and he now cried out, 'Why, you walk as if you were pursued by all the CABIRI in a body.'

Much as Johnson enjoyed this visit to Oxford, his second visit in 1759 seems to have afforded him even greater pleasure. Warton was now Professor of Poetry and he himself, largely due to the intercession of Warton supported by Dr Adams, was a Master of Arts; but he behaved almost as though he were a young undergraduate once more. He had taken up drinking again since his wife's death, and on one occasion apparently he drank 'three bottles of port without being the worse for it', a fact that he remembered with evident pride for the rest of his life.

He stayed with Dr Robert Vansittart, the future Regius Professor of Civil Law, then thirty-one years old and a Fellow of All Souls. And he wrote delightedly to a friend, '[Van] is now making tea for me. I have been in my gown ever since I came here. It was at my first coming quite new and handsome. I have swum thrice which I had disused for many years. I have proposed to Vansittart climbing over the wall, but he has refused me. And I have clapped my hands till they are sore' at the speech made by Dr William King upon the occasion of the installation of the Jacobite Earl of Westmorland as Chancellor.

No one who knew Johnson and his sudden whims to perform some exacting and unusual physical feat could have been in the least surprised at his proposing to Vansittart that they should climb over the walls of All Souls. What was surprising was that Vansittart did not agree to undertake the climb with him.

For Vansittart, a very tall and very thin young man, was renowned for his lively eccentricities and his debauched and licentious habits. A fellow member with John Wilkes of the Hell Fire Club, whose orgies were conducted at Sir Francis Dashwood's country house, he once presented to the club a baboon which had been sent to him from India by his brother, Henry, Governor of Bengal; and it had become Dashwood's habit to administer the Eucharist to Vansittart's baboon at the club's meetings.

Remembering his deep affection for Richard Savage and Harry Hervey, Johnson's Oxford friends could well understand his fondness for Robert Vansittart and for another clever young rake he now met, Topham Beauclerk.

Beauclerk was only nineteen at the time of this visit of Johnson to Oxford. He had matriculated at Trinity College in 1757 in the same term as Bennet Langton, two years his senior, and the two undergraduates—the one serious and rather prim, the other careless, vivacious and very wanton —soon became intimate friends. 'Their opinions and modes of life were so different that it seemed utterly improbable that they should at all agree,' wrote a mutual acquaintance. But Beauclerk had 'so ardent a love of literature, so acute an understanding, such elegance of manners' that he won the immediate affection not only of Langton but also of Johnson to whom Langton introduced him. 'I love the acquaintance of young people,' Johnson later told another young man whose company he also much enjoyed, 'because in the first place, I don't like to think myself growing old. In the next place, young acquaintances must last longest, if they do last; and then, Sir, young men have more virtue than old men; they have more generous sentiments in every respect. I love the young dogs of this age, they have more wit and humour and knowledge of life than we had; but then the dogs are not so good scholars. Sir, in my early years I read very hard. It is a sad reflection but a true one, that I knew almost as much at eighteen as I do now. My judgment, to be sure, was not so good; but I had all the facts.' 'I am always on the young people's side when there is a dispute between them and the old ones,' he told a woman friend, 'for you have at least a chance for virtue till age has withered its very root.' Men commonly grew wickeder as they grew older, changing the vices of youth, 'headstrong passion and wild temerity, for treacherous caution and desire to circumvent'.

Both Langton and Beauclerk had more to recommend them than youth and intelligence.

If Johnson had been gratified to hear that Langton was of the same ancient family as the thirteenth-century cardinal, he was even more contented when he learned that Langton's young friend was the son of Lord Sydney Beauclerk and grandson of the first Duke of St Albans, Nell Gwyn's son by King Charles II to whom he bore an unmistakable resemblance.

Dissipated, kind-hearted, as easy in conversation as in manners, Topham Beauclerk was also extremely rich, having succeeded when only four years old to the estates which his father, a notorious fortune-hunter, had inherited from Richard Topham, Member of Parliament for Windsor. He lived in great style in Bloomsbury, his library of some 30,000 volumes being housed in a building which, so Horace Walpole said, stretched half way from there to Highgate.

Johnson was fascinated by him, and delighted in his company to the consternation or amusement of his maturer friends. 'What a coalition,' exclaimed Garrick, voicing a general concern. 'I shall have my old friend to bail out of the Round house.' And certainly one night soon after Johnson's return from Oxford to his rooms in Inner Temple Lane, Johnson came close to being locked up.

He was in bed when at three o'clock in the morning there was a violent rapping at his door. He got out of bed, picked up a poker with which to defend himself from the ruffians who had, he supposed, come to attack him, and went to the window in his nightshirt with his little black wig on the top of his head instead of a nightcap. In the street were Topham Beauclerk and Bennet Langton, who had dined well at a tavern, and were now off for a ramble. Would Mr Johnson join them?

'What, is it you, you dogs!' he called back in great good humour. 'I'll have a frisk with you.'

He went back, soon appeared dressed, and marched off with his young friends to Covent Garden 'where the green grocers and fruiterers were beginning to arrange their hampers, just come in from the country. Johnson made some attempts to help them; but the honest gardeners stared so at his figure and manner, and odd interference, that he soon saw his services were not relished. They then repaired to one of the neighbouring taverns, and made a bowl of that liquor called bishop which Johnson had always liked; while in joyous contempt of sleep, from which he had been roused, he repeated the "festive lines" from Lord Lansdowne's Drinking Song to Sleep, "*Short, very short be then thy reign, For I'm in haste to laugh and drink again.*"'

When they had finished their bishop 'they walked down to the Thames, took a boat and rowed to Billingsgate. Beauclerk and Johnson were so well pleased with their amusement, that they resolved to persevere in dissipation for the rest of the day: but Langton deserted them, being engaged to breakfast with some young ladies. Johnson scolded him for "leaving his social friends to go and sit with a set of wretched *un-idea'd* girls".'

When David Garrick was told how Johnson had spent the night, he said to him rather crossly, 'I heard of your frolick t'other night. You'll be in the *Chronicle*.' But Johnson was gratified rather than upset by this rebuke, knowing that Garrick, who had been married for ten years to a rather managing Austrian woman, would never have been allowed such freedom of behaviour. '*He* durst not do such a thing,' Johnson observed with some complacency. 'His wife would not *let* him.'

Johnson, for his part, often had occasion to rebuke Beauclerk both for his reckless behaviour and for his cruel tongue. Everything he did displayed his 'love of folly', and everything he said his 'scorn of fools'. 'You never open your mouth,' Johnson once scolded him, 'but with intention to give pain; and you have often given me pain, not from the power of what you said, but from seeing your intention.' Yet Johnson could never remain put out by Beauclerk for long; he was too amusing, his fundamental good-nature was too beguiling.

Even the dour and censorious John Hawkins spoke highly of Beauclerk's character and attainments: 'To the character of a scholar, and a man of fine parts, he added that of a man of fashion. . . . Travel, and a long residence at Rome, and at Venice, had given the last polish to his manners, and stored his mind with entertaining information. . . . His conversation was of the most excellent kind: learned, witty, polite, and where the subject required it, serious; and over all his behaviour there beamed such a sunshine of cheerfulness, and good humour, as communicated itself to all around him.' His body might be 'all vice', as Johnson told him, but his mind was 'all virtue'; and when Beauclerk did not seem too pleased with this observation, Johnson added, 'Nay, Sir, Alexander the Great, marching in triumph into Babylon, could not have desired to have had more said of him.'

It was astonishing to Johnson's friends what liberties he would allow Beauclerk to take with him, though there were, indeed, times when the younger man went too far. There was, for instance, the well-remembered occasion several years later when they quarrelled about the intentions of a man who was found with two pistols in his possession. The original cause of the dispute was the case of the Rev James Hackman, who shot the Earl of Sandwich's beautiful mistress through the head when she refused to marry him, and then, with another pistol, attempted to shoot himself. Johnson argued illogically that Hackman's being in possession of two pistols was 'proof that he meant to shoot two persons'. Beauclerk disagreed, contending that every wise man who intended to shoot himself 'took two pistols that he might be sure of doing it at once'. He cited the case of a peer's cook, who had failed to kill himself instantly with one pistol and had lingered in agony for ten days, and of a more practical gentleman 'who loved buttered muffins, but durst not eat them because they disagreed with his stomach, and resolved to shoot himself: and then he ate three buttered muffins for breakfast, before shooting himself, knowing that he should not be troubled with indigestion; *he* had two charged pistols; one was found lying charged upon the table by him, after he had shot himself with the other.'

'"Well," said Johnson, with an air of triumph, "you see one pistol was sufficient." Beauclerk replied smartly, "Because it happened to kill him." And either then or a very little afterwards, being piqued at Johnson's triumphant remark, added, "This is what you don't know, and I do." There was then a cessation of the dispute; and some minutes intervened, during which, dinner and the glass went on cheerfully; when Johnson suddenly and abruptly exclaimed, "Mr Beauclerk, how came you to talk so petulantly to me, as 'This is what you don't know, but what I know?' One thing *I* know, which *you* don't seem to know, is that you are very uncivil."'

Beauclerk immediately riposted, 'Because *you* began by being uncivil (which you always are).' At first Johnson did not reply to this, and the others round the table thought that, perhaps, he had not heard the last four offensive words, which Beauclerk had added parenthetically as an after-thought. But as Johnson himself later confessed he was merely wondering whether he ought to resent the remark and then, considering that there were present in the company 'a young lord and an eminent traveller, two men of the world with whom he had never dined before', he was apprehensive that 'they might think they had a right to take such liberties with him as Beauclerk did, and therefore resolved he would not let it pass'. So when the conversation turned on the violence of Hackman's temper, he resumed the attack:

'It was his business to *command* his temper, as my friend Mr Beauclerk should have done some time ago.'

'I should learn of *you*, Sir.'

'Sir, you have given *me* opportunity enough of learning, when I have been in *your* company. No man loves to be treated with contempt.'

Beauclerk decided that the quarrel had lasted long enough. He turned to Johnson politely and said, 'Sir, you have known me twenty years, and however I may have treated others, you may be sure I could never treat you with contempt.'

'Sir, you have said more than was necessary.'

Thus it ended. Beauclerk's coach did not come for him until very late, and Johnson waited with him a long time after the rest of the company, with one exception, had gone home. They were dining together again in perfect amity the following week.

Very different from Johnson's feelings for Topham Beauclerk were those he entertained for Samuel Richardson. He much admired Richardson's work—'Sir,' he once said, 'there is more knowledge of the heart in one letter of Richardson's than in all *Tom Jones*'[9]—and he was grateful for the readiness with which Richardson lent him money when he was pressed. Yet Johnson could feel little affection or respect for him.[10] Although he maintained with truth that he had never 'sought much after any body', he *had* sought out the celebrated author of *Clarissa*, had been a frequent visitor to his house in the 1730s, and was still friendly enough with him in 1758 to pass on to him a pheasant which Bennet Langton had sent him from his Lincolnshire estate. But there was something displeasing and irritating about Richardson. He was kindly and generous, to be sure, yet his hypochondriacal self-concern, his obvious delight in the most abject flattery, his circle of admiring ladies, his short, plump, pompous, fresh-faced figure made him more than a little ridiculous. 'He was ever thinking of his writings,' John Hawkins thought, 'and listening to the praises which, with an emulous profusion, his friends were incessantly bestowing on them. He could scarce enter into free conversation with any-one that he thought had not read *Clarissa* or *Sir Charles Grandison*, and at best, he could not be said to be a companionable man. . . . He was austere in the government of his family, and issued his orders to some of his servants in writing only. His nearest female relations [he had five daughters], in the presence of strangers, were mutes, and seemed to me, in a visit I once made him, to have been disciplined in the school of Ben

Jonson's Morose, whose injunction was, "Answer me not but with your leg." In short, they appeared to have been taught to converse with him by signs; and it was too plain to me, that on his part, the most frequent of them were frowns and gesticulations, importing that they should leave his presence.'

It was his passion for flattery that most exasperated Johnson. 'You think I love flattery,' he once said to a woman friend, 'and so I do; but a little too much always disgusts me: that fellow Richardson, on the contrary, could not be contented to sail quietly down the stream of reputation, without longing to taste the froth from every stroke of the oar.'

One day at his country house at Hammersmith, at a large dinner party, a gentleman who had just returned from Paris, willing to please his host, mentioned to him 'a very flattering circumstance—that he had seen his *Clarissa* lying on the King's brother's table [it was translated into French in 1741]. Richardson observing that part of the company was engaged in talking to each other, affected then not to attend to it. But by and by, when there was a general silence, and he thought that the flattery might be fully heard, he addressed himself to the gentleman, "I think, Sir, you were saying something about—", pausing in a high flutter of expectation. The gentleman, provoked at his inordinate vanity, resolved not to indulge it, and with an exquisitely sly air of indifference answered: "A mere trifle, Sir, not worth repeating." The mortification of Richardson was visible, and he did not speak ten words more the whole day. Johnson was present, and appeared to enjoy it much.'

Johnson's distaste for Richardson was aggravated, so Joshua Reynolds's sister, Frances, thought, by the resentment he felt on account of 'Richardson's success with certain literary ladies (especially Miss [Hester] Mulso and Miss [Elizabeth] Carter), previously of his circle, and by whom he now felt himself to be neglected, on Richardson's account'.

Certainly, he strongly disliked being neglected by any of his friends. As he said himself of Elizabeth Montagu, 'Mrs Montagu has dropt me. Now, Sir, there are people whom one should very much like to drop, but would not wish to be dropped by.' Certainly, too, he strongly believed that a man 'should keep his friendship in constant repair' and, looked upon 'every day to be lost in which' he did 'not make a new acquaintance'. For the more acquaintances he had, the less likely was he to find himself alone; and solitude, he feared, was 'dangerous to reason'.

6

Tea Cups and Dinner Plates

'Johnson to be sure has a roughness in his manner; but no man alive has a more tender heart. He has nothing of the bear but his skin.'
Oliver Goldsmith

Now that Johnson was in his fifties his fear of solitude was more intense than ever. In the tavern at night he was usually among the last to leave—often begging Joshua Reynolds to go home with him so that he would not be alone in the coach—and, however late it was, he would invariably call at Miss Williams's lodgings before going home to his own. On occasions he knocked on her door at four or even five o'clock in the morning. And one morning he said to her, 'Take notice, Madam, that for once I am here before others are asleep. As I turned into the court, I ran against a knot of bricklayers.'

'You forget, my dear Sir, that these people have all been a-bed, and are now preparing for their day's work.'

'Is it so, then, Madam? I confess that circumstance had escaped me.'

Yet Miss Williams—'dressed in scarlet made in the handsome French fashion of the time,' in Laetitia-Matilda Hawkins's recollection, 'with a lace cap, with two stiffened projecting wings on the temples and a black lace hood'—would always be sitting up for him to give him tea before he went to bed, keeping her fingers inside the rim of his cup as she poured it out for him so that she could judge when the cup was full. Every night, however, there came a time when there would be no further excuse for staying up, and he would have to say good-night to Miss Williams, and walk home to Inner Temple Lane. And there, when the moods of depression were upon him, he could no longer escape what Frances Reynolds once referred to as his 'terrifying melancholy, which he was sometimes apprehensive bordered on insanity'.

'I have often heard him lament,' Miss Reynolds continued, 'that he inherited from his father a morbid disposition both of body and mind—an apprehensive melancholy, which robbed him of the common enjoyments of life. Indeed, he seemed to struggle almost incessantly with some mental evil, and often, by the expression of his countenance and the motion of his lips, appeared to be offering up some ejaculation to Heaven to remove it.'

However much he might have diverted himself during the day, even at those times when he had come out of the dreaded stage of the manic depression which would probably be the modern diagnosis of his complaint, at night time, alone in his room, he would fall victim to his recurrent fears. He was as terrified of madness as he was of death; and he dreaded that divine punishment which would follow death and from which he did not believe his faith sufficient to save him. 'O Almighty God, merciful Father, who has continued my life another year,' he prayed on his fifty-first birthday, 'grant that I may spend the time thou shalt yet give me in such obedience to thy word and will that finally I may obtain everlasting life. Grant that I may repent and forsake my sins before the miseries of age fall upon me, and that while my strength yet remains I may use it to thy glory and my own salvation, by the assistance of thy Holy Spirit, for Jesus Christ's sake. Amen.'

He made a list of resolutions for the following year: he must make no vows to God that he might break—he had, no doubt, broken such vows in the past[1]—and he must combat his depraved imaginings, those 'tumultuous imaginations' of sexual fantasy. He was again firmly resolved:

> To apply to Study
> To rise early
> To study Religion
> To go to Church
> To drink less strong liquors
> To keep Journal
> To oppose laziness, by doing what is to be done

But six months later, at Easter 1761, he was painfully conscious that he had failed to keep his resolves. 'Since the Communion of last Easter, I have led a life so dissipated and useless,' he wrote, 'and my terrors and perplexities have so much increased, that I am under great depression and discouragement.' Once more he steadfastly purposed to lead a new life, and, though he was 'afraid to resolve again', he listed his sadly familiar rules for an improved life. He prayed that God would look down upon his 'misery with pity' and so strengthen him that he might 'overcome all sinful habits', that 'all corrupt desires' might be 'extinguished, and all vain thoughts dispelled'.

Feeling the need of a change of air he went up to Lichfield that winter but he was not much taken with what he found. It was the first time that he had visited the town for over twenty years and, so he wrote to a friend, the streets were 'much narrower and shorter than I thought I had left them, inhabited by a new race of people to whom I was very little known. My playfellows were grown old, and forced me to suspect that I was no longer young. My only remaining friend has changed his principles, and has become the tool of the predominant faction. My daughter-in-law [Lucy Porter who was still living with Catherine Chambers in the house by the market place], from whom I expected most, and whom I met with sincere benevolence, has lost the beauty and gaiety of youth, without having gained much of the wisdom of age. I wandered about for five days, and took the first convenient opportunity of returning to a place, where, if there is not much happiness, there is at least a diversity of good and evil, that slight vexations do not fix upon the heart.'

Much of Johnson's troubles stemmed from his increasing inability to settle down to work and consequently to improve his standard of living. Arthur Murphy was no doubt painting an excessively gloomy picture when he described 1 Inner Temple Lane as 'the abode of wretchedness' and depicted Johnson living in 'poverty' and 'total idleness'. But it was true that Johnson had written very little since the last number of *The Idler* had appeared on 5 April. A few reviews, an occasional dedication or introduction, one or two short prefaces were almost all that he managed to produce; and the work was not done with much care. He had once written a preface for Rolt's *Dictionary of Trade Etc.*, without either meeting its compiler or even reading the book. 'Sir, I never saw the man, and never read the book,' he replied to an enquiry about it. 'The booksellers wanted a preface to a Dictionary of Trade and Commerce. I knew very well what such a Dictionary should be, and I wrote a preface accordingly.'

Sometimes the work was done out of kindness, without expectation of payment. He wrote, for example, a brief life of Roger Ascham—and perhaps did all the editorial work as well—for the *English Works of Roger*

Ascham which was nominally the work of James Bennet, an indigent schoolmaster, who had excited his pity. And in December 1759 he wrote three letters to the *Daily Gazeteer*, attacking Robert Mylne's designs for elliptical arches for the new Blackfriars Bridge not, as was said, because Mylne was a Scotchman, but because alternative designs for semicircular arches had been submitted by an acquaintance of his.

In October 1761 an edition of *The Idler* was published in two volumes by John Newbery, but they did not sell very well, and Johnson had, in any case, already got himself deep into Newbery's debt. Three times he had been obliged to apply to him for small sums while he was working on the dictionary, and in May 1759 and March 1760 he had borrowed considerably larger sums totalling nearly £73. He had finally managed, after over seventeen years, to pay off the debt on the mortgage on the Lichfield house, but this was only because he had taken subscriptions for a new edition of Shakespeare which was barely even started.

The idea of a new edition of Shakespeare, a more satisfactory edition than those of Rowe, Pope and Theobald, had occurred to him years before; and in 1745 he had started work on the project. But the magnitude of the task had daunted him. Even when the subscription money began to come in, he put off from day to day and from week to week the time when he would have to get down to work on it again, paying scant regard to the claims that his subscribers now had upon his time. One day a bookseller's young apprentice called with yet another subscription, and was surprised to see the author pocket the money without making any note of the customer's name or address. He diffidently suggested that the name and address might be taken down so that they be properly inserted in the printed list of subscribers. Johnson replied emphatically and with 'great abruptness', '*I shall print no list of subscribers*'. Then, evidently supposing that this startling announcement required some explanation, he added, 'Sir, I have two very cogent reasons for not printing any list of subscribers—one, that I have lost all the names, the other, that I have spent all the money.'

There was so much else that he would rather do than write, so much else to be enjoyed in conversation and society. 'No man but a blockhead ever wrote, except for money,' he once announced, and laid it down as a general rule that 'we would all be idle if we could'. Working on Shakespeare would at least be congenial, friends urged him. But no, it was all just work. 'I look upon this as I did upon the dictionary,' he replied to John Hawkins who suggested the labour would be enjoyable; 'it is all work, and my inducement to it is not love or desire of fame, but the want of money, which is the only motive to writing that I know of.'

It was, indeed, as much to have an excuse not to write as because he was both constitutionally inquisitive and compulsively magisterial that he welcomed every opportunity to settle the affairs of the outside world and to give his advice upon every problem for the solution of which it was invoked. When, therefore, he was invited to be a member of a committee appointed to investigate the Cock Lane ghost he accepted with alacrity. He held, as a Christian, that 'a total disbelief of [ghosts] is adverse to the opinion of the existence of the soul between death and the last day; the question simply is, whether departed spirits ever have the power of making themselves perceptible to us'. Certainly he 'knew one friend, who was an honest and sensible man, who told him that he had seen a ghost, old Mr Edward Cave, the printer at St John's Gate. He said, Mr Cave did not like to talk of it, and seemed to be in great horror whenever it was mentioned.' Johnson himself, as an undergraduate at Pembroke while turning the key of his room, had heard his mother distinctly call his name.

But he made 'a distinction between what a man may experience by the mere strength of his imagination, and what imagination cannot possibly produce. Thus, suppose I should think that I saw a form, and heard a voice cry, "Johnson you are a very wicked fellow, and unless you repent you will certainly be punished"; my own unworthiness is so deeply impressed upon my mind, that I might *imagine* I thus saw and heard, and therefore I should not believe that an external communication had been made to me. But if a form should appear, and voice should tell me that a particular man had died at a particular place, and a particular hour, a fact which I had no apprehension of, nor any means of knowing, and this fact, with all its circumstances should afterwards be unquestionably proved, I should, in that case, be persuaded that I had supernatural intelligence imparted to me.' Or, as he put it more succinctly on an earlier occasion, 'Prodigies are always seen in proportion as they are expected'.

He condemned John Wesley, who accepted the existence of ghosts unquestioningly, for believing in them without 'sufficient authority'. Yet when he once remarked in Anna Seward's presence that he was 'sorry that John did not take more pains to enquire into the evidence' for his belief in one particular ghost at Newcastle, and Miss Seward, with an incredulous smile, exclaimed, 'What, Sir! About a ghost?', Johnson turned on her with solemn vehemence, 'Yes, Madam: this is a question, which, after five thousand years, is yet undecided; a question, whether in theology or philosophy, one of the most important that can come before the human understanding.'

It was then, with great seriousness that he applied himself to the problem of the Cock Lane ghost, which was reported to be giving messages from beyond the grave to an eleven-year-old girl at 33 Cock Lane in the slums of Smithfield. The messages came in the form of strange scratching sounds that could be heard when this girl was lying in bed. The girl's father, William Parsons, alleged that the sounds came from the ghost of his sister-in-law, Fanny, who had recently died. It was believed at the time that she had died of smallpox, but the mysterious noises, according to Mary Frazer, a friend of the family, who claimed that she could interpret them, indicated that she had in reality died of arsenical poisoning. The arsenic, Mary Frazer said, had been administered by a neighbour named Kent with whom the Parsons family had previously lodged and with whom they had quarrelled.

When the story became known, the whole town of London thought of nothing else, Horace Walpole said, and, accompanied by the Duke of York and others, he went to see the girl. He could not at first get into the house so great was the crowd; and when he did eventually gain admittance to the small and crowded room in which the girl lay, he was disappointed to be told that the ghost would not make itself heard before seven o'clock the next morning.

By the time Johnson went to see the girl she had been removed to the house of the Rev Stephen Aldrich, rector of St John's, Clerkenwell. Here, at ten o'clock at night, Johnson, Sir John Fielding, the blind magistrate, the Rev John Douglas, later Bishop of Salisbury, a Scottish divine who was 'a great detector of impostures', and other members of the committee of investigation met in a chamber when the girl 'with proper caution had been put to bed by several ladies'. For an hour they listened and, hearing nothing, went downstairs to interrogate her father 'who denied in the strongest terms, any knowledge or belief of fraud'.

'While they were enquiring and deliberating,' Johnson reported in an account that was published in the *Gentleman's Magazine*, 'they were summoned into the girl's chamber by some ladies who were near her bed, and who had heard knocks and scratches. When the gentlemen entered, the girl declared that she felt the spirit like a mouse upon her back.'

The girl was asked to keep her hands outside the bed. 'From that time no evidence of any preternatural power was exhibited. . . . It is, therefor, the opinion of the whole assembly,' Johnson concluded his report, 'that the child has some art of making or counterfeiting a particular noise [it was afterwards discovered that she scratched a piece of wood which she had beneath the blanket] and that there is no agency of any higher cause.'

Although he felt confident that he had acted wisely in the matter and, in later years, 'related with much satisfaction how he had assisted in detecting the cheat', Johnson came in for a good deal of ridicule for having taken the matter so seriously in the first place; and those who had cause to dislike him made the most of their opportunity.² One of these was John Wilkes's friend, the poet Charles Churchill, of whose recent production, *Night*, Johnson had justifiably spoken with some scorn as being the work of a 'shallow fellow'. Recognising in the Cock Lane affair an opportunity to be revenged upon 'Pomposo—insolent and loud, vain idol of a scribbling crowd' whose 'features so horrid, were it light, would put the devil himself to flight'—Churchill published a poem entitled *The Ghost* in which both Johnson's appearance and conversational manner, as well as his failure to provide the subscribers to his edition of Shakespeare with the books for which they had paid, were all roundly condemned:

> For 'tis with him a certain rule,
> The folly's proved when he calls fool,
> Who to increase his native strength,
> Draws words six syllables in length,
> With which, assisted with a frown,
> By way of club, he knocks us down . . .
> He for subscribers baits his hook,
> And takes their cash—but where's the book?
> No matter where—wise fear, we know,
> Forbids the robbing of a foe;
> But what, to serve our private ends,
> Forbids the cheating of our friends . . .

Thereafter, Johnson was in the habit of talking very contemptuously of Churchill's poetry, contending that it would soon 'sink into oblivion', that 'it had a contemporary currency only from its audacity of abuse, and being filled with living names'. When it was suggested to him that he was not quite a fair judge as Churchill had attacked his own name so violently, he protested, 'Nay, Sir, I am a very fair judge. He did not attack me violently till he found I did not like his poetry; and his attack on me shall not prevent me from continuing to say what I think of him, from an apprehension that it may be ascribed to resentment. No, Sir, I called the fellow a blockhead at first, and I will call him a blockhead still. However, I will acknowledge that I have a better opinion of him now, than I once had; for he has shewn more fertility than I expected. [*The Ghost* had been followed in quick succession, by three far superior satires, *The Author, The Epistle to William Hogarth* and *The Duellist*.] To be sure, he is a tree that cannot produce good fruit; he only bears crabs. But, Sir, a tree that produces a great many crabs is better than a tree which produces only a few.'

While the town was still discussing his part in the affair of the Cock Lane ghost, Johnson gave his enemies surer grounds upon which to attack him.

One day in July 1762 when Johnson was fifty-two, Arthur Murphy called at 1 Inner Temple Lane on an errand for the Government. Murphy, Thomas Sheridan, the Irish actor and father of the playwright, and some other of Johnson's friends had persuaded Alexander Wedderburn, a close friend of the Prime Minister, the Earl of Bute, to suggest that Samuel Johnson be granted a state pension. Murphy had been deputed by the Government to approach Johnson informally and to sound him out on the matter. Unsure himself as to how Johnson would react, Murphy broached the subject cautiously until at last 'by slow and studied approaches the message was disclosed'.

Johnson's immediate reaction was to ask if the offer were seriously intended, and then, on being assured that it was, he fell into silence and deep thought. Pensions were not usually given without it being tacitly understood that the recipients would perform occasional services for their benefactors in return for them. On occasions they were given to troublesome authors on the understanding that they would write no more or write in a different way, as in the case of John Cleland, an impoverished former employee of the East India Company whose novel the *Memoirs of a Woman of Pleasure* [Fanny Hill] had procured for him a pension of £100 a year on condition that he made a 'worthier use of his talents'.

Moreover, Johnson could not but be aware that his definition of 'pension' in his dictionary would be constantly quoted against him. Murphy assured him that 'he, at least, did not come within the definition'; but Johnson hesitated still. Finally, he said he would like time to think about it, and asked Murphy to dine with him at the Mitre in Fleet Street, his favourite tavern, the next day.

Before meeting Murphy again he went to Joshua Reynolds for his advice. Reynolds was much younger than Johnson, but in the ten years since they had first met, he had become the most distinguished and fashionable portrait painter of his day; and Johnson's letters repeatedly refer to his ever-increasing fame and fortune with a certain wistful envy: 'Mr Reynolds has within these few days raised his price to twenty Guineas a head' (January 1759); 'Reynolds is without a rival, and continues to add thousands to thousands' (June 1761); 'Mr Reynolds gets six thousand a year' (July 1762); 'Reynolds still continues to increase in reputation and in riches' (December 1762). But as well as being rich and famous, Reynolds was a man with a wide knowledge of the world, sympathetic, tactful and sensible. Johnson once said of him that 'if he had a month given to him to find fault with him he should at the end of the month be as much at a loss as at the beginning'. He could not have chosen a better adviser.

He went round to see Reynolds at his house at 47 Leicester Fields (now Leicester Square), told him of the offer that had been made to him, and said that he 'wished to consult his friends as to the propriety of his accepting this mark of the royal favour, after the definitions which he had given in the Dictionary of *pension* and *pensioners*. He said he should not have Sir Joshua's answer till next day, when he would call again, and desired he might think of it.'

Reynolds replied that there was no need for him to come back the next day, for he had no doubt at all that he ought to accept the offer; there 'could be no objection to his receiving from the King a reward for literary merit'; 'the definitions in his Dictionary were not applicable to him'.

Evidently satisfied by this, Johnson told Murphy that he would be happy to accept the offer, and he was then conducted by Wedderburn to call upon Lord Bute to thank him. Lord Bute 'behaved in the handsomest manner', replying to Johnson's question, 'Pray, my Lord, what am I expected to do for this pension?' with the assurance that it was not offered with any design that he should 'dip his pen in faction'. 'It is not given you for anything you are to do, but for what you have done,' Bute said; and, to emphasise the point, or to make sure that Johnson had distinctly heard the words, he repeated them twice.

'Bounty always receives part of its value from the manner in which it is bestowed,' Johnson wrote in an elegant letter of thanks to Lord Bute. 'Your Lordship's kindness includes every circumstance that can gratify delicacy, or enforce obligation. You have conferred your favours on a man who has neither alliance nor interest, who has not merited them by services, nor courted them by officiousness; you have spared him the shame of solicitation, and the anxiety of suspense.

'What has been thus elegantly given will, I hope, not be reproachfully enjoyed; I shall endeavour to give your Lordship the only recompense which generosity requires—the gratification of finding that your benefits are not improperly bestowed.'

He wrote to Lucy Porter in simpler terms: 'If I write but seldom to you, it is because it seldom happens that I have anything to tell you that can give you pleasure, but last Monday I was sent for by the Chief Minister, the Earl of Bute, who told me that the King had empowered him to do something for me, and let me know that a pension was granted me of three hundred a year. Be so kind as to tell Kitty.'

Three hundred a year was a very generous sum, ten times the amount he had proposed as an income upon which a man might live in London when he had first arrived there twenty-five years before. Although such comparisons are inevitably misleading, it might be considered the equivalent of over four thousand pounds a year today.

To Johnson it was riches. It was scarcely enough, a friend pointed out to him, to keep a coach; but he had never desired to keep a coach. He had never wanted to dress expensively either, except on that joyous occasion when he had astonished the audience at Drury Lane in his scarlet waistcoat and gold-laced hat; and, in fact, he continued to wear for the rest of his life the same dingy clothes to which he had grown accustomed. He had, he readily confessed, 'no passion for clean linen'.

Johnson did not even make any immediate plans to move out of his first floor lodgings at Inner Temple Lane to a house more suitable to his new station. But he was full of gratitude that he could now do this, and many other things, if he wanted to. When a friend remarked that there were certain things he could not do, he replied contentedly that he had no reason to complain. 'It is rather to be wondered at that I have so much. My pension is more out of the usual course of things than any instance I have known. Here, Sir, was a man avowedly no friend to Government at the time, who got a pension without asking for it. I never courted the great; they sent for me.'[3]

The numerous and expected reflections that were thrown out against him for having accepted the Government's money appeared to distress him not in the least. 'Why, Sir,' he said, with a hearty laugh, 'it is a mighty foolish noise they make. I have accepted of a pension as a reward which has been thought due to my literary merit; and now that I have this pension, I am the same in every respect that I have ever been; I retain the same principles. It is true that I cannot now curse the House of Hannover; nor would it be decent for me to drink King James's health in the wine that King George gives me money to pay for. But, Sir, I think that the pleasure of cursing the House of Hannover, and drinking King James's health, are amply overbalanced by three hundred pounds a year.'[4]

In this contented mood he set off on a holiday to Devon with Joshua Reynolds, who was born at Plympton-Earl's, where his father, a clergyman, had been master of the grammar school. Johnson was 'much pleased with this jaunt'. He was 'entertained at the seats of several noblemen and gentle-men in the west of England', and it was while walking in the garden of one of them that he gave his answer to the question 'Are you a botanist, Mr Johnson?' '"No, Sir,"(answered Johnson) "I am not a botanist; and, (alluding, no doubt, to his near sightedness) should I wish to become a botanist, I must first turn myself into a reptile."'

Most of this time Reynolds and Johnson spent in Plymouth where the Commissioner of the Dockyard provided a yacht for the two distinguished visitors to his town to sail out to the Eddystone rocks upon which John Smeaton's lighthouse had just been built. Johnson amused himself and his companion by affecting to share to a passionate degree the detestation of the citizens of Plymouth for the inhabitants of a new town that had been built two miles from the old for the benefit of those who worked on the docks. He protested that it was his duty to stand by the established town, and so warmly entered into its interests on behalf of its unreasonable inhabitants, that upon every occasion he 'talked of the *dockers*, as the inhabitants of the new town were called, as upstarts and aliens'. 'I HATE a docker!' he exclaimed with the utmost vehemence. And when he was told that the dockers had applied for a conduit from Plymouth's water supply which was so abundant that it ran to waste in the town, he came out in the most violent opposition. 'No, no, no! I am against the *dockers*. I am a Plymouth man. Rogues! Let them die of thirst! They shall not have a drop!'

Soon after Johnson's return to London he learned that the unaccountable Robert Levett, though past his sixtieth year, had married a young prosti-tute. He had been in the habit of meeting her in a coal shed in Fetter Lane where she had succeeded in persuading him that, despite the lowliness of their chosen place of congress, she was closely related to a 'man of fortune but was injuriously kept by him out of large possessions'. She for her part had been satisfied that he was a physician with a considerable practice. Compared with the marvels of this transaction, so Johnson himself declared when relating them, the tales in the Arabian Nights' Entertain-ments seemed quite commonplace occurrences.

The marriage had been no more successful than might have been expected. After four months a writ was taken out against Levett for debts incurred by his wife, and they were obliged to go into hiding. Having no taste for so secluded a life, Mrs Levett ran away from her husband and was soon afterwards arrested as a pickpocket.

Her husband, it was said, was with difficulty dissuaded from going to give evidence against her at the Old Bailey in the hope that she would be hanged. She was, on the contrary, acquitted. With Johnson's help, however, Levett managed to arrange a separation from his ill-chosen bride, and he then became a permanent member of Johnson's household as he had, it seems, on occasions been a temporary one in the past.

Thereafter visitors who called of a morning at Temple Lane found Johnson half undressed, and Levett pouring out tea 'for himself and his patron alternately, no conversation passing between them', as they drank and ate their bread and butter. Levett was not a dependant, Johnson insisted; he just had house-room, 'his share in a penny loaf at breakfast, and now and then a dinner on a Sunday'. When surprise was expressed by a man who did not know Johnson well that he should admit such a character into his home, a friend who knew him better replied that Levett was poor and honest which was 'recommendation enough to Johnson', and since Levett was now miserable as well as poor, Johnson's protection of him was assured.

Levett's habitual silence in no way interfered with his companion's enjoyment of his Sunday dinner, for it was Johnson's habit, even when dining out, to eat in silence himself, concentrating on his food with a gluttonous intensity, so totally absorbed in it that his 'looks seemed rivetted to the plate'. 'Unless in very high company,' a friend said of him, he would not 'say one word or even pay the least attention to what was said by others, till he had satisfied his appetite, which was so fierce, and indulged with such intenseness, that while in the act of eating, the veins of his forehead swelled, and generally a strong perspiration was visible.'

'It was, at no time in his life, pleasing to see him at a meal,' John Hawkins confirmed disapprovingly. 'The greediness with which he ate, his total inattention to those among whom he was seated, and his profound silence in the hour of refection, were circumstances that at that instant degraded him, and showed him to be more a sensualist than a philosopher. Moreover, he was a lover of tea to an excess hardly credible; whenever it appeared, he was almost raving, and by his impatience to be served, his incessant calls for those ingredients which make that liquor palatable, and the haste with which he swallowed it down, he seldom failed to make that a fatigue to everyone else, which was intended as a general refreshment.'

But although he was ready to condemn himself for so many other failings, both real and imaginary, although he recorded more than once his resolve to drink less strong liquors or wine, he never accused himself of gluttony or thought it necessary to make any apology for his passion for tea. On the contrary, he proudly described himself as 'a hardened and shameless tea-drinker, who has, for many years, diluted his meals with only the infusion of this fascinating plant; whose kettle has scarcely time to cool; who, with tea amuses the evening, with tea solaces the midnights, and with tea welcomes the morning'. He was certainly, as Hawkins said, very troublesome whenever tea was produced in a tavern; and at tea-time in private houses he exhausted his hostess by emptying his cup as fast as she could fill it. Once at the house of Richard Cumberland, the drama-tist, Sir Joshua Reynolds annoyed him by remarking that he had drunk eleven cupfuls. 'Sir,' Johnson reprimanded him, 'I did not count your glasses of wine, why should you number my cups of tea.' Then, laughing in perfect good humour, he added, 'Sir, I should have released the lady from any further trouble, if it had not been for your remark; but you have re-minded me that I want one of the dozen, and I must request Mrs Cumberland to round up my number.'

'When he saw the readiness and complacency, with which my wife obeyed his call,' Richard Cumberland recalled, 'he turned a kind and cheerful look upon her and said, "Madam, I must tell you for your com-fort you have escaped much better than a certain lady did awhile ago, upon whose patience I intruded greatly more than I have done on yours; but the lady asked me for no other purpose but to make a Zany of me, and set me gabbling to a parcel of people I knew nothing of; so, Madam, I had my revenge of her; for I swallowed five and twenty cups of her tea, and did not treat her with as many words." I can only say my wife would have made tea for him as long as the New River could have supplied her with water.'

Nor would Johnson have any suggestion made that he was wrong to take so great an interest in the food which he ate in such extraordinary quanti-ties. He would speak with disdain of other gluttons, and one number of *The Rambler* is a 'masterly essay against gulosity'. Yet he seemed not to look upon himself as greedy at all, preferring to consider that he was a discern-ing, not to say fastidious epicure, as experienced an expert in the art of cookery as he was in good breeding. 'I, Madam, who live at a variety of good tables, am a much better judge of cookery, than any person who has a tolerable cook but lives much at home,' he intimidatingly addressed a lady at whose house he had been invited to dine; 'for his palate is gradually adapted to the taste of his cook; whereas, Madam, in trying by a wider range, I can more exquisitely judge.'[5]

'Some people,' he observed on an earlier occasion, 'have a foolish way of not minding, or pretending not to mind, what they eat. For my part,' he affirmed, 'I mind my belly very studiously, and very carefully; for I look upon it, that he who does not mind his belly will hardly mind anything else.' He had no doubt that he could write a better cookery book himself than any that had yet been written. 'You shall see,' he exclaimed warming excitedly to his theme, 'what a Book of Cookery I shall make! I shall agree with Mr Dilly for the copyright!'[6]

The memory of a good dinner would delight him, and he would describe it in the minutest detail and with the warmest and most earnest expressions. After an especially memorable one at the house of Edmund Allen, the printer, whose old housekeeper knew well how to please him, he exclaimed joyously, 'Sir, we could not have had a better dinner, had there been a *Synod of Cooks*'. A plain and simple meal, on the other hand, would not please him at all. Oh yes, he would agree after such a one, it was 'a good dinner enough to be sure: but it was not a dinner to *ask* a man to'. As for a poor dinner, it would bring out in him the most extravagant anger. Once after dining at a certain nobleman's house where every dish was a wretched performance he vehemently cried out that if he could have his way he'd throw the rascally cook into the river.

In spite of his odd behaviour at the dining-table and in front of the teapot, Johnson was rarely without visitors when he was having breakfast or without an invitation when it was dinner-time. His neighbour, who kept the shop on the corner of Inner Temple Lane, said that all the time he lived there, more enquiries were made for Mr Johnson than for all the other inhabitants of the Inner and Middle Temple put together. He was scarcely ever to be found at home in the morning without at least 'some people', and often was surrounded by a 'numerous levee'. 'All who visited him at these hours were welcome,' Hawkins said, 'and whoever withdrew, went too soon.' 'Nay, don't go, Sir,' he would say when the last of the company rose and threatened to leave him alone. 'I am obliged to any man who visits me.'

The immediate impression he gave to those who visited him was, however, no more alluring now that it had been before the pension had given him ease in his circumstances. A young visitor who called for the first time in the summer of 1763 recalled that he was received 'very courteously: but, it must be confessed that his apartment, and furniture, and morning dress, were sufficiently uncouth. His brown suit of cloaths looked very rusty: he had on a little old shrivelled unpowdered wig, which was too small for his head; his shirt-neck and knees of his breeches were loose; his black worsted stockings ill drawn-up; and he had a pair of unbuckled shoes by way of slippers.' His shoes indeed were often unbuckled, since, although he could not be bothered to buckle them himself, he was unwilling that Frank should do them for him. 'No, Frank,' he would say, 'time enough yet. When I can do it no longer, then you may.' Laetitia-Matilda Hawkins confirmed that his clothes—which he put on in a great hurry, believing that 'everyone should get the habit' of dressing quickly—were always far from neat. They 'hung loose about him,' she said, 'and the pocket on the right hand swung violently, the lining of his coat being always visible. I can now call to mind his brown hand, his metal sleeve-buttons, and my surprise at seeing him with plain wristbands when all gentlemen wore ruffles; his coat-sleeve being very wide showed his linen almost to the elbow. His wig in common was cut and bushy.'

Some days the slovenliness of the chambers would be emphasised by an unpleasant smell that emanated from the garret above. For this room had been fitted out by Johnson as a laboratory where, surrounded by spirit lamps, retorts, tubes, bottles and all manner of other vessels including an alembic, he conducted various chemical experiments. No one was quite sure what these experiments entailed, but they seemed mainly to do with the distilling of various substances such as peppermint and the dregs of strong beer from which he extracted a strong and very nauseous spirit that few of his visitors could be persuaded to taste though none could fail to smell. He also conducted experiments on his own body, shaving the hairs on his arms and chest to see how long it took them to grow, measuring the length of a cut finger nail so that, as he recorded in his journal, he might 'know the growth of nails'.[7]

When it was time for dinner, he would go downstairs, amble out into the lane, and lumber off to a tavern or a private house. Only once in his whole life, he told a friend, had he refused one of the numerous invitations to dinner that he received, and that was because he had made a resolution to do some work, a resolution he failed to keep. In the evenings he would have supper at a favourite tavern, sometimes the Mitre, sometimes the Turk's Head in the Strand, a place he frequented because the mistress was 'a good civil woman' and had 'not much business'. And after supper he would unfailingly walk round to Miss Williams in Bolt Court for his nightly cup of tea, carrying a vast oak stick, or rather a small tree, which was over six feet in length and almost three inches in diameter at the upper end where the root had been trimmed to the size of an orange.

To be invited to accompany him to Miss Williams was a mark of high favour, much sought after by his intimates; and Oliver Goldsmith's proud cry, 'I go to Miss Williams' as he strutted off with Johnson, was remembered years later with exasperation and envy by a younger man upon whom the honour had not yet been bestowed.

Goldsmith, the son of an Irish clergyman, was almost twenty years younger than Johnson. Having failed to earn a reasonable living either as a physician or as a schoolmaster, he had become a literary hack; and when Johnson first visited his lodgings at No 6 Wine Office Court, Fleet Street, in May 1761 he had begun to make a name for himself as a contributor to John Newbery's newspaper, the *Public Ledger*, and as editor of the *Lady's Magazine*. Johnson arrived at Wine Office Court dressed with uncommon neatness for he had heard that Goldsmith, who spent far more on his clothes than he could well afford, had cited him as an example of slovenly habits. He had found the young writer sufficiently complimentary and respectful, however, and thereafter they had seen a great deal of one another.

To some of Johnson's other friends the intimacy seemed a curious one. For Goldsmith had the reputation of being rather a fool. Garrick described him as one 'for shortness called Noll, who wrote like an angel, and talked like poor Poll'; while Horace Walpole, referred to him as 'an inspired idiot'. It would have been much better, it was generally agreed, if he had followed Addison's example, who, having no talent for conversation, had made no attempt to shine at it. Undoubtedly he did often join in conversations with very little knowledge of the subject under discussion, would frequently contradict himself and sometimes become incoherent. There was no doubt, too, that he was extremely vain, excessively hostile to criticism, anxious at every opportunity to leap into the limelight, and morbidly jealous of the reputation of other literary characters, indeed of anyone praised in more lavish terms than himself.

'Whenever I write anything,' he once complained to Johnson 'in ludicrous terms of distress', 'the public *make a point* to know nothing about it.' He readily confessed to feeling sick with envy at Johnson's reputation. 'He had so much envy,' Johnson remarked, 'that he could not conceal it. He was so full of it that he overflowed. He talked of it to be sure often enough. Now, Sir, what a man avows, he is not ashamed to think; though many a man thinks what he is ashamed to avow. We are all envious naturally; but by checking envy we get the better of it.' Goldsmith, however, could never check his envy, and remembered with painful distress every occasion upon which it had been provoked. He remembered with particular bitterness a night when he was talking with Johnson and Graham, the author of *Telemachus*, who was a master at Eton. 'Doctor,' said Graham, rather drunk, before departing, 'I shall be happy to see you at Eton.'

'I shall be happy to wait upon you,' answered Goldsmith, thinking the invitation was addressed to him.

'No, 'tis not you I mean, Dr *Minor*; 'tis Dr *Major* there.'

Graham, Goldsmith afterwards decided in furious exasperation, was a 'fellow to make one commit suicide'.

There were also well-known stories of how, when travelling through France with two beautiful young ladies Goldsmith was 'seriously angry' that they received more attention from the inhabitants for their looks than he did for his talents; and of how, during an exhibition of *fantoccini*, he had been so put out by the praise lavished upon the dexterity of the puppets in tossing a pike that he had exclaimed with some warmth, 'Pshaw! I can do it better myself!' On his way home to supper after the performance, in attempting to show how much better he could jump over a stick than the puppets could, he had broken his shin.

John Hawkins related numerous anecdotes to show just how absurdly 'this idiot' behaved. 'At the breaking up of an evening at a tavern,' one of these anecdotes went, 'he entreated the company to sit down, and told them if they would call for another bottle they should hear one of his *bons mots*. They agreed, and he began thus: "I was once told that Sheridan, the player, in order to improve himself in stage gestures, had looking glasses, to the number of ten, hung about his room, and that he practised before them; upon which I said, 'then there were ten ugly fellows together'." The company were all silent. He asked why they did not laugh, which they not doing, he, without tasting the wine, left the room in anger.'

Goldsmith was a short man, his features were coarse and much marked by smallpox, his 'deportment that of a scholar awkwardly affecting the easy gentleman'. He was, also, Johnson contended, extraordinarily ignorant; it was 'amazing' how little he knew. 'Sir, he knows nothing,' he commented dismissively when Goldsmith had said, 'As I take my shoes from the shoemaker, and my coat from the tailor, so I take my religion from the priest.' 'Sir, he knows nothing; he has made up his mind about nothing.'

Johnson, indeed, found much fault with his friend, particularly as a conversationalist. Since he had 'no settled notions upon any subject', he talked 'always at random'; it seemed to be 'his intention to blurt out whatever was in his mind, and see what would become of it'; he was always being 'catched in an absurdity', yet this did not 'prevent him from falling into another the next minute'. All in all, Goldsmith was 'not an agreeable companion'; he talked 'always for fame'.

On other occasions Johnson observed of him: 'Sir, he is so much afraid of being unnoticed that he often talks merely lest you should forget that he is in the company. . . . Rather than not speak he will talk of what he knows himself to be ignorant. . . . He goes on without knowing how he is to get off. . . . He should not be for ever attempting to shine in conversation: he has not temper for it, he is so much mortified when he fails. . . . When he contends, if he gets the better, it is a very little addition to a man of his literary reputation: if he does not get the better, he is miserably vexed.'

Sometimes Goldsmith's vexation was so great that he could not control his temper. Once, during an after-dinner argument in which he had not yet taken part, he sat in restless agitation waiting for an opportunity to put in his oar, but, finding himself excluded, he took up his hat to go. Yet he could not bring himself to leave the room, and stood by the door, hat in hand, hesitating. At last he spoke; but Johnson himself was speaking so loudly that his observation went unheard. In a passion he threw his hat to the floor, looked furiously at Johnson and shouted, 'Take it!'

At this violent interruption Johnson fell silent, and as one of the other members was about to say something, Johnson turned to him 'uttering some sound'. 'Sir,' exclaimed Goldsmith, 'the gentleman has heard you patiently for an hour: pray allow us now to hear him.'

'Sir, I was not interrupting the gentleman. I was only giving him a signal of my attention. Sir, you are impertinent.'

Goldsmith did not reply to this, but later on, seeing him brooding silently in a corner, Johnson called out to him in a loud voice, 'Dr Goldsmith, something passed today when you and I dined; I ask your pardon.'

'It must be much from you, Sir, that I take ill', Goldsmith answered, placated immediately as most men were by Johnson's gruff apologies.

Yet always Johnson's superiority in conversation and debate rankled with Goldsmith. He complained that those who spoke of him as though he were entitled to the honour of unquestionable superiority were 'making a monarchy of what should be a republic'. And he was particularly mortified that one day as he was talking with unaccustomed fluency, and as he thought, to the admiration of all who were present, a German who was sitting next to him and who saw Johnson rolling himself about in his chair as though he were about to speak, suddenly interrupted him, crying out, 'Stay! stay! Toctor Shonson is about to say something.'

Condemn him as he would for his ignorance and inept, pushful conversation, tease him as he would for his love of splendid clothes, the 'absurd colour' of the 'bloom-coloured coat' in which he proudly strutted about before a dinner party one afternoon, and his affectation that he did not care whether or not the King attended his new play, Johnson deeply respected Goldsmith's artistry, 'his great merit'. No man was 'more foolish' when he did not have a pen in his hand, 'or more wise when he had'. He teased him often enough to be sure: When Goldsmith complained about the acclaim accorded to James Beattie's *Essays on Truth*, 'Here's such a stir about a fellow that has written one book, and I have written many', Johnson immediately replied, 'Ah, Doctor, there go two-and-forty six-pences you know to one guinea'. But his respect for Goldsmith's worth as a writer was quite sincere, all the same.

'Whether, indeed, we take him as a poet, as a comic writer, or as an historian he stands in the first class,' Johnson insisted; there had not been a finer poem than Goldsmith's *Traveller* since the time of Pope; he knew of no comedy that had 'so much exhilarated an audience', that had 'answered so much the great end of comedy' as *She Stoops to Conquer*. Goldsmith, he concluded, 'is one of the first men we now have as an author, and he is a very worthy man too'. Consequently Johnson did not join in the general laughter at his expense when Goldsmith complained naïvely that he had met Lord Camden, the Lord Chancellor, at Lord Clare's country house and, said Goldsmith indignantly, 'he took no more notice of me than if I had been an ordinary man'.

'Nay, Gentlemen,' protested Johnson at the loud laughter with which this complaint was greeted. 'Dr Goldsmith is in the right. A nobleman ought to have made up to such a man as Goldsmith; and I think it is much against Lord Camden that he neglected him'.[8]

Johnson even allowed Goldsmith to take the occasional liberty with him that was denied to all other men other than Beauclerk—as, for instance, when Johnson treated slightingly a proposal for having a third theatre in London for the exhibition of new plays, a proposal that would give play-wrights opportunities at present denied them by the unadventurous managements of Drury Lane and Covent Garden. Goldsmith objected, 'Ay, ay, this may be nothing to you who can now shelter yourself behind the corner of a pension'. Johnson, according to Beauclerk, accepted the well-phrased rebuke with 'good-humour'. And when Goldsmith was talk-ing about the writing of fables, how it was necessary to make the animals talk in character, to make little fishes talk like little fishes, Johnson shook his sides with laughter. 'Why, Dr Johnson,' he said smartly and effectively, 'this is not so easy as you seem to think; for if you were to make little fishes talk, they would talk like WHALES.' Johnson appears to have accepted this rebuke also in silence.[9]

Indeed, Goldsmith insisted that Johnson was not nearly so fierce as he was reputed to be by those who did not know him well. 'Johnson, to be sure, has a roughness in his manner,' he observed, denying the justice of applying to him the epithet of a bear; 'but no man alive has a more tender heart. He has nothing of the bear but his skin.'[10]

So Johnson and Goldsmith maintained their friendship to the end; and in the early 1760s, before Goldsmith had achieved anything like Johnson's fame, they dined together regularly. On Friday 1 July 1763 they were having dinner at the Mitre when they were joined by a young Scotchman whose name was James Boswell.

7

A Young Man from Edinburgh

'He is very slovenly in his dress and speaks with a most uncouth voice. Yet his great knowledge and strength of expression command vast respect and render him very excellent company. He has great humour and is a worthy man. But his dogmatic roughness of manners is disagreeable. I shall mark what I remember of his conversation.' James Boswell

James Boswell had arrived in London from Scotland a few months before, 'all life and joy', as he recorded in his journal, singing songs about pretty girls and giving three cheers as the coach went briskly in. He was then just twenty-two. His father was Alexander Boswell, eighth Laird of Auchinleck in Ayrshire, and as a judge of the Scottish Courts of Session, and in the High Court of Justiciary, entitled to call himself Lord Auchinleck. His mother, a pious Presbyterian, who seems to have been almost a stranger to the eldest of her three sons, was of even more ancient lineage, being descended from the grandfather of Lord Darnley, husband of Mary, Queen of Scots.

James was born in his father's town house in Edinburgh and was sent to the High School there, and then, at the age of thirteen, he entered the University. Although at the University, he still lived at home under the guidance of his strict, domineering father and of a succession of domestic tutors, all of them preparing to enter the ministry of the Church of Scotland. He was a shy, timid, uneasy boy, dark-haired, swarthy and rather fat, suffering from bouts of deep depression; and, when he was sixteen, from some sort of nervous breakdown. After his recovery his character appeared to change and his constitution to become more robust. Somewhat priggish and decidedly withdrawn before his illness, he was now both sensual and gregarious. He had as many love affairs as could be conducted out of sight of his father's watchful eye, and at twenty-one he became the father of an illegitimate child.

It was Lord Auchlinleck's wish that he should continue the family tradition and become a lawyer; he had no sympathy with his son's literary ambitions and felt nothing but contempt for his unconventional, artistic acquaintances. Nor did he sympathise with his desire to become an officer of the Foot Guards, suspecting—and rightly suspecting—that this was no more than an excuse to live in London.

In the spring of 1760, desperately unhappy in his studies of civil law, Boswell ran away, or rather rode away, to London where he was received into the Roman Catholic Church, a fact which his father, and indeed most of his friends, never discovered. After three months' hectic enjoyment of London life, during which he renounced his new faith, he acceded to his father's request to return home.

Unwillingly continuing with his legal studies, making love to any woman who would have him, he brought to his father's notice whenever the opportunity offered and whenever he dared, his unabated ambition to become an army officer. At length Lord Auchinleck gave way. Making him an allowance of £200 a year, he agreed that he might go to London with an introduction to the Duke of Queensberry and endeavour to gain a commission with the Duke's influence, provided he passed his civil law examinations. So James Boswell had arrived in London, full of hope, eagerness and confidence.

He was a young man of little dignity and much vanity, with an overwhelming interest in self-analysis, a compelling need for self-revelation, and astonishing resilience. There were times when he seemed absurd in his passionate quest for fame and favour, but he did have talent and he did have charm. He could be unthinkingly cruel, but he was never malicious. His main interest in life, other than women and himself, was people; and although he was still so young, he had already cultivated the friendship of a wide variety of men who found his company congenial. In Scotland he had seen much of Lord Kames, the philosopher and author of *The Elements of Criticism*; and had held long conversations with David Hume, Adam Smith, and the Rev Hugh Blair, Professor of Rhetoric at the University, all of them many years his senior. He had met Thomas Sheridan, who had gone to Edinburgh to give lectures on English elocution, and Sheridan had taken to him as he himself had taken to Sheridan. He shared a confidential friend, Sir David Dalrymple, with his father; and he had a number of close friends of his own age to whom he could outpour his feelings about his present, his past, his future, his career, his needs, his character. Some were rakes like himself, but others, such as William Temple, were high-minded young men of the most impeccable virtue.

Already Boswell had proved his ability as a writer. His verses were abysmal; when he touched upon philosophy he became tedious; but his skill in sharply delineating the foibles of the human character and in recording conversations was already remarkable. This skill was given much practice, for he was a compulsive writer. He did not write—as Johnson claimed only to write—for money; he wrote because he felt the urgent need to write. If he had nothing else to write about he would set down a memorandum for himself, reminding him to do something which he could not possibly have forgotten to do. He was to find in London a marvellous abundance of material for that busily scratching pen. He was to find, too, material for conversation which, as one of his early memoranda indicates, was his first purpose in seeking out 'all the Literati'. By being able to talk about famous people from first-hand knowledge he would make himself the more interesting.

Within four days of his arrival in London he had dined with the Earl of Eglinton, a Scottish nobleman and acquaintance of his father's, and had met Robert Mylne, the architect, whose design for Blackfriars Bridge had been accepted despite Johnson's objections. A few days later John Bear, manager of Covent Garden, took him to the Beefsteak Club where he drank wine and punch 'in plenty and freedom', and sang a number of songs with a merry company that included Charles Churchill and John Wilkes. Within the next two or three months he met almost all the people he wanted to meet from Lord Elibank, the Duke of Queensberry and the Prince of Mecklenburg to Oliver Goldsmith, 'a curious, odd, pedantic fellow with some genius', and David Garrick with whose kindness and flattering attention he was 'quite in raptures'.

Yet the months passed, and the spring of 1763 came, and still he had not managed to meet Samuel Johnson. His name, of course, had frequently cropped up in conversation. Dr Blair had spoken of a visit to 1 Inner Temple Lane and of having 'found the Giant in his den'. Goldsmith at a dinner party at the house of Thomas Davies, the actor and bookseller, had —after denying the merit of Shakespeare—spoken of Johnson's 'exceeding great merit', of his *Rambler* as being 'a noble work'; and Davies had said, 'He is a most entertaining companion. And how can it be otherwise, when he has so much imagination, has read so much, and digested it so well?'

In Scotland, too, the conversation had often turned to Johnson. Thomas Sheridan would expatiate on Johnson's extraordinary knowledge, talents, and virtues, repeat his pointed sayings, describe his peculiarities, and boast of his 'being his guest sometimes till two or three in the morning'. After a talk with David Hume on the same fascinating subject, Boswell had recorded: 'Mr Samuel Johnson has got a pension of £300 a year. Indeed his Dictionary was a kind of national Work so he has a kind of claim to the Patronage of the state. His stile is particular and pedantic. He is a man of enthusiasm and antiquated notions, a keen Jacobite yet hates the Scotch. Holds the Episcopal Hierarchy in supreme veneration and said he would stand before a battery of cannon to have the Convocation restored to its full powers. He holds Mr Hume in abhorrence and left a company one night upon his coming.'

Boswell had hoped for an introduction to Johnson from Samuel Derrick, the Irish author. He had 'unluckily got acquainted with this creature' when he was first in London in 1760, and, while making use of his knowledge of the town in 'all its variety of departments, both literary and sportive', had decided that he was 'a little blackguard pimping dog'. Johnson, however, had a 'great kindness for Derrick', even claiming to have respect for his merits as a writer, a literary judgement he later modified when, in reply to a question about the relative worth of Derrick and Christopher Smart, he said that there was 'no settling the point of precedency between a louse and a flea'. But although Derrick gave Boswell reason to hope that he would introduce him to Johnson, and although Johnson afterwards said that he 'might very well' have introduced him, he never found the opportunity to do so.

Boswell had also hoped that Thomas Sheridan, who had spoken so warmly of Johnson in Edinburgh, might introduce him. But since Sheridan's return to London he had quarrelled bitterly with Johnson about their respective pensions. For, upon hearing that Sheridan, a mere actor, had been granted a pension of £200 a year, Johnson had exploded in indignation, 'What! Have they given *him* a pension? Then it is time for me to give up mine. However,' he added, a little later, correcting himself, 'I am glad that Mr Sheridan has a pension, for he is a very good man.'

Sheridan, to whom the first part of Johnson's remark was repeated but not the amendment, never forgave him for the insult, declined all overtures to make it up with him, and refused to dine in the same house with him again. 'It was the greatest ingratitude,' he insisted, 'for it was I and Wedderburn that first set the thing agoing [for *his* pension].' Nor did Johnson trouble to mend their quarrel by subsequently speaking well of Sheridan or of his work as an actor and elocutionist. Of his influence on the English language, he said it was 'burning a farthing candle at Dover to shew light at Calais'; on his threat to go to America where his talents might be more appreciated, he remarked that he hoped he *would* go, that the Americans certainly had no need to learn oratory but nor had the English need of Sheridan; and commenting on Sheridan's intellect he observed, 'Why, Sir, Sherry is dull, naturally dull; but it must have taken him a great deal of pains to become what we now see him. Such an excess of stupidity, Sir, is not in Nature.' It was not to be expected, then, that Boswell could hope for much in the way of an introduction to Johnson from Sheridan.

Thomas Davies, the bookseller, a 'friendly and very hospitable man' and an 'entertaining' if 'somewhat pompous' companion, more than once suggested that Boswell should come to meet Johnson at his house at 8 Russell Street, Covent Garden. 'Mr Davies recollected several of Johnson's remarkable sayings,' Boswell wrote, 'and was one of the best of the many imitators of his voice and manner, while relating them. He increased my impatience more and more to see the extraordinary man whose works I highly valued, and whose conversation was reported to be so peculiarly excellent.' When on Monday 16 May the meeting at last came, however, it came by chance.

Boswell was sitting in the parlour behind the shop with Davies and his wife, a former actress celebrated for her beauty. They had just finished tea when Davies, looking up, saw through the glass panel of the door the great bulk of Johnson approaching through the shop. He entered the parlour, and Davies introduced Boswell to him. Boswell confessed that he was 'much agitated' and in his agitation, with a kind of nervous jocularity, cried out to Davies, 'Don't tell where I come from.'

'From Scotland,' explained Davies 'roguishly'.

'Mr Johnson,' said Boswell, more nervous and self-conscious than ever. 'I do indeed come from Scotland, but I cannot help it.'

'Sir,' replied he, 'that, I find, is what a very great many of your countrymen cannot help.'

'This stroke,' poor Boswell confessed, 'stunned me a good deal; and when we had sat down, I felt myself not a little embarrassed, and apprehensive of what might come next.'

What did come next was further humiliation. For Johnson, turning to Davies said, 'What do you think of Garrick? He has refused me an order for the play for Miss Williams, because he knows the house will be full, and that an order would be worth three shillings.' And, Boswell, over-eager to please, not knowing that however ill Johnson sometimes spoke of Garrick he would not let anyone else do so in his presence, made an embarrassing attempt at flattery: 'Oh, Sir, I cannot think Mr Garrick would grudge such a trifle to you.'

Johnson turned once again upon the impertinent and rather fat young man with the full sensual lips and the fleshy nose. 'Sir,' he said to him, with what his victim described as a stern look, 'I have known David Garrick longer than you have done: and I know no right you have to talk to me on the subject.'

It does not appear that Boswell made any further effort to interrupt the talk which then ensued. He acknowledged that he had probably deserved the rebuke; for it was 'rather presumptuous' of him, an entire stranger, to express any doubt of the justice of Johnson's animadversion upon his old acquaintance and pupil. All the same he was much mortified, he admitted, and began to think that the hope which he had long indulged of obtaining Johnson's acquaintance was blasted. 'And, in truth,' he added, 'had not my ardour been uncommonly strong, and my resolution uncommonly persevering, so rough a reception might have deterred me for ever from making any further attempts. Fortunately, however, I remained upon the field not wholly discomfited.'

This characteristic display of resilience was rewarded. For when he rose to go, after listening to Johnson talk for three hours, he had decided that though there was a roughness in his manner, there was no ill-nature in his disposition. During part of the time, Mr and Mrs Davies had left the room, and he had ventured to make an observation now and again which, instead of being rebuffed, was 'received very civilly'. At the door he murmured something to Davies about the hard blows which Johnson had dealt him earlier; and Davies consoled him by saying, 'Don't be uneasy. I can see he likes you very well.'

Certainly Boswell was determined that now he had made the acquaintance of the great man at last, he would not remain content with that one taste of his conversation. 'Mr Johnson is a man of most dreadful appearance,' the entry for that day in his journal recorded. 'He is a very big man, is troubled with sore eyes, the palsy, and the King's evil. He is very slovenly in his dress and speaks with a most uncouth voice. Yet his great knowledge and strength of expression command vast respect and render him very excellent company. He has great humour and is a worthy man. But his dogmatic roughness of manners is disagreeable. I shall mark what I remember of his conversation.'

And so he did. Assured by Davies that Johnson would welcome a visit from him, he called upon him at his lodgings the next week, was received 'very courteously', and was begged to stay on the first two occasions when he rose to take his leave. He listened with close attention and 'much satisfaction' to all the interesting and important things that the 'great oracle' said to him, and afterwards wrote them down. 'I begged that he would favour me with his company at my lodgings some evening,' he noted at the end of his account of their conversation. 'He promised he would. I then left him, and he shook me cordially by the hand. Upon my word, I am very fortunate. I shall cultivate this acquaintance.'

From that day until 5 August when he left London—having failed to get a commission in the Guards and having agreed to go to Holland to continue his legal studies—Boswell saw Johnson regularly. On 13 June he visited him again at his lodgings, and found him, as before, very civil to him; he never was with 'this great man' without feeling himself 'bettered and rendered happier'. 'He again shook me by the hand at parting,' Boswell recorded, 'and asked me why I did not come oftener to him. Trusting that I was now in his good graces, I answered that he had not given me much encouragement, and reminded him of the check I had received from him at our first interview. "Poh, poh, (said he, with a complacent smile,) never mind these things. Come to me as often as you can. I shall be glad to see you" . . . Can I help being vain at this?'

Less than a fortnight later, having in the meantime had his pocket picked by a street-walker while he was 'indulging sensuality' with her in Privy Garden, Boswell met Johnson by chance at Temple Bar. He invited him to go to the Mitre with him knowing this to be his favourite tavern; but Johnson said it was too late: 'They won't let us in. But I'll go with you another night with all my heart.'

The following Saturday they met again by chance at Clifton's eating-house in Butcher Row where Johnson and a cantankerous Irishman got into a dispute about the reason why some races had black skins. Johnson's pronouncement on this problem, listened to by the diners at the various separate tables in the room, for some reason drove the Irishman to fury, and Johnson, having finished his meal got up and walked away from him. Boswell followed him to the door and asked him if he would go to the Mitre with him that evening. Johnson agreed; so Boswell called for him at nine o'clock and they walked to Fleet Street together.

They had a good supper followed by two bottles of port, and they sat talking until after one o'clock in the morning. Finding him in a pleasant humour, Boswell ventured to bring his own character and career into the conversation. He gave him a little sketch of his life (to which Johnson appeared to listen with great attention) and acknowledged that, although he was educated very strictly in the principles of religion, he had for some time been 'misled into a certain degree of infidelity'. He was now, how-ever, 'come to a better way of thinking, and was fully satisfied of the truth of the Christian revelation', though still not clear as to every point con-sidered to be orthodox. At the end of this confession, Johnson suddenly stretched out his arm and said affectionately, 'Give me your hand. I have taken a liking to you.' Later on in the evening, after Boswell had remarked, with obvious sincerity despite the bottle of port, how he would have exulted if it had been foretold some years ago that he would pass an even-ing with the author of *The Rambler*, Johnson said, 'Sir, I am glad we have met. I hope we shall pass many evenings, and mornings, too, together.'

They were again at the Mitre on 1 July, this time with Goldsmith; and on the 6th Boswell gave a little supper party there for Goldsmith, Johnson, Tom Davies, the bookseller, the Rev John Ogilvie, the Scottish poet, and an acquaintance of Davies, a rich Irishman named Eccles. Boswell had intended giving the party at his lodgings in Downing Street but he had quarrelled with his landlord after a noisy, drunken evening there with Temple and his brother the night before, and had resolved not to spend another night in the house. When he had called on Johnson to explain this and had presented it as a matter of serious distress, Johnson had laughed and said, 'Consider, Sir, how insignificant this will appear in a twelvemonth hence. There is nothing in this mighty misfortune; nay, we shall be better at the Mitre.'

It was a most successful party. Goldsmith was 'in his usual style, too eager to be bright'; but 'the stupendous Johnson' was 'exceeding good company' all the evening, and the Scotchman, Ogilvie, was 'rapt in admiration' of him.

As well as being, in Johnson's estimation, an indifferent poet—when Boswell had asked permission to introduce him, Johnson had stipulated, 'with a sly pleasantry', 'but he must give us none of his poetry'—Ogilvie was also in Boswell's description, a 'rank Scot' and chose for the topic of his conversation the praises of his native country. 'He began with saying, that there was very rich land around Edinburgh. Goldsmith, who had studied physick there, contradicted this, very untruly, with a sneering laugh. Disconcerted a little by this, Mr Ogilvie then took a new ground, where, I suppose, he thought himself perfectly safe; for he observed, that Scotland had a great many noble wild prospects. JOHNSON. "I believe, Sir, you have a great many. Norway, too, has noble wild prospects; and Lap-land is remarkable for prodigious noble wild prospects. But, Sir, let me tell you, the noblest prospect which a Scotchman ever sees, is the high road that leads him to England." '

A roar of applause greeted this most excellent sally; but whether or not the unfortunate Ogilvie joined in it Boswell does not say. The party continued happily, however, until one o'clock in the morning, and the host congratulated himself warmly upon its success. 'I was well dressed and in excellent spirits, neither muddy nor flashy. I sat with much secret pride, thinking of having such a company with me. I behaved with ease and propriety, and did not attempt at all to show away; but gently assisted conversation by those arts which serve to make people throw out their sentiments with ease and freedom. . . . I was very happy.'

The next week Johnson and Boswell once more had supper at the Mitre by themselves. It was a very rainy night, and Boswell made some hum-drum remark about the 'depression of spirits' which such weather oc-casioned, though the rain was good for the 'vegetable creation'. Johnson would not suffer his friends to fill up chasms in conversation with remarks upon the weather. He was in a good humour and was looking forward too much to his supper to be put off by a bit of rain. With a smile of ridicule, he answered, 'Why, yes, Sir, it is good for vegetables, and for the animals who eat those vegetables, and for the animals who eat those animals.' Soon he was demolishing a good supper with his accustomed relish. When it was over he settled down to port. On their coming in he had said that they would only drink one bottle of port that night; but as soon as the one bottle was finished he called for another pint, and as Boswell was carefully pouring out the last of that, Johnson said, 'Come, you need not measure it so exactly.'

'Sir, it is done.'

'Well, Sir, are you satisfied? Or would you choose another?'

'Would you, Sir?'

'Yes, I think I would. I think two bottles would seem to be the quantity for us.'

Boswell was now perfectly at ease with his new friend, much more so, as he told him, than he was with his father who was not much older; and characteristically he asked Johnson what was the reason for this. 'Why, Sir,' replied Johnson complacently, 'I am a man of the world. I live in the world, and I take, in some degree, the colour of the world as it moves along. Your father is a Judge in a remote part of the island, and all his notions are taken from the old world. Besides, Sir, there must always be a struggle between a father and son, while one aims at power and the other at independence.' It was on this evening, as though he had found in

Boswell the son he had never had, just as Boswell had found in him the father he would have liked to have had, that Johnson suddenly stretched out his hand to him, and warmed by the port, exclaimed, 'My dear Boswell, I do love you very much.'

On 20 July Boswell entertained Johnson, together with Dr John Boswell, his uncle, and his friend George Dempster, a Scottish lawyer and Member of Parliament, at the new chambers which he had taken in Farrar's Buildings close to Johnson's at the bottom of Inner Temple Lane; and two days later they supped together in a private room at the Turk's Head coffee-house. Here it was that Boswell confessed he was subject to periods of melancholy, a hereditary complaint in the family. Replying that he, too, was greatly distressed with it and had been 'obliged to fly from study and meditation to the dissipating variety of life', Johnson advised Boswell to 'have constant occupation of mind, to take a great deal of exercise, and to live moderately; especially to shun drinking at night'.[1] 'Melancholy people,' he said, 'are apt to fly to intemperance, which gives a momentary relief but sinks the soul much lower in misery', adding that labouring men 'who work much and live sparingly are seldom or never troubled' with low spirits.

This mutual confession to bouts of deep depression brought them closer together than ever. 'There are few people whom I take so much to as you,' Johnson assured him; and when Boswell spoke of his imminent departure for Holland, Johnson said, with an affection that almost made the young man cry, 'My dear Boswell, I should be very unhappy at parting, did I think we were not to meet again.'[2]

The next week, over another supper in private at the Turk's Head, Johnson proposed a day out together at Greenwich. Boswell had been pestering him for a plan of study which would enable him to make the most of the time he was to spend in Holland; and Johnson had been reluctant to think about it. But now he said abruptly, 'Come, let us make a day of it. Let us go down to Greenwich and dine and talk of it there.' Boswell immediately agreed. The following Saturday was fixed for this excursion.

On their way home that night, walking arm in arm down the Strand, a prostitute accosted them in the 'usual enticing manner'. 'No, no, my girl,' said Johnson, though not harshly, 'No, it won't do.' They talked then of the wretched life of such women and Boswell, who had been in the habit of what he called 'rogering' them both before and after his meetings with Johnson, agreed that 'much more misery than happiness upon the whole is produced by illicit commerce between the sexes'.

The excursion to Greenwich was a happy one. They took a boat at Temple Stairs, and on the way discussed the value of education, Johnson insisting that everyone profited by it, even if their work did not require it.

'And yet,' argued Boswell, 'people go through the world very well, and carry on the business of life to good advantage, without learning.'

'Why, Sir, that may be true in cases where learning cannot possibly be of any use; for instance, this boy rows as well without learning as if he could sing the song of Orpheus to the Argonauts', adding—for the benefit of the boy—the information that the Argonauts were 'the first sailors'.

He then asked the boy, 'What would you give, my lad, to know about the Argonauts?'

'Sir,' said the boy. 'I would give what I have.'

Johnson was so much pleased with this answer that he gave the boy a double fare. 'Sir,' he concluded optimistically, 'a desire of knowledge is the natural feeling of mankind; and every human being, whose mind is not debauched, will be willing to give all that he has, to get knowledge.'

They landed at the Old Swan Stairs to avoid the danger of shooting the fast-flowing water under London Bridge where so many boats overturned, walked downstream to Billingsgate and re-embarked there. On stepping ashore at Greenwich, Boswell picked a copy of Johnson's *London* from his pocket, and, as he had earlier practised, read aloud with enthusiasm:

> On Thames's banks in silent thought we stood,
> Where Greenwich smiles upon the silver flood:
> Pleas'd with the seat which gave Eliza birth,
> We kneel, and kiss the consecrated earth.

Then suiting the action to the word, Boswell actually did kneel down and kiss the earth. Johnson seems not to have commented on this display. Instead he turned to the buildings around him and remarked—one of his very rare comments on architecture—that the structure of Greenwich Hospital, built seventy years before by Christopher Wren, was 'too magnificent for a place of charity, and that its parts were too much detached to make one great whole'.

After disposing of the business of the day in 'an animating blaze of eloquence'—of which Boswell could remember little other than advice to select some particular branch of knowledge to excel in but to 'acquire a little of every kind'—Johnson said, as they walked through the Park in the evening, 'Is not this very fine?'

Having 'no exquisite relish of the beauties of Nature and being more delighted with the "busy hum of men"', Boswell replied, 'Yes, Sir, but not equal to Fleet Street.'

It was Johnson's sentiment entirely: 'You are right, Sir.'

The day had been warm and fine, but it had now turned cold; and on the return upstream, Boswell shivered in the boat. Johnson was not pleased to see this; he could not sympathise with displays of such frailty in young men, and had once scolded another young friend who complained of a head-ache, 'At your age, Sir, I had no head-ache'. Now he spoke sternly to Boswell, 'Why do you shiver?'

They were 'very social' once more, however, when they sat down to supper at the Turk's Head. Johnson listened attentively and approvingly as Boswell talked about his family estate, the 'romantick seat' of his ancestors, describing the new house built in the style made fashionable by Robert Adam, and the Old Castle now in ruins. Johnson burst out, 'I must be there, Sir, and we will live in the Old Castle; and if there is not a room in it remaining, we will build one.'

At parting, Johnson said that when Boswell sailed for Holland he would see him off at Harwich; and Boswell could not find words to express what he felt 'upon this unexpected and very great mark of his affectionate regard'.

Boswell was due to leave for Harwich on 5 August and there was opportunity for only two further meetings with Johnson in London. On the morning of Tuesday 2nd Johnson called at his chambers, remarking that he 'always felt an inclination to do nothing', and making good Boswell's claim to be 'a privileged man' by inviting him to accompany him to tea with Miss Williams that afternoon. Boswell thought Miss Williams an 'agreeable woman, though stone-blind' with a good turn of conversation; 'but her particular value was the intimacy in which she had long lived with Johnson, by which she was well acquainted with his habits, and knew how to lead him on to talk'. After tea Johnson took him to what he called his walk, 'a paved long court overshadowed by some trees in a neighbouring garden', where he gave him some fatherly advice on how to study while he was abroad—'to read with a keenness after knowledge' when he was settled in a particular spot, and, when he was travelling about, 'to read diligently the great book of mankind'.

On 3 August they had their last meal together at the Turk's Head; but Boswell, who had sat up all night writing and had spent the night before with a fine fresh lass who had tapped him on the shoulder in the Strand, was so tired he almost went to sleep, 'even in Mr Johnson's company'.

They set out for Harwich in the stage-coach early on the morning of the 5th as planned. Johnson, in high good humour, fell into conversation with a fat, talkative, elderly gentlewoman who said that she had done her best to educate her children and had never suffered them to be idle for a moment.

'I wish, Madam, you would educate me too: for I have been an idle fellow all my life.'

'I am sure, Sir, you have not been idle.'

'Nay, Madam, it is very true; and that gentleman there,' pointing to Boswell, 'has been idle. He was idle at Edinburgh. His father sent him to Glasgow, where he continued to be idle. He then came to London where he has been very idle; and now he is going to Utrecht, where he will be as idle as ever.'

Later Boswell asked him how he could expose him so, but Johnson would have none of the complaint, 'Poh, poh!' he said. 'They knew nothing about you, and will think of it no more.'

In the afternoon the old lady began to talk violently against the Roman Catholics and of the horrors of the Inquisition. To the utter astonishment of everyone present, except Boswell who knew by now that he would talk on any side of a question, Johnson defended the Inquisition warmly, maintaining that a false doctrine should be checked on its first appearance, that the civil power should unite with the church in punishing those who dared to attack the established religion, that none but such as these had ever been punished by the Inquisition.

Having disposed of that matter, he picked a book out of his pocket and holding it close up to his good eye, as was his wont, he buried himself in ancient geography.

At one of the stages he noticed Boswell ostentatiously give a shilling to the coachman when the custom was to give only sixpence. Drawing him aside he reprimanded him, saying that what he had done would make the coachman dissatisfied with all the rest of the passengers who gave him no more than his due.

They spent the night at Colchester, which Johnson talked about with veneration since it had withstood a siege for Charles I. Here a fellow-traveller, a Dutchman who spoke English tolerably well, favourably compared the criminal jurisprudence of England with that of Holland and inveighed against the barbarity of using torture to force confessions. But Johnson was as ready for this as for the Inquisition and found as sound arguments for the practical benefits, as even, indeed, for the humaneness of the Dutch system.

After the Dutchman had gone to bed, Johnson suggested he might go over to Holland himself the following summer and accompany Boswell on a tour of the Netherlands. When Boswell appeared dejected again at the thought that he would be all by himself in Holland until then, Johnson drew his attention to a moth that had burnt itself by fluttering round the candle. 'That creature,' he said, 'was its own tormentor, and I believe its name was Boswell.'

The next day they arrived at Harwich, and they walked down to the beach together. 'We embraced and parted with tenderness and engaged to correspond by letters,' Boswell recalled. 'I said, "I hope, Sir, you will not forget me in my absence."'

'Nay, Sir,' Johnson replied, 'it is more likely you should forget me, than that I should forget you.'

As the vessel put out to sea, Boswell kept his eyes upon Johnson for a considerable time, while he remained 'rolling his majestic frame in his usual manner'. At length he turned on his heel, walked back into the town and disappeared.

Boswell remembered the conversations he had had with Johnson with an extraordinary clarity. Some of them he recorded at the time; others he wrote down years later from notes in his journal. Johnson had spoken of all manner of things in those first few weeks of their friendship. He had talked of the British Constitution, of the King of Prussia, of Rousseau and of London. He had talked of Bishop Berkeley and his theory of the non-existence of matter, and when Boswell had observed that, although we are satisfied that the doctrine is not true it was impossible to refute it, Johnson had answered, with an alacrity that Boswell could 'never forget', striking his foot with mighty force against a large stone, 'I refute it thus'.[3] He had talked of writers, of Swift—'a higher reputation than he deserves'; of Gray—'not a first-rate poet; he has not a bold imagination, nor much command of words'; of Colley Cibber—'by no means a blockhead'; of William Whitehead, the poet-laureate—'*grand* nonsense is insupportable'; of Adam Smith—'I was once in company with Smith, and we did not take to each other; but had I known that he loved rhyme as much as you tell me he does, I should have HUGGED him'; of David Hume—'Why, Sir, his style is not English; the structure of his sentences is French'; and of James Macpherson, the genuineness of whose translations of the poems of the legendary third century Gaelic hero, Ossian, Johnson took strong leave to doubt. 'Yes, Sir,' he announced when asked if any man of a modern age could possibly have written them, 'Yes, Sir, many men, many women, and many children.' He added subsequently that 'a man might write such stuff for ever, if he would *abandon* his mind to it'.

On several occasions he had discussed subordination, a favourite theme of his: 'I am a friend to subordination, as most conducive to the happiness of society. There is a reciprocal pleasure in governing and being governed. . . . Subordination tends greatly to human happiness. Were we all upon an equality, we should have no other enjoyment than mere animal pleasure. . . . I would no more deprive a nobleman of his rank, than of his money. I consider myself as acting a part in the great system of society, and I do to others as I would have them do to me. I would behave to a nobleman as I should expect he would behave to me, were I a nobleman and he Sam Johnson. Sir, there is one Mrs Macaulay in this town, a great republican. One day when I was at her house, I put on a very grave countenance, and said to her, "Madam, I am now become a convert to your way of thinking. I am convinced that all mankind are upon an equal footing; and to give you an unquestionable proof, Madam, that I am in earnest, here is a very sensible, civil, well-behaved fellow-citizen, your footman; I desire that he may be allowed to sit down and dine with us." I thus, Sir, shewed her the absurdity of the levelling doctrine. She has never liked me since. Sir, your levellers wish to level *down* as far as themselves; but they cannot bear levelling *up* to themselves. They would all have some people under them; why not then have some people above them?'[4]

In a happy analogy he had denied that Boswell's genial friend, Dempster, had been right not to join in the composition of a pamphlet harshly criticising a tragedy acted at Drury Lane on the grounds that, although it was a bad tragedy, he himself could not have written one nearly as good: 'Why, no, Sir; this is not just reasoning. You *may* abuse a tragedy, though you cannot write one. You may scold a carpenter who has made you a bad table, though you cannot make a table. It is not your trade to make tables.'

Boswell had delighted in remarks like these, in the quickness and fertility of Johnson's mind, his sharp insights, his marvellously inventive humour. 'The notion of liberty amuses the people of England, and helps to keep off the *tedium vitae*. When a butcher tells you that *his heart bleeds for his country*, he has, in fact, no uneasy feeling.' 'Truth, Sir, is a cow which will yield such people [sceptics] no more milk, and so they are gone to milk the bull.' There was nothing surprising about Boswell's acquaintance, the 'impudent fellow from Scotland, who affected to be a savage, and railed at all established systems'. He merely wanted 'to make himself conspicuous. He would tumble in a hogstye, as long as you looked at him and called to him to come out. But let him alone, never mind him, and he'll soon give it over.' And as for maintaining that there was no distinction between vice and virtue. 'Why, Sir, if the fellow does not think as he speaks, he is lying; and I see not what honour he can propose to himself from having the character of a lyar. But if he really does think that there is no distinction between virtue and vice, why, Sir, when he leaves our houses let us count our spoons.'

A few days after recording these comments in his journal, Boswell had made a note of what was to become the most celebrated and most often quoted of all Johnson's remarks. Under the date Sunday 31 July 1763, he wrote in his journal: 'In the forenoon I was at a Quakers' meeting in Lombard Street [where I heard a woman preach], and in the afternoon at St Paul's where I was very devout and very happy. After service, I stood in the centre and took leave of the church, bowing to every quarter. I cannot help having a reverence for it. Mr Johnson says the same. Mr Johnson said today that a woman's preaching was like a dog's walking on his hinder legs. It was not done well, but you were surprised to find it done at all.'

'My *journal*,' Boswell later decided with well justified content, 'will afford materials for a very curious narrative.'

8

The Turk's Head Oracle

'Johnson is a man of a very clear head, great power of words, and a very gay imagination; but there is no disputing with him. He will not hear you, and having a louder voice than you, must roar you down.'   The Rev John Taylor

Soon after Boswell's departure for Holland, Johnson was assured of a wider audience for his table-talk by Reynolds's proposition that they should form a club to meet every Monday evening at seven at the Turk's Head in Gerard Street. Although other members were later admitted, Johnson proposed that at first there should be no more than nine of them in all, the same number as had constituted the earlier club that had met at the King's Head in Ivy Lane. It was an ideal number, Johnson thought; and when Goldsmith proposed an infusion of new blood on the grounds that the present members had travelled thoroughly over each other's minds, Johnson turned on him angrily: 'Sir, you have not travelled over *my* mind, I promise you.'

In addition to Johnson and Reynolds, the nine members were John Hawkins, formerly a member of the Ivy Lane Club, now a magistrate with an extremely rich wife; Anthony Chamier, a charming and highly intelligent man of French Protestant descent who had made a considerable fortune as a stockbroker and was now Deputy Secretary at War; Christopher Nugent, a Roman Catholic physician of whom Johnson had a high opinion and to whom he listened with close attention; Oliver Goldsmith, Topham Beauclerk, Bennet Langton and Edmund Burke.

Burke, then little known as an author and not yet a Member of Parliament, was, in Johnson's opinion, 'a great man by nature', and he rarely spoke of him without affection and respect. When he entered Parliament in 1765, John Hawkins expressed surprise at his being able to obtain a seat, but Johnson would have no criticism of his young friend. 'Now we who know Mr Burke,' he said, 'know that he will be one of the first men in the country.' 'He is an extraordinary man,' he later decided. 'His stream of mind is perpetual. . . . Take up whatever topic you please, he is ready to meet you. . . . Burke, Sir, is such a man that if you met him for the first time in a street when there was a shower of cannon bullets & you & he ran up a stair to take shelter he'd talk to you in such a manner that when you came down you'd say, "This is an extraordinary man."' At the Club Burke had already displayed remarkable powers as a disputant, and invariably succeeded in putting Johnson on his mettle. 'That fellow calls forth all my powers,' Johnson admitted one day when he was feeling ill and not up to the effort of heated argument. 'Were I to see Burke now it would kill me.'

Burke, for his part, never attempted to out-talk Johnson; and one evening in their company, Bennet Langton felt that he was being unduly modest. On their way home Burke remarked how very great Johnson had been that night; Langton agreed but said he wished he could have heard more from 'another person' who could have illustrated many of the topics discussed with 'extensive knowledge and richness of expression'. 'Oh, no,' replied Burke, 'it is enough for me to have rung the bell to him.'

Although Garrick was an intimate friend of Burke and of other members of the Club and would certainly have liked to join it, he was not admitted until 1773. The reason for this, said Hawkins, was that Johnson, who was still envious of his former pupil's success and affected to despise his profession, refused to have him elected. When his candidature was discussed, Johnson said, 'He will disturb us by his buffoonery', and saw to it that his name was never formally proposed. Garrick took the rebuff very patiently, though on his way home to Hampton he would often call at Hawkins's house at Twickenham to ask such questions as 'Were you at the Club on Monday night?' 'What did you talk of?' 'Was Johnson there?' 'I suppose he said something of Davy—that Davy was a clever fellow in his way, full of convivial pleasantry; but no poet, no writer, ha?'

Boswell, on the other hand, says that it was Garrick's own conceit that prevented his becoming a member. Reynolds was speaking about the Club to Garrick, who was in Italy with his wife at the time of its formation, and Garrick said, 'I like it much, I think I shall be of you.'

'*He'll be of us!*' exclaimed Johnson, when Reynolds told him what

Garrick had said. 'How does he know we will *permit* him? The first Duke in England has no right to hold such language.'

The early meetings of the Club were entirely to Johnson's satisfaction. He frequently congratulated himself on the wise selection of members, who, soon after the first meeting, included Samuel Dyer, a member of the Ivy Lane Club, recently returned from the army in Germany where he had unaccountably failed to make his fortune as a commissary.

The hours which Johnson spent in this society, Hawkins wrote, seemed the happiest of his life. Although the conversation was chiefly literary, they talked on all manner of subjects, only politics, 'the most vulgar of all topics', being excluded. Johnson led the conversation, 'as indeed he did everywhere'.

The breadth of his knowledge was truly astonishing and he was constantly adding to it. 'All knowledge is of itself of some value,' he said. 'There is nothing so minute or inconsiderable that I would not rather know it than not.' On a visit to Warley Camp, where Bennet Langton was stationed as a captain in the Lincolnshire Militia, he asked if he could accompany the major of the regiment on his rounds at night so that he could observe the exact forms of visiting the guards. In Scotland he asked to be shown precisely how the women *waulked* their cloth, and asked repeated questions about the operation. Little escaped his notice. 'Did you never observe,' he once asked a friend, 'that dogs have not the power of comparing? A dog will take a small bit of meat as readily as a large when both are before him.' In London he attended the office of Saunders Welch, the magistrate, 'for a whole winter to hear the examination of the culprits', and obtained permission to experiment at the Chelsea China Works where, for a time, he spent two days a week.[1]

He could talk, as though he had been bred to the trades, of tanning and brewing, of butchery and coining, of threshing and thatching. He knew all about the manufacture of gunpowder, the various uses to which the poor put the bones they picked up in the street, how to make orange-butter. He was happy to give advice on agriculture and the growing of fruit, on forestry and the cost of building. He could discuss dancing with a dancing-master who protested at the end of some discourse that Johnson knew more about it than himself; and his fellow-travellers, on a stage-coach journey, were amazed when he occasionally put aside the book he was reading, not merely to quote various authors as accurately as if the works had been in his hands, but even to speak upon one subject that attracted him—the digestion of dogs—as though that had been his special field of study. Admittedly, as Reynolds said, he would rarely admit that he did not know anything and would attempt to cover his ignorance by talking in generalities, but it was rarely that he did not know.

In Johnson's own opinion the essential requirements of a good conversationalist were knowledge, a command of words, presence of mind, imagination, 'to place things in such view as they are not commonly seen in', and finally, 'a resolution that is not to be overcome by failures'. 'This last is an essential requisite,' he thought. 'For want of it many people do not excel in conversation. Now *I* want it; I throw up the game upon losing a trick.'

No one who had heard Johnson in full flood could possibly agree, however, that he gave up the game upon losing a trick. It would have been truer to say that upon the rare occasions when he was defeated, he forced his opponents to give up their game by kicking over the table.

'There is no arguing with Johnson,' said Goldsmith, in the words of one of Cibber's comedies; 'for when his pistol misses fire, he knocks you down with the butt end of it.' The Rev John Taylor, who was occasionally aroused to a pitch of bellowing by his old friend's Toryism, agreed with Goldsmith. 'Johnson is a man of a very clear head, great power of words, and a very gay imagination; but there is no disputing with him. He will not hear you, and having a louder voice than you, must roar you down.'

His powers of invective were wonderfully developed; he was a match any day for the Thames boatmen whose custom it was to shout the most outlandish insults at their fellow-oarsmen and their passengers as their craft passed by each other on the river. Johnson, being attacked one day with some coarse raillery, immediately shouted back, 'Sir, your wife, under pretence of keeping a bawdy-house, is a receiver of stolen goods.' Even in more polite society, Johnson's powerful, pungent conversation was often too strong for delicate palates. It was, as one of his women friends said, like mustard in a young child's mouth.

He delighted in his powers of overthrowing his opponents. 'Well, we had good talk,' he said to Boswell with satisfaction one morning after an evening at the Crown and Anchor during which he had shown himself even more disputatious than usual. 'Yes, Sir,' replied Boswell, 'you tossed and gored several persons.'

The elegant and witty Earl of Eglinton ventured to regret that Johnson had so much aggression and so little tact, that he had not been 'educated with more refinement and lived more in polished society'. 'No, no, my

Lord,' it was objected, 'do with him what you would, he would always have been a bear.' 'True,' answered Eglinton, 'but he would have been a *dancing* bear.'

This, though, was not Johnson's manner. He revelled in hard argument, provided he was allowed to put the case and was not interrupted or sharply contradicted. When asked if there had been 'good conversation' at a friend's house where there had been 'a very pretty company', he said, 'No, Sir. We had *talk* enough, but no *conversation*; there was nothing *discussed*.'

He had little patience with those whom he deemed incapable of keeping up an argument ágainst him. 'Sir, you don't see your way through that question,' he would say, or, 'Sir, you talk the language of ignorance.' To Boswell he would cry out in exasperation, 'My dear Boswell, let's have no more of this; you'll make nothing of it. I'd rather have you whistle a Scotch tune'; or he would say angrily, 'Nay, Sir, there is no talking with a man who will dispute what everybody knows. Don't you know this?'

There were very few people indeed whose conversational powers impressed him. One man, for instance, had a great deal of learning but it did not lie straight; he never had one idea by the side of another. General Oglethorpe had a variety of knowledge, but he never *completed* what he had to say. Others were afraid to talk at all in front of him, as Boswell told him, citing one particular worthy friend of his: 'Sir,' commented Johnson, 'he need not have been afraid, if he had anything rational to say. If he had not, it was better he did not talk.' Even Charles James Fox, so Gibbon said, was 'very shy of saying anything in Dr Johnson's presence'; at Aberdeen University, 'the professors seemed afraid to speak'; and at a meeting of the Essex Head Club when Johnson made a mistaken criticism of Edmund Burke, William Windham contented himself by whispering an objection to his neighbour.

It was not only Johnson's tongue of which the speaker had to beware. That was sharp and quick enough: he had no 'formal preparation, no flourishing with his sword; he was through your body in an instant'. Sometimes he would actually lay hands on an offender. Normally he was content to cry out, 'Don't attitudinise' to a man who was gesticulating too flamboyantly for his taste; but it was not unknown for him to fairly seize a man's hands and hold them down on the table.

He could be devastatingly rude. 'Sir, I have found you an argument,' he would say impatiently to a man who confessed his inability to comprehend it; 'I am not obliged to find you an understanding.' To a dull country magistrate who gave a tedious account of having sentenced four convicts to transportation, Johnson, in an agony of impatience, exclaimed, 'I

heartily wish, Sir, that I were a fifth.' He made a similar remark to Boswell
who, advancing the usual arguments in favour of drinking, observed to
him, 'You know, Sir, drinking drives away care, and makes us forget
whatever is disagreeable. Would you not allow a man to drink for that
reason?' 'Yes, Sir,' Johnson growled, 'if he sat next *you*.' And to another
tiresome gentleman who spent seven or eight minutes complaining
exactly how and precisely why barristers upon circuit at Shrewsbury were
much bitten by fleas, he burst out, 'It is a pity, Sir, that you have not seen
a lion; for a flea has taken you such a time, that a lion must have served
you a twelvemonth.'

This outburst, however, was delivered not with what one of Garrick's
correspondents described as 'the sneer of one of Johnson's ghastly smiles',
but playfully, in the same manner that he gave a rebuke to a junior tutor
at St John's College, Oxford, who had been bred a Whig, 'Sir, you are a
young man, but I have seen a great deal of the world, and take it upon my
word and experience, that where you see a Whig you see a rascal.'[2]
Indeed, Johnson insisted himself, he was 'much misunderstood'; he was
not 'an uncandid or severe man'. On the contrary, he maintained one day
to the utter astonishment of all his hearers, 'You may observe that I am
well-bred to a degree of needless scrupulosity. No man is so cautious not to
interrupt another; no man thinks it so necessary to appear attentive when
others are speaking; no man so steadily refuses preference to himself, or
so willingly bestows it on another, as I do. Nobody holds as strongly as I
do the necessity of ceremony, and the ill effects which follow the breach of
it. Yet people think me rude.'

He sometimes, he admitted, said more than he meant 'in jest', and
people were apt to believe him serious. He also, Miss Reynolds thought,
sometimes said more than he would have done had it not been for his
deafness—which blurred the expression in other peoples' voices—and for
his poor eyesight, which did not allow him, so she heard him say, to
'distinguish any man's face half a yard distant from him'. If he had been
able to see the expressions on the faces opposite him when, in his loud
voice, he was disparaging a man who was present in the room, it might not
have been necessary for Garrick to nudge him under the table. As it was he
called out in exasperation, 'David, David, is it you? What makes you
tread on my toes so?'

Neither his eyes nor his deafness, however, could be pleaded as excuses
for his rudeness one day at the Reynolds's dinner table when he interrupted Isaac Wilkes, to say, 'I hope, Sir, what you are going to say may be
better worth hearing than what you have already said.' Later he turned to

another guest who had praised the Venetian form of government and said, 'Yes, Sir, all republican rascals think as you do.'[3] Nor could easy excuses be found for his retort to a self-satisfied gentleman who observed to him, 'Dr Johnson, we have had a most excellent discourse today.' 'That may be,' Johnson replied, 'but it is impossible that you should know it.' Richard Cumberland recorded a similar example of Johnson's offensiveness to a man whom he did not like. 'What provokes your risibility, Sir?' he asked when the man laughed too ingratiatingly at one of Johnson's remarks, 'Have I said anything that you understand? Then I ask pardon of the rest of the company.' And to a young man who lamented that he had lost all his Greek, he said, 'I believe it happened at the same time, Sir, that I lost all my large estate in Yorkshire.'

But although he said more than he meant in jest, his victims were not always prepared to accept his caustic comments and sardonic railleries as playful jokes.[4] The physician, who insisted that Johnson was mistaken in thinking that they had never met before, cannot, for example, have been much amused when Johnson, in reply to the contention that his notice must have been caught by the very fine coat its owner was wearing, replied sharply, 'Sir, had you been dipped in Pactolus, I should not have noticed you.'

Boswell, of course, came in for much of this treatment. One day when Johnson was abusing the Americans with characteristic vehemence, Boswell said something in their favour and added that he was sorry that his friend always damned them so. 'This, it seems exasperated him, though he said nothing at the time,' Boswell recalled. 'The cloud was charged with sulphurous vapour, which was afterwards to burst in thunder.—We talked of a gentleman who was running out his fortune in London; and I said, "We must get him out of it. All his friends must quarrel with him and that will soon drive him away." JOHNSON. "Nay, Sir, we'll send *you* to him. If your company does not drive a man out of his house, nothing will." This was a horrible shock for which there was no visible cause. I afterwards asked him why he had said so harsh a thing. JOHNSON. "Because, Sir, you made me angry about the Americans." BOSWELL. "But why did you not take your revenge directly?" JOHNSON (smiling). "Because, Sir, I had nothing ready. A man cannot strike till he has his weapons." This was a candid and pleasant confession.'

So the insult was forgiven. Usually, indeed, no offence was taken, for the insult was no more than a pleasantry, as when in Scotland Johnson hurried to Boswell to tell him to save him from the company of some Scotch professors who were exasperating him with questions: '"O ho,

Sir!" said I. "You are flying to me for refuge." He never, in any situation, was at a loss for a ready repartee. He answered with a quick vivacity, "It is of two evils choosing the least." I was delighted with this flash.'

The form of questioning to which the Scotch professors had subjected him always exasperated Johnson. 'Questioning,' he advised Boswell sternly, 'is not the mode of conversation among gentlemen.' And he exploded in anger when Boswell bothered him persistently with trivial questions: 'I will not be put to the question. Don't you consider, Sir, that these are not the manners of a gentleman? I will not be baited with *what* and *why*. What is this? Why is a cow's tail long? Why is a fox's tail bushy?' Boswell, who was put a good deal out of countenance by this, said, 'Why, Sir, you are so good that I venture to trouble you.' 'Sir, my being so *good*,' Johnson retorted, 'is no reason why you should be so *ill*.'[5] 'When Boswell gets wine,' he later complained to Langton, 'his conversation consists all of questions.'[6]

Boswell's persistent questions about his personal life, however, rarely ruffled Johnson's temper. He refused to tell him the reason for his always carrying bits of dried orange-peel in his pockets; but he refused good-humouredly.[7] And, when in Scotland he was taxed about his reasons for not wearing a night-cap, patiently he replied, 'Sir, I had this custom by chance; and perhaps no one shall ever know whether it is best to sleep with or without a night-cap. . . . Nobody before,' he added, laughing, 'was ever foolish enough to ask whether it was best to wear a night-cap or not. This comes of being a little wrong-headed.'

What did irritate Johnson was Boswell's tendency to bestow praise extravagantly. 'What is all this rout about the Corsicans?' he burst out violently after Boswell had eulogised their heroism. 'They have been at war with the Genoese for upwards of twenty years, and have never yet taken their fortified towns. They might have battered down their walls, and reduced them to powder in twenty years. They might have pulled the walls in pieces and cracked them with their teeth in twenty years!' Boswell thought better of advancing the Corsicans' lack of artillery as a possible reason for their failure, for Johnson was 'not to be resisted for the moment'.

Indeed, he still revelled in taking up a contradictory position merely for the sake of opposition. 'Why, Sir, as to the good or evil of card-playing . . .', he would slowly open a discourse on the subject: and, as Garrick said, he was merely giving himself time to decide which side of the argument he would take. Garrick knew this habit of Johnson's only too well. One day when Garrick was extolling Dryden, Johnson interrupted him to ask him to repeat twenty lines that were worthy of such praise. Garrick chose twenty which he had previously heard Johnson commend, but which were *now* held up to ridicule as containing no less than sixteen faults.

Johnson himself readily admitted that he often talked in a spirit of contradiction. When he and Burke took opposing views as to how the defence of one of their friends should be conducted in a court of law, George Steevens afterwards remarked that he thought the argument had been conducted with rather too much warmth. 'It may be so, Sir,' replied Johnson, 'for Burke and I should have been of one opinion, if we had not had an audience.'

'I may perhaps have said this,' he agreed when it was pointed out to him that he had once observed that the happiest part of a man's life was spent lying awake in bed in the morning. 'For nobody, at times, talks more laxly than I do.'

Offensive as he sometimes was, Johnson usually took the trouble to make amends when he realised—as very often he did not—that he had given offence.[8] He would drink the offended person's health, direct some polite remark to him, rise to shake his hand when he left the room, or go to sit near him in the drawing-room after the meal was over. Sometimes, so Hawkins said, he had tears in his eyes when he apologised to those whom he had offended by contradiction or roughness of behaviour. Frances Reynolds recorded a characteristic example of his penitence:

I shall never forget with what regret he spoke of the rude reply he made to Dr [Thomas] Barnard [Dean of Derry] on his saying that men never improved after the age of forty-five. 'That is not true, Sir,' said Johnson. 'You, who perhaps are forty-eight, may still improve, if you will try: I wish you would set about it; and I am afraid,' he added, 'there is great room for it'; and this was said in rather a large party of ladies and gentlemen at dinner. Soon after the ladies withdrew from the table, Dr Johnson followed them, and, sitting down by the lady of the house, he said, 'I am very sorry for having spoken so rudely to the dean.' 'You very well may, Sir.' 'Yes,' he said, 'it was highly improper to speak in that style to a minister of the Gospel, and I am the more hurt on reflecting with what mild dignity he received it.' When the dean came up into the drawing room, Dr Johnson immediately rose from his seat, and made him sit on the sofa by him, and with such a beseeching look for pardon, and with such fond gestures—literally smoothing down his arms and his knees— tokens of penitence, which were so graciously received by the Dean as to make Dr Johnson very happy.

Often, as though to make amends for a rude remark or a curt rebuff, Johnson would summon all his powers to talk so well and entertainingly that the company might forgive him for his lapse, as one day when he was musing by the fire in a country house and a young gentleman called out to him suddenly, 'Mr Johnson, would you advise me to marry?' Johnson, angry at being disturbed in this disrespectful way, replied crossly, 'I would advise no man to marry, Sir, who is not likely to propagate understanding.' And with that he lumbered out of the room. Soon afterwards, however, he returned, and, pulling up a chair joined in the conversation which he eventually brought round to marriage, 'where he laid himself out in a dissertation so useful, so elegant, so founded on the true knowledge of human life, and so adorned with beauty of sentiment, that no one ever recollected the offence, except to rejoice in its consequence'.

Yet Joshua Reynolds noticed that Johnson was quite indifferent when his overtures were sullenly rebuffed, considering that he had done all that was required of him and that the other person was now in the wrong. Sometimes he would leave the apology until the following day as he did when staying at High Wycombe with Maurice Morgann, under-secretary of State to Lord Lansdowne, to whom he said earnestly in the breakfast-room, 'Sir, I have been thinking about our dispute last night—*You were in the right.*' Or he would send Frank round with a note like the ones he sent to Tom Davies: 'Come, come, dear Davies, I am always sorry when we quarrel; send me word that we are friends.'

Boswell recorded several characteristic examples of Johnson's readiness both to receive and accept an apology. He was arguing once with Dr Thomas Percy about the merits as a travel writer of Thomas Pennant who had made Percy cross by writing disrespectfully of Alnwick Castle and of Northumberland generally.

JOHNSON 'Pennant, in what he has said of Alnwick, has done what he intended; he has made you very angry.'
PERCY 'He has said the garden is trim, which is representing it like a citizen's parterre, when the truth is, there is a very large extent of fine turf and gravel walks.'
JOHNSON 'According to your own account, Sir, Pennant is right. It *is* trim. Here is grass cut close, and gravel rolled smooth. Is not that trim? The extent is nothing against that; a mile may be as trim as a square yard.'
PERCY 'He pretends to give the natural history of Northumberland, and yet takes no notice of the immense number of trees planted there of late.'

JOHNSON 'That, Sir, has nothing to do with the *natural* history; that is *civil* history. A man who gives the natural history of the oak, is not to tell how many oaks have been planted in this place or that. A man who gives the natural history of the cow, is not to tell how many cows are milked at Islington . . .'
PERCY 'Pennant does not describe well.'
JOHNSON 'I think he describes very well.'
PERCY 'I travelled after him.'
JOHNSON 'And I travelled after him.'
PERCY 'But my good friend, you are short-sighted, and do not see as well as I do.'

I wondered at Dr Percy's venturing this. Dr Johnson said nothing at the time: but inflammable particles were collecting for a cloud to burst. In a little while Dr Percy said something more in disparagement of Pennant.

JOHNSON (pointedly) 'This is the resentment of a narrow mind, because he did not find everything in Northumberland.'
PERCY (feeling the stroke) 'Sir, you may be as rude as you please.'
JOHNSON 'Hold, Sir! Don't talk of rudeness; remember, Sir, you told me (puffing hard with passion, struggling for a vent) I was short-sighted. We have done with civility. We are to be as rude as we please.'
PERCY 'Upon my honour, Sir, I did not mean to be uncivil.'
JOHNSON 'I cannot say so, Sir; for I *did* mean to be uncivil, thinking *you* had been uncivil.'

Dr Percy rose, ran up to him, and taking him by the hand, assured him affectionately that his meaning had been misunderstood; upon which a reconciliation immediately took place.

JOHNSON 'My dear Sir, I am willing you shall *hang* Pennant.'

In the last year of his life he showed himself to be as ready to apologise to a young gentleman, who argued with him about the difference between intuition and sagacity, as Percy had been ready to apologise to him. The young man 'persisted much too long, and appeared to Johnson as putting himself forward as his antagonist with too much presumption; upon which he called to him in a loud tone, "What is it you are contending for if you *be* contending?"—And afterwards, imagining that the gentleman retorted upon him with a kind of smart drollery, he said, "Mr *****, it does not become you to talk so to me. Besides, ridicule is not your talent; you have there neither intuition nor sagacity."—The gentleman protested that he had intended no improper freedom, but had the greatest respect for Dr Johnson. After a short pause, during which we were somewhat uneasy:—
JOHNSON. 'Give me your hand, Sir. You were too tedious and I too short.'
Mr *****. 'Sir, I am honoured by your attention in any way.'

JOHNSON. 'Come, Sir, let's have no more of it. We offended one another by our contention; let us not offend the company by our compliments.'

It was widely agreed that the unique excellence of Johnson's conversation lay not so much in its content as in his inimitable manner of utterance —no one other than Garrick could imitate it well and he not perfectly[9]— and in his extraordinary fluency and delightfully eccentric vocabulary. Nor was there any doubt that the width and depth of his knowledge were as remarkable as his sound common sense. 'This man is just a *hogshead* of sense,' commented Dr Alexander Maclean after hearing him talk at dinner on the island of Mull. 'Oh, that his words were written in a book!' exclaimed another admirer, Joseph Cradock, the author and High Sheriff of Leicestershire.

There were certain subjects he would not discuss, and certain talk he would not listen to. When Charles James Fox was expatiating one day upon the Catiline conspiracy, he withdrew his attention and 'thought about Tom Thumb'. Nor could he often be persuaded to talk about politics. 'Sir,' he once said irritably, 'I'd as soon have a man to break my bones as talk to me of public affairs, internal or external.' And although his capacity to draw characters was praised by Boswell as being 'as rare as good portrait painting', Reynolds thought it was overdone: 'in order to mark the characters which he draws, he overcharges them, and gives people more than they really have, whether of good or bad.'

Also he had a tendency, which some people found embarrassing and others irritating, to laugh immoderately at things the rest of the company found only faintly amusing, if that. As Garrick said, when Johnson was at his best, his wit and humour were irresistible: 'Rabelais and all other wits are nothing compared with him. You may be diverted by them; but Johnson gives you a forcible hug, and shakes laughter out of you, whether you will or no.' When he appeared to be shaking laughter out of himself, however, he was less pleasing. He would run on and on, repeating variations of jokes on the same theme, laughing uproariously, 'like a rhinoceros', Tom Davies once said, until the company was quite exhausted by him.

Boswell, with evident reluctance, records several instances of this: 'I have known him at times exceedingly diverted at what seemed to others a very small sport. He now laughed immoderately, without any reason that we could perceive, at our friend's [Bennet Langton's] making his will; called him the testator, and added, "I dare say he thinks he has done a mighty thing. He won't stay till he gets home to his seat in the country to produce this wonderful deed: He'll call up the landlord of the first inn on the road; and after a suitable preface upon mortality and the uncertainty of life, he will tell him that he should not delay in making his will; and here, Sir, will he say, is my Will, which I have just made, with the assistance of one of the ablest lawyers in the kingdom; and he will read it to him, (laughing all the time). He believes he has made this will, but he did not make it: you, Chambers, [Langton's lawyer] made it for him. I trust you have had more conscience than to make him say, "being of sound understanding; Ha! ha! ha!"'

He was running on uncontrollably like this on another occasion, Bennet Langton said, 'while all the company were grave about him. Only Garrick, in his significant smart manner, darting his eyes around, exclaimed "*very* jocose, to be sure!"'

These were rare occasions. Normally Johnson was unfailingly entertaining once he had been persuaded to join in the conversation. He did not like to introduce a subject for discussion; he said that he liked best the description of him by Tom Tyers who observed that 'like the ghost he never spoke till he was spoken to'. Sometimes, in fact, he could not be prevailed upon to speak at all: at one dinner party at Bennet Langton's in 1778, he did not utter a single word before the meal, except, 'Pretty baby!' to one of Langton's children. And when he did speak it was only to fulfil the boast that he could repeat word for word an entire chapter of Horrebow's *Natural History of Iceland*:

'Chapter LXXI
Concerning Snakes
There are no snakes to be met with throughout the whole island.'

But once the conversation was under way, the company waited for Johnson—rolling in his chair, his head on one side, his mouth opening and closing as though rehearsing what was now to come—to join in with that measured, magnificent eloquence that would hold the table in thrall. It was an eloquence that appeared entirely natural, but in fact had been acquired through long practice; and he continued, on occasions, to practise it in public: "Talking of the comedy of 'The Rehearsal'," he said, "It has not wit enough to keep it sweet." This was easy. He therefore caught himself, and pronounced a more rotund sentence, "It has not vitality enough to preserve it from putrefaction."'

This, too, was easy. He took greater pleasure in introducing the most abstruse words he could think of. Having asked Bennet Langton if his parents had sat for their portraits, which he thought each generation of a

family ought to do, and being informed that they opposed it, he pronounced, 'Sir, among the *anfractuosities* of the human mind, I know not if
it may not be one, that there is a superstitious reluctance to sit for a
picture.' And when discussing *The Beggar's Opera* he said, 'I do not deny
that it may have some influence, by making the character of a rogue
familiar, and in some degree pleasing.' Then, collecting himself, rolling
about and obviously preparing himself for his heavy stroke, he added,
'There is in it such a *labefactation* of all principles as may be injurious to
morality.'

At this Boswell, Reynolds, Gibbon and the rest of the company sat 'in
a comical sort of restraint smothering a laugh', which they were afraid
might burst out.

Sometimes the laughter could not possibly be contained. Boswell, in one
of his most vivid, disarming and celebrated passages, preserved one such
occasion for posterity:

> Talking of a very respectable author, he told us a curious circum-
> stance in his life, which was, that he had married a printer's devil.
> REYNOLDS. 'A printer's devil, Sir! Why, I thought a printer's devil was
> a creature with a black face and in rags.' JOHNSON. 'Yes, Sir. But I
> suppose he had her face washed, and put clean clothes on her. (Then
> looking very serious and very earnest.) And she did not disgrace him;—
> the woman had a bottom of good sense.' The word bottom thus intro-
> duced, was so ludicrous when contrasted with his gravity, that most
> of us could not forbear tittering and laughing; though I recollect
> that the Bishop of Killaloe kept his countenance with perfect steadi-
> ness, while Miss Hannah More slyly hid her face behind a lady's
> back who sat on the same settee with her. His pride could not bear that
> any expression of his should excite ridicule, when he did not intend
> it; he therefore resolved to assume and exercise despotick power,
> glanced sternly round, and called out in a strong tone, 'Where's the
> merriment?' Then collecting himself, and looking awful, to make us
> feel how he could impose restraint, and as it were searching his mind
> for a still more ludicrous word, he slowly pronounced, 'I say the
> woman was fundamentally sensible'; as if he had said, hear this now,
> and laugh if you dare. We all sat composed as at a funeral.

The imperiousness was never entirely pretended, even on this occasion.
He bridled furiously when anyone attempted to interrupt him in the
middle of his flowing talk, though he interrupted others often enough,
Boswell more often than most; and one of the very few criticisms he ever
voiced about Topham Beauclerk—whose keenness of mind he compared

favourably, and with unusual modesty, with his own delivery: 'Everything comes from him so easily. It appears to me that I labour, when I say a good thing'—was that Beauclerk 'assumed a predominance over his company'. The dominant position he appeared to consider was his, and his alone.

His deafness naturally made it difficult to conduct an ordinary conversation with him as he grew older. There was, for example, an evening in 1775 when someone raised an objection to the antiquity of the poetry said to be Ossian's on the grounds that there were no wolves mentioned in it. The mention of wolves evidently led Johnson to think of other wild animals. For, while Langton and Reynolds were subsequently carrying on an earnest conversation together about something quite unrelated to the previous topic, and while the rest of the company were listening to them, Johnson suddenly broke out, 'Pennant tells of bears . . .'. And he went on telling what Pennant told of bears, oblivious of the dialogue still being conducted by Reynolds and Langton. These two continued to talk, so that, despite his loud voice, much of what Johnson said was lost. The word 'bear', however, was heard at regular intervals which, since that was the nickname by which he was sometimes known, caused a great deal of ill-suppressed laughter. Reynolds and Langton at last fell into silence; but Johnson carried on, 'We are told that the black bear is innocent; but I should not like to trust myself with him.' Edward Gibbon muttered under his breath, 'I should not like to trust myself to *you.*'

Few people did. There were certain rules to be observed in his presence. Firstly he was never to be made to look ridiculous. A man who once made a joke at his expense was so terrified by a tremendous snarl that he immediately apologised. 'Indeed, indeed, Doctor, believe me,' he said, 'I meant nothing.' 'Sir,' growled Johnson, 'if you *mean* nothing *say* nothing.'[10]

Nor did Johnson like men either to swear in his presence or to talk laxly about the Christian religion. Tom Davies said that Arthur Murphy had paid Johnson the 'highest compliment that ever was paid to a layman by asking his pardon for repeating some oaths in the course of telling a story'. Johnson forgave Murphy but was less ready to excuse those for whom he did not entertain so high a regard. To a gentleman-farmer who said that Lord Eglinton was a 'damned fool' to have advanced on Mungo Campbell after Campbell had threatened to shoot him if he did, Johnson angrily replied, 'He was not a *damned* fool,' stressing the word with a ferocious frown. 'He did not believe Campbell would be such a *damned* scoundrel, as to do so *damned* a thing.' On other occasions Johnson had been known to leave the room if a man persisted in swearing.[11]

It was also unwise to wander too far from the truth in recounting anecdotes, or, as Samuel Foote was prone to do, to invent them altogether. Johnson himself, though given to exaggeration in his descriptions of characters and in his praise or condemnation of them, was always believed when he told a story, however unlikely it appeared. Boswell gave as an example an incident which Johnson related as having happened to him one night in Fleet Street. ' "A gentlewoman (said he) begged I would give her my arm to assist her in crossing the street, which I accordingly did; upon which she offered me a shilling, supposing me to be the watchman. I perceived that she was somewhat in liquor." This, if told by most people, would have been thought an invention; when told by Johnson it was believed by his friends as much as if they had seen what passed.'

Johnson's attitude towards drunkenness was equivocal. He once gave it as his opinion that the only time a man was happy was when he was drunk; and he himself had enjoyed getting drunk in his earlier years. Indeed, in later life he confessed that it was not so much the taste as the effect of wine that he enjoyed; he used often to pour capillaire into his port.[12]

Twice in his life he succeeded in giving up alcohol altogether for long periods. 'For what ferments the spirits may also derange the intellects,' he explained, 'and the means employed to counteract dejection may hasten the approach of madness.' The trouble was, as he often confessed, that he could not drink in moderation. 'I can't drink a *little*, child,' he told Hannah More, 'therefore I never touch it. Abstinence is as easy to me as temperance would be difficult.'

'I am *sure* you would not carry it too far,' Lady Macleod once protested. 'Nay, madam,' Johnson replied, 'it carried me.' He did not find that it affected his powers of thinking, he told his friend William Bowles, but it did affect his limbs.

During his periods of abstinence there were occasional lapses. On a visit to Cambridge with Beauclerk in 1765 he managed to subsist for most of the time on his 'large potations of tea', but on the last night, so Dr John Sharp recorded, 'several persons got into his company . . . at Trinity, where, about twelve, he began to be very great; stripped poor Mrs Macaulay to the very skin, then gave her for his toast, and drank her in two bumpers'. Also, that same year after going to church on the anniversary of Tetty's death, he could not resist a glass or two of wine which he much regretted the next morning.

Towards the end of his life he returned to his earlier habit of drinking wine regularly; and he returned to it with relish as anyone who saw him draining his glass could testify, though, according to George Steevens, he was known only once to have drunk too much, 'a circumstance which he himself discovered on finding that one of his sesquipedalian words hung fire. He then started up and gravely observed, "I think it time we should go to bed."'

Usually he drank only when he was alone: 'I have then often wished for it, and often taken it . . . to get rid of myself, to send myself away. Wine gives great pleasure: and every pleasure is of itself a good. It is a good unless counterbalanced by evil. A man may have strong reason not to drink wine; and that may be greater than the pleasure. Wine makes a man better pleased with himself. I do not say that it makes him more pleasing to others.'

Although he liked sweet wines—he sometimes dropped a lump of sugar in his evening glass of port—he did not like light ones. 'A man would be drowned' by claret before it made him drunk: 'No, Sir, claret is the liquor for boys; port for men; but he who aspires to be a hero must drink brandy. . . . Brandy will do soonest for a man what drinking *can* do for him.' He rarely censured a man for drinking too much; when once a friend appeared drunk at a tavern a mutual acquaintance, thinking to make trouble between them and to provoke a severe rebuke from Johnson, afterwards asked him what the friend had said by way of apology. 'Sir,' Johnson answered, 'he said all that a man *should* say: he said he was sorry for it.'

When Boswell was suffering from a hangover, Johnson teased him affectionately; and even when Boswell, after getting drunk at the Duke of Montrose's, walked into Miss Monckton's drawing-room 'in extraordinary spirits and above all fear of awe', Johnson—by whom he sat down 'to let the company know' how he 'could contend with Ajax'—merely evaded his questions, attempted to keep him quiet, and later accepted his apology 'with the most friendly gentleness'.

Yet he was not always so tolerant. A Newcastle ship-master infuriated him in Scotland by talking in his cups of 'Wilkes and Liberty'. How could such a fellow, he asked Boswell indignantly, 'come into *our* company who was fit for *no* company?' A man had to have the 'art of getting drunk', he said on another occasion; and he denied that there was any virtue in the maxim *in vino veritas*: 'Why, Sir, that may be an argument for drinking if you suppose men in general to be liars. But, Sir, I would not keep company with a fellow, who lies as long as he is sober, and whom you must make drunk before you can get a word of truth out of him.'

He also denied, in argument with Reynolds, that drinking improved a man's conversational powers. 'No, Sir,' he said. 'Before dinner men meet with great inequality of understanding; and those who are conscious of their inferiority have the modesty not to talk. When they have drunk wine, every man feels himself happy, and loses that modesty, and grows impudent and vociferous; but he is not improved. He is only not sensible of his defects.'

'I am,' persisted Reynolds, 'in very good spirits when I get up in the morning. By dinner time I am exhausted; wine puts me in the same state as when I got up; and I am sure that moderate drinking makes people talk better.'

'No, Sir. Wine gives not light, gay, ideal hilarity; but tumultuous, noisy, clamorous merriment. I have heard none of those drunken—nay, drunken is a coarse word—none of those *vinous* flights.'

'Because you have sat by, quite sober, and felt an envy of the happiness of those who were drinking.'

'Perhaps contempt . . .'

The Club had not long been founded when Johnson's temporarily cheerful spirits began to decline. On Good Friday that year, 1764, he mournfully castigated himself for having made no reformation in his idle life, for having lived totally uselessly, more sensual in thought and more addicted to wine. He resolved to put his rooms in order, disorder being 'one great cause of Idleness'. The rooms in the garret where he kept his books were, in particular, almost always in an appalling muddle. Levett once showed them to Boswell who found the books very dusty and in great confusion and the floor strewn with manuscripts. Not all the books were his own, for a man foolhardy enough to lend him a book rarely received it back; amongst them was a book he had taken out of Pembroke College library as an undergraduate. Yet it was upon the rarest of occasions that he could bring himself to put his books in order or, indeed, to tidy up any of his other possessions. He was always losing things and because he declined to wear spectacles—though he 'could recollect no production of art to which man has superior obligations' and mentioned the name of their original inventor with reverence—it was extremely difficult for him to find what he had mislaid. William Fitzherbert who visited him once and asked if he could write a letter found that Johnson could not put his hand on pen, ink or paper. He once lost five guineas that he had hidden to avoid the trouble of locking them up and had then forgotten the hiding place. But this was not necessarily due to advancing years, he insisted. 'There is a wicked inclination in most people to suppose an old man decayed in his intellects. If a young or middle-aged man, when leaving a company, does not recollect where he laid his hat, it is nothing; but if the same inattention is discovered in an old man, people will shrug up their shoulders, and say, "His memory is going."'

On Easter Saturday, having fasted all the day before, he was in lower spirits than ever, blaming himself for his 'grosser sluggishness', his 'wilder negligence', his thoughts 'clouded with sensuality'. 'Except that from the beginning of this year I have in some measure forborn excess of Strong Drink my appetites have predominated over my reason. A kind of strange oblivion has overspread me, so that I know not what has become of the last year, and perceive that incidents and intelligence pass over me without leaving any impression.' On Easter Sunday, with tears in his eyes as he thought of Tetty, he made his usual resolutions and prayed earnestly for amendment. He went to church, arriving late as he so often did, endeavoured to attend the service and to listen to the sermon, and 'privately' gave a crown to a poor girl who moved him to pity as she knelt to receive the Sacrament, although he saw in her hand a copy of Hart's *Hymns,* an extremely evangelical, 'enthusiastic' production of which he strongly disapproved.

After church he went home to pray, then had dinner with Miss Williams. In the evening he went to Tom and Susanna Davies with whom he spent the evening 'not pleasantly'. Succeeding in his resolve not to drink too much wine, he 'tempered a few glasses with sherbert'. At home he prayed intently for deliverance from his 'habitual wickedness and idleness' and from 'distresses of vain terrour'.

In his depression this year he thought he was losing his reason, and confessed to Dr Adams that he would 'consent to have a limb amputated to recover' his spirits. Dr Adams found him 'in a deplorable state, sighing, groaning, talking to himself, and restlessly walking' up and down. 'He looked miserable,' Adams recorded, 'his lips moved, tho he was not speaking[;] he could not sit long at a time—was quite restless, sometimes walked up and down the room, sometimes into the next room, and returned immediately.' According to Hawkins he sought relief in opium which he was later to take in large quantities and to which he already had a 'strong propensity'. 'His practice was to take it in substance, that is to say, half a grain levigated with a spoon against the side of a cup half full of some liquid which, as a vehicle, carried it down.'

Earlier in the year he had been cheerful enough during a visit to the Langton family in Lincolnshire, and in August he went north again to stay with Dr Thomas Percy, at that time Vicar of Easton-Maudit in Northamptonshire. But on his fifty-sixth birthday in September, Johnson sadly recorded his unhappiness: 'I have outlived many friends. I have felt many sorrows. I have made few improvements. Since my resolution formed last Easter I have made no advancement in knowledge or in goodness; nor do I recollect that I have endeavoured it. I am dejected . . . O God for Jesus Christ's sake have mercy upon me. . . . I have now spent fifty-five years in resolving, having from the earliest times almost that I can remember, been forming schemes of a better life. I have done nothing; the need of doing therefore is pressing, since the time of doing is short.' Afterwards he made his usual resolutions and undertook to keep accounts as well as a journal, to study the scriptures by reading 640 verses every Sunday, to take care of his health by washing more frequently, and, of course, to rise early: 'Not later than six if I can, I hope sooner, but as soon as I can.' Yet, as the new diary which he began on 1 January 1765 reveals, he was still up at three o'clock in the morning, and got out of bed as late as ever. 'Have mercy, eternal Father, if thy gift has been wasted,' he wrote on 3 January in Latin, the language he used for entries of an important, personal nature. He felt more miserable than ever.

Within a week, however, he was to meet a man and his wife whose friendship was to alter his life.

The Market Place,
Lichfield. Samuel
Johnson was born in
the house above his
father's bookshop
which stands opposite
St Mary's Church

Michael Johnson,
Samuel's father

Lichfield as seen across Stowe Pool, the spires of the Cathedral on the right and the tower of St Mary's Church on the left

Lichfield Grammar School where Johnson was educated from 1717, when he was seven and a half, to 1725

An early portrait of Samuel Johnson, 'not much of a scholar to look at'

Pembroke College, Oxford, where Johnson was entered as a commoner in October 1728. His rooms were over the gateway at the top of the tower

Left: Mrs Harry Porter, the young wife of a Birmingham mercer, whom Johnson married at Derby in 1735, ten months after the death of her first husband, when she was forty-five.

Below: Edial Hall, near Lichfield, a school opened in 1736 with his wife's money where young gentlemen were to be 'boarded and taught the Latin and Greek languages by Samuel Johnson'

Edward Cave

Joshua Reynolds

Topham Beauclerk

Oliver Goldsmith

A pomade pot on the lid of which Johnson is depicted being kept waiting for an interview in Lord Chesterfield's ante-room

DICTIONARY

OF THE

ENGLISH LANGUAGE:

IN WHICH

The WORDS are deduced from their ORIGINALS,

AND

ILLUSTRATED in their DIFFERENT SIGNIFICATIONS

BY

EXAMPLES from the beft WRITERS.

TO WHICH ARE PREFIXED,

A HISTORY of the LANGUAGE,

AND

An ENGLISH GRAMMAR.

BY SAMUEL JOHNSON, A. M.

In TWO VOLUMES.

VOL. I.

> Cum tabulis animum cenforis fumet honefti :
> Audebit quæcunque parum fplendoris habebunt,
> Et fine pondere erunt, et honore indigna ferentur.
> Verba movere loco ; quamvis invita recedant,
> Et verfentur adhuc intra penetralia Veftæ :
> Obfcurata diu populo bonus eruet, atque
> Proferet in lucem fpeciofa vocabula rerum,
> Quæ prifcis memorata Catonibus atque Cethegis,
> Nunc fitus informis premit et deferta vetuftas.   Hor.

LONDON

Printed by W. STRAHAN,

For J. and P. KNAPTON ; T. and T. LONGMAN ; C. HITCH and L. HAWES ;
A. MILLAR ; and R. and J. DODSLEY.

MDCCLV.

The title page of Johnson's dictionary, the first edition of which was published on 15 April 1755

Johnson's Court, Fleet Street, where Johnson lived from 1765 to 1776

Johnson's house in Bolt Court where he lived from 1776 until his death

Miss Anna Williams, the blind lady with whom Johnson shared his home for many years and with whom he drank tea every night before going to bed

Francis Barber, Johnson's negro servant who was in his service almost continually from 1752 until his master's death

Edmund Burke

David Garrick

Giuseppe Baretti

Rowlandson depicts Dr Johnson at tea

Above left: Fanny
Burney. *Above right:*
Mrs Montagu. *Left:*
Mrs Thrale with her
eldest daughter,
Queeney

Johnson in late
middle age

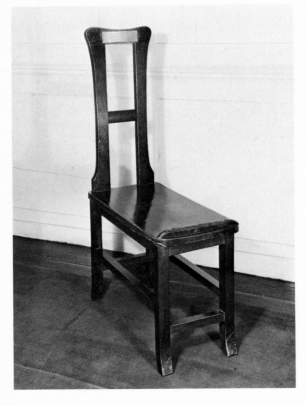

A chair from the Old
Cock Tavern where it
was known as 'Dr
Johnson's chair'. The
style was favoured by
men suffering from
gout

Left: Johnson in travelling dress on the Isle of Mull. *Below left:* Loch Lomond. *Below right:* Lord Monboddo

Charles Burney

James Boswell

Bennet Langton

Mrs Thrale at the time
of her widowhood

Gabriel Piozzi

The Thrales' house
at Streatham

A portrait by Reynolds which was presented to Boswell

A portrait by Opie to whom Johnson sat in 1783

'Well, Sir,' said Johnson. 'I think my friend Joe Nollekens can chop out a head with the best of them.' He was, however, very much displeased with the way in which the sculptor loaded his head with hair which was modelled from the ample locks of an Irish beggar

Part III

❧

1765–1775

9
New Friends and Old Rambles

*'We liked each other so well that the next Thursday was appointed
for the same company to meet . . . and since then Johnson has
remained till this Day, our constant acquaintance, Visitor, Companion and Friend.'*   Hester Thrale

Johnson's record of his first encounter with Mr and Mrs Thrale could
scarcely be briefer: 'At Mr Trails.' His hostess was more explicit:

It was the second Thursday of the Month of January 1765. that I
first saw Johnson in a room. Murphy was one day dining with us at
our house in Southwark; and was zealous that we should be acquainted
with Johnson, of whose Moral and Literary Character he spoke in the
most exalted terms; and so whetted our desire of seeing him soon, that
we were only disputing *how* he should be invited, *when* he *should* be
invited, and what should be the pretence. At last it was resolved that
one Woodhouse, a Shoemaker [James Woodhouse], who had written
some verses [published under the title *Poems on Several Occasions*] and
been asked to some Tables, should likewise be added to ours, and made
a Temptation to Mr Johnson to meet him: accordingly he came and
Mr Murphy at four o'clock brought Mr Johnson to dinner—we liked
each other so well that the next Thursday was appointed for the same
company to meet—exclusive of the Shoemaker, and since then Johnson
has remained till this Day, our constant acquaintance, Visitor, Companion and Friend.[1]

Henry Thrale was in a thriving way of trade as a brewer. He had
inherited the business from his father who, after working in it for a number

of years, had managed to acquire it following the marriage of the owner's only child to a nobleman. It not being considered fit that a peer should continue it, the business had been made over to Thrale's father who ran it so successfully that within eleven years he was able to pay the purchase money. By the time of his death he had acquired a considerable fortune which had provided his only son with an excellent education and, after he had come down from Oxford and completed the Grand Tour, with a splendid allowance of £1,000 a year.

Henry Thrale was a silent man, tall, stately, dignified, controlled and authoritative. He was not, therefore, a man to arouse deep affection, but he did merit respect; and after Johnson had become a regular guest in his house and had cause to feel indebted to his generosity, he repeatedly professed his esteem for him. Mr Thrale was a man of excellent principles, he said, a good scholar, well skilled in trade, and of a sound understanding. His wife, Hester, after thirteen years of marriage, painted an extraordinarily dispassionate picture of him. She did not love him, but she had grown fond of him, and was ready to overlook his numerous, though decorously conducted, love affairs, from one of which he had contracted a venereal infection.

Mr Thrale's Person is manly, his Countenance agreeable, his Eyes steady and of the deepest Blue; his Look neither Soft nor severe, neither sprightly nor gloomy, but thoughtful and Intelligent: his Address is . . . unaffectedly civil and decorous; and his Manner more completely free from every kind of Trick or Particularity than I ever saw any person's. . . . He loves Money & is diligent to obtain it; but he loves Liberality too, & is willing enough both to give generously & spend fashionably. His Passions either are not strong, or else he keeps them under such Command that they seldom disturb his Tranquility. . . . His regard for his Father's Memory is remarkably great, and he has been a most exemplary Brother; though when the house of his favourite Sister was on Fire, & we were alarmed with the Account of it in the Night, I well remember that he never rose, but bidding the Servant who called us, go to her Assistance; quietly turned about & slept to his usual hour. . . . Mr Thrale's sobriety, & the Decency of his Conversation being wholly free from all Oaths Ribaldry and Profaneness make him a Man exceedingly comfortable to live with, while the easiness of his Temper and slowness to take Offence add greatly to his Value as a Domestic Man: Yet I think his servants do not much love him, and I am not sure that his Children feel much Affection for him: low People almost all indeed agree to abhorr him, as he has not of that officious & cordial Manner which is universally required by them

—nor any Skill to dissemble his dislike of their Coarseness—with Regard to his Wife, tho' little tender of her Person, he is very partial to her Understanding. . . . Johnson has a great Degree of Kindness and Esteem for him, and says if he would talk more, his *Manner* would be very completely that of a perfect Gentleman.

At the time that Johnson first met them, Mr Thrale was about thirty-five, his wife twenty-four. They had been married just over a year.

Hester was the daughter of an ineffectual, ill-tempered and improvident Welsh gentleman who had soon run through the estate left him by his father, John Salusbury, a descendant of Richard Clough, and had been obliged to move to a small cottage and then to Nova Scotia. Her mother, left behind in Wales with Hester, sought the help and protection of various members of her family, first of all of her brother Sir Robert Cotton, who died without providing for Hester as he had promised to do, then of Sir Lynch Cotton, and finally of her brother-in-law, Thomas Salusbury, who had married an heiress and agreed to give the child an allowance of £200 a year and then £10,000 if she married with her mother's consent. Various suitors were dismissed as unsuitable, and then her uncle Thomas told her one day that he had found her an entirely eligible husband in Henry Thrale. Her father, who had by now returned to England, strongly objected to the match, protesting, 'If you marry that scoundrel he will catch the pox and for your amusement set you to make his poultices.' But John Salusbury died in December 1762, and a marriage contract between his daughter and Thrale was drawn up; Hester was provided with a rich husband; Thrale was given a wife with a good dowry, a fit mother for his children and an engaging hostess for his table. They were married in October 1763, and it was not until 'after the nuptial Ceremony' was past, as the bride put it, that she was allowed to be alone with Henry for more than five minutes.

Although she admitted that many a worse husband might have been found for her, there were many disadvantages in being Mrs Henry Thrale. Her husband had a pleasant country house at Streatham as well as the town house in Southwark near the brewery, but she was not allowed to ride there—and she loved riding—because he thought it a too masculine pastime. Nor was she allowed into the kitchen, since he was a dedicated gourmet and liked to consider the supervision of the cooking staff his personal responsibility. 'I know no man,' commented Johnson after he had grown to know them both well, 'who is more master of his wife and family than Thrale. If he but holds up a finger, he is obeyed.' There were compensations for Hester, however. Henry did not say much, but he liked to entertain people who did talk well; and so his wife, a sprightly talker herself, was never short of amusing company. Once Samuel Johnson had become a frequent guest at their dinner table, attracting other celebrated figures and literary luminaries, her house became the sort of centre that she had longed to make it.

She was an attractive young woman, though not beautiful in any way, rather plump and very short. Her early experiences had combined to make her something of a cynic, even hard in her personal relationships; but they had also taught her how to please older men with her vivacity, her bright, if rather superficial intelligence, her flattering attentions. Johnson was much taken by her. He professed not to think much of her learning, which was 'that of a schoolboy in one of the lower forms', and he condemned her malicious tongue, but he enjoyed talking to her both in company and alone, and he enjoyed teasing her flirtatiously as though she were a precociously responsive child. 'You little creatures should never wear those sort of clothes,' he once chided her when she appeared in a dark-coloured gown. 'They are unsuitable in every way. What! Have not all insects gay colours!' 'Your malice defeats itself, for your censure is too violent,' he told her on another occasion. 'And yet,' he added, looking at her with what Boswell described as a 'leering smile', 'she is the first woman in the world, could she but restrain that wicked tongue of hers— she would be the only woman, could she but command that little whirligig.'

From the very beginning of his friendship with the Thrales, Johnson's spirits seem to have risen; and in a far more contented frame of mind than he had been of late, he thought about moving at last out of his chambers in Inner Temple Lane. He settled upon a good house in Johnson's Court, Fleet Street, where he was to remain for the next ten years. Miss Williams, Robert Levett and Frank Barber all moved in with him, Miss Williams being given an apartment on the ground floor and Levett a room in the garret. Frank spent much of his time in a little ante-room where the Rev Noel Turner found him one day when his master was out. He was with a 'group of his African countrymen sitting round the fire,' Turner said, and 'on their all turning their sooty faces at once to stare at me, they presented a curious spectacle.'

Johnson himself had a pleasant, light apartment on the first floor, with 'some furniture which', so John Hawkins said, 'would not have disgraced a better dwelling'. Assured always now of company, if not of domestic harmony, Johnson awaited the publication of his Shakespeare which had at long last been completed.

This new edition of Shakespeare, which Johnson had first proposed in 1756, was published in October 1765 under the title, *The plays of William Shakespeare, in eight volumes, with the Corrections and Illustrations of Various Commentators: To which are added notes by Samuel Johnson.* Also added was a preface of some seventeen thousand words, one of the most accomplished, incisive and perceptive of all Johnson's writings. There were some adverse comments from a few critics, in particular from Dr William Kenrick, a man who had, in Johnson's dismissive opinion, made himself '*publick*' without making himself '*known*'. Kenrick's attack was answered by an Oxford undergraduate, not entirely to the satisfaction of Johnson, who believed adverse criticisms were best ignored and did not, in any case, feel disposed to welcome so young and untried a champion. But on the whole the work was as well received as it was successful, going through several impressions and forming the basis of more than one subsequent edition. There was no doubt that such an edition was sorely needed.

For generations Shakespeare's plays had been mangled and adapted for the stage by self-professed improvers, who thought nothing of rewriting scenes, adding dialogue, altering endings and cutting out unwelcome or obtrusive characters. Garrick, himself, while posing as the 'restorer' of Shakespeare, was almost as guilty as other theatrical managers, adding, for instance, a dramatic dying speech with which to round off his performance as Macbeth. At the same time there was a growing feeling in the country, fostered by certain scholars and critics, that Shakespeare should be treated as a hallowed classic, that it was a kind of sacrilege, as well as an insult to the English nation, when Voltaire referred to him as a 'barbarous mountebank'. George III, who exclaimed to Fanny Burney, Queen Charlotte's Assistant Keeper of the Wardrobe, 'Was there ever such stuff as great part of Shakespeare?' felt obliged to add, 'Only one must not say so! But what think you? What? Is there not sad stuff? What?—What? . . . Oh, I know it is not to be said. . . . It's Shakespeare and nobody dare abuse him. . . . One should be stoned for saying so.'

Johnson had approached his task not as an abuser, and certainly not as an idolator. He had already expressed the opinion that 'Shakespeare never has six lines together without a fault. Perhaps you may find seven; but this does not refute my general assertion. If I come to an orchard and say, "There's no fruit here." And then comes a poring man who finds two apples and three pears and tells me, "Sir, you are mistaken. I have found both apples and pears", I should laugh at him.' Nor, it must be confessed, had Johnson set about his task altogether as a scholar should. He complained in his Preface that he had not been able to see all the existing texts because he had 'not found the collectors of these varieties very communicative'. But, in fact, he had not put himself out to collate those he could have obtained. David Garrick, whom many thought Johnson had deliberately snubbed by not mentioning in his Preface, had an extensive collection of material yet Johnson had not consulted any of it, although, as Garrick himself told Boswell, he had been made welcome to it and the servants at Hampton Court had been instructed 'to have a fire and every convenience for him'. It was not just that Johnson felt disinclined to do any more work than he had to do, but, as he himself implied when discussing the offer with Boswell, he resented the way in which Garrick had made it: Garrick had wanted to be 'courted' for the material, and it was not for *him* to court Garrick, it was for *Garrick* to court him.

But if Johnson might have been more scholarly in his approach, his well-considered, impartial comments and sound common-sense were wonderfully refreshing; and his interpretations of numerous passages are enlightening even now. In Adam Smith's opinion the Preface was the most '*manly* piece of criticism that was ever published in any country'.

Johnson disliked much of Shakespeare's language, the punning and the word-play, failed even to notice the bawdy and complained strongly of his carelessness in structure and his failure to impose, except in *Macbeth* (Johnson's favourite play), any moral order. 'He sacrifices virtue to convenience,' Johnson wrote, 'and is so much more careful to please than to instruct, that he seems to write without any moral purpose. . . . It is always a writer's duty to make the world better.' Yet he brought to his task rare gifts of learning and insight; and from his work on the dictionary, and his editions of Sir Thomas Browne and Roger Ascham, he was able to bring to it a sound knowledge of the English spoken in Shakespeare's day. In his concise accounts of the plays his mastery of paraphrase is everywhere apparent, and in his observations on the characters he shows how well he understood the complexities of the human mind.

Unlike his predecessor, Warburton, who had emended the plays with extraordinary licence, altering obscure passages and even adding lines, Johnson's purpose was to restore the texts, as well as he could, to the texts which Shakespeare wrote and which, for all the faults his independent mind found in them, he so deeply admired.[2]

'The business of him that republishes an ancient book,' he wrote, 'is to correct what is corrupt, and to explain what is obscure.' It was not to profess to understand passages that were found to be incomprehensible, and it was not to alter what the author wrote to what the editor thought he ought to have written and would have written had he lived at a later time. Previous editors, for example, had altered the phrase in *Hamlet* 'in hugger mugger to inter him' to 'in private to inter him'. Johnson, however, respected the original text, explaining, 'that the words now replaced are better, I do not undertake to prove; it is sufficient that they are Shakespeare's: If phraseology is to be changed as words grow uncouth by disuse, or gross by vulgarity, the history of every language will be lost; we shall no longer have the words of any author; and, as these alterations will be often unskilfully made, we shall have very little of his meaning.'

For three years after the publication of his Shakespeare, Johnson did scarcely any work at all. Shortly before it appeared he had an idea to study law and offered up a prayer that God would enable him to 'attain such knowledge' as would qualify him to 'direct the doubtful, and instruct the ignorant; to prevent wrongs and terminate contentions'. A few weeks later he composed another prayer entitled 'Engaging in Politicks with H——n', from which it appears that he had come to some arrangement with William Gerard Hamilton, the rich Member of Parliament for Pontefract for whom Edmund Burke had worked as a kind of private secretary for several years. 'This Mr Hamilton,' a female acquaintance wrote of him, 'is extremely tall and handsome, has an air of haughty and fashionable superiority, is intelligent, dry, sarcastic and clever. I should have received much pleasure from his conversational powers had I not previously been prejudiced against him by hearing that he is infinitely artful, double, and crafty.' He had become famous overnight as a young man of twenty-five when he made an astonishingly accomplished maiden speech, lasting from two o'clock in the afternoon until two o'clock the next morning, which Johnson was said to have written for him.

Johnson, who had been intimate with Hamilton for many years and had a high opinion of his talents and conversational powers, once said to him, 'I am very unwilling to be left alone, Sir, and therefore I go with my company down the first pair of stairs, in some hopes that they may, perhaps, return again. I go with you, Sir, as far as the street door.'

For some unknown reason nothing came of the proposed association with Hamilton, and Johnson's final attempt to enter the law was abandoned.[3] It was certainly not abandoned so that he could devote more time to literature. A pamphlet on the Corn Laws, written in consultation with Hamilton, and dedications to Percy's *Reliques*, rewritten from Percy's own draft, to Payne's *Geometry*, to Hoole's translation of *Metastasio*, to Adams's *Globes* and Gwynn's *London and Westminster Improved* were almost all that he wrote between 1765, when he was created Doctor of Laws by Trinity College, Dublin, and the spring of 1769 when he went on a round of extended visits to Oxford, Lichfield and to Brighton with the Thrales. He helped a young friend, Robert Chambers, Blackstone's successor as Vinerian Professor of Law at Oxford, to write some lectures, and he helped Miss Williams produce a volume of *Miscellanies* which included a poem 'On the Death of Stephen Gray, the Electrician'. This poem was obviously his work; but when Miss Williams, who was growing increasingly cantankerous with each passing year, was asked outright if it were by him, she haughtily replied, 'Sir, I wrote that poem before I had the honour of Dr Johnson's acquaintance.' 'It is true, Sir,' Johnson confirmed, 'that she wrote it before she was acquainted with me.' Yet he felt obliged to add, 'But she has not told you that I wrote it all over again, except two lines.'

He recorded his intention of writing a 'History of Memory' and a commentary on the Book of Common Prayer; but neither project was realised. Yet although he continued to reprimand himself for his indolence, he professed to believe that he had earned the right to rest from his literary labours and could now devote himself to conversation. One evening in the spring of 1766 he said as much to Goldsmith and Boswell (now returned from his travels) who had called upon him hoping to persuade him to go out to supper with them at the Mitre. He was not feeling very well and declined their invitation. 'Come then,' Goldsmith said, 'we will not go to the Mitre tonight, since we cannot have the big man with us.' So Johnson sent for a bottle of port for his guests and ordered water for himself.

'I think, Mr Johnson, you don't go near the theatre now,' Goldsmith said. 'You give yourself no more concern about a new play, than if you had never had anything to do with the stage.'

'Why, Sir, our tastes alter greatly. The lad does not care for the child's rattle, and the old man does not care for the young man's whore. . . . As we advance in the journey of life we drop some of the things that have pleased us; whether it be that we are fatigued and don't choose to carry so many things any farther, or that we find other things which we like better.'

'But, Sir,' Boswell asked him, 'Why don't you give us something in some other way?' 'Ay, Sir,' Goldsmith urged him, 'we have a claim upon you.'

'No, Sir,' Johnson insisted, 'I am not obliged to do any more. No man is obliged to do as much as he can do. A man is to have part of his life to himself. If a soldier has fought a good many campaigns, he is not to be blamed if he retires to ease and tranquility. A physician, who has practised long in a great city, may be excused if he retires to a small town, and takes less practice. Now, Sir, the good I can do by my conversation bears the same proportion to the good I can do by my writings, that the practice of a physician, retired to a small town, does to his practice in a great city.'

Some months later, however, he was urged not to give up writing altogether for conversation by a man whose encouragement he found it more difficult to ignore. This was King George III whom he met one day in the library of the Queen's House. It was a meeting which much gratified Johnson's 'monarchical enthusiasm', and which he loved to relate with all its circumstances, when requested by his friends.

The King, learning of Dr Johnson's occasional visits to the library, asked to be informed next time he came there; so one day, when Johnson was sitting by the fire, deep in the study of a book, the librarian went to tell the King of his opportunity. The King rose immediately, followed the librarian who lit the way with a candle, and came to a private door which he opened with his own key. Johnson was still in a profound study by the fire. The librarian went up to him and whispered, 'Sir, here is the King.' 'Johnson started up, and stood still. His Majesty approached him, and at once was courteously easy.'

They spoke of Oxford and Cambridge, of Lord Lyttelton's *History of the Life of Henry the Second* which had just been published, and of the controversy between William Warburton, Bishop of Gloucester, and Robert Lowth, Bishop of St David's; they discussed literary journals, and the egregious Dr John Hill, a prolific writer on all manner of subjects, the fifth edition of whose *Old Man's Guide to Health and Longer Life* had appeared not long before. The King observed that he supposed Dr Johnson must have read a great deal; and Johnson replied that he thought more than he read now, but that he had read a great deal 'in the early part of his life'.

'His Majesty enquired if he was then writing anything. He answered, he was not, for he had pretty well told the world what he knew, and must now read to acquire more knowledge. The King . . . then said, "I do not think you borrow much from anybody." Johnson said, he thought he had already done his part as a writer. "I should have thought so too, (said the King,) if you had not written so well."'

No man could have paid a handsomer compliment than that, Johnson decided, 'and it was fit for a King to pay. It was decisive.' When, later, His Majesty expressed a desire to have the literary biography of this country ably executed, and proposed to Dr Johnson to undertake it, 'Johnson signified his readiness to comply with his Majesty's wishes'.

After the interview was over, and the King had left, Johnson turned to the librarian and observed, 'Sir, they may talk of the King as they will; but he is the finest gentleman I have ever seen'; and he later added, 'Sir, his manners are those of as fine a gentleman as we may suppose Lewis the Fourteenth or Charles the Second.'

While relating the details of the interview at Sir Joshua Reynolds's house, someone asked him if he had made any reply to the King's high compliment as to the merits of his work. 'No, Sir,' he replied. 'When the King had said it, it was to be so. It was not for me to bandy civilities with my Sovereign.'

It was generally agreed that Johnson had carried out the conversation very well. The librarian reported that he had spoken to the King 'with profound respect, but still in his firm manly manner, with a sonorous voice, and never in that subdued tone which is commonly used at the levee and in the drawing room'. Even Goldsmith was moved to overcome his envy and pay a rare compliment.

He had listened to Johnson's account in silence, ruminating gloomily on a sofa at a distance from the others; but at length 'the simplicity of his natural character prevailed'. He sprang up from the sofa, walked across the room and 'in a kind of flutter from imagining himself in the situation which he had just been hearing described, exclaimed, "Well, you acquitted yourself in this conversation better than I should have done; for I should have bowed and stammered through the whole of it."'

Although Johnson had 'signified his readiness to comply with the King's wish that he write the literary biography of the country', it was not to be for many years that he felt able to settle down to so formidable a task. For, as he confessed in a letter to Frank Barber, whom he had now sent to school at Bishop's Stortford in Hertfordshire, urging him to 'be a good boy' there, he was 'very much out of order'.

For several months after the publication of his Shakespeare he had been feeling well and active enough. For the first time in his life since leaving Oxford he had managed to get out of bed at a reasonable time in the morning—'every morning by eight; at least, not after nine'—until, shortly before midsummer 1766, he had gone to stay with the Thrales and 'the irregularity of that family' had broken his habit. He had 'indeed done but little' in the longer mornings he had gained for himself, as he had had to admit to Bennet Langton, yet it had been 'no slight advancement' to obtain for so many hours more, 'the consciousness of being'. In the spring of 1766 he had moved into a new study at Johnson's Court, 'an upper room with the advantages of a good light and free air'; he had even bought himself a new brown wig. And although he lapsed into his old habits of lying abed in the mornings during the three months he spent at Streatham in the summer and autumn of 1766, he was able to rise regularly for early prayers during a subsequent month's visit he paid to Oxford. But then, towards the end of 1766 and, throughout the next two years, he seems to have been in poor physical health and deep mental distress.

There were periods when he appeared content and even cheerful. During one of his visits to Oxford to help Chambers with his lectures, Boswell who followed him there found Johnson in expansive and talkative mood and in excellent conversational form.

When Boswell asked him whether he, 'as a moralist did not think that the practice of the law, in some degree, hurt the nice feeling of honesty', he gave a characteristically forceful reply, concluding, 'Why, no, Sir. Everybody knows you are paid for affecting warmth for your client; and it is, therefore, properly no dissimulation: the moment you come from the bar you resume your usual behaviour. Sir, a man will no more carry the artifice of the bar into the common intercourse of society, than a man who is paid for tumbling upon his hands will continue to tumble upon his hands when he should walk on his feet.'

They talked, too, of course, of Scotland; and Johnson teased Boswell with all his former zest when it was suggested that the Scotch had made a 'great advancement' in literature.

'Sir, you have learned a little from us, and you think yourselves very great men. Hume would never have written History, had not Voltaire written it before him. He is an echo of Voltaire.'

'But, Sir, we have Lord Kames.'

'You *have* Lord Kames. Keep him; *Ha, ha, ha!* We don't envy you him. . . . Do you ever see Dr Robertson?'

'Yes, Sir.'

'Does the dog talk of me?'

'Indeed, Sir, he does and loves you,' Boswell replied, and thinking he now had Johnson in a corner, asked him what he thought of Robertson's *History of Scotland.*

But Johnson escaped: 'Sir, I love Robertson, and I won't talk of his book.'

The conversation then turned to 'the future life of brutes', a doctrine which was supported by a gentleman 'who seemed fond of curious speculation'. This talk was not at all to the taste of Johnson who 'did not like to hear of anything concerning a future state which was not authorized by the regular canons of orthodoxy'.

He endeavoured to discourage the talk, and, when it continued, waited for an opportunity to knock the 'poor speculatist' down. He did not have long to wait. 'But really, Sir, when we see a very sensible dog,' said the gentleman, with what Boswell described as 'a serious metaphysical pensive face', 'we don't know what to think of him.'

'Johnson, rolling with joy at the thought which beamed in his eye, turned quickly round, and replied, "True, Sir: and when we see a very foolish *fellow*, we don't know what to think of *him*." He then rose up, strided to the fire, and stood for some time laughing and exulting.'[4]

But these moods when he could roll with joy were transitory, and, on occasions, he seemed close to that complete mental collapse which had threatened him in 1764 when Dr Adams had discovered him pacing up and down his rooms, talking to himself in the utmost agitation. In November 1766 his diary jottings became incoherent:

Remember—Mother one Sunday between Church and supper lay with the children on the bed.
Mother after my father's death.
Christ did not dye in vain.
Lucy there are six days in the week.

Soon after this was written he was staying once more in his father's house, where, in August 1767, to his great grief and perturbation, Kitty Chambers lay dying. He took communion with her on 17 August and kissed her and 'was for some time distracted'. When the end at last came he 'desired all to withdraw,' as he recorded in his diary, 'then told her that we were to part for ever, that as Christians we should part with prayer, and that I would, if she was willing, say a short prayer beside her. She expressed great desire to hear me, and held up her poor hands, as she lay in bed, with great fervour, while I prayed, kneeling by her. . . . I then kissed her. She told me that to part was the greatest pain that she had ever felt, and that she hoped we would meet again in a better place. I expressed with swelled eyes and great emotion of tenderness the same hopes. We kissed and parted, I humbly hope, to meet again, and to part no more.'

Towards the end of the year, he left Lichfield. He had been a long while there, he told a friend on his return to London, 'but he had grown very weary before he left it'. He had also been, as his diary shows, 'disturbed and unsettled . . . without resolution to apply to study or to business'. He gave up eating supper and drinking wine; he doctored himself with purges; and for a time he obtained some relief. But on his fifty-ninth birthday on 18 September 1768, while staying with Francis Brooke, an attorney and friend of the Thrales, at Townmalling in Kent, he felt constrained to write in his diary, 'How the last year has past I am unwilling to terrify myself with thinking. This day has been past in great perturbation. I was distracted at Church in an uncommon degree, and my distress has had very little intermission. . . . This day it came into my mind to write the history of my melancholy. On this I purpose to deliberate. I know not whether it may not too much disturb me.'

Evidently, he decided it would much disturb him; and as he later told Boswell, it was as well to make it an invariable and obligatory law never to mention your own mental diseases. 'If you are never to speak of them, you will think on them but little, and if you think little of them, they will molest you rarely.'

Yet he did not forbear to write about his own mental distress in his journal, while recording his physical ailments with meticulous care. He appears to have been in almost continual pain or discomfort, from intermittent attacks of diarrhoea, from breathlessness, from 'Spasms in the throat and in the stomach', from 'Lumbago, or Rheumatism in the Loins, which often passes to the muscles of the belly, where it causes equal, if not greater, pain'. In the night, he complained, this pain 'is so troublesome as not very easily to be born. I lye wrapped in Flannel with a very great fire near my bed, but whether it be that a recumbent posture encreases the pain, or that expansion by moderate warmth excites what a great heat dissipates, I can seldom remain in bed two hours at a time without the necessity of rising to heat the parts affected at the fire.' Even when not kept awake by the pain of the rheumatism, he was woken by his bladder, closing his mind to the idea that this might be due to the enormous quantities of tea he drank before going to bed, and often he would lie awake troubled by 'terrours' and by 'bad and troublesome thoughts'. He sought relief in opium; he laid blisters to his back; he had hot baths—though as he admitted, he had no greater a passion for immersion than he had for clean linen—he was often blooded. But he gained only intermittent relief. On his sixtieth birthday in 1769 he wrote of the past year having been spent 'in a slow progress of recovery', though he was conscious of having 'grown fat too fast' and the 'perturbation' of his nights was still 'very distressful'. A few weeks later he was praying to God to look down with pity upon the diseases of his body and the continuing perturbations of his mind, a prayer he repeated some weeks later, on New Year's Day 1770.

On Good Friday that year he went back to Johnson's Court from the Thrales so that he could spend the day fasting unobserved. He did not go to church in the morning, because it was cold and he did not want to aggravate his rheumatism, but thinking that he might be using his ill-health as an excuse, he went in the afternoon, arriving late as usual. He succeeded in maintaining his fast all day long, having 'nothing but water once in the morning and once at bedtime. I refused tea,' he noted, 'after some hesitation', adding pathetically, as though this made his abstinence less commendable, 'they did not press it'. In the evening he returned to the Thrales where he passed 'a very tedious and painful night'. 'The pain harrasses me much,' he recorded, 'yet many have the disease perhaps in a much higher degree with want of food, fire, and covering.' He, on the other hand, though his suffering was 'grievous', had all 'the succours that riches and kindness can buy and give'.

Indeed, the kindness, the comforts, the reassuring and continuing companionship, the shelter of family life that the Thrales provided for him had now become the mainstays of his life.

10
Streatham Park

'How many times has this great, this formidable Doctor Johnson kissed my hand, ay and my foot too upon his knees! Strange Connections there are in this odd World.'   Hester Thrale

When not so ill that he was forced to stay in bed, Johnson found as much contentment at the Thrales as he had ever found anywhere. Though quite at home he was 'yet looked up to with an awe, tempered by affection, and seemed to be equally the care of his host and hostess'.

He needed their care for he was not an easy guest, requiring almost constant companionship and attention. There was usually someone other than his hostess who could be prevailed to sit up with him at night while he drank his tea at Streatham, but when he was her guest in Southwark she often was reluctantly persuaded to sit up with him until four o'clock in the morning herself. She did not resent this in the early years of their friendship, for her affection for him was as deep as her respect. 'Well does he contradict the Maxim of Rochefoucault, that no Man is a Hero to his Valet de Chambre,' she wrote in her diary. 'Johnson is more a hero to me than to anyone—and I have been more to him for Intimacy, than ever was any Man's Valet de Chambre.' For his part, he continued to treat her with that same playful, teasing, affectionate fondness which he displayed to all young ladies to whom he was attracted, as when he would lightly reproach her for her malicious and chattering tongue. 'I have been thinking this Morning what Creature you most resemble,' he once told her, ''tis the Rattle Snake; I am sure you have its

Attractions, I think you have its *Venom* too, and all the World knows you have its *Rattle*.'

Conscious of how much he owed to his hospitality and generosity, Johnson treated Henry Thrale with unfailing courtesy and respect, never attempting to beat him down in conversation or to question his commands; and this, on one memorable occasion, led Hester to burst out in anger against him. It was after a dinner party during which the master of the household had cruelly displayed his susceptibility to the charms of the beautiful, seductive Sophy Streatfeild. Hester, in the last stages of one of her numerous pregnancies and very low-spirited, had been sitting at dinner between Johnson and Edmund Burke when her husband asked her to change places with Sophy who was 'threatened with a sore throat and might be injured by sitting near the door':

> I had scarcely swallowed a spoonful of soup when this occurred [Mrs Thrale recalled], and was so overcast by the coarseness of the proposal, that I burst into tears, said something petulant—that perhaps ere long, the lady might be at the head of Mr T's table, without displacing the mistress of the house &c., and so left the apartment. I retired to the drawing-room, and for an hour or two contended with my vexations, as I best could, when Johnson and Burke came up. On seeing them, I resolved to give a *jobation* to both, but fixed on Johnson for my charge, and asked him if he had noticed what passed, what I had suffered, and whether allowing for the state of my nerves, I was much to blame? He answered, 'Why, possibly not, your feelings were outraged.' I said, 'Yes, greatly so; and I cannot help remarking with what blandness and composure you *witnessed* the outrage. Had this transaction been told of others your anger would have known no bounds; but, towards a man who gives good dinners, &c., you were meekness itself!' Johnson coloured, and Burke, I thought, looked foolish; but I had not a word of answer from either.

Johnson also meekly accepted his host's decision that there would be no more chemical experiments performed at Streatham when Johnson was found one day, surrounded by children and servants, about to astonish them by the mysteries of science. He even accepted the rebukes of his host when he was being overbearing or unduly loquacious at the dinner table. 'There, there, now we have had enough for one lecture, Dr Johnson,' Thrale would say, or something like this. 'We will not be upon education any more till after dinner, *if* you please.' And Johnson would obediently desist.

He also raised no objection when Thrale's valet-de-chambre, on instructions from his master, took to the regular habit of standing by the parlour door when the bell rang for dinner and of offering Dr Johnson a decent wig in exchange for the one he wore, the foretop of which, like all its fellows, was burned down to the very network through its owner's practice of short-sightedly reading books in bed so close to the flame of a candle that the hairs were scorched off.

When Henry Thrale was not there to control him, Johnson's behaviour at the dinner table was frequently intimidating. After one particular dinner party at Streatham, William Weller Pepys trusted that it would never be his fate to pass such a day again. Pepys had gently criticised one of Johnson's works, and, 'the moment the cloth was removed', Johnson challenged him 'to *come out* (as he called it)', and say what he had to object to it. 'Come forth, man,' Johnson shouted, 'What have you to say, Sir. . . . What are your objections? If you have anything to say, let's hear it. Come forth, man, when I call you.' 'This, as you see,' Pepys explained to a friend, 'was a call which, however disagreeable to myself and the rest of the company, I could not but obey, and so *to it we went* for three or four hours without ceasing . . . We shook hands, however, at parting.'

While the dispute lasted, so Fanny Burney said, Johnson 'was so red, poor Mr Pepys so pale. . . . He fairly bullied him into a quarrel. . . . He was unreasonably furious and grossly severe. . . . His vehemence and bitterness [were] almost incredible.'

Mrs Thrale was so upset that upon being given a tumbler of champagne by the butler, instead of the water she had asked for, she drank it off without noticing the difference until she had finished it. Then, after upbraiding the butler for his mistake, she became so frightened by having drunk so much champagne that she drank glass after glass of water, 'and that occupied her, so entirely, that she could attend to nothing at all else'.

Fortunately the quarrel was brought to an end by the ludicrous and persistent interventions of John Cator, a timber merchant who gave his opinion 'quite uncalled', Fanny Burney wrote in her diary, 'upon everything that was said by either party, and that with an importance and pomposity, yet with an emptiness and verbosity, that rendered the whole dispute, when in his hands, nothing more than ridiculous, and compelled even the disputants themselves, all inflamed as they were, to laugh'.

Mr Cator could not exactly speak to the purpose as he had not actually read the work in question, though he had read another in the same series. He had bought it, however, for he had ordered it the week before, and it had arrived on Thursday, together with the other in the series which he had begun to read first. But he had heard that the subject of the book under discussion had a steward who had dunned William Shenstone for his rent. Now, if Shenstone was, indeed, a tenant of his, why had he not paid the rent? After dinner, Mr Cator had started to read the book so that he could better understand the cause; and later, in the drawing-room, he entered the dispute once more. He had not yet got quite through the book, so what he was going to say must be considered as being only said aside, but what he was going to say was . . .

Here Mrs Thrale, recovered from her champagne, interrupted her tiresome guest. 'I wish, sir, that it had been *all* set aside. . . . I should be very glad to hear no more of it.' This request, uttered with great spirit and dignity, brought the disputants to silence; and, after a pause, Johnson said, 'Well, Madam, you *shall* hear no more of it. Yet I will defend myself in every part and every atom.'

Sometimes Johnson's behaviour at table was positively alarming, as when, after being repeatedly pressed to eat something by a lady sitting next to him—an importunity that frequently enraged him—he suddenly rose to his feet, his knife in his hand, exclaiming loudly, 'I vow to God I cannot eat a bit more,' to the great terror, it was said, of the entire company.[1] He would also 'bolt up in the midst of a mixed company', Adam Smith recalled, 'and without any previous notice, fall upon his knees behind a chair, repeat the Lord's Prayer and then resume his seat at table. He has played this freak over and over, perhaps five or six times in the course of an evening. It is not hypocrisy, but madness.' Joshua Reynolds's sister, Frances, confirmed that 'in Lent, or near the approach of any great festival, he would generally retire from the company to a corner of the room, but most commonly behind a window-curtain, to pray, and with such energy, and in so loud a whisper, that every word was heard distinctly, particularly the Lord's Prayer and the Apostles' Creed, with which he constantly concluded his devotions. Sometimes some words would emphatically escape him in his usual tone of voice.'

He would also rise from the table when he wanted to blow his nose, holding it ill-mannered to use a pocket-handkerchief at meals. On these occasions he would retreat some distance from his chair and, with his back towards the company, perform the operation as silently as possible. This was but one expression of his confidence in himself as an authority on good manners. 'Every man of education,' he once said to the astonishment of the assembled company, 'would rather be called a rascal than accused of deficiency in *the graces*.' And he obviously meant to include himself. To be sure, he ate fish with his fingers; but this, he explained, was merely because otherwise he could not find the bones. As a self-professed expert on polite conduct, he did not hesitate to criticise the ill behaviour of others at table, so Miss Reynolds said; 'particularly for their perversion of the idea of refinement in the use of a water-glass, a very strange perversion indeed he thought it. . . . It was amazing,' she added, 'so dim-sighted as Dr Johnson was, how very observant he was of appearances in Dress, in behaviour, and even of the servants, how they waited at table, etc., *the more particularly so, seeming as he did to be stone-blind to his own* dress and behaviour. One day as his man Frank was waiting at Sir Joshua's table, he observed with some emotion, that he had the salver under his arm.' On other occasions he lamented that the art of carving had been lost in England. No one understood this art better than himself, he insisted, and he deeply regretted that, being so nearsighted, it would be highly indecorous of him to attempt it in company as it required a sus-pension of his breath during the operation. 'It must be owned, indeed,' Miss Reynolds commented, 'that it was to be regretted that he did not practise a little of that delicacy in eating, for he appeared to want breath more at that time than usual.'

Miss Reynolds explained that Johnson was able to notice such things as Frank holding a salver under his arm, to describe minutely a person's dress and appearance, because he did not hesitate to get close enough to them to see them well. Certainly Arthur Murphy saw him one day as he sat at table next to 'the celebrated Mrs Cholmondeley', take hold of her hand, in the middle of dinner, and lift it up 'close to his eye, wondering at the delicacy and whiteness, till, with a smile, she said, "Will he give it to me again when he has done with it."'

Although he was usually gallantry itself in the presence of ladies he could not always control his irritation if they were stupid or verbose. William Seward, a rich young dilettante whom Johnson often met at the Thrales, recorded that he was 'one day in company with a very talkative lady, of whom he appeared to take very little notice. "Why, Doctor, I believe you prefer the company of men to that of the ladies." "Madam," replied he, "I am very fond of the company of ladies, I like their beauty, I like their delicacy, I like their vivacity, and I like their *silence*."' And the writer, the Rev Percival Stockdale, when tutor to the eldest son of Lord Craven, overheard Johnson deliver another flattening snub to one Mrs Bruce, an old Scottish widow who spoke in the full dialect of her country. 'Dr Johnson,' she said to him in the manner of a dominie, 'you tell us in your Dictionary that in England oats are given to horses; but that in Scotland they support the people. Now, Sir, I can assure you, that in Scotland we give oats to our horses, as well as you do in England.' Johnson threw her what Stockdale described as 'a contemptuous leer', but deigned to answer, 'I am very glad, Madam, to find that you treat your horses as well as you treat yourselves.'

Usually, however, he was far more ready to stand corrected by a lady than by a man, particularly by a pretty young lady, though few of these could be found with courage enough to stand up to him. During dinner one day at Sir Joshua Reynolds's the conversation turned to music of which Johnson spoke as disdainfully as usual, remarking that 'no man of talent, or whose mind was capable of better things, ever would or could devote his time to so idle and frivolous a pursuit. A niece of Sir Joshua, who was fond of music, whispered as Johnson reached the end of his provocative condemnation, 'I wonder what Dr Johnson thinks of King David.'

'Madam, I thank you,' said Johnson with great good humour. 'I stand rebuked before you, and promise that, on one subject at least, you shall never hear me talk nonsense again.'[2]

Sometimes, of course, he felt that young ladies required correction. When, for instance, he was visiting the house of a rich merchant who, in displaying his treasures, observed of one of them, 'And this, Dr Johnson, is *Vesuvius* Caesar', a young lady present could not suppress a titter. Johnson strongly rebuked her with words that discomfited the merchant as much as herself. 'What is the child laughing at? Ignorance is a subject for pity—not for laughter.'

Nor did he like young ladies to flatter him excessively, fond though he was of praise. To one who persisted in her extravagant compliments after he had told her to desist, he said, 'My dear, before you are so lavish of your praise, you ought to consider whether it be worth having.' Two others, who visited him as he sat at work, obliging him to lay down his pen while one of them recited a lengthy and enthusiastic effusion to which they awaited his response with bated breath, he deflated by replying, 'Fiddle-de-dee, my dears.'[3]

Usually, though, as he said himself, he loved 'to see a knot of little misses dearly', and he behaved towards them, and to their mothers, with the most fastidious courtesy, escorting them down the stairs, out into the court and then down Fleet Street to their carriage, however far away it was stationed, with such an air of importance and courtliness that crowds gathered to watch the diverting performance.

Topham Beauclerk recalled one such occasion when Madame de Boufflers, on her first visit to London, called upon him. Having taken her leave of him, she was accompanied downstairs by Beauclerk when all at once a noise like thunder shook the building.

This [Beauclerk related] was occasioned by Johnson, who, it seems, upon a little recollection, had taken it into his head that he ought to have done the honours of his literary residence to a foreign lady of quality, and eager to show himself a man of gallantry, was hurrying down the stair-case in violent agitation. He overtook us before we reached the Temple-gate, and brushing in between me and Madame de Boufflers, seized her hand, and conducted her to her coach. His dress was a rusty brown morning suit, a pair of old shoes by way of slippers, a little shrivelled wig sticking on the top of his head, and the sleeves of his shirt and the knees of his breeches hanging loose. A considerable crowd of people gathered round, and were not a little struck by his singular appearance.

Ladies of rank particularly appealed to Johnson. 'Adventitious accomplishments may be possessed by all ranks,' he told Dr William Maxwell, 'but one may easily distinguish the *born gentlewoman*.' If the gentlewoman were also young and lively so much the greater, of course, was Johnson's admiration; and if she praised his work intelligently or complimented him gracefully he was enchanted. 'Boswell,' he would sometimes call out—as Samuel Richardson might have done—when wishing to draw attention to a particularly pleasing compliment which had been paid to him by Lady Anne Lindsay, 'what was it that the young lady of quality said of me at Sir Alexander Dick's?'

He was also enchanted by the Hon Mary Monckton, who later became the Countess of Cork and Orrery, to whom he used to talk 'with all imaginable ease'. One day they disagreed about Sterne's writings which she thought 'very pathetic' and he did not. 'I am sure,' she persisted, 'that they have affected me.'

'Why,' said Johnson, rolling about and smiling at her, 'that is, because, dearest, you are a dunce.'

Sometime afterwards she reminded him of this observation, and he assured her warmly, 'Madam, if I had thought so, I certainly should not have said it.'

Another particular favourite of his was Hannah More whose poetry he praised with flattering extravagance and in whose presence he nearly always seems to have been 'very good-humoured and gay'. 'Hush!

Hush!' he commanded the guests at a party where poetry was being discussed in her presence. 'It is dangerous to say a word of poetry before her. It is talking of the art of war before Hannibal.' She was delighted, she later told him, by his approbation of her work. 'And so you may,' he answered her, 'for I give you the opinion of a man who does not rate his judgement in these things very low, I can tell you.'

Tuesday evening we drank tea at Sir Joshua's with Dr Johnson [Sarah More told another of her sisters]. Hannah is certainly a great favourite. She was placed next to him, and they had the entire conversation to themselves. They were both in remarkably high spirits; it was certainly her lucky night! I never heard her say so many good things. The old genius was extremely jocular, and the young one very pleasant. You would have imagined we had been at some comedy had you heard our peals of laughter.

Provocative, rude, ill-mannered and freakish as Johnson appears in the recollection of those, like Adam Smith, who did not like him, to others his behaviour seemed only mildly idiosyncratic. Richard Cumberland, for instance, claimed never to have found him morose or ill-humoured, but cheerful, kind and even, at this period of his life, neatly clothed.[4] 'He presented himself always in his fashion of apparel,' Cumberland wrote. 'A brown coat with metal buttons, black waistcoat and worsted stockings, with a flowing bob wig was the style of his wardrobe, but they were in perfectly good trim, and with the ladies, which he generally met, he had nothing of the slovenly philosopher about him; he fed heartily, but not voraciously, and was extremely courteous in his commendations of any dish, that pleased his palate: he suffered his next neighbour to squeeze the China oranges into his wine glass after dinner, which else perchance had gone aside, and trickled into his shoes, for the good man had neither straight sight nor steady nerves.'

No one denied, however, that Johnson's behaviour in the street and when rambling about in the country was often inexplicably eccentric. When walking by himself in London he lumbered clumsily along, rolling his head about constantly from side to side, yet he nevertheless got about at a great pace, moving in a zig-zag course from one side of the street to the other so far as crowds and carriages would allow, often knocking into other pedestrians while remaining unaware of the collision, tapping the street posts with his stick and going back if he missed one. Bennet Langton saw him one day suddenly lurch to one side and bump into a porter, pushing the load off his back. Johnson walked on briskly, unconscious of what he had done. The porter 'was very angry, but stood still, and eyed the huge figure with much earnestness, till he was satisfied that his wisest course was to be quiet, and take up his burthen again'.

Johnson's left arm remained fixed across his breast, the hand under his chin; in his right hand he carried his heavy stick; his pockets bulged with books. On occasions he would suddenly stop as though he had forgotten something and then move on once more appearing to count his steps. If for some reason the count was unsatisfactory he would retrace his steps and begin the process all over again. Sometimes when he came to one of his abrupt halts, he would turn round and lumber off in the opposite direction; and Boswell recalled one evening, when they were going together to have supper with Beauclerk, Johnson 'suddenly stopped and said, "I cannot go", adding with emphatic earnestness, *"But I do not love Beauclerk the less."*'

On other occasions when he suddenly stopped in his tracks, he would perform with his feet and hands a series of antics so strange that a crowd would gather around him laughing or staring. As if oblivious to their presence, he would either hold out his arms with some of the fingers bent, as though he had been seized by cramp, or he would hold them high and stiff above his head, or, alternatively, close to his chest, when he would agitate them up and down in the manner of a jockey holding the reins of a horse galloping at full speed. At the same time he formed his feet into the shape of a V with either the heels together or the toes. Having twisted his limbs into the required postures, with many corrections and alterations of their relative positions, he would finally take a great leap forward and walk on with the satisfied air of a man who had performed a necessary duty and who seemed totally unconscious of having done anything odd.

Thomas Tyers, an occasional author, joint-manager of Vauxhall gardens, a great favourite with Johnson, believed that these gestures were involuntary, a kind of St Vitus's dance, for Johnson was 'to the last a *convulsionary*'. Tyers said that when walking with Johnson he 'often looked another way, as the companions of Peter the Great were used to do', when Johnson 'stept aside, to let nature do what she could with him'. A more exact observer, Frances Reynolds, however, thought that his 'extraordinary gestures or anticks with his hands and feet' were deliberately calculated for some reason rather than the 'natural effects of a nervous disorder'. For, as her brother confirmed, he sat perfectly still when having his portrait painted without even rolling his body about as he otherwise did almost perpetually. Moreover, he was able to control himself if someone spoke to him while he was in the middle of his manœuvres. When he and Sir Joshua Reynolds had been on their way to Devonshire in 1762 they had called to see Corfe Castle, the owner of which, John Bankes, showed them round 'with great civility, politely attending them through the apartments, etc., in the finest of which Dr Johnson began to exhibit his Anticks, stretching out his legs alternately as far as he could possibly stretch; and at the same time pressing his foot on the floor as heavily as he could possibly press, as if endeavouring to smooth the carpet, or rather perhaps to rumple it, and every now and then collecting all his force, apparently to effect a concussion of the floor. Mr Bankes, regarding him for some time with silent astonishment, at last said, "Dr Johnson, I believe the floor is very firm"; which immediately made him desist.'

Sir Joshua's sister remembered one Sunday morning walking with him in Twickenham meadows when he stopped in his tracks and deliberately began 'his ludicrous beat' which was 'so extraordinary that men, women and children gathered round him, laughing. At last we sat down on some logs of wood by the river side and they nearly dispersed, when he pulled out of his pocket Grotius's "De Veritate Religionis" [it being his custom always to carry a religious treatise in his pocket on a Sunday] over which he see-sawed at such a violent rate as to excite the curiosity of some people at a distance to come and see what was the matter with him.'

Johnson was particularly prone to carry out his gyrations at the threshold of a door; and Miss Reynolds graphically described how in entering her brother's house 'with poor Mrs Williams, a blind lady who lived with him, he would quit her hand, or else whirl her about on the steps as he whirled and twisted about to perform his gesticulations; and as soon as he had finish'd, he would give a sudden spring, and make such an extensive stride over the threshold, as if he was trying for a wager how far he could stride, Mrs Williams standing groping about outside the door, unless the servant, or the mistress of the House more commonly, took hold of her hand to conduct her in, leaving Dr Johnson to perform at the Parlour Door much the same exercise over again.'

He would even sometimes go through this procedure in the middle of a room, 'as if trying to make the floor to shake'; and he would greatly alarm ladies sitting round a tea-table by tapping his feet on the floor while at the same time stretching out his arm in every direction with a full cup of tea in his hand to the 'imminent danger of their cloaths. Sometimes he would twist himself round with his face close to the back of his chair, and finish his cup of tea, breathing very hard, as if making a laborious effort to accomplish it.' Boswell confirmed that 'while talking or even musing as he sat in his chair, he commonly held his head to one side towards his right shoulder, and shook it in a tremulous manner, moving his body backwards and forwards, and rubbing his left knee in the same direction, with the palm of his hand. In the intervals of articulating he made various sounds with his mouth; sometimes as if ruminating, or what is called chewing the cud, sometimes giving a half whistle, sometimes making his tongue play backwards from the roof of his mouth, as if chucking like a hen, and sometimes protruding it against his upper gums in front, as if pronouncing quickly under his breath, "*Too, too, too.*" All this accompanied sometimes with a thoughtful look, but more frequently with a smile. Generally when he had concluded a period, in the course of a dispute, by which time he was a good deal exhausted by violence and vociferation, he used to blow out his breath like a whale. This I suppose was a relief to his lungs; and seemed in him to be a contemptuous mode of expression, as if he had made the arguments of his opponents fly like chaff before the wind.'

Why did he do all these extraordinary things, a young child, Christopher Smart's niece, asked him innocently one day. 'From bad habit,' he replied gently. 'Do you, my dear, take care to guard against bad habits.'

Out of doors his sudden whims to perform some physical feat were often as disconcerting as his necromantic gestures. On a visit to Langton he once took it into his head to take a roll down a very steep hill behind the house. Bennet Langton and his father endeavoured to dissuade him; but he was determined to do it, insisting that he had not had a roll for a long time. So, emptying his pockets of keys, pencil, purse and penknife, he lay down at the summit, turned himself over it and rolled over and over to the bottom. Similarly when staying with John Taylor he suddenly decided to increase the flow of a waterfall in the grounds. He seized a long pole which was lying on the bank and worked frantically until he was quite out of breath levering away the branches of trees and other obstacles in the water's path.

He strongly fancied himself as a fast runner, and one day when a spacious lawn prompted a young lady to boast that she could run faster than anybody, he immediately challenged her. 'Madam, you cannot run faster than me'; and nor indeed could she. She outstripped him at first; but he kicked off his shoes and then caught up with her, overtook her, and won the race easily. This done, he led her back to the house 'highly delighted' by his achievement. An even easier victory was scored over John Payne, the Castle Street bookseller, a tiny man, whom Johnson challenged to a race while they were out together on a country ramble. They ran along side by side for a time until Johnson picked up his little adversary, placed him on the bough of a tree and, having thus disposed of competition, went on to win the race. He then returned and exultantly picked down his friend from his uncomfortable perch.

As well as enjoying running and rolling, Johnson never lost his taste for climbing trees and jumping over gates. He was getting on for sixty when he exclaimed, 'Why I can swarm it now,' in answer to someone who pointed out a large tree in the grounds of Gunnersbury House that he had climbed as a boy. To prove the boast was not an idle one, he climbed it there and then, and when at last he came down again 'with a triumphant air' he encouraged his companions to suppose that his making such a climb was an everyday occurrence. Similarly, on his visits to Lichfield he delighted in jumping over the stiles that he had vaulted as a boy; and on arriving late for dinner one day at a house outside Lichfield on Stowe Hill he astonished his hostess, Mrs Gastrell, by climbing over the great carriage gate at the end of the drive instead of using the smaller gate for foot passengers. Mrs Gastrell asked him if he had forgotten the smaller gate. 'No, my dear lady,' he replied, 'but I had a mind to try whether I could climb a gate now as I used to when I was a lad.'

He was obviously very proud of these sorts of accomplishments, and of his great physical strength which allowed him, his friend, Wickens, was astonished to discover, to tug out a nail driven into the trunk of a plum tree. When, after 'Herculean' efforts he had accomplished his task, he exclaimed, 'There, Sir, I have done *some* good to-day; the tree might have festered. I make a rule, Sir, to do some good every day of my life.'

He took great pride in having had an uncle, Andrew—his father's brother—who, as a bookseller's apprentice had been a notable boxer and wrestler and had held the ring at Smithfield against all comers for a whole year and never was thrown or conquered. He was also pleased to remember how as a young man he was attacked one night in a street in London by four men and had succeeded in holding them all at bay until the watch came up. He was sorry, he said, that prize-fighting had gone out; the art of defence was surely important and prize-fighting made people 'accustomed not to be alarmed at seeing their own blood, or feeling a little pain from a wound'. Mrs Thrale said that he was himself 'very conversant in the art of attack and defence by boxing' and would descant upon it 'much to the admiration of those who had no expectation of his skill in such matters'.

It was well known that he could practise what he preached and could never be intimidated by the threat of physical violence. When he was threatened by James Macpherson, the authenticity of whose translations of Ossianic poems he denied, Johnson, in acknowledging his 'foolish and impudent letter', defied his rage. And when Samuel Foote announced that he would imitate Johnson on the stage, Johnson asked Thomas Davies the common price of an oak stick. On being informed it was sixpence, Johnson said, 'Why then, Sir, give me leave to send your servant to purchase me a shilling one. I'll have a double quantity; for I am told Foote means to *take me off*, as he calls it, and I am determined the fellow shall not do it with impunity.' Davies told Foote of Johnson's intentions, and the project of taking Johnson off was abandoned.

As an instance of Johnson's strength, Garrick recalled an evening in Lichfield when a troupe of travelling players were performing in the Guildhall. Johnson had a seat on the stage between the side screens which he left for a time and which, upon his return, he found occupied by a local innkeeper. Johnson told the man the place was his and asked him to give it up to him. The man, encouraged by a Scottish officer who had conceived a dislike for Johnson, refused; so Johnson picked up the chair with the innkeeper in it and hurled them both 'at one jerk into the pit'. When the hubbub had abated, he sat through the rest of the performance with 'great composure'.

No compliments delighted Johnson more than those paid to his strength or agility as when at Brighton with the Thrales one of the 'dippers' on the beach said to him as he emerged from a swim in the sea, 'Why, Sir, you must have been a stout-hearted gentleman forty years ago!' And when Johnson was told that William Gerard Hamilton had exclaimed upon seeing him ride a horse across Sussex Downs, 'Why Johnson rides as well, for aught I see, as the most illiterate fellow in England!' it seemed to Mrs Thrale that he had never been better pleased by a compliment in his life.

He did not enjoy riding, however, and although he occasionally hunted with Thrale for fifty miles on end, priding himself on the fact that he rode harder at a fox chase than anybody—unlike the French who capered about on managed horses and would as soon have leaped a hedge as mounted a breach—he did not take much pleasure in hunting either. 'It is very strange and very melancholy,' he thought, 'that the paucity of human pleasures should persuade us ever to call hunting one of them.'

It was the domestic enjoyments and gastronomic delights of Streatham that really pleased him.

The house was large and imposing when Mrs Thrale first moved into it, and her husband was constantly making additions and alterations, adding a new wing in 1773, remodelling and redecorating the interior, making a lake in 1777, until to one visitor, Fanny Burney's sister, Susan, it seemed 'a little Paradise . . . worthy of the charming inhabitants. . . . Cattle, poultry, dogs all running freely about without annoying each other.' The park extended to a hundred acres; and in the greenhouses and kitchen gardens grew those fruits and vegetables that appeared in such profusion and variety on the dining-room table. Johnson alone regularly accounted for as many as sixteen peaches a day, devouring eight before breakfast and another eight or so after dinner.

One of the greatest pleasures of Streatham in addition to the fruit—of which Johnson thought no man could ever get enough—were the children to whom Mrs Thrale gave birth with seasonal regularity. Johnson once told her that if he had a child of his own he did not think that he would have had much fondness for it. Knowing how fond he was of her children, she protested, 'Nay, Sir, how can you talk so?' And he replied, 'At least I never wished to have a child.'

To the Thrale children, however, he was devoted, particularly to the eldest of the girls, Hester Maria, known as Queeney.[5] As soon as she was old enough to understand them he wrote little poems for her, he played games with her, made collections of 'curiosities' with her, took her for rides on his back, and directed her education with care. By the time she was six he thought her 'cadence, variety, and choice of tones in reading verse [were] surpassed by nobody not even Garrick himself'. When she was eight and he was staying with John Taylor at Ashbourne he wrote the second of his surviving letters to her:

Dear Sweeting,

Your pretty letter was too short. If Lucy is not good, you must try to mend her by good advice, and good example, for all the little girls will try to be like you. I am glad to hear of the improvement and prosperity of my hen. Miss Porter has buried her fine black cat. So things come and go. Generations, as Homer says, are but like leaves; and you now see the faded leaves falling about you.

You are sorry to come to town, and I am sorry for dear Grandmama
that will be left in the country, be sure that you make my compliments
to her.

I am, Dear Miss,
Your most obedient servant
Sam: Johnson

In another letter written that same month, he told her how much he
would love reading her own, 'if they were a little longer. But we shall
soon, I hope,' he went on, 'talk matters all over. I have not had the luck
this journey to pick up any curiosities for the cabinet. I would have been
glad to bring you something, if I could have found it. . . . You said
nothing of Lucy, I suppose she is grown a pretty good scholar, and a very
good playfellow; after dinner we shall have good sport playing all
together, and we will none of us cry. Make my compliments to Grandmama, and Papa, and Mama, and all the young ones.'[6]

It was the opinion of Queeney's mother that it was the 'memory of
what had passed in his own childhood' that made Johnson 'very solicitous
to preserve the felicity of children'. He insisted that they ought to be
indulged—although he also insisted that they ought to be beaten if they
did not do their lessons properly—and was even, Mrs Thrale said,
'scrupulously and ceremoniously attentive not to offend them. He had
strongly persuaded himself of the difficulty people always find to erase
early impressions either of kindness or resentment, and said, "he should
never have so loved his mother when a man, had she not given him coffee
she could ill afford, to gratify his appetite when a boy."'[7]

He was also insistent that children should never be asked to perform
in front of adults as he had been made to do by his father; and when a
proud parent suggested that his two sons recite alternate verses of Gray's
Elegy so Johnson could judge which had the better delivery, he immediately replied, 'No, pray, Sir, let the dears both speak it at once; more
noise by that means will be made, and the noise will be sooner over.'

He could, of course, be highly intimidating as well as indulgent, kind
and playful, humiliating children for the deficiencies or follies of their
parents, as when he took Thomas Percy's little daughter on his knee and
asked her what she thought of *Pilgrim's Progress*. She told him that she had
not read it. 'No,' said Johnson, 'then I would not give one farthing for
you.' He put her down and took no more notice of her. A little girl at
Mrs Gastrel's had a similar experience. She was sent to recite to him
Cato's soliloquy. She got through it successfully, but was unable to

answer his questions about its meaning. Mrs Gastrel intervened on her behalf, saying that the child was much too young to understand such things. So he asked the child, 'My dear, how many pence are there in *sixpence?*' Extremely nervous by now, the girl replied, 'I cannot tell, Sir.' 'Now, my dear lady,' Johnson protested crossly to Mrs Gastrel. 'Can anything be more ridiculous than to teach a child Cato's soliloquy who does not know how many pence there are in sixpence?'

Normally, however, he delighted in the company of children and though he insisted they were 'always cruel', he was constantly giving them sweetmeats, and took the trouble to write to them in a large round hand, resembling printed characters. In the last year of his life he thus addressed his god-daughter, Jane Langton, who was six: 'My dearest Miss Jenny, I am sorry that your pretty letter has been so long without being answered; but when I am not pretty well, I do not always write plain enough for young ladies. I am glad, my dear, to see that you write so well, and hope that you mind your pen, your book, and your needle.'

He knew exactly how to entertain children, and how to amuse them. He liked to pretend, talking in a deep, hollow voice, that he was a giant and that he would take them away with him to his lair. He told one little girl 'that he lived in a cave, and had a bed in the rock, and she should have a little bed cut opposite it!'

His manner or appearance never seems to have frightened children other than those whose behaviour displeased him. Boswell was delighted that his four-month-old daughter, Veronica, was not in the least alarmed by him: 'She had the appearance of listening to him. His motions seemed to her to be intended for her amusement; and when he stopped, she fluttered, and made a little infantine noise, and a kind of signal for him to begin again. She would be held close to him; which was a proof, from simple nature, that his figure was not horrid. Her fondness for him endeared her still more to me, and I declared she should have five hundred pounds of additional fortune.'

One of the greatest pleasures in life, Johnson thought, was to be driven rapidly along in a post-chaise. On one such journey he remarked contentedly to his fellow-passenger, 'Life has not many things better than this.' 'If I had no duties, and no reference to futurity,' he later observed, 'I would spend my life in driving briskly in a post-chaise with a pretty woman; but she should be one who could understand me, and would add something to the conversation.'

'He loved indeed the very act of travelling,' Mrs Thrale said, 'and I cannot tell how far one might have taken him in a carriage before he would have wished for refreshment. He was therefore in some respects an admirable companion on the road, as he piqued himself upon feeling no inconvenience, and on despising no accommodations. On the other hand, however, he expected no one else to feel any, and felt exceedingly inflamed with anger if any one complained of the rain, the sun, or the dust. "How (said he) do other people bear them?"' He also became angry if anyone expressed concern about the possibility of an accident, as accidents, he insisted, with that wild hyperbole he so much condemned in others, 'never happened'.

It was not only the sensation of travelling, 'the very act of going forward', that delighted him. He enjoyed being in a coach because he was assured of companionship there; the other passengers were shut in with him and could not escape as they could out of a room. Moreover, he had no difficulty in hearing what people said for they all sat so close together.

In the late 1760s and early 1770s he was continually on the move, more so than he had ever been in his life before, travelling between Johnson's Court and Streatham, to Lichfield, Oxford, Ashbourne and the south coast.

In the autumn of 1769, after visits earlier in the year to Lichfield and, with Miss Williams, to Oxford, he went on holiday with the Thrales to Brighton which ever since the publication of Dr Richard Russell's *A Dissertation Concerning the use of sea Water in Diseases of the Glands* had been renowned as a health resort. In the spring of the following year he was once more with Robert Chambers at Oxford; in July he went up to Lichfield again and from there went on to Ashbourne to stay with John Taylor; and in the winter he spent a week visiting a friend aboard the *Ramillies* where he felt obliged to rebuke a naval officer for swearing. In 1772 he was again in the Midlands, spending nearly two months at Lichfield and Ashbourne. In all this time he did very little work. Indeed, his friend, Dr William Maxwell, was surprised that he found time to do any work at all and supposed that 'he wrote chiefly in the night'.

Maxwell commonly visited him at noon and found him in bed, 'or declaiming over his tea, which he drank very plentifully. He generally had a levee of morning visitors, chiefly men of letters . . . and sometimes ladies. . . . He seemed to be considered as a kind of public oracle, whom everybody thought they had a right to visit and consult.' Visitors unacquainted with each other were punctiliously introduced by their host who believed that others were most remiss in this respect and who

demonstrated how it should be done by not only enunciating the name
slowly, loudly and distinctly but even by spelling them out—not alway
accurately—letter by letter. Old friends were greeted by the nicknames he
had given them—Bozzy, Lanky, Beau and Mur. Goldsmith was called
Goldy, though he did not like it, thinking it undignified; and in the day
before their quarrel Sheridan was sometimes Sherry, at others Sherry
Derry.

Maxwell could 'scarcely recollect that he ever refused going to a
tavern' with any friend or casual visitor who invited him, and he often
went to Ranelagh, which he deemed 'a place of innocent recreation'
particularly when they had fireworks there. He loved fireworks. He went
to Marylebone Gardens once with George Steevens to see Torré's fire
works, and was so disappointed when the management announced to the
few people present that a shower of rain had dampened the powder and
that consequently the show could not be given, he exclaimed in anger to
Steevens, 'This is a mere excuse to save their crackers for a more profitable
company. Let us both hold up our sticks, and threaten to break those
coloured lamps that surround the orchestra, and we shall soon have our
wishes gratified.' Some young men nearby, hearing his words, immedi
ately attacked the lamps as he had recommended, whereupon the
management agreed to try to set the fireworks off; but they were, as they
had said, too damp to light.

On Sundays, which he insisted should not be kept 'with rigid severity
and gloom, but with a gravity and simplicity of behaviour', Johnson
usually dined at home; and one Sunday, to his 'great surprize', Boswell
received an invitation to a meal. A previous guest had 'hated to see the
victuals paw'd by poor Mrs Williams, that would often carve, though ston
blind'; another, Fanny Burney, had accepted an invitation with pro
found reluctance, afraid that the meal might not be wholesome 'on accoun
of poor blacky'; and, from all that Boswell had heard of Johnson'
domestic arrangements, he supposed that they would 'scarcely hav
knives and forks and only some strange, uncouth, ill-drest fish'. But, o
the contrary, he found everything 'in very good order'.

'I have generally a meat pye on Sunday,' Johnson had told him. 'It
baked at a publick oven, which is very properly allowed, because one ma
can attend it; and thus the advantage is obtained of not keeping servan
from church to dress dinners.' On this occasion, however, Johnson, Mi
Williams, Boswell, and a young woman whom Boswell did not know, sa
down to 'a very good soup, a boiled leg of lamb and spinach, a veal py
and a rice pudding'.

After dinner they sat talking, and Boswell asked Johnson if he would communicate to him the particulars of his early life. 'You shall have them all for two-pence,' Johnson replied. 'I hope you shall know a great deal more of me before you write my life.' He then 'mentioned many circumstances' which Boswell wrote down as soon as he got home.

After his guest had gone, Johnson settled down to read the Bible which he had recently determined to study both in English and Greek with closer attention than he had ever previously found time to give it; and in the evening he went to church and 'was composed'.

To be composed in church was for him an unusual occurrence that merited comment in his journal; for usually he was so disturbed and restless that he found it impossible to sit still. That morning, in fact, he changed his pew three times during Matins at which he had already created a mild disturbance, as he invariably did, by arriving late and lumbering up the aisle at the beginning of the prayers. On other occasions he drew attention to himself by standing up, while the rest of the congregation were receiving the Sacrament, instead of sitting down, a posture which, though usual, he thought improper.

On Good Friday 1773 he went to the church of St Clement Danes with Boswell who had first called at his house in Johnson's Court for breakfast. Boswell had been given tea, made by '*Doctor* Levet, as Frank called him', and cross-buns, but Johnson had nothing but one cup of tea without milk which later made him 'fretful and impatient', unable to fix his mind or govern his thoughts. During the service Boswell found Johnson's behaviour, as he had imagined it, 'solemnly devout'. 'I shall never forget,' he said, 'the tremulous earnestness with which he pronounced the aweful petition in the Litany: "In the hour of death, and at the day of judgment, good Lord deliver us."' 'I hope in time,' Johnson recorded in his journal when the service was over, 'to take pleasure in publick Worship.' He was 'convinced' that he ought to attend divine service more frequently than he did, but the 'provocations given by ignorant and affected preachers too often' disturbed his mental calm. 'I am apt,' he confessed to a friend, 'to whisper to myself on such occasions.'

That Good Friday night he slept very badly and felt a 'very uneasy sensation' both in his stomach and head, 'compounded as it seemed of laxity and pain'. Once more he was deeply concerned about the state of his mind. 'My mind is unsettled and my memory confused,' he wrote. 'I have of late turned my thoughts with a very useless earnestness upon past incidents. I have yet got no command over my thoughts; an unpleasing incident is almost certain to hinder my rest.' He was above all anxious about those 'sinful and corrupt imaginations' that so much distressed him, those 'inordinate desires' and 'wicked thoughts' which he could not drive out of his mind and which he believed it not only dangerous to his sanity to linger upon but also sinful even to entertain. He was constantly disturbed by them. When James Beattie, the poet and philosopher, confessed to him that he was 'at times troubled with shocking impious thoughts', Johnson replied, 'Sir, if I was to divide my life into three parts, two of them have been filled with such thoughts.'

While he was alive Mrs Thrale thought that she alone knew how afraid Johnson was of going mad. He entrusted her with this 'Secret far dearer to him than his Life . . . about the Years 1767 or 1768,' she recorded in her diary in 1779. 'Such however is his nobleness, and such his partiality, that I sincerely believe he has never since that Day regretted his Confidence, or ever looked with less kind Affection on her who had him in her Power.' She did not at that time mention what the secret was 'lest by dying first [her diaries], might be printed and the secret'—for such she thought it—'discovered'. But on reading the *Gentleman's Magazine* for December 1784 she came across an obituary by his friend, Thomas Tyers, in which his fear of insanity was mentioned. 'Poor Johnson!' she then wrote. 'I see they will leave *nothing untold* that I laboured so long to keep secret; and I was so very delicate in trying to conceal his fancied Insanity, that I retained no proofs of it—or hardly any—nor ever mentioned it in these books.'

There was another, deeper secret too. Johnson hinted to Boswell what this might have been in a 'serious conversation on melancholy and madness' which they had together in 1777, a conversation which Boswell modified before describing it in his biography: 'Said he: "A man indulges his imagination while it is pleasing, till at length it overpowers his reason." This I have experienced frequently in a certain degree. He said, "A Madman loves to be with people whom he fears; not as a dog fears the lash, but of whom he stands in awe." This I almost ever experience. . . . He said, "Madmen are all sensual in the lower stages of the distemper. But when they are very ill, pleasure is too weak for them, and they seek pain."'

That Johnson was commenting on his own case seems more than likely, though Boswell clearly had no suspicion of this. In May 1779 Mrs Thrale wrote in her diary, 'And yet says Johnson a Woman has *such* power between the Ages of twenty five and forty five, that She may tye a

Man to a post and whip him if She will.' And to this entry she later added a marginal note, presumably after his secret fear of insanity had been revealed to the world by Thomas Tyers: 'This he knew of him self was *literally* and *strictly* true I am sure.'

A few months after the date of her original entry, in December 1779, Mrs Thrale made a comparable entry which was annotated in a similar way. The entry ran: 'How many Times has this great, this formidable Doctor Johnson kissed my hand, ay and my foot too upon his knees! Strange Connections there are in this odd World! his with me is mere *Interest* tho'; he loves Miss Reynolds best.' To this was afterwards added the marginal note: 'a dreadful and little suspected Reason for *ours*, God knows—but the Fetters and Padlocks will tell Posterity the Truth.'

Some years before this Johnson had actually given Mrs Thrale a pad-lock which was found amongst her belongings after her death with a label attached to it reading, 'Johnson's padlock, committed to my care in 1768'. That Johnson's self-styled 'sinful and corrupt imaginations' had, at least upon one occasion, formed themselves into a fantasy about such devices is shown by an entry in his diary in 1771, an entry which he could bring himself to record in his journal only in a brief Latin note: '*De pedicis et manicis insana cogitatio*' ('Insane imaginings about foot-fetters and handcuffs'). It appears from an extraordinary correspondence between him and Mrs Thrale while he was staying at Streatham in 1773 that actual fetters and handcuffs may perhaps have been used there.

Johnson's letter, scarcely intelligible, was written in French—presum-ably so that any servant into whose hands it might fall would not be able to read it—and begins, 'Madame Trés *Honorée*.' He asks where he may confine himself 'within prescribed bounds', and goes on: 'I beg you to spare me the obligation of constraining myself, by taking away from me the power of leaving the place where you want me to be. . . . You must act the Mistress completely, so that your judgment and your vigilance may come to the aid of my weakness.' He begs her not to forget so many promises, not to condemn him to 'solicitations repeated so many times that the recollection of them fills [him] with horror'; and he ends, 'You must either grant me this, or refuse me; and you must remember what you grant. I want always to be sensible of your rule, my patroness, and I want you to hold me in that slavery which you know so well how to render pleasant.'

Mrs Thrale replied, 'What Care can I promise my dear Mr Johnson that I have not already taken. . . . You were saying but on Sunday that of all the unhappy you was the happiest, in consequence of my Attention to your Complaint. . . . If it be possible shake off these uneasy Weights, heavier to the Mind by far than Fetters to the body. Let not your fancy dwell thus upon Confinement and severity.—I am sorry you are obliged to be so much alone; I foresaw some ill Consequences of your being here while my Mother was dying thus; yet could not resist the temptation of having you near me. . . . Dissipation is to you a glorious Medicine, and I believe Mr Boswell will be at last your best Physician. For the rest you really are well enough now if you will keep so; and not suffer the noblest of human minds to be troubled with fantastic notions which rob it of all its Quiet. — I will detain you no longer, so farewell and be good; and do not quarrel with your Governess for not using the Rod enough. H.L.T.'

Whether or not the rod was actually used, whether or not Johnson's fantasies about manacles and fetters were erotic and masochistic in their nature, it is impossible now to say. But it does seem certain that Johnson, who cannot have fully understood the real nature of his malady, did insist on occasions that he should be kept close confined at Streatham Park. Mrs Thrale clearly did not recognise the implications of the role that Johnson wished her to play, but she realised only too well how desperately afraid he was at times of going mad. He often talked to her and to Boswell about the means by which a man might hold on to sanity, of the importance of having something to occupy the mind. 'He should have a lamp constantly burning in his bed chamber during the night,' he thought, 'and if wakefully disturbed, take a book, and read, and compose himself to rest. To have the management of the mind is a great art, and it may be attained in a considerable degree by experience and habitual exercise. . . . Let him take a course of chymistry, or a course of rope-dancing, or a course of anything to which he is inclined at the time. Let him contrive to have as many retreats for his mind as he can.' Women were fortunate in that they had so many petty occupations 'which contributed to the lengthening of their lives and preserving their minds in a state of sanity'. He was much struck, and used to repeat, the observation of a lady who remarked to him one day, 'A man cannot hem a pocket-handkerchief, and so he runs mad, and torments his family and friends.' He himself, to make sure that his mental faculties were not impaired, once began to teach himself Dutch, though he gave it up when he found he could learn it pretty well.

'His over-anxious care to retain without blemish the perfect sanity of his mind, contributed much to disturb it,' Mrs Thrale wrote. 'He had studied medicine diligently in all its branches; but had given particular attention to the diseases of the imagination, which he watched in himself with a solicitude destructive of his own peace, and intolerable to those he trusted. Dr Lawrence told him one day, that if he would come and beat him once a week he would bear it; but to hear his complaints was more than *man* could support. 'Twas therefore that he tried, I suppose, and in eighteen years contrived to weary the patience of a *woman*. When Mr Johnson felt his mind, or fancied he felt it, disordered, his constant recurrence was to the study of arithmetic; and one day that he was totally confined to his chamber, and I enquired what he had been doing to divert himself; he shewed me a calculation which I could scarce be made to understand, so vast was the plan of it, and so very intricate were the figures.'

II

Scotland

'Being told that Dr Johnson did not hear well, [the Laird of Lochbuy] bawled out to him, "Are you of the Johnstons of Glencro, or of Ardnamurchan?" Dr Johnson gave him a signifi-cant look, but made no answer; and I told Lochbuy that he was not Johnston but Johnson, and that he was an Englishman.'[1]

James Boswell

On the evening of Saturday, 14 August 1773, Dr Johnson arrived at Boyd's Inn at the corner of Canongate and St Mary's Wynd, Edinburgh. For years he had entertained a wish to visit the Hebrides, an account of which his father had shown him as a child; and soon after his first meeting with Boswell he had suggested that they should one day go there together. When Boswell was at Ferney in 1764 he had told Voltaire of this design; and Voltaire, out of spirits and annoyed at being disturbed by the importunate young man—for he had been in bed when he called—had looked at him as if he had talked of going to the North Pole.

It was not, however, until nine years later, shortly before his sixty-fourth birthday and after Boswell's marriage, that Johnson had set out on his first journey outside England.

It was a remarkable enterprise for a man of his age and temperament, for a man who treasured his comforts, who professed to take no pleasure in either 'wild prospects' or wild people, who would be forced to travel on horseback through a hard and rugged countryside 'upon which, perhaps, no wheel had ever rolled'.

It seemed, in fact, to William Scott of University College, Oxford, in whose company he had travelled from Newcastle, that Johnson had no sooner arrived in Edinburgh than he regretted having left London. At

Boyd's, a 'crowded and confused' inn, according to a correspondent in the *Gentleman's Magazine*, he had called for lemonade which proved not to be sweet enough for his taste. He had accordingly asked for it to be made sweeter, upon which the waiter had lifted up a lump of sugar in his greasy fingers and had dropped it into the jug. In high indignation, Johnson threw the lemonade out of the window; and Scott was afraid that having done so he was then going to knock the waiter down.

When Boswell arrived, Johnson had calmed down. He embraced him warmly, and gladly accepted his offer of a room in Boswell's house in James's Court. 'Shall I see your Lady?' he asked him.

'Yes.'

'Then I'll put on a clean shirt.'

''Tis needless. Either don't see her tonight, or don't put on a clean shirt.'

'Sir, I'll do both.'

They walked up the High Street arm in arm and Johnson, calling Boswell's attention to the stench that arose from the open sewers of Scotland's capital, grumbled in his ear, 'I smell you in the dark.'

Warned by her husband, Mrs Boswell was waiting for Dr Johnson behind a teapot. He 'shewed much complacency,' his host wrote, 'upon finding that the mistress of the house was so attentive to his singular habit; and as no man could be more polite when he chose to be so, his address to her was most courteous and engaging; and his conversation soon charmed her into a forgetfulness of his external appearance'.

Boswell said that he was very glad to see him under his roof, to which Johnson replied, 'And 'tis a very noble roof.' The drawing-room, he added with one of his highly extravagant compliments, was the pleasantest room he had ever been in. After Mrs Boswell had left them they sat up in it talking until two o'clock in the morning.

From the beginning Johnson was in excellent spirits. He lost no opportunity, of course, of voicing disrespectful opinions about the Scotch and their country throughout his travels. On seeing a number of people walking about barefooted at Inchkeith, he remarked to Boswell, 'I suppose you all went so before the Union.' And on their way to Talisker he maintained it was not only shoes the Scotch lacked before the Union with England; they had 'hardly any trade, any money, or any elegance'. 'We have taught you,' he went on, 'and we'll do the same in time to all barbarous nations,—to the Cherokees,—and at last to the Ouran-Outangs'; and at this conceit he laughed 'with as much glee' as if Lord Monboddo— the Scottish judge who believed that these animals were a class of the human species—had himself been present.

'We had wine before the Union,' Boswell protested.

'No, Sir; you had some weak stuff, the refuse of France, which would not make you drunk.'

'I assure you, Sir, there was a great deal of drunkenness.'

'No, Sir; there were people who died of dropsies, which they contracted in trying to get drunk.'

On the island of Mull he lost his big oak walking stick and claimed to be quite convinced that the Scotch had stolen it. 'No, no, my friend,' he insisted when Boswell endeavoured to persuade him that this was most unlikely. 'It is not to be expected that any man in Mull, who has got it, will part with it. Consider, Sir, the value of such a *piece of timber* here.'

Timber, he claimed, was indeed to be found scarcely anywhere in the country; and he could not abide a landscape without trees. That was the trouble with Brighton Downs, 'a country so desolate that if one had a mind to hang one's self from desperation, it would be difficult to find a tree on which to fasten the rope'. Sir Allan Maclean, lessee of the island of Inchkenneth and anxious for the honour of the neighbouring island of Mull, pointed out some woods in the distance. 'Sir,' replied Johnson, 'I saw at Tobermory what they called a wood, which I unluckily took for *heath*. If you shew me what I shall take for *furze*, it will be something.' Some time later Sir Allan asked Johnson to agree that Scotland at least had the advantage over England in that it had more water. Of course, Scotland had more water, Johnson agreed; but 'we would not have your water to take the vile bogs which produce it. You have too much! . . . Your country consists of two things, stone and water. There is, indeed, a little earth above the stone in some places, but a very little; and the stone is always appearing. It is like a man in rags; the naked skin is still peeping out.' He even affected to find Edinburgh Castle a poor place in comparison to any comparable structure that could be found at home. He admitted to Boswell when he first saw it that it was 'a great place', but when Lord Elibank talked of it with the natural elation of a Scotchman, Johnson would have none of its praises—well, he grudgingly allowed, it might make 'a good *prison* in ENGLAND'.

Yet for all the pleasure he took in such sallies, his enjoyment of his holiday was obvious as soon as the tour began on 18 August, and he and Boswell left Edinburgh for St Andrews. To be sure, when Boswell remarked that the view of the Firth of Forth from the Castle Hill, Edinburgh, was surely the finest prospect in Europe after the views to be enjoyed in Constantinople and Naples, Johnson curtly gave it as his opinion that water was 'the same everywhere'; and when Boswell insisted on 'scottifying' Johnson's palate by getting him to eat a piece of spelding, a kind of salted and dried fish, like Bombay Duck, which was eaten by the Scotch as a relish, Johnson did not like it. But when they arrived at St Andrews on a very fine day, Johnson 'seemed quite wrapt up in the contemplation of the scenes which were now presented to him'. They walked over the ground upon which the cathedral had stood, and Johnson punctiliously took off his hat.

The professors at the University entertained the two visitors to 'a very good dinner' before which the Principal, having said grace in English, asked Johnson if it were true that at Oxford and Cambridge they never said grace in English but repeated the Latin words '*Benedictus benedicat*'. Johnson, 'in very good humour', replied that he had never heard those words used at an English university. 'For my part,' he continued, 'I remember perfectly the words which were used, in the University of Oxford, by one of the heads of the college, of which I was a member, and for your satisfaction I shall repeat them.' He thereupon said a grace in Latin which one of the guests remembered as being a 'pretty long' one.

From St Andrews, Johnson and Boswell rode north for Dundee, and then on towards Montrose. At Montrose, at a very poor inn, a waiter again put a lump of sugar into Johnson's lemonade with his fingers, at which Johnson called him a rascal. 'It put me in great glee,' Boswell reported, 'that our landlord was an Englishman. I rallied the Doctor upon this, and he grew quiet. . . . Then he was angry at me for purposing to carry lemons with us to Sky, that he might be sure to have his lemonade. "Sir, (said he) I do not wish to be thought a feeble man who cannot do without anything. Sir, it is very bad manners to carry provisions to any man's house, as if he could not entertain you."'

From Montrose they drove on towards Aberdeen, where Johnson, 'much pleased' to be presented with the freedom of the city, walked about the town with the burgess-ticket stuck in his hat according to the usual custom. Boswell was uncertain whether or not to go to Aberdeen by way of Monboddo, and to take Johnson to see Lord Monboddo whose views about the origins of society and language expressed in his six-volume work on the subject and whose admiration for the primitive life, Johnson so frequently derided. Lord Monboddo talked 'a great deal of nonsense' about savages, Johnson had told Boswell several years before; so, too, did Rousseau, 'but Rousseau *knew* he was talking nonsense and laughed at the world for staring at him'. 'Why, Sir, a man who talks nonsense so well, must know that he is talking nonsense. But I am *afraid* (chuckling and

laughing) that Monboddo does *not* know that he is talking nonsense.'
When the suggestion of a visit to Monboddo was made to him, however,
Johnson readily agreed; and the meeting was a great success. Boswell was
delighted that the two men got on together 'like two brothers'. There had
been an awkward moment at first when Lord Monboddo, pointing to the
coat of arms above his front door, remarked, 'In such houses our ancestors
lived who were better men than we.'

'No, no, my Lord,' Johnson had immediately objected, always angry,
as he confessed himself, when he heard previous centuries praised at the
expense of modern times. 'No, we are as strong as they, and a great deal
wiser.' And, after he had left the house, Johnson expressed his disapproval
that Lord Monboddo, a judge, should call himself 'farmer Burnett' (his
family name) and go about with a little round hat; for, as he afterwards
said, 'A judge may be a farmer; but he is not to geld his own pigs; a judge
may play a little at cards for his amusement; but he is not to play at
marbles, or chuck farthing in the Piazza.' The two men had also had a
'slight difference in adjusting the claims of merit between a Shopkeeper
of London, and a Savage of the American wildernesses'. Johnson naturally
took the side of the London shopkeeper, but he pressed his case 'without
full conviction' and admitted that he might well have taken the side of the
savage had Monboddo taken up the cause of the shopkeeper.

'He was much pleased with Lord Monboddo,' Boswell thought, and
'would have pardoned him for a few paradoxes when he found he had so
much that was good.' Johnson was also much pleased with Monboddo's
black servant, Gory, who accompanied them as a guide from Monboddo
to the main road to Aberdeen.

Johnson had left Frank at home in London, but Boswell's Bohemian
servant, Joseph Ritter, was with them; and Johnson laughed to see the
two of them riding along together so cordially in front of the carriage.
'Those two fellows,' he said, 'one from Africa, the other from Bohemia,
seem quite at home.' When Gory was about to leave them, Johnson called
to him, 'Mr Gory, give me leave to ask you a question! Are you baptised?'
Gory said he was—and confirmed by the Bishop of Durham. On receipt
of this satisfactory intelligence, Johnson produced his purse and gave
him a shilling.

Despite the rigours of the journey, he was still in excellent spirits. The
night before, tired by the long and tedious drive, he had said peevishly
that if they had to drive as much as that every day they would not go any
further, 'and there's an end on't'. This day, however, he was so cheerful
that Boswell felt able to tease him: 'Why, Sir, you seemed to me to despond

yesterday. You are a delicate Londoner; you are a macaroni; you can't ride.'

'Sir, I shall ride better than you. I was only afraid I should not find a horse able to carry me.'

He rarely complained again. Indeed, Boswell could not but praise his resolution and perseverance, while Johnson in his turn wrote home to Mrs Thrale of his companion's 'good humour and perpetual cheerfulness'. When on foot Johnson strode purposefully, if irregularly along, in his boots and huge brown cloth greatcoat with its enormous pockets which Boswell thought almost commodious enough to contain the two folio volumes of his dictionary. In his hand was his immense oak stick, which, until he lost it on Mull, served not only as a help to his knees, weakened by his illness in 1776, but also as a measure, since two nails were driven into it, one at a distance of a foot from the end, the other at a yard. It could also serve him as a weapon should the occasion arise. He had brought two pistols with him to Edinburgh, together with some gunpowder and a quantity of bullets; but on being assured by Boswell that he would meet no robbers on his journey he had left these in a drawer at the house in St James's Court.

They drove in a chaise as far as Inverness, and there hired four horses, one each for Johnson and Boswell, one for Joseph and one for their portmanteaus. Two Highlanders walked beside them as guides. Johnson 'rode very well', said Boswell confirming the opinion of William Gerard Hamilton. One day, while riding along a mountain path so narrow that there was no room for him to dismount in the usual way, he fell at his length upon the ground, but he got up immediately and carried on. 'To strive with difficulties and to conquer them,' he had written in the *Adventurer*, 'is the highest human felicity.'

It was not until the last day of their ride on the mainland, when they were coming down into Glenelg opposite the Isle of Skye, that Johnson fell utterly out of humour. It had been a difficult and exhausting ride down the mountain from Glenshiel, and Johnson had grumbled because his horse did not go well. One of the Highland guides, walking by the horse's head, did all he could to cheer the grumpy Englishman up, talking as much as he could and '(having heard him in the forenoon, express a pastoral pleasure on seeing the goats browzing), just when the Doctor was uttering his displeasure, the fellow cried, with a very Highland accent, "See, such pretty goats!" then he whistled, *whu!* and made them jump.'

The performance did not much entertain Johnson who rode on, as it grew dark, in gloomy silence. As they approached Glenelg, Boswell went ahead to make arrangements at the inn and to hire a boat; but he was peremptorily called back by 'a tremendous shout'. Boswell rode back to Johnson and found him, so he said, 'in a passion with me for leaving him. I told him my intentions, but he was not satisfied, and said, "Do you know I should as soon have thought of picking a pocket, as doing so."'

'I am diverted with you, Sir.'

'Sir,' Johnson replied with extraordinary warmth, 'I could never be diverted with incivility. Doing such a thing makes one lose confidence in him who has done it, as one cannot tell what he may do next.'

The accommodation at the inn at Glenelg made Boswell even more apprehensive. A maid showed them up into a damp and dirty room with 'bare walls, a variety of bad smells, a coarse black greasy fir table, and forms of the same kind; and out of a wretched bed started a fellow from his sleep, like Edgar in King Lear'. The inn was furnished with 'not a single article' that they could either eat or drink. There was 'no bread, no eggs, no wine, no spirits but whisky, no sugar but brown grown black'.

'Boswell blustered,' Johnson told Mrs Thrale, 'but nothing could be got.' The landlord prepared some mutton chops which were inedible, then killed two hens which were almost equally so. Johnson had nothing but a bit of bread that they had brought with them and some lemonade that Joseph made for him with a lemon that he had prudently carried from Inverness. Yet Johnson was calm, not from vanity, he assured Boswell, but from philosophy. Boswell sent for hay to make beds for themselves, and Johnson lay down, buttoned up in his greatcoat, bearing all the discomforts of the inn without a murmur, remarking that they were better than they had been on the mountain.[2] He was 'still violent', though, upon the subject of being left with Joseph and the guides on the mountain. 'Sir, had you gone on,' he said, 'I was thinking that I should have returned to Edinburgh, and then have parted from you, and never spoken to you more.'

But in the morning he admitted he had spoken in a passion, that he would not really have done what he threatened, and that if he had done his behaviour would have been ten times worse than Boswell's. Finally he said, 'Let's think no more on't.'

During the next few weeks there were other occasional outbursts. One day at Dunvegan on the Isle of Skye, Johnson gravely remarked, 'I have often thought that, if I kept a seraglio, the ladies should all wear linen gowns—or cotton—I mean stuffs made of vegetable substance. I would have no silk; you cannot tell when it is clean. . . .'

The thought of Johnson keeping a harem struck Boswell as so ludicrous that he could not help bursting out into laughter. But Johnson, who would never allow himself for a moment to be the object of ridicule, 'instantly retaliated', Boswell remembered, 'with such keen sarcastick wit, and such a variety of degrading images, of every one of which I was the object, that, although I can bear such attacks as well as most men, I yet found myself so much the sport of all the company, that I would gladly expunge from my mind every trace of this severe retort'. Although Boswell declined to say so in his published *Tour*, Johnson had decided that his travelling companion would make 'a very good eunuch'.

'I take it,' Boswell had countered, 'better than you would do your part.'

'I have not told you what was to be my part,' Johnson had admonished him, 'and then at once,' so Boswell recorded in his journal, 'he returned to my office as eunuch and expatiated upon it with such fluency that it really hurt me. He made me quite contemptible for the moment.'

It was not only Boswell who was humiliated for offending Johnson. A presbyterian minister, who spoke slightingly of the bishops and deans of the Church of England, was silenced with the furious retort, 'Sir, you know no more of our Church than a Hottentot.' And his hostess on the island of Mull, Lady Lochbuy, was stunned by the vehemence of his refusal of her offer of a dish that was common enough on Scottish breakfast tables but was certainly not to his taste first thing in the morning.

'Do you choose,' asked Lady Lochbuy when her guest entered the dining-room, 'any cold sheep's head, Sir?'

'"No, MADAM," said he, with a tone of surprise and anger. "It is here, Sir," said she, supposing he had refused it to save the trouble of bringing it in. They thus went on at cross purposes, till he confirmed his refusal in a manner not to be misunderstood.'

Occasionally, too, there would be complaints about the countryside through which he rode. 'O, Sir,' he lamented gloomily when riding through a dreary part of Mull, 'O, Sir, a most dolorous country.' Also, the manner in which he and his companions had to ride along the narrow paths in single file distressed him; not only was it unsociable but 'you cannot indulge in meditation by yourself, because you must be always attending to the steps which your horse takes'. Then, before he lost his oak stick on Mull, he lost his spurs while crossing from Skye to Raasay. They had been entrusted to Joseph's care and he flared into anger, observing that there was 'something wild in letting a pair of spurs he carried into the sea out of a boat'. But his anger soon cooled, and he added that, as Janes, the naturalist, had said on losing his pocket-book, it was rather an inconvenience than a loss.

Indeed, these were rare outbursts and they were soon over. Johnson was delighted with the way the Scottish people received him, and of his fame amongst them. At Ellon the landlady of the inn where they breakfasted asked Boswell, 'Is not this the great Doctor that is going about through the country?'

'Yes.'

'Ay. We heard of him. I made an errand into the room on purpose to see him. There's something great in his appearance. It is a pleasure to have such a man in one's house, a man who does so much good. If I had thought of it I would have shewn him a child of mine, who has had a lump on his throat for some time.'

'But, he is not a doctor of physick.'

'Is he an oculist?'

'No, he is only a very learned man.'

'They say he is the greatest man in England, except Lord Mansfield.'

He was certainly treated as such. Wherever he went, he told Norman Macleod, he met with 'kind treatment'. And to Boswell he exclaimed, 'Wherever we have come, we have been received like princes in their progress!'

This was not true, unfortunately, of their reception at Sir Alexander Macdonald's house at Armadale, where a most 'improper parsimony' was observed and where, so Johnson said, 'the lady had not the common decencies of her tea table. We picked up our sugar with our fingers. Boswell was very angry.' Little better was their reception at Sir John Dalrymple's house at Cranston where they arrived very late to find Sir John 'not in very good humour' and the conversation 'not brilliant'. They went to bed in ancient rooms, cold and comfortless. At breakfast the next morning Lady Darylmple asked them what they would like for dinner, fore-leg or hind-leg of mutton, and suggested fore-leg. On learning that in Scotland fore-leg meant shoulder, Johnson said, 'I vote hind-leg to be sure.' Poor Lady Dalrymple looked 'much disconcerted'.

'Sir, this is an odious woman,' Johnson decided afterwards. 'Were I Dalrymple, I'd go and entertain my friends at Edinburgh and leave her to herself. Did you observe when we voted leg? Sir, she looked as if we had voted for roasting one of her children.'

In the event they did not get either fore-leg or hind-leg; and thinking they would be more comfortable at the inn at Blackshiels two miles nearer Edinburgh, they went there in the evening. Their experiences at

Armadale and Cranston were exceptional, however; and Boswell told Johnson that all the people they visited on their tour had said to him of the Doctor, '*Honest man!*'—a high compliment in these regions—'*Honest man!* He's pleased with everything; he's always content.' Certainly, he bore the hardships of the journey with remarkable imperturbability. When he got soaked to the skin one morning crossing Loch Awe in a ferry-boat, he resolutely kept all his clothes on and stood quietly on the far bank, letting them steam, before a smoky turf fire. He got soaked again that afternoon in another torrent of rain, yet sitting in his wet clothes in an inn in the evening, he remained in excellent heart. To Boswell's surprise, he called for a gill of whisky, the first time he had tasted any alcohol since the tour began. 'Come,' he said gaily, 'let me know what it is that makes a Scotchman happy!'

'He drank it all but a drop, which I begged leave to pour into my glass, that I might say we had drunk whisky together,' Boswell recorded. 'I proposed Mrs Thrale should be our toast. He would not have *her* drunk in whisky, but rather "some insular lady"; so we drank one of the ladies whom we had lately left.—He owned tonight that he got as good a room and bed as at an English inn.'

As he bore the hardships and discomforts of the journey uncomplainingly, so he bore its dangers. He had never been a cautious man, and had always been ready to act decisively when other men drew back. John Hawkins said that it was one of Johnson's maxims that a man who was afraid of anything was a scoundrel. Hawkins also recorded that when out in the hunting field Johnson thought nothing of leaping over or breaking through 'many of the hedges that obstructed him. This he did, not because he was eager in the pursuit, but, as he said, to save the trouble of alighting and remounting.'

Topham Beauclerk remembered an occasion when two large ferocious dogs were fighting at his house in the country. Johnson 'looked steadily at them for a little while; and then, as one would separate two little boys who are foolishly hurting each other, he ran up to them, and cuffed their heads till he drove them asunder'. Beauclerk's friend Langton related a similar incident when he had been swimming near Oxford. Langton warned Johnson of a pool which was reckoned 'particularly dangerous'; Johnson immediately swam into it. There was also the occasion when he was warned of the danger that a gun might burst if charged with many balls; he put in six or seven and fired them off against a wall.

The crossing between Skye and Raasay was a very rough one, but though the seas lashed and tossed the boat, he remained quite composed.

Boswell, who was of a much more nervous disposition, admitted that he 'did not like it'. Johnson, on the other hand, happily declared, 'This now is the Atlantick. If I should tell at a tea-table in London, that I have crossed the Atlantick in an open boat, how they'd shudder, and what a fool they'd think me to expose myself to such danger.'

Another storm violently tossed and plunged the boat that took them from Skye to Coll and threatened to drive it upon the rocky shore. Boswell, clinging to a rope, listening to the sailors shouting to each other in Gaelic above the roar of the wind, and looking in terror upon the 'prodigious sea, with immense billows' lashing against the vessel, 'trembled lest she should be overset'. He recklessly vowed to live ten times better if God would only preserve him. Even Donald Maclean, the young Laird of Coll, was frightened and cried in relief when the harbour of Loch Eatharna was sighted at last, 'Thank God, we are safe.'

All this time Johnson had been lying below on one of the bunks, quiet and unconcerned, 'in philosophick tranquillity' with one of Maclean's greyhounds at his back, keeping him warm.

At the end of the journey, when reports had appeared in the newspapers of his being drowned, so many compliments had been paid to him upon his safe return, he was 'really ashamed' of the congratulations. 'We are addressed,' he remarked to Boswell, 'as if we had made a voyage to Nova Zembla, and suffered five persecutions in Japan.'

He had been ready to see even more islands than they had visited; and when Boswell had said it might be dangerous since the uncertainty of the season might lead them to being stranded on one of them, he commented, 'I have more the spirit of adventure than you.'

Day by day he showed how much he was enjoying himself. On 13 August, a delightful day, while he and his companions were riding along the shores of Loch Ness in the shade of the birch trees beneath the towering hills, they saw a little hut with an old woman at the door. 'Let's go in,' said Johnson. It was a wretched mud hovel with a hole in the wall, stopped by a piece of turf that served as a window, and with a second hole in the roof to let out the smoke of the peat fire. There was a pot on the fire with a bit of goat's flesh boiling in it. Johnson was curious to know where the woman slept, so one of the guides asked her this in Gaelic; but the wretched old hag was unwilling to show them, for she was afraid, so she said, that they wanted to go to bed with her.

Afterwards Johnson and Boswell were 'very merry' about this outlandish suspicion. Boswell said it was Johnson who had alarmed the poor woman's virtue.

'No, Sir,' objected Johnson, 'she'll say, "There came a wicked young fellow, a wild dog, who I believe would have ravished me, had there not been with him a brave old gentleman who repressed him: but when he gets out of the sight of his tutor, I'll warrant you he'll spare no woman he meets, young or old."'

'No, Sir,' replied Boswell, 'she'll say, "There was a terrible ruffian who would have forced me, had it not been for a gentle mild-looking youth who, I take it, was an angel sent from heaven to protect me."'

The next day they were on the way to Anoch when they passed a party of soldiers at work upon the road. They gave them two shillings to spend on drink, and finding them later making merry in a barn attached to the inn where they were to spend the night, Johnson said, 'Come, let's go and give 'em another shilling a-piece.' This they did, and Johnson, to his obvious pleasure, was addressed as 'My Lord' by all of them. 'He is really generous,' commented Boswell affectionately, 'loves influence and has the way of gaining it. He said, "I am quite feudal, Sir." Here I agree with him.'

In the afternoon the landlord's daughter, who made tea for them, much pleased Johnson by her modesty, neatness and civility. 'I presented her with a book, which I happened to have about me,' Johnson afterwards wrote in his account of his *Journey to the Western Isles of Scotland*, 'and should not be pleased to think that she forgets me.' The title of this book gave rise to much subsequent speculation; and the public were greatly surprised to learn that it was Edward Cocker's *Arithmetic*. 'Is it not somewhat singular,' Johnson was asked, 'that you should *happen* to have Cocker's Arithmetic about you on your journey?'

'Why, Sir,' Johnson replied, 'if you are to have but one book with you upon a journey, let it be a book of science. When you have read through a book of entertainment, you know it, and it can do no more for you; but a book of science is inexhaustible.'

That night Boswell and Johnson slept in the same room in two beds divided from each other by a woman's gown hung on a rope as a curtain. They were undecided as to whether or not to undress, but supposing that there would be less harbour for vermin about him if he took his clothes off, Boswell cried, 'I'll plunge in!' And so saying he stripped. Johnson said that he felt like a man hesitating whether to go into the cold bath but then he, too, 'resolved'.

'He was in excellent humour,' Boswell said, and 'after we had offered up our private devotions, and had chatted a little from our beds, he said, "God bless us both, for Jesus Christ's sake! Good night!"—I pronounced

Amen!—He fell asleep immediately.' He was wearing, as was his usual habit, a coloured handkerchief tied round his neck in place of a nightcap.

He was still fast asleep when Boswell got up in the morning and it was with difficulty that he was aroused and persuaded to get up himself. They were down to breakfast early, however, and were on the road again by eight o'clock. They rode through Glenshiel, and at Auchnashiel they sat down to rest on a green turf-seat at the end of a house. Dishes of milk were brought out to them, one of them frothed up like a syllabub by the woman of the house with a stick. A crowd of people gathered about them, inspecting them closely, chattering to each other in Gaelic. It was like being with a tribe of Indians, Boswell observed. 'Yes, Sir,' agreed Johnson, 'but not so terrifying.'

Boswell gave them each a bit of wheat bread which they had never tasted before; and to any who chose them, little packets of snuff and tobacco which he had had made up for him at Fort Augustus;[3] to the children he gave a penny. Not to be outdone, Johnson called to Joseph and the guides to bring him change for a shilling. Then he had the children all lined up in a row in front of him, and solemnly dealt about his copper.

Throughout their time in the Hebrides the two travellers were handsomely entertained by the various lairds and chieftains of the islands, who warmly welcomed Johnson because of his reputation and Boswell because of his family. 'It is very convenient to travel with him,' Johnson told Mrs Thrale; 'for there is no house where he is not received with kindness and respect.' The Laird of Raasay gave a substantial dinner for them, after which a fiddler appeared and there was a little ball; and a 'kind of wild man' was called in and 'made much jovial noise'. Johnson was delighted with this scene—though he thought the Laird's wife made 'no very sublime appearance for a Sovereign'—and he said to Boswell, 'I know not how we shall get away.' Boswell, in the intervals of dancing, was happy to see his friend so content, sometimes in deep meditation, sometimes smiling with satisfaction, sometimes looking into Nathaniel Hooke's *Roman History*, which he had picked from a bookshelf in the house, sometimes talking to one of the other guests. The Laird's family had owned the island for over four hundred years. 'This is truly the patriarchal life,' Johnson remarked approvingly. 'This is what we came to find.'

There was another party a few days later on the Isle of Skye. Here he was more convivial than ever, 'and though he drank no fermented liquor, toasted Highland beauties with great readiness. His conviviality engaged them so much, that they seemed eager to shew their attention to him, and vied with each other in crying out, with a strong Celtic pronounciation, "Toctor Shonson, Toctor Shonson, your health!"'

One of them, a lively pretty little married girl of sixteen, sat upon his knee. She had taken a bet to do so, and to kiss him, with some other girls who said he was 'too ugly for any woman to kiss'. She put her hands round his neck and pressed her lips against his cheek. 'Do it again,' he said, 'and let us see who will tire first.' He kept her on his knee for some time while they drank tea together. 'All the company were much entertained to find him so easy and pleasant.'

He showed himself happy to share all the customs of his hosts. On the island of Coll, in a farmhouse where Boswell enjoyed the best goose that he ever ate, they were entertained with a primitive heartiness. Whisky was served round in a shell, according to the old Highland custom; and Johnson, being desirous to do the honour of the modes 'of other times', drank some water out of it. Later in the house of Donald Maclean, the Laird of Coll, he made himself immediately comfortable, and as though to demonstrate that he was now quite at home with the forms of Highland address, called out with 'a spirited familiarity' as soon as he had sat down, 'Now, Coll, if you would get us a dish of tea.'

Another day he greatly delighted Sir Allan Maclean, Chief of the Clan Maclean, by strutting about the room with a broad-sword and target. He made, said Boswell, a 'formidable appearance; and, another night, I took the liberty to put a large blue bonnet on his head'. It was a Sunday and Sir Allan informed his guests that it was the custom of his house to have prayers in the evening. His daughter then read the evening service. Johnson said that it was the most agreeable Sunday that he had ever passed.

Johnson even, after initial hesitations, relished Scottish food, particularly Scottish breakfasts which he reckoned were probably the best in the world. At Aberdeen he ate several platefuls of Scotch broth with barley and peas in it one after the other. Boswell remarked that he had never eaten that dish before. 'No, Sir,' he replied with satisfaction. 'But I don't care how soon I eat it again.' Barley broth, he wrote home, 'is a constant dish and is made well in every house'.

He took pleasure in a good deal else, particularly in roasted kid, which he tasted for the first time at an inn in Inverness, and roasted venison (eaten to the sound of bagpipes). At the Red Lion in Elgin he was served beef collops and mutton chops which he could not eat; but this was the first, and except for one other, the last time that he had cause to complain of a Scottish meal. After a particularly excellent dinner at Fort George, he observed, 'I shall always remember this fort with gratitude.'

Naturally, he pretended to believe that his fortune was exceptional. 'Come, Dr Johnson,' Boswell said to him at a dinner party at his house in Edinburgh, 'it is commonly thought that our veal in Scotland is not good. But here is some which I believe you will like.'

'Why, Sir, what is commonly thought, I should take to be true. *Your* veal may be good; but that will only be an exception to the general opinion; not a proof against it.'

For all his hits against the Scotch, however, Johnson met very few during this tour with whom he could not get on well. One of the few was the Rev Kenneth Macaulay, the minister of Cawdor and author of the *History of St Kilda* which Johnson was convinced he had not written, for Macaulay was not only as 'obstinate as a mule' but 'as ignorant as a bull', 'the most ignorant booby and the grossest bastard'. After a visit to Cawdor Castle, near which were some ancient trees, Macaulay began to talk disdainfully of the lower English clergy. Johnson gave him a frowning look and said crossly, 'This is a day of novelties. I have seen old trees in Scotland and I have heard the English clergy treated with disrespect.'

Macaulay's brother, John, the grandfather of the historian, also angered Johnson one evening at an inn in Inveraray by attempting to interrupt him. 'Mr Macaulay, Mr Macaulay!' Johnson expostulated. 'Don't you know it is very rude to cry, "Eh! Eh!" when one is talking.'

Macaulay subsequently gave further offence by remarking that he had 'no notion of people being in earnest in their good professions, whose practice was not suitable to them'. This was a subject on which Johnson held strong views, as might well have been expected from the concern that his own failures to keep his resolutions always gave him. He went so far as to give credit to Dr John Campbell for taking off his hat when he passed a church though he never went inside one; he showed that he had at least good principles.[4] He now turned upon the unfortunate Macaulay and exclaimed, 'Sir, are you so grossly ignorant of human nature, as not to know that a man may be very sincere in good principles without having good practice?'

Johnson also had trouble with Lady Macleod at Dunvegan who protested that a certain author did not practise what he preached. 'I cannot help that, madam. That does not make his book the worse. . . . No man practises so well as he writes. I have, all my life long, been lying till noon; yet I tell all young men, and tell them with great sincerity, that nobody who does not rise early will ever do any good.' Later in their discussion Lady Macleod asked if no man was naturally good.

'No, madam, no more than a wolf.'

'Nor no woman, sir,' interposed Boswell.

'No, sir.'

Lady Macleod started at this response and murmured in a low voice, 'This is worse than Swift.'[5]

Johnson had already startled Lady Macleod, whom he afterwards described as a 'fine lady', at tea-time when, after pouring him out upwards of sixteen dishes of tea, she asked him if a small basin would not be more agreeable to him and save him trouble. 'I wonder, Madam,' he answered her with that vehemence that such suggestions always aroused in him, 'why all the ladies ask me such impertinent questions? It is to save yourselves trouble, Madam, and not me.'

Johnson grew quite as impatient with the Rev Hector Maclean, the minister of Coll, a deaf old man who could not hear what Johnson said any better than Johnson could hear him. They began to argue about Leibnitz, Johnson affirming in a lengthy lecture that he was as 'paltry a fellow' as he knew, Maclean simultaneously asserting, as he stood with his back to the fire and pulled down the front of his periwig, what a great man Leibnitz was.

Johnson's most unfortunate encounter, however, was with Boswell's father, Lord Auchinleck, as convinced a Whig and a Presbyterian as Johnson was a Tory and a Church of England man. Boswell brought them together with much trepidation, knowing that his father strongly disapproved of Johnson as '*a Jacobite fellow*'. Boswell begged Johnson not to bring up the subjects of either Whiggism or Presbyterianism, and not, on any account, to mention Sir John Pringle, his father's friend of whom Johnson strongly disapproved on both political and religious grounds. Johnson replied, 'I shall certainly not talk on subjects which I am told are disagreeable to a gentleman under whose roof I am; especially, I shall not do so to *your father*.'

The first meeting went off smoothly enough, Johnson not touching upon the fatal topics. The next day, too, was free from argument, though another of Lord Auchinleck's visitors riled Johnson by asking him how he liked the Highlands. 'How, Sir,' replied Johnson heatedly, 'can you ask me what obliges me to speak unfavourably of a country where I have been hospitably entertained? Who *can* like the Highlands? I like the inhabitants very well.'

On the last day but one of the visit, however, the inevitable explosion came when Lord Auchinleck was showing Johnson a coin of Oliver Cromwell, and the fateful subjects of Charles I and Toryism were thereby introduced. A violent altercation ensued, an altercation in which Boswell 'durst not interfere' and the details of which he forbore to record in his *Tour*. Johnson challenged his father to name any theological work of merit written by a Presbyterian minister in Scotland: 'My father, whose studies did not lie much in that way, owned to me afterwards, that he was somewhat at a loss how to answer, but that luckily he recollected having read in catalogues the title *Durham on the Galatians*; upon which he boldly said, "Pray, Sir, have you read Mr Durham's excellent commentary on the Galatians?" "No, Sir," said Dr Johnson.'

'You may buy it at any time for half a crown or three shillings.'

'Sir, it must be better recommended,' Johnson retorted rudely, 'before I give half the money for it.'

The next day was a Sunday. Boswell and his father went to church, but Johnson declined to attend a Presbyterian service. In Edinburgh he had already refused a similar invitation when Dr William Robertson was preaching. 'I will hear him,' he said, 'if he will get up into a tree and preach; but I will not give a sanction, by my presence, to a Presbyterian assembly.'[6]

The following day Boswell and Johnson left Auchinleck for Edinburgh, and Lord Auchinleck, his son gratefully acknowledged, 'was very civil to Dr Johnson, and politely attended him to the post-chaise'. But Auchinleck, who had been predisposed to dislike his son's unsuitable friend, was confirmed in his view of him. 'With more warmth than common' he afterwards reported to a friend, 'that the great Dr Johnson of whom he had heard wonders, was just a *dominie*, and the worst-bred dominie he had ever seen.'

It was an uncommon verdict. In most houses in Scotland, Johnson was well received and well-behaved, particularly well-behaved in the houses of men of high rank to whom he always displayed the deference which he considered they deserved. At Inveraray he was placed next to the Duke of Argyll at dinner, and Boswell had 'never seen him so gentle and complaisant'. Boswell complimented him upon his 'wonderfully courteous' behaviour, adding, 'You were quite a fine gentleman when with the Duchess.' Johnson accepted the compliment as no more than his due. 'Sir,' he said, 'I look upon myself as a very polite man.' And politeness, he often insisted, was of great consequence in society. 'Depend upon it,' he said, 'the want of it never fails to produce something disagreeable. . . . I know not how it is, but I cannot bear low life; and I find others, who have as good a right as I to be fastidious, bear it better, by having mixed more with different sorts of men. You would think that I have mixed pretty well too.'

He was always careful, though, to make a distinction between politeness and servility. 'One day at Inveraray,' Boswell recorded, 'a gentleman [Lieutenant-Colonel Adam Livingston, Member of Parliament for Argyllshire] in company after dinner, was desired by the Duke to go to another room, for a specimen of curious marble, which his grace wished to shew us. He brought a wrong piece, upon which the duke sent him back again. He could not refuse; but, to avoid any appearance of servility, he whistled as he walked out of the room, to show his independency. Upon my mentioning this afterwards to Dr Johnson, he said it was a nice trait of character.' He did not speak so highly, however, of Colonel Livingston's conversation: 'A mighty misty man, the Colonel.'

Johnson and Boswell left Inveraray towards the end of October and arrived, on 9 November, in Edinburgh, where Johnson was once again entertained by Mrs Boswell, who did not, her guest now realised, much care for his presence in her house. She behaved with the most 'assiduous and respectful attention' to him; but although he was studiously attentive to her in turn, his clumsiness and untidiness exasperated her. It distressed her to think that so uncouth a man should have such influence over her husband to whom she crossly remarked, 'I have seen many a bear led by a man; but I never before saw a man led by a bear.'[7]

Mrs Boswell was particularly annoyed by the tiresomely irregular hours he kept and by the way he turned the candles upside down when they did not burn brightly enough, so that the wax dropped on to her carpets. She was accordingly deeply thankful when towards the end of the month, Johnson took the coach for London, the 'fountain of intelligence and pleasure'.

Riding in the rain one evening on the Isle of Skye he had said how much he longed 'to be again in civilised life'; and on arriving in Glasgow towards the end of the tour, he 'enjoyed in imagination the comforts' he could then command and 'seemed to be in high glee'. He put up a leg on each side of the grate at the Saracen's Head and said, with a mock solemnity by way of soliloquy, but loud enough for Boswell to hear, 'Here am I, an ENGLISHMAN, sitting by a *coal* fire.' Yet he had greatly enjoyed his travels and looked back upon them with deep pleasure—and with the satisfaction that most of his preconceptions about Scotland and Scottish society had been confirmed.[8] He had never had much taste for 'rural beauties'—though he did admit that the situation of Slains Castle was the noblest he had ever seen—and from his personal experiences he could now heartily laugh 'at the ravings of those absurd visionaries who have attempted to persuade us of the superior advantages of a *state of nature*'.

Of the Hebrides, 'it must be confessed,' he wrote, 'that they have not many allurements, but to the lover of naked nature. The inhabitants are thin, provisions scarce, and desolation and penury give little pleasure.' His hosts had nevertheless given him much enjoyment, and he remembered them with affection. Even the discomforts and dangers of the journey had their uses, and indeed their pleasures. Describing one peculiarly hazardous ride, he told Henry Thrale, 'about ten miles of this day's [23 October] journey were uncommonly amusing. We travelled with very little light, in a storm of wind and rain, we passed about fifty-five streams that crossed our way, and fell into a river that for a very great part of our road, foamed and roared beside us. All the rougher powers of Nature, except thunder were in motion. . . . I should have been sorry to have missed any of the inconveniences, to have had more light, or less rain, for their co-operation crowded the scene, and filled the mind.'

From London he wrote to Boswell to say 'the expedition to the Hebrides was the most pleasant journey' he had ever made. 'Such an effort annually would give the world a little diversification.' Later he said it was the pleasantest part of his life; and he assured the man who had shared it with him that he would not 'lose the recollection of it for five hundred pounds'.

12

Wales and France

*'Dr Johnson asked of one of our sharp currents in North Wales,
"Has this* BROOK *e'er a name?" And received for answer,
"Why, dear Sir, this is the* RIVER *Ustrad." "Let us," said he,
turning to [Henry Thrale], "jump over it directly, and shew
them how an Englishman should treat a Welch* RIVER.*"'*

Hester Lynch Thrale

In letters as long as any he had ever brought himself to write, Johnson had kept Mrs Thrale fully informed about his progress through the Highlands; and he had twice been angry with Boswell for referring to her with insufficient respect—once when Boswell had suggested that they drink her health in whisky, and once when he proposed writing a poetical letter to Johnson on his return from Scotland 'in the style of Swift's humorous epistle in the character of Mary Gulliver to her husband, Captain Lemuel Gulliver, on his return to England from the country of the Houyhnhnms'.

Johnson laughed and asked Boswell in whose name he would write it. Boswell said Mrs Thrale's, at which Johnson flared up in anger.

'Sir, if you have any sense of decency or delicacy, you won't do that!' Soon after his return, being 'very ill of a cold and cough', Johnson went to stay with his 'honoured Mistress' at Streatham so that he could be 'taken care of'.

The Thrales' house had been considerably enlarged and altered during the summer of the year before; a whole new library wing had been added, and many of the rooms had been remodelled. All this had been done despite a crisis in Henry Thrale's business affairs.

The brewery had been brought to the verge of bankruptcy by Thrale's foolhardy endorsement of the ideas of one Humphrey Jackson who claimed to have discovered a revolutionary way of making beer without hops or malt. Tempted by the fortune to be made from Jackson's improbable process, Thrale risked a great deal of money upon it, abandoning conventional brewing for a year and spending two thousand pounds upon huge new copper vats. At the end of the year he had no beer and enormous debts. To add to his worries his family continued to grow, while his mistresses became increasingly troublesome and expensive.

His wife, energetic and resilient as ever, was never cast down for long. Even the death of her mother in June 1773, and, in the following October, of her uncle Sir Thomas Salusbury—from whom she inherited a small and rather tumbledown estate in Flintshire instead of the money she had hoped for—had not upset her for long. In the spring of 1774, the brewery being back in business again, she decided that it was time for a little holiday. It was years since she had been back to Wales and there was now a good reason for a visit—an inspection of Bach-y-Graig, her inheritance in Flintshire. Her husband agreed to go with her; and they decided to take their eldest daughter, Queeney, now ten years old. Johnson, who had expressed his readiness 'to begin a new journey' immediately upon his return from Scotland, was asked to join them.

They left Streatham on the morning of Tuesday 5 July and set out for Barnet, where they stopped for forty minutes at the Mitre, and then went on to a 'good cold' dinner with some relatives of Henry Thrale at St Albans. From St Albans they travelled to Lichfield by way of Dunstable, Johnson reading Cicero on the road and, although Thrale was bearing his expenses, characteristically taking careful note of the cost of travel.

He was in cheerful spirits; he settled back in the coach, after it had become too dark to read, with the contented comment, 'How much pleasanter it is travelling by night than by day!' He was obviously looking forward to seeing Lichfield again and to showing it and its inhabitants to his friends. So when next morning Mrs Thrale came down to breakfast in the Swan at Lichfield, Johnson was distressed to see her wearing a 'morning nightgown and close cap' in his native city. 'My dress did not please him,' she recorded in her diary, 'and he made me alter it entirely before he would stir a step with us about the town, saying most satirical things about the appearance I made.'

Once clothed to his satisfaction, Mrs Thrale was taken to see the famous museum of Richard Greene, the apothecary, a 'bustling, good-humoured little man', whose wonderful collection 'both of antiquities and natural curiosities and ingenious works of art' was later to impress

Boswell; then she was taken to a service in the Cathedral, and after that to the house where he was born, to Lucy Porter, and to Stowe Hill to call upon Elizabeth Aston, Molly's sister.

During the course of the next two days they had breakfast with Dr Erasmus Darwin, the physiologist and poet, Charles Darwin's grandfather, and with Peter Garrick, David's eldest brother; they had tea with Mrs Thomas Cobb, and paid visits to Andrew Newton, a rich wine-merchant and brother of the Bishop of Bristol, to Mary Vyse, daughter of the man, now dead, who had tried to give Johnson a pair of new shoes at Oxford and who had afterwards became Archdeacon of Salop, and to Anna Seward. On Saturday, 9 July they left for Ashbourne to stay with John Taylor.

Taylor took them over to see the Duke of Devonshire's house at Chatsworth. Johnson who had been there before and had, on that occasion, been given a display of the fountains and cascade, was not greatly impressed on this second visit by either the house or its furniture. He was again struck by some of the waterworks in the grounds, in particular by a willow tree that spouted out streams of water from its every bough at the touch of a concealed spring; but to a man who had 'seen the Ocean, cascades were but little things'. Of all the Duke's possessions he confessed that he liked Atlas, one of his handsome racehorses, the best.[1]

Nor did Johnson entertain a much higher opinion of Lord Scarsdale's new house at Kedleston which they visited after a walk over Dovedale—a place that deserved a visit but did not answer his expectations. Kedleston, recently finished by Robert Adam, had a 'very stately' hall, a 'very richly furnished' state bedchamber, and the dining parlour was 'more splendid with gilt plate' than any he had ever seen. Yet the whole displayed 'more cost than judgement'; it was all 'very costly but ill-contrived'.

From Kedleston they went to Derby, where Johnson 'remarked a particular manner of propagating motion from a horizontal to a vertical wheel', and noted that Mr Thrale's bill at the inn for dinner was '0 – 18 – 10'. From Derby they went to Macclesfield—'a very large town in Cheshire, little known. It has a silk mill.'

The next day, Johnson continued in his diary, as though recording the bare, dull facts out of a sense of unwelcome duty, 'We came to Congleton where there is likewise a silk mill. Then to Middlewich, a mean old town, without any manufacture, but I think a corporation. Thence we proceeded to [Nantwich], an old town, from the Inn, I saw scarcely any but black timber houses. I tasted the brine water, which contains much more salt than the sea-water. By slow evaporation they make large crystals of salt, by quick boiling small granulations. It seemed to have no other preparation. At evening we came to Combermere [Hall, the home of Sir Lynch Salusbury Cotton, Mrs Thrale's uncle], so called from a wide lake. 22 [July]. We went upon the Mere. I pulled a bulrush of about ten feet. 23 [July]. We visited Lord Kilmurrey's house [Shavington Hall]. It is large and convenient, with many rooms, none of which are magnificently spacious. The furniture was not splendid. The bed curtains were guarded. Lord K. [an 'extremely offensive' man, in Mrs Thrale's opinion] showd the place with too much exultation. He has no park, and little water. 24 [July]. We went to a Chapel built by Sir Lynch Cotton for his tenants. It is consecrated and therefore, I suppose, endowed. It is neat and plain. . . . 26 [July] . . . In the afternoon we came to West Chester (my father went to the fair when I had small pox). We walked round the walls which are compleat and contain one Mile, three quarters, and one hundred and one yards[;]within them are many gardens. They are very high, and two may walk very commodiously side by side. On the inside is a rail; there are towers from space to space not very frequent, and I think not all compleat.'

Johnson was not sure whether or not they were complete because it was late and almost dark when they finished their walk, and Mrs Thrale, who wanted to go to bed, grew tired and cross, and was afterwards put 'fairly out of countenance' when Johnson commented, 'I have known *my mistress* fifteen years and never saw her fairly out of humour but on Chester wall.'

They remained at Chester the next day and saw the Cathedral, which, in Johnson's opinion, was 'not of the first rank'. Chester, he added laconically, had 'many curiosities'. He did not enjoy looking at them, though. For he liked to take his time, 'was slow, and heavy, and short-sighted', in Mrs Thrale's words, and while he was still examining or discussing one object, the brisk, impatient guide would rush him off to see another. He kept his temper as long as he could, then suddenly demanded of Mrs Thrale, 'Pray, what is this gentleman's name, who accompanies us so officiously?'

'I think they called him *Harold*,' replied Mrs Thrale, 'and perhaps you will find him to be of the family of *Harold Harefoot*, he runs with us at such a rate.'

At this Johnson turned on her in fury; she had 'seldom seen him much more angry'. 'Oh, Madam,' he said, 'you had rather crack a JOKE, I know, than stop to learn anything I can teach; so take the road you were born to run.'

The next day the travellers entered Wales and Johnson's diary continued its dry story, by turns laborious and perfunctory. Having inspected Bach-y-Graig without much enthusiasm, they went to St Asaph where the Cathedral, though not large, was judged to have 'something of dignity and Grandeur' and the Bishop was 'very civil'. They went to Denbigh and inspected the ruined castle, once 'a prodigious pile'. They visited Holywell, 'a Market town neither very small nor mean'; they saw St Winifred's Well and the bath 'completely and indecently open'; and a woman bathed in it while they all looked on.² They travelled on to Rhuddlan Castle, 'a very noble ruin'; and to Bodryhddan where Johnson grew cross when made to trudge unwillingly on to see a cascade which turned out—he admitted he was not sorry to find it so—completely dry.

Mrs Thrale lost her purse here, and expressed so much uneasiness that Johnson concluded the sum to be very great; when he learned it was only seven guineas he was 'glad to find she had so much sensibility of money'. They went on to Lleweney and to Conway, to Anglesey and Beaumaris Castle, 'a mighty pile'; they travelled to Bangor—where all four of them were stuffed into one filthy bedroom in the inn and where the 'Quire [of the Cathedral was] mean and the service not well read'. Then they went on to Snowdon where they saw a huge herd of goats, and Mr Thrale said he would give his daughter a penny for every one she counted; Johnson kept the score, which, as he meticulously noted in his journal, was 149. From Snowdon they drove to Bodvil, 'the place where Mrs T. was born'. 'Mrs T. remembred the rooms and wandered over them with recollections of her childhood. This species of pleasure is always melancholy. The walk was cut down and the pond was dry.'

The church was mean and neglected 'to a degree scarcely imaginable'; the earth floor was full of holes; the pews were rude benches; there was a hole in the roof; and on the desk there was a Welsh black letter bible which the curate had great difficulty in reading.

Although the country appeared to be 'full of very splendid houses', Johnson did not think very highly of most of the people who lived in them. It was not until they reached Gwaynynog that they were made to feel welcome, and it was not until they met John Myddleton, their kind and hospitable host there, that Johnson found anyone in Wales to whom he could talk of literature. At Llanrhaiadur their entertainment by the vicar was 'poor'; at Carnarvon when they dined at Sir Thomas Wynn's it was 'mean'. Lady Catherine Wynn [daughter of the second Earl of Egmont] 'set a vile dinner before us,' Mrs Thrale confirmed, 'and on such linen as shocked one; no plate, no china to be seen, nothing but what was as despicable as herself'. Lady Catherine was 'an empty woman of quality, insolent, ignorant and ill bred, without either beauty or fortune to atone for her faults. . . . Mr Johnson compared her at our return to sour small beer; she could not have been a good thing, he said, and even that poor thing was spoilt.'

Even at Gwaynynog Mrs Thrale thought the other women guests were 'gross' and their conversation 'contracted'.[3] But if she could not boast of the elegance of the society of the 'Welch folks' at Gwaynynog, she was quite derisive about the conversation offered to Johnson by various Welsh parsons whom they met elsewhere. At Chirk Castle the conversation of the 'ridiculous' chaplain made her 'ready to burst with laughing'; and she found it 'impossible not to laugh when a Welch parson of mean abilities' struck with reverence at the sight of Dr Johnson, whom he had heard of as the greatest man living, could not find any words to answer his enquiries concerning a motto round somebody's arms which adorned a tomb-stone in Ruabon church-yard. 'If I remember right the words were Heb Dw, Heb Dym, Dw o' diggon,' Mrs Thrale wrote. 'And though no very difficult construction, the gentleman seemed wholly confounded, and unable to explain them; till Mr Johnson having picked out the meaning by little and little, said to the man, "Heb is a preposition, I believe, Sir, is it not?" My countryman recovering some spirits upon the sudden question, cried out, "So I humbly presume, Sir," very comically.'

But generally in Wales with the Thrale family, Johnson was treated with nothing like the respect he had been accorded in Scotland with Boswell; and three years after his return, when Boswell expressed a desire to see Wales, he strongly dissuaded him. What was there in Wales, he wanted to know, except the woods of Bach-y-Graig?—and even these received scant praise in his diary. What was there that could 'fill the hunger of ignorance, or quench the thirst of curiosity'? Wales offered 'nothing to the speculation of the traveller'. His diary shows that he was not as blind to the beauties of nature as he often affected to be; but whenever Mr Thrale pointed out a particularly fine view to him he dismissed it as abruptly as he had dismissed the prospect of the Firth of Forth from Leith to which Boswell had too eagerly drawn his attention.

'Mr Thrale loved prospects,' his wife wrote, 'and was mortified that his friend could not enjoy the sight of those different dispositions of wood and water, hill and valley, that travelling through England and France affords a man. But when he wished to point them out to his companion: "Never heard such nonsense," would be the reply: "a blade of grass is always a blade of grass whether in one country or another: let us if we *do* talk, talk about something: men and women are my subjects of enquiry; let us see how these differ from those we have left behind. . . ." Walking in a wood when it rained was, I think, the only rural image he pleased his fancy with; "for (says he) after one has gathered the apples in an orchard, one wishes them well baked, and removed to a London eating house for enjoyment."' The best gardens were those which produced most roots and fruit; the water most to be prized was that which contained most fish.

'Has this BROOK e'er a name?' was a typical enquiry made of Mrs Thrale in north Wales. Why, he was assured, this was the *River* Ustrad. 'Let us jump over it directly,' he then said, turning to Thrale, 'and show them how an *Englishman* should treat a *Welch* RIVER.'

Often Mrs Thrale, to make up for her rather surly ten-year-old daughter, Queeney, her silent husband and his grumpy friend, behaved towards their hosts and guides with what Johnson took to be excessive civility. A young friend of Mrs Thrale later recorded this comment of hers to Johnson at Streatham: 'I remember, Sir, when we were travelling in Wales, how you called me to account for my civility to the people. "Madam," you said, "let me have no more of this idle commendation of nothing. Why is it, that whatever you see, and whoever you see, you are to be so indiscriminately lavish of praise?" "Why, I'll tell you, Sir," said I, "when I am travelling with you and Mr Thrale and Queeney, I am obliged to be civil for four."'

Certainly there were times when Johnson, for one, was appallingly rude. At Sir Robert Cotton's, Mrs Thrale said, she had 'meant to please him particularly with a dish of very young peas'. Were they not charming? she asked him, while he was eating them. 'Perhaps,' he said, 'they would be so—to a pig.'⁴ She remembered another day, while riding with him in their carriage, that Johnson told her husband that he had never sought to please till past thirty years old, considering the matter hopeless, but that since then he had 'always been studious not to make enemies'. So saying he had taken a book out of his pocket and started reading. He had continued reading when George Cholmondeley, 'a gentleman of no small distinction for his birth and elegance', had rode up to the carriage to pay its occupants his compliments. Since Johnson took no notice, Cholmondeley tapped him gently on the shoulder; there being still no response, Thrale said, ''Tis Mr Cholmondeley.' 'Well, Sir,' said Johnson sternly at last, lifting his eyes for but a moment from his book, 'and what if it is Mr Cholmondeley!'⁵

Frances Reynolds records a somewhat similar response to the efforts of a man to introduce a new member to him at the Club. 'This, Sir, is Mr Vesey,' the man said. 'I see him,' Johnson replied and immediately turned away. No more fortunate was the person who approached Johnson to say, 'Will you permit me, Sir, to present to you the Abbé Raynal?'

'No, Sir,' was Johnson's very loud reply before he turned on his heels and moved off.

Yet Johnson continued always to think of himself as good-humoured. 'It is wonderful, Sir, how rare a quality good humour is in life,' he observed one day on a coach journey. 'We meet with very few good-humoured men. . . . I look upon *myself*,' he added, shaking his head, stretching himself at ease in his seat, and smiling with much complacency, 'I look upon *myself* as a good-humoured fellow.' He also continued to look upon himself as a 'very polite man'. A man had no more right to *say* an uncivil thing than to *act* one, he informed Bennet Langton, 'no more right to say a rude thing to another than to knock him down'.

'Sir, you need say no more,' he assured Burke who had begun his recommendation of Agmondesham Vesey for membership of the Club by saying that he was a man of gentle manners. 'When you have said a man of gentle manners, you have said enough.'

Certainly Johnson seems often to have been quite unaware of his rudeness and abruptness, and when made aware of it by a sharp retort to have been—at best—anxious to make amends, or—at worst—apparently unoffended. The American historian, Gilbert Stuart, was introduced to Johnson by his fellow-countryman, Benjamin West, the painter. After they had been talking for some time, Johnson turned to West and said to him that his young friend spoke very good English. Then, turning to Stuart, he asked him where he learned it.

The young American very promptly and effectively replied, 'Sir, I can better tell you where I did not learn it—it was not from your dictionary.' Johnson seemed satisfied of his own impertinence and was not offended.

For much of the time in Wales Johnson had not been feeling well. One day he was so out of sorts, that he actually refused both coffee and tea after dinner, something he could not remember ever having done before. He took wine of antimony and tartar emetic, both depressants, without success; and took a number of ipecac pills which had little better effect. He returned to England out of health and consequently out of temper. It was *very* difficult, as he had often said to Mrs Thrale, for a sick man not to be a scoundrel.

Nevertheless, when the Thrales, accompanied again by Queeney—and this time also by Giuseppe Baretti, Queeney's Italian tutor whom Johnson had known for over twenty years—visited Paris the next year and asked Johnson to go with them, he accepted the invitation readily.

He had never been abroad before; and he affected all the narrow, insular Englishman's distrust of foreigners. He admitted that his own countrymen were too reserved towards strangers, that two of them 'shewn into a room together at a house where they are both visitors [would] probably go each to a different window, and remain in obstinate silence'; but even that was to be preferred to the chatter of Frenchmen who were always talking whether they knew anything or not. In fact, in almost every respect, Englishmen were far superior to other people. Needless to say, Africans and Asiatics could not be compared with them. Ten thousand Londoners could drive all the people of Peking; 'they would drive them like deer'.

When Boswell commended the people of Tahiti, Johnson cut him short with the tart retort, 'Don't cant in defence of savages.'

'They have the art of navigation,' Boswell persisted.

'A dog or a cat can swim.'

'They carve very ingeniously.'

'A cat can scratch, and a child with a nail can scratch.'

Even the Chinese in Johnson's opinion, were savages. But had they not arts? Boswell suggested.

'They have pottery.'

'What do you say to the written characters of their language?'

'Sir, they have not an alphabet. They have not been able to form what all other nations have formed.'

'There is more learning in their language than any other, from the immense number of their characters.'

'It is only more difficult from its rudeness, as there is more labour in hewing down a tree with a stone than with an axe.'

As for Americans, well they, he assured Dr John Campbell, were 'a race of convicts, and ought to be thankful for anything we allow them short of hanging'. He was willing to love all mankind, he averred on a later occasion, '*except an American*'. Although he numbered several Americans among his friends and 'set a high value' upon their friendship—he met Benjamin Franklin at a meeting of a society interested in financing schools for Negroes in the American colonies—Americans were in general 'rascals, robbers and pirates'; he would 'burn and destroy them'. Anna Seward, who was present when this outburst took place, remarked that it was an instance 'that we are always most violent against those whom we have injured'. This made him more furious than ever and he roared out another tremendous volley that Boswell thought might have been heard across the Atlantic.

The French were little better than the Americans; but when the Thrales offered to take him on a trip to Paris, he felt it was an opportunity which should on no account be missed. He had long been an advocate of foreign travel and always spoke of it with uncommon animation. Within a few days of meeting Boswell he urged him to go to Spain, a good deal of which had 'not been perambulated'; and he later proposed that they should go together upon a tour of the Baltic countries. When Boswell expressed a wish to see the wall of China, Johnson pressed him to go. 'Sir,' he said urgently, 'by doing so, you would do what would be of importance in raising your children to eminence. There would be a lustre reflected upon them from your spirit and curiosity. They would at all times be regarded as the children of a man who had gone to visit the wall of China. I am serious, Sir.' He would himself, he said, have gone to Constantinople to study Arabic if his pension had come to him twenty years before. The only two places he did not particularly want to see were America, which had nothing to offer but natural curiosities, and Ireland. In fact, he told Boswell, Ireland is 'the last place where I should wish to travel'.

'Should you not like to see Dublin, Sir?'

'No, Sir. Dublin is only a worse capital.'

'Is not the Giant's Causeway worth seeing?'

'Worth seeing? Yes. But not worth going to see.'

What *was* worth any man's going to see was Italy; but you had to be of a suitable age to appreciate it. He disapproved of young men going off on the Grand Tour too young; it would be much better for them to spend the time studying, though, indeed, 'if a young man is wild, and must run after women and bad company, it is better this should be done abroad'. Most young men added nothing to their conversation by having travelled. Only once had he ever heard one certain young Lord 'talk of what he had seen, and that was of a large serpent in one of the pyramids of Egypt'.

A man was always conscious of an inferiority, however, 'from his not having seen what it is expected a man should see. The grand object of travelling is to see the shores of the Mediterranean. On those shores were the four great empires of the world: the Assyrian, the Persian, the Grecian and the Roman. All our religion, almost all our law, almost all our arts, almost all that sets us above savages, has come to us from the shores of the Mediterranean.'

Paris was not the Mediterranean, but it was a step in the right direction.
Dr Johnson explored Paris with all the conscientious industry of an
earnest young man on his Grand Tour. He went to the École Militaire,
and the observatory, to the Chartreuse, the foundling hospital in the
Faubourg St Antoine, the Courts of Justice, the Palais Royal, and the
Palais Bourbon, to several *hôtels* and to many churches. He took the
coach out to Versailles. He walked in the Place Vendôme and in the
Tuileries. He inspected the King's cabinet, a natural history museum
where there was displayed a wonderful variety of shells, fossils, precious
stones and dried animals: it was 'very neat, not, perhaps, perfect'. He
also went to the King's library in the Rue Richelieu, to the libraries of
the Sorbonne and St Germain, and to the royal menagerie—apparently
the first proper zoo he had ever seen. In his diary he carefully listed the
animals, the black stags and brown bears, the camels and dromedaries, a
rhinoceros—'the skin folds like loose cloth double over his body . . . a vast
animal, though young'—and a baby elephant with his tusks just appearing. The tigers he did not see very clearly. 'Among the birds was a pelican,
who being let out, went to a fountain, and swam about to catch fish. His
feet well webbed: he dipped his head, and turned his long bill sidewise.
He caught two or three fish, but did not eat them.'

He went to watch the royal family at dinner and noticed that the
'King fed himself with his left hand as we'; he saw the Queen riding side-
saddle in the forest at Fontainebleau, and went over the stables which
were 'cool', though the gutters were filthy. The horses were 'not much
commended', the dogs 'almost all English' and 'degenerate'. He gratified
his curiosity about the manufactures of Paris by visiting the Gobelins
tapestry factory, the porcelain works at Sèvres, the workshops where the
best looking-glasses were wrought, M. Santerre's brewery and the King's
watchmaker. He went over the house of the Marquis de Paulmy d'Argen-
son, which was almost entirely covered with looking glasses, and the
house of Gagny, Intendant des Finances, where he saw rooms 'furnished
with a profusion of wealth and elegance' that he had never seen before—
'the whole furniture said to have cost 125,000 L'. He dined with the
Marquis Blanchetti, with Count Manucci, and with the Benedictines,
who gave him, it being unfortunately a fast day, 'soup meagre, herrings,
eels, both with sauce. Fryed fish. Lentils, tasteless in themselves'.

He watched the rope- and egg-dancing on the boulevards; and he
walked through the galleries of the Palais de Justice where he bought a
snuff box for Lucy Porter, a table-book, and three pairs of scissors. He
visited the convent of the English Austin nuns, Notre Dame de Sion, and

it was probably here that he made the remark to the prioress that he later related to Boswell: 'Madam, you are here, not for the love of virtue, but the fear of vice.'[6] He spoke always in Latin, for 'it was a maxim with him that a man should not let himself down by speaking a language which he speaks imperfectly', and, according to Foote, who was in Paris at the same time, he 'obstinately continued' to wear exactly the same brown clothes, black stockings and plain shirt that he wore in London, quite astonishing the inhabitants by this strange attire and by his stranger antics which Foote succeeded in making appear 'abundantly ludicrous'. Before the end of his holiday, however, he acquired a new hat, at least two pairs of white stockings and was seen parading the streets in 'a French-made wig of handsome construction'.

He returned home satisfied that Paris could not hold a candle to London and that the French were no match for Englishmen. He was not in the least surprised that a rage for everything English had prevailed in their country since the end of the Seven Years' War, for, so he said, 'we had drubbed those fellows into a proper reverence for us. . . . Their national petulance required periodical chastisement.'

'Paris is not so fine a place as you would expect,' he told Lucy Porter. 'The palaces and churches, however, are very splendid and magnificent: and what would please you, there are many very fine pictures; but I do not think their mode of life commodious or pleasant.' Their meals, he had decided immediately upon arrival, were 'gross'; and they had once been served a 'Hare not tainted but putrified'. 'The meat in the markets is such as would be sent to a gaol in England; and Mr Thrale justly observed, that the cookery of the French was forced upon them by necessity; for they could not eat their meat, unless they added some taste to it. The French are an indelicate people; they will spit upon any place. At Madame [du Boccage], a literary lady of rank, the footman took the sugar in his fingers, and threw it into my coffee. . . . The spout of the tea-pot did not pour freely; she bade the footman blow into it.[7] France is worse than Scotland in everything but climate. . . . The French are a gross, ill-bred, untaught people; a lady will spit on the floor and rub it in with her foot. What I gained by being in France was learning to be better satisfied with my own country.'

Frances Reynolds recorded a conversation in which Johnson elaborated his complaints:

JOHNSON: 'The French, Sir, are a very silly People, they have no common life. Nothing but the two ends, Beggary and Nobility. . . .

Sir, they are made up in every thing of two extremes. They have no common sense, they have no common manners, no common learning, gross ignorance or *les belles lettres.* . . . They are much behind-hand, stupid, ignorant creatures. At Fountainblue I saw a Horse-race, everything was wrong, the heaviest weight was put upon the weakest Horse, and all the jockies wore the same colour coat.'

GENTLEMAN: 'Had you any acquaintance in Paris?'

JOHNSON: 'No, I did not stay long enough to make any. I spoke only Latin, and I could not have much conversation. There is no good in letting the French have a superiority over you every word you speak. . . . Baretti was sometimes displeased with us for not liking the French.'

LADY: 'Perhaps he had a kind of partiality for that country, because it was in the way to Italy, and perhaps their manners resembled the Italians.'

JOHNSON: 'No. He was the showman, and we did not like his show; that was all the reason.'[8]

Miss Reynolds thought that Johnson and Baretti never got on well together after this trip to Paris and what perhaps 'entirely extinguished' their friendship was 'a most mendacious falsehood' that Baretti told Johnson about his having twice beaten the South Sea Islander, Omai, at chess; 'for the very reverse was true'.

'Do you think,' he said to Johnson, 'that I should be conquered at chess by a savage?'

'I know you were.'

Baretti continued to insist upon the contrary which brought Johnson from his seat in a most violent rage, crying 'I'll hear no more.' In a fright, Baretti flew out of the house, Miss Williams told Miss Reynolds, 'and perhaps never entered it after. I believe he was never invited.'

Baretti, for his part, never afterwards spoke of Johnson with his earlier reverence. 'Johnson is a nasty old man [*un vecchiaccio*],' he told his brothers the following year, 'a giant both in body and mind, always absent-minded, fierce, touchy, dirty, full of unpleasant habits, always shifting his body when he is seated, and always moving his jaw like an ox chewing the cud; but as he is rightly believed to possess more learning than any other man in this kingdom, he is feared and respected by all, perhaps more than he is loved. Although he is a great critic in French, and knows almost as much Italian as I do, he can speak neither language; but he speaks Latin as vehemently as Cicero. . . .'

Part IV

1776–1784

13
'Whole Nests of People in his House'

'He is tall and stout; but stoops terribly; he is almost bent double. His mouth is almost constantly opening and shutting as if he was chewing. He has a strange method of frequently twirling his fingers, and twisting his hands. His body is in continual agitation, see-sawing up and down; his feet are never a moment quiet; and, in short, his whole person is in perpetual motion.'
Fanny Burney

Although he spoke with such enthusiasm of the benefits of foreign travel, there can be no doubt that Johnson was pleased, as always, to return to the comforts of Streatham. Here, as he now advanced into old age, he appeared to be as happy as he had ever been in his life. He enjoyed to the full the family life and family jokes, the parties, the constant stream of guests and visitors. He was always assured of company, and never got up in the morning until he was sure there would be people about, though once he arrived first in the breakfast-room and was much put out to find himself alone for a considerable time. 'Madam,' he afterwards said reproachfully to Mrs Thrale, who twitted him for normally being so late, 'I do not like to come down to vacuity.'

He happily played charades and undemanding parlour games; and, although he did not usually like to be reminded of his birthday, 'an awful day' that brought fears of death, he dearly loved the celebrations which were held on 17 September, Queeney's birthday, and on his own birthday, the next day, when all the servants and their friends were given a dance and supper and allowed the use of the summer house 'to fill with acquaintance and merriment'. He took delight in gently teasing the pretty young girls who came to tea and in romping with the children. When Mrs Thrale's cousin, Margaret Owen, came to stay, he gave it out that she had declined his hand in marriage and warned other potential suitors that since she had not accepted him she was unlikely to take to them. When Mrs Thrale's mother was alive, he had riotously indulged her passion for foreign news by inventing global wars and shattering battles being fought that very moment upon the Continent.[1] He made mottoes and jokes and exercised his talent for reciting extempore verse. Once when Queeney was discussing with a friend whether or not to wear a new gown and a new hat he suddenly, to her surprise—for she thought he was out of earshot—advised her,

> Wear the gown and wear the hat,
> Snatch thy pleasures while they last,
> Hadst thou nine lives like a cat,
> Soon those nine lives would be past.

Similarly, when Mrs Thrale went into his room on the morning of her thirty-fifth birthday, complaining that no one sent her verses any more, he immediately recited to her—

> Oft in danger, yet alive,
> We are come to thirty-five;
> Long may better years arrive,
> Better years than thirty-five.
> Could philosophers contrive
> Life to stop at thirty-five,
> Time his hours should never drive
> O'er the bounds of thirty-five.
> High to soar, and deep to dive,
> Nature gives at thirty-five.
> Ladies, stock and tend your hive,
> Trifle not at thirty-five:
> For howe'er we boast and strive,
> Life declines from thirty-five:
> He that ever hopes to thrive
> Must begin by thirty-five;
> And all who wisely wish to wive
> Must look on Thrale at thirty-five.

'And now,' he added as she was writing the lines down, 'you may see what it is to come for poetry to a dictionary-maker; you may observe that the rhymes run in alphabetical order exactly.'

Mrs Thrale also recalled how when a guest was giving what Johnson deemed excessive praise to these verses of Lope de Vega:

> Se a quien los leones vence
> Vence una muger hermosa
> El de mas flaco s'averguence
> O ella de ser mas furiosa,

'Mr Johnson instantly observed that they were "founded on a trivial conceit; and that conceit ill-explained, and ill-expressed beside. That lady, we all know, does not conquer in the same manner that the lion does. 'Tis a mere play of words, and you might as well say that,

> If the man who turnips cries,
> Cry not when his father dies,
> 'Tis a proof that he had rather
> Have a turnip than his father."'

Also at Streatham, Johnson was able to indulge his taste for reading aloud to a small audience. His skill at this was widely renowned. According to Arthur Murphy, 'his manner of reciting verses . . . was wonderfully impressive'; while Mrs Thrale said that 'whoever once heard him repeat an ode of Horace, would be long before they could endure to hear it repeated by another'. He delighted in reading verses from Pope which he did to wonderful effect; 'but what was very remarkable', in Miss Reynolds's opinion, 'was that though his cadence in reading poetry was so judiciously emphatical as to give a double force to the words he utter'd, yet in reading prose, particularly common and familiar subjects, narrations, essays, letters, etc., nothing could be more injudicious than his manner, beginning every period with a pompous accent, and reading it with a whine, or with a kind of spasmodic struggle for utterance; and this, not from any natural infirmity, but from a strange singularity, in reading on, in one breath, as if he had made a resolution not to respire until he had closed the sentence'.

William Cooke said that Johnson was never so impressive as when he was reciting prayers or hymns; and once 'fired by someone quoting the nineteenth psalm, he took off his hat and recited the hymn, "The Spacious Firmament on High". . . . His habitually harsh features were, on this occasion, transformed as if it had been the face of an angel.' Sometimes, when reciting particularly moving passages he would break down and weep.

Of all the pleasures to be enjoyed at the Thrales none, perhaps, was more to Johnson's taste than the joy of a dinner party with fine food and excellent company, marred only by a large, ill-behaved spaniel, named Belle, whose 'frequent solicitations to be fed' made him very cross. At the big table in the dining-room he could enjoy sitting next to attractive young women like the beautiful Sophy Streatfeild whose knowledge of Greek was scarcely less remarkable than her ability to shed tears upon request. Johnson confessed that he loved her much; she was a 'sweet creature', though it had to be admitted that, 'taking away her Greek, she was as ignorant as a butterfly'. He could also enjoy talking to those friends and acquaintances of his whom the Thrales' hospitality brought out to Streatham. Reynolds, Goldsmith, Burke and Garrick were all regular guests; Boswell was invited when he was staying in London; Charles Burney was often there as he taught music to the children; Giuseppe Baretti, as Queeney's tutor, stayed in the house for months on end. Portraits of all these and of other frequent visitors were commissioned from Reynolds and hung in the library, arranged around Johnson's portrait which was given the best position over the fireplace.

Naturally all her dinner parties did not go off as smoothly as the hostess would have liked since the temper of the guest, whose presence at her table was the principal reason for its fame, became more and more unpredictable as he grew older. One afternoon in March 1775 Dr Thomas Campbell, the Irish clergyman, came to dine, and afterwards recorded his most unfavourable impressions in his diary:

Johnson you are the very man Lord Chesterfield describes. A Hottentot indeed. And tho' your abilities are respectable, you never can be respected yourself. He has the aspect of an Idiot—without the faintest ray of sense gleaming from any one feature. With the most awkward garb & unpowdered grey wig on one side only of his head, he is forever dancing the Devils jig, & sometimes he makes the most driveling effort to whistle some thought in his absent paroxisms. He came up to me and took me by the hand—then sat down on a sofa, & mumbled out that he had hear'd two papers had appeared against him in the course of this week. . . . His awkwardness at table is just what Chesterfield described and his roughness of manner kept pace with that. When Mrs Thrale quoted something from Fosters Sermons he flew in a passion & said that Foster was a man of mean ability, & of no original thinking. All of which tho' I took to be most true yet I held it not meet to have so set down. . . . The Doctor—as he drinks no wine—retired soon after dinner—& Baretti who, I see, is a sort of literary toad-eater to

Johnson told me that he was a man nowise affected by praise or dispraise. . . . The Doctor however returned again, & with all the fond anxiety of an author I saw him cast out all his nets to know the sense of the town about his last pamphlet, *Taxation no Tyranny*—which he said did not sell. Mr Thrale told him such and such members of both houses admired it—And why did you not tell me this—quoth Johnson. —Thrale asked him what Sir Joshua Reynolds said of it? Sir Joshua, quoth the Doctor has not read it. I suppose, quoth Thrale he has been busy of late. No! sayd the Doctor but I never look at his pictures, so he won't read my writings. Was this like a man insensible to glory.

A few years later Johnson made a similarly unfavourable impression upon two Quakers who came to dinner, one of whom made some remark about the defence of Gibraltar which aroused Johnson's ire. 'I would advise you, Sir,' said he, with what his hostess described as a 'cold sneer', 'never to relate this story again. You really can scarce imagine how *very poor* a figure you make in the telling of it.'

The crushed Quaker dared not raise his voice again, contenting himself with a few quiet remarks to the friend who sat next to him. After they had gone, Johnson said to Mrs Thrale, 'very seriously', 'I did not quarrel with those Quaker fellows.'

'You did perfectly right for they gave you no cause of offence.'

'No offence!' he exclaimed in an altered tone of voice. 'And is it nothing to sit whispering together when *I* am present, without ever directing their discourse towards me, or offering me a share in the conversation?'

From most accounts of Johnson at Streatham, however, we derive an impression not so much of cantankerousness and conceit as of geniality, good nature and generosity. He laughed more heartily, his hostess wrote in her journal, than almost any man she had ever known; and his laugh was 'irresistible'. Certainly Dr Burney's daughter, Fanny, provided in her diary a very different portrait of Dr Johnson than that drawn by Dr Campbell.

Fanny, small, shy and extremely short-sighted, had not been sent to France to be educated as her sisters had been after the early death of their mother. Instead she had been left more or less to her own devices at home, and had scarcely been educated at all. But she was intelligent and quick, and if her nervous, fluttering timidity seemed almost assumed at times and therefore irritating, she was a responsive girl, warm-hearted and understanding. In 1777, unknown to her father, her brother took the manuscript of her anonymous novel, *Evelina*, to a bookseller and sold the copyright for £20. It sold so well she might have made £15,000 out of it;

but she did not mind about the money. *Evelina* was as highly praised by Burke as by Gibbon. Joshua Reynolds became so absorbed in it over dinner one day that he had to be fed, and he stayed up all night to finish it. Its little author was made famous; and when he met her Johnson assured her emphatically that his admiration for her novel was as great as anyone's.

Fanny Burney had long wanted to meet Dr Johnson. She had heard so many stories about him in their house; she had read with awe and admiration his *Rasselas*; she knew how devoted to him her father was;[2] how Johnson's praise of his *Tours* had given him the 'highest delight', coming as it did from one whom he revered 'above all authors living or dead': 'What would I not go through to see Dr Johnson!' she wrote in her diary in the spring of 1772. 'Mr Bewley [William Bewley to whom Johnson later sent copies of some of his works inscribed to 'The broom gentleman'] accepted as a present or relic, a tuft of his hearth broom, which my father secretly cut off, and sent to him in a frank. He thinks it more precious than pearls.'[3]

Fanny's desire to meet Dr Johnson had been increased by hearing David Garrick, during a breakfast-time visit to their house—formerly Sir Isaac Newton's house—in St Martin's Street, give his celebrated imitation of his former schoolmaster:

'David, will you lend me [your Petrarch]?'
'Yes, sir.'
'David, you sigh.'
'Sir, you shall have it certainly.'
Accordingly, the book, stupendously bound, was sent; but scarce had he received it, when uttering a Latin ejaculation (which Mr Garrick repeated) in a fit of enthusiasm,—all over his head goes poor [Petrarch], —Russian leather and all![4]

It was not, however, until March 1777 that Fanny met her hero for the first time. He had been invited to a morning party at St Martin's Street with Mrs Thrale and Mrs Thrale's cousin, Miss Owen. The party from Streatham arrived first. Miss Owen was 'good humoured and sensible . . . a sort of butt, and, as such, a general favourite'. Mrs Thrale was 'a very pretty woman still [she was then thirty-seven] extremely lively and chatty', with 'no supercilious or pedantic airs', 'really gay and agreeable'. Her daughter, however, who looked about twelve years old (if it was Queeney, as it seems to have been, she was actually fifteen) was, on the contrary, 'stiff and proud' or, possibly, 'shy and reserved'.

While Fanny's two elder sisters, Esther and Susan, were playing a duet on the harpsichord in the library, in strode Dr Johnson. Fanny could not help but be somewhat unnerved by his appearance even though she knew well enough what to expect. 'He is indeed very ill-favoured,' she wrote to her father's old friend and her own confidant, Samuel Crisp, who had encouraged her in her writings and had urged her to keep a journal. 'He is tall and stout; but stoops terribly; he is almost bent double. His mouth is almost constantly opening and shutting, as if he was chewing. He has a strange method of frequently twirling his fingers, and twisting his hands. His body is in continual agitation, *see-sawing* up and down; his feet are never a moment quiet; and, in short, his whole person is in *perpetual motion*. His dress, too, considering the times, and being engaged to dine in a large company, was as much out of the common road as his figure; he had a large wig, snuff-colour coat, and gold (or, peradventure, brass) buttons, but no ruffles to his shirt, doughty fists, and very coarse black worsted stockings.'

Fanny's young sister Charlotte, however, thought that Dr Johnson was 'immensely *smart*, for *him*,—for he had not only a very decent tidy suit of cloathes on, but his hands, face, and linnen were clean, and he treated us with his *worsted wig* which Mr Thrale made him a present of, because it scarce ever gets out of curl'.

'He is shockingly near-sighted,' Fanny continued, 'and did not, till she held out her hand to him, even know Mrs Thrale. He *poked his nose* over the keys of the harpsichord, till the duet was finished, and then my father introduced Hetty [my sister] to him, and he cordially kissed her!'

He then turned away to the bookcases and pored over them, shelf by shelf, his good eye so close to the spines that he almost touched them with his eyelashes as he read the titles. 'At last having fixed upon one, he began without further ceremony, to read to himself, all the time standing at a distance from the company. We were all very much provoked, as we perfectly languished to hear him talk; but it seems he is the most silent creature, when not particularly drawn out, in the world.'

Since there seemed no likelihood of conversation yet awhile Charles Burney sat down at the harpsichord and played another duet with his daughter, Esther. Johnson remained deep in a volume of the *British Encyclopaedia*, apparently oblivious of what was going on. When the duet was finished, however, and Mrs Thrale and Dr Burney were talking about a Bach concert that had been performed the night before, Burney, endeavouring to draw his guest into the conversation, made some remark to him about it:

257

The Doctor, seeing his drift, good-naturedly put away his book, and said very drolly, 'And pray, Sir, *who* is Bach? Is he a piper?' Many exclamations of surprise you will believe followed this question. 'Why you have read his name often in the papers,' said Mrs Thrale; and then gave him some account of this Concert, and the number of fine performances she had heard at it.

'Pray,' said he gravely, 'Madam, what is the expence?'

'Oh!' answered she, 'much trouble and solicitation to get a Subscriber's Ticket, or else, half a guinea.'

'Trouble and solicitation,' said he, 'I will have nothing to do with; but I would be willing to give eighteen pence.' Chocolate being then brought, we adjourned to the drawing-room. And here, Dr Johnson being taken from the books, entered freely and most cleverly into conversation; though it is remarkable he never speaks at all, but when spoken to; nor does he ever *start*, though he so admirably *supports*, any subject.

To her delight, Fanny was given another opportunity of savouring Dr Johnson's conversation when she was invited to stay at Streatham the following year. By then, knowing how highly he had praised her *Evelina*, comparing it favourably with the work of Samuel Richardson, she had developed 'so true a veneration for him' that the 'very sight of him inspired her with delight and reverence notwithstanding the cruel infirmities' to which he was subject. She was placed next to him at dinner, and afterwards thought that it had been the 'most consequential day' of her life. He had been so attentive and so flattering, had told Mrs Thrale how proud he had been to sit by Miss Burney.[5]

'Miss Burney,' said Mrs Thrale laughing, 'you must take great care of your heart if Dr Johnson attacks it; for I assure you he is not often successless.'

'What's that you say, Madam? Are you making mischief between the young lady and me already?'

He was in excellent form; he drank Fanny Burney's health; he laughed, he talked of Garrick and how he looked much older than he was, for his face, changing its expression from one moment to the next, had 'double the business of any other man's . . . and such an eternal, restless, fatiguing play of the muscles, must certainly wear out a man's face before its real time'. They spoke, too, of Sir John Hawkins, and Mrs Thrale said, 'Why now, Dr Johnson, he is another of those whom you suffer nobody to abuse but yourself. Garrick is one, too. . . .'

'Why, madam, they don't know when to abuse him, and when to praise him; I will allow no man to speak ill of David that he does not deserve. And as to Sir John, why really I believe him to be an honest man at the bottom: but to be sure he is penurious, and he is mean, and it must be owned he has a degree of brutality, and a tendency to savageness, that cannot easily be defended.'

They all laughed, as he meant them to do, at this 'curious manner of speaking in Sir John's favour'; and when the laughter had subsided, he told them, in illustration of his friend's meanness, how he had asked to be excused from paying his share of the cost of the supper on the first night of his admission to the Club on the grounds that he had not eaten anything. 'We all scorned him and admitted his plea. For my part I was such a fool as to pay my share for wine, though I never tasted any. But Sir John was a most *unclubable* man!'

On a second longer visit to Streatham, later on that month, Fanny found Dr Johnson in as high spirits as ever, 'full of mirth and sport'. He kissed her hand at breakfast, talked about the characters in her book, told her that she was a toad and a sly young rogue to have created them, and that one of them—Mr Smith—was so good a character that Fielding never drew a better; there was 'no character better drawn anywhere—in any book or by any author'.

During this and later visits, Fanny grew to respect Dr Johnson more and more, to find increasing enjoyment in those 'thousand delightful conversations' she had with him, to grow accustomed to his plea, when she rose to leave—'Don't go little Burney!'—to feel a thrill of pleasure when he put his huge arm round her as she sat beside him on a sofa and urged her, 'half-laughing, half-serious', to be a good girl and not to be so fond of the Scotch. He spoke to her quite openly about the other people in the house, 'neither diminishing faults, nor exaggerating praise', trusting to her discretion. It deeply flattered her vanity to be treated as a special case, to be singled out for his attentions, to join in conversations with him and Mrs Thrale in which he compared them favourably with other women, with, for example

A Mrs Somebody who spent a day here once, and of whom he asked, 'Can she read?'

'Yes, to be sure,' answered Mrs Thrale; 'we have been reading together this afternoon.'

'And what book did you get for her?'

'Why, what happened to be in the way, Hogarth's *Analysis of Beauty*.'

'Hogarth's *Analysis of Beauty*! What made you choose that?'

'Why, Sir, what would you have had me take?'

'What she could have understood—*Cow-hide*, or *Cinderella*!'

'Oh, Dr Johnson,' cried Fanny, "'tis not for nothing you are feared.'

'Oh, you're a rogue!' said he, laughing, 'and they would fear *you* if they knew you.'

He delighted her, too, by the way he said the drollest things in the gravest possible manner, see-sawing in his chair, and by the manner in which he suddenly interrupted a conversation to pay her a compliment—on her cap, for intance: '"Nay, it's very handsome!"

'"What, sir," cried I, amazed.

'" Why, your cap. I have looked at it some time, and I like it much. It has not that vile bandeau across it, which I have so often cursed." Did you ever hear anything so strange? Nothing escapes him.'

One day it was announced that the formidable and contentious Mrs Montagu was coming to dinner, and Johnson turned to Fanny and said to her with great animation, 'Down with her, Burney! Down with her! Spare her not! Attack her, fight her, and down with her at once! You are a rising wit, and she is at the top; and when I was beginning the world, and was nothing and nobody, the joy of my life was to fire at all the established wits. And then everybody loved to halloo me on. But there is no game now; everybody would be glad to see me conquered: but then, when I was new, to vanquish the great ones was all the delight of my poor little dear soul! So at her, Burney—at her, and down with her.'

There was one particularly delightful conversation Fanny remembered about the flamboyant *demi-monde* of Johnson's earlier years. He talked of Bet Flint, 'habitually a slut and a drunkard, and occasionally a thief and harlot', who brought him verses to correct. Bet 'advertised for a husband, but she had no success. . . . Then she hired very handsome lodgings and a footboy; and she got a harpsichord, but Bet could not play; however, she put herself in fine attitudes, and drummed. . . . When she found herself obliged to go to jail, she ordered a sedan chair, and bid her footboy walk before her. However, the boy proved refractory, for he was ashamed, though his mistress was not. . . . Oh, I loved Bet Flint.'

Then he told them of Laurinda who also wrote verses and stole furniture, and of Hortensia who walked up and down the park repeating a book of Virgil, and of the famous Mrs Pinkethman who owed all her misfortune to her wit, for she was so unhappy as to marry a man who thought himself also a wit and this 'occasioned much contradiction and ill-will'.

There was also, he said, a very fine lady (Fanny could not remember her name) who 'had not quite the same stock of virtue nor the same stock of honesty as Bet Flint'. But Johnson supposed that she 'envied her accomplishments, for she was so little moved by the power of harmony, that while Bet Flint thought she was drumming very divinely, the other jade had her indicted for a nuisance!'

'Oh!' said Fanny. 'How we all laughed.'

She was quite as diverted by the studiedly solemn account of the domestic economy of his own numerous household which Dr Johnson gave in answers to questions put to him one tea-time by Mr Thrale, with occasional interpolations by his wife:

'And pray, sir,' Mr Thrale asked him. 'Who is clerk of your kitchen?'

'Why, sir, I am afraid there is none; a general anarchy prevails in my kitchen, as I am told by Mr Levett who says it is not now what it used to be.'

'Mr Levett, I suppose, sir, has the office of keeping the hospital in health, as he is an apothecary?'

'Levett, madam, is a brutal fellow, but I have a good regard for him.'

'But how do you get your dinners drest?'

'Why, Desmoulins has the chief management of the kitchen; but our roasting is not magnificent, for we have no jack.'

'No jack! Why how do they manage without?'

'Small joints, I believe, they manage with a string, and larger are done at the tavern. I have some thoughts (with a profound gravity) of buying a jack, because I think a jack is some credit to a house.'

'Well, but you'll have a spit, too?'

'No, sir, no. That would be superfluous, for we shall never use it; and if a jack is seen a spit will be presumed.'

'And, pray, sir, who is the Poll you talk of? . . .

'Why, I took to Poll very well at first, but she won't do upon a nearer examination.'

'How came she among you, sir?'

'Why, I don't rightly remember, but we could spare her very well from us. Poll is a stupid slut. I had some hopes of her at first. But when I talked to her tightly and closely, I could make nothing of her. She was wiggle-waggle, and I could never persuade her to be categorical.'

The arrival of Poll Carmichael, 'a Scotch wench', at Johnson's house, 8 Bolt Court, to which he had moved from 7 Johnson's Court in 1776, was far from welcome to its other inhabitants who had good cause to consider it overpopulated already.[6] In particular Poll's advent annoyed Mrs Desmoulins who was required to share her room with her, although she was sharing it with her daughter already. Miss Williams also strongly disapproved of the new arrival; but then Miss Williams, increasingly cantankerous as she grew older, disapproved as strongly of all her fellow guests as she did of the servants. 'Williams hates everybody,' Johnson commented with sad resignation, 'Levett hates Desmoulins, and does not love Williams; Desmoulins hates them both; Poll loves none of them.'

After a particularly violent quarrel with Mrs Desmoulins, Miss Williams threatened to go away. Johnson pleaded with her to stay; and she was persuaded to stay. But thereafter she became more ill-tempered than ever and, as Johnson himself admitted, she 'rather got the upper hand'. When she went into the country for a time to try to recover her health, he had to bribe the maid half a crown a week above her wages to stay with her.

The dissensions were further aggravated when Frank, some time after Levett had disposed of his unsatisfactory wife, got married himself. Frank had always been 'eminent for his success among girls', and in 1764 a lovesick Lincolnshire farm-girl had followed him back to London after a visit with his master to Bennet Langton's. His bride was another white girl, 'eminently pretty' in Mrs Thrale's opinion, and he was violently jealous. One year, at the annual servants' party at Streatham, he left in a fury, having taken offence at the attentions paid to her, and began to walk back to London. Johnson, driving home himself with Mrs Thrale for company, overtook him on the road and called out to him in a solicitous tone of voice, 'What is the matter, child, that you leave Streatham? Art sick?'

'He is jealous,' whispered Mrs Thrale.

'Are you jealous of your wife, you stupid blockhead?' Johnson cried out in a very different tone of voice.

Frank hesitated, and then stammered out, 'To be sure, Sir. I don't quite approve, Sir.'

'Why, what do they *do* to her, man? Do the footmen kiss her?'

'No, Sir, no. Kiss my *wife*, Sir. *I hope not*, Sir.'

'Why what *do* they do to her, my lad?'

'Why, nothing, Sir, I'm sure, Sir.'

'Why then go back directly and dance you dog, do; and let's have no more of such empty lamentations.'

There were further lamentations, however, when Mrs Barber became pregnant, and Frank succeeded in convincing himself that he was not the father. It was only after the birth of the baby that he was satisfied.[7]

In the domestic squabbles that so frequently erupted at Bolt Court, Johnson usually took Frank's side. His fondness for the young man was undoubted and deep, and he frequently indulged him in a way that few eighteenth-century masters would have considered proper. He shared the view of most of his contemporaries that the negroes were a racially inferior people. But he abominated slavery, demanding in *Taxation No Tyranny* how it was that the 'loudest *yelps* for liberty' came from the drivers of negroes, and shocking a dinner party at Oxford by proposing a toast to the next negro uprising in the West Indies.

Although he took Frank's side in the household quarrels, Johnson remained as courteous and kind to Miss Williams, for all her peevishness, as he had always been. He frequently took her out with him though her blindness and growing clumsiness in sickness and old age made her an even more distressing sight when eating than her companion was, a distasteful offence to 'the delicacy of persons of nice sensations'. And when he went out on his own, he still invariably took the trouble to ask her what she would like for her dinner, 'a chicken, a sweetbread or any other nice little thing', which he would send to her from the tavern ready cooked.

Miss Williams had a little income of her own, about £40 a year, and except when Johnson bought her a special dinner, she appeared, according to her friend, Lady Knight, to live almost entirely upon tea and bread and butter, so she was not so great an expense to him as she might otherwise have been. But Mrs Desmoulins lived almost entirely upon his charity, receiving from him half a guinea a week, more than a twelfth part of his pension. For a time he also gave a guinea a week to James Compton, a convert to the Anglican faith from the convent in Paris, until Compton managed to establish himself in London.

The sums he allowed to his various dependants or gave away to needy acquaintances or strangers were, quite, astonishing. His diaries are full of such entries as 'gave to Coxeter 10s. 6d., to Lucy 5s. 3d. . . . Gave Reid a guinea to free him from the Spunging house, with 10s. 6d. before'. These regular disbursements of charity were quite often given to people he could not bring himself to like. The Coxeter who received half a guinea was, for instance, in his opinion, a 'slight and feeble' boy, 'worth nothing'; but he was the son of the worthy antiquary, Thomas Coxeter, and therefore deserved helping on that account. And the man who was given a guinea to free him from a sponging-house appears to have been one of those tiresome would-be authors who plagued Johnson by reading their works to him. 'I never did the man an injury,' he said of him. 'But he *would* persist in reading his tragedy to me.'[8]

When he had no money of his own to give, he would borrow some. He once borrowed a guinea from William Strahan—the printer to whom he had addressed the remark, 'There are few ways in which a man can be more innocently employed than in getting money'—to give to a poor boy from the country whom Strahan had taken on as an apprentice upon Johnson's recommendation. Bending down over the little shy, awkward, short-legged boy, Johnson addressed him as though he were an intelligent adult, it being his belief that a man should never, 'let himself down to the capacity of his hearer', but speak 'uniformly, in as intelligible a manner' as he could.

'Well, my boy, how do you go on?'

'Pretty well, Sir; but they are afraid I an't strong enough for some parts of the business.'

'Why, I shall be sorry for it,' Johnson told him with slow and sonorous solemnity, 'for when you consider with how little mental power and corporeal labour a printer can get a guinea a week, it is a very desirable occupation for you. Do you hear—take all the pains you can; and if this does not do, we must think of some other way of life for you. There's a guinea.'

Another boy, a schoolboy at the Charterhouse, who had been sent by his father to see Johnson at an earlier period of his life, received, as well as a long lecture 'on the course of his education and other particulars', half a guinea; and he believed, from the appearance of the room and its occupant, that his benefactor had probably not got another half guinea in the world.

Johnson's generosity, indeed, had long been notorious. According to the Rev William Maxwell, the poor watched for him to leave his house to go out to dinner for they knew he could usually be prevailed upon to part with all the silver in his pocket. He told Miss Reynolds that as he returned home at one or two o'clock in the morning, he often saw poor children asleep on thresholds and stalls, and that he used to put pennies into their hands to buy them a breakfast.

'His liberality in giving his money to persons in distress was extraordinary,' Boswell confirmed. 'Yet there lurked about him a propensity to paltry saving. One day I owned to him, that "I was occasionally troubled with a fit of narrowness."'

'Why, Sir (said he,) so am I. *But I do not tell it.*' He has now and then borrowed a shilling of me; and when I asked him for it again, seemed to be rather out of humour. A droll little circumstance once occurred: as if he meant to reprimand my minute exactness as a creditor, he thus addressed me, 'Boswell, *lend* me sixpence—*not to be repaid.*'

This great man's attention to small things was very remarkable. As an instance of it, he one day said to me, 'Sir, when you get silver in change for a guinea, look carefully at it; you may find some curious piece of coin.'

Nor did Johnson hesitate to solicit contributions for those he thought in need from men who could well afford to be generous. To Bennet Langton he once wrote a characteristic letter:

Dear Sir,

I have an amanuensis in great distress. I have given what I think I can give, and begged till I cannot tell where to beg again. I put into his hand this morning four guineas. If you could collect three guineas more, it would clear him from his present difficulty.

I am, Sir, Your most humble servant,
Sam: Johnson

He would go to immense trouble to help his friends and acquaintances in this way, though, as Mrs Thrale discovered, he became extremely angry if importunately pressed to bestow small favours without good cause. One evening as she dropped him from her carriage at his door, she reminded him of his promise, so far unfulfilled, to write a recommendatory letter of a little schoolboy to his master. 'Do not forget dear Dick,' she said, as he stepped out of the coach. At these words he turned back, stood still for two full minutes rolling about on the carriage step, and then burst out, 'When I have written my letter for Dick, I may hang myself, mayn't I?' He shambled off into the house in a very ill humour indeed.

Although he expressed the opinion that it was 'better to spend money than to give it away', and told Boswell that raising the wages of day-labourers was wrong—for it did not make them live better, but only made them idler—he would not accept the criticism of those who objected to his indiscriminate charity. He did not believe in giving large sums. 'No, no, Sir, we must not *pamper* them,' he said when an acquaintance offered what he considered too much for a person in distress; but when a woman

265

asked him why he constantly gave money to beggars, he answered her 'with great feeling', 'Madam, to enable them to beg on.' He strongly denied that some scoundrels made a lot of money by begging; the trade was far too overstocked for that. His friend Saunders Welch, a former High Constable of Holborn, assured him that Johnson's own guess that twenty people a week died in London of starvation was an under-estimate. 'And you may depend upon it,' he assured Boswell, 'there are many who cannot get work. A particular kind of manufacture fails; those who have been used to work at it, can, for some time, work at nothing else. You meet a man begging; you charge him with idleness. He says, "I am willing to labour. Will you give me work." "I cannot." "Why, then, you have no right to charge me with idleness."' 'A decent provision for the poor,' he insisted, 'is the true test of civilization.'

'Well, my dear,' he once chided a lady who objected that a woman, to whom he had given half-a-crown, had expended the money on long sleeves and ribands to wear in church, 'and if it gave the woman pleasure, why should she not wear them.' 'Why should they be denied such sweeteners of their existence?' he demanded on another occasion when it was objected that giving alms to beggars merely enabled them to lay it down on gin and tobacco. 'It is surely very savage to refuse them every possible avenue to pleasure, reckoned too coarse for our own acceptance. Life is a pill which none of us can bear without gilding; yet for the poor we delight in stripping it still barer, and are not ashamed to show even visible displeasure if ever the bitter taste is taken from their mouths.' He even reprimanded a lady who strongly condemned drunkenness in the lower classes, 'I wonder, Madam,' he expostulated, 'that you have not penetration enough to see the strong inducement to this excess; for he who makes a *beast* of himself gets rid of the pain of being a man.'

'In consequence of these principles,' as Mrs Thrale said, 'he nursed whole nests of people in his house where the lame, the blind, the sick and the sorrowful found a sure retreat from all the evils whence his little income could secure them.' One of these poor unfortunates was a sick woman he found lying, half naked on a pile of straw, as he was walking home up Fleet Street in the early hours of the morning. She told him she had been turned out of her rooms by an 'inhuman landlord', and begged him to help her. He immediately assured her that he would look after her and, having failed to find a coach, he wrapped her up in his coat and carried her home on his back. Next day a doctor examined her and, finding that she was suffering from a venereal disease, advised him to get rid of her. He refused to do so on the grounds that the disease might be 'as much her misfortune as her fault', and kept her for over thirteen weeks. When she had been cured, he raised money for her to set up as a milliner in the country where she afterwards 'lived in good repute'.

According to John Hawkins, by no means all of Johnson's dependants were either grateful to him for his charity, or even worthy of it. One of them, a dancing master, was 'a worthless fellow', a cheat and a drunkard; another, a younger brother of Lord Southwell, was a wastrel who 'seldom went sober to bed, and as seldom rose from it before noon'. 'Even those intruders who had taken shelter under his roof, and who, in his absence from home, brought thither their children, found cause to murmur.' They complained that their provision of food was scanty or their dinners ill-cooked; yet he bore with their reproaches, and went so far as to borrow money for them, and, by recommending them for credit, enabled them to contract debts which were never repaid.

He also took the trouble to ensure that they, as well as the rest of the household, were managing to get along all right under Levett's supervision when he was staying at Streatham, generally coming home on a Saturday to give them 'three good dinners and his company'.

On special occasions, as when Boswell dined at Bolt Court with Johnson, Levett, Miss Williams, Mrs Desmoulins, Alexander Macbean (one of his former amanuenses who had fallen on hard times), and Edmund Allen (the printer who was his landlord), the host proudly got out 'some handsome silver salvers' which he had purchased in 1767. At night it was still his custom as in the past to sit in Miss Williams's room where the table 'had a singular appearance, being covered with a heterogeneous assemblage of oysters and porter and tea for himself'.

The oysters also served for his cat Hodge to whom Johnson was devoted, as he had been to his previous cat, which Tetty had once beaten in front of the maid. Johnson had rebuked her, for the maid might now 'treat puss with cruelty and plead her mistress's example'. Johnson always bought Hodge's oysters himself in case the servants, being put to that trouble on a cat's behalf, might take against the 'poor creature'.[9] Boswell recollected Hodge 'one day scrambling up Dr Johnson's breast, apparently with much satisfaction, while my friend, smiling and half whistling, rubbed down his back, and pulled him by the tail; and when I observed he was a fine cat, saying "Why, yes, Sir, but I have had cats whom I liked better than this"; and then as if perceiving Hodge to be out of countenance, adding, "but he is a very fine cat, a very fine cat indeed."'

Recounting this anecdote reminded Boswell of a 'ludicrous account' which Johnson gave Bennet Langton, of the 'despicable state of a young gentleman of good family. "Sir, when I heard of him last, he was running about town shooting cats." And then in a sort of kindly reverie, he bethought himself of his own favourite cat, and said, "But Hodge shan't be shot; no, no, Hodge shall not be shot."'

14
Mr Wilkes and Mr Edwards

'O, that his words were written in a book.'
Joseph Cradock

Shortly before his sixty-eighth birthday, Johnson had been approached by the representatives of 'forty of the most respectable booksellers of London' to write short biographies and prefaces for a new edition of the works of the English poets. He had been asked to name his own terms and had mentioned the sum of two hundred guineas which had been eagerly accepted. It had been a long time, however, before he had settled down to any concentrated work. There were so many distractions, so many other things that he would rather do.

There were visits with the Thrales to Brighton—where he swam regularly in the sea, though he did not think it did him much good—and to Bath, where the inn was so bad that Johnson could only describe its horrors by saying that Boswell, who joined them for a few days, wished to be in Scotland. There were visits also to Oxford—where it was 'a great thing to dine with the canons of Christ Church'—and to the Midlands, to Birmingham, Ashbourne and Lichfield.

At Ashbourne, he still enjoyed the generous hospitality of the Rev John Taylor, although his talk was now all of bullocks; and at Lichfield, he had the pleasure of staying in the handsome new house which Lucy Porter had built with part of the fortune she had inherited from her brother, the naval officer.

In 1776 Boswell accompanied Johnson on his visit to Lichfield, which had become by then almost an annual event, and was 'pleased to find that Johnson was so much *beloved* in his native city'.

It touched Boswell, too, to discover how proud of Lichfield and its inhabitants Johnson was. The Lichfeldians, Johnson assured his young friend, were 'the most sober, decent people in England, the genteelest in proportion to their wealth, and spoke the purest English'. They were also, he assured another friend, more orthodox in their religion than the people of 'any other town in the kingdom'. They were not much troubled by industry, and when Boswell, who could find 'very little business going forward', said they were an idle set of people, Johnson corrected him: 'Sir, we are a city of philosophers, we work with our heads, and we make the boobies of Birmingham work for us with their hands.'

Johnson was very proud, also, of Lichfield's more distinguished and enterprising sons; and was highly gratified that his own portrait by Sir Joshua Reynolds could be inspected there, for, as he told the artist, 'every man has a lurking wish to appear considerable in his native place'. Johnson was particularly proud of Richard Greene, the apothecary and collector who was distantly related to him, and he made a practice of taking visitors to see his museum to which he had proudly conducted the Thrales. 'Sir,' he said to Greene, 'I should as soon have thought of building a man of war, as of collecting such a museum.'

Even the dullest of Lichfield's citizens were treated with unusual respect by Johnson, particularly if they had been at school with him. One of these was a Mr Jackson, a red-faced, ale-swilling man in a coarse grey coat, black waistcoat, greasy leather breeches, and a yellow uncurled wig. He had failed as a cutler in Birmingham and now had plans to set himself up as a leather-dresser employing new methods. Johnson listened with patient courtesy to the man's long and indistinct account of his supposedly revolutionary process, so as to be able to give him the benefit of his advice upon it.

Johnson seems to have done no writing when he was on what he called his rambles, and did not do a great deal of reading either, although on this occasion he had with him a novel, *Il Palmerino d'Inghilterra*. He was studying this—without enjoyment—for the language, he told Boswell, in preparation for a trip to Italy which he hoped soon to make with the Thrales.

Once back in London there could always be found even more reasons not to settle down to work than could be found in the Midlands. There were the meetings of the Club, whose membership was now augmented to thirty; there were the early afternoon levees at Bolt Court; there were the dinner parties which he attended with all his old enthusiasm, dinner parties like the celebrated one given in May 1776, soon after his return from Lichfield, at Dilly's, the bookseller's, where Boswell engineered a meeting between himself and Jack Wilkes, the rakish demagogue whose principles, or lack of them, Johnson abhorred.

The thought of Wilkes and Johnson meeting in his house had at first horrified Edward Dilly; and when Boswell suggested it, he had said, 'Not for the world. Johnson would never forgive me.'

'Come, if you'll let me negotiate for you, I will be answerable that all shall go well.'

'Nay, if you will take it upon you, I am sure I shall be very happy to see them both here.'

Suspecting that a direct invitation would elicit the response, 'Dine with Jack Wilkes, Sir! I'd as soon dine with Jack Ketch', Boswell contrived to obtain Johnson's agreement in an artful way, of which he was clearly rather proud. He said to him casually, 'Mr Dilly, Sir, sends his respectful compliments to you, and would be happy if you would do him the honour to dine with him on Wednesday next along with me, as I must soon go to Scotland.'

'Sir, I am obliged to Mr Dilly. I will wait upon him.'

'Provided, Sir, I suppose, that the company which he is to have is agreeable to you?'

'What do you mean, Sir? What do you take me for? Do you think I am so ignorant of the world, as to imagine that I am to prescribe to a gentleman what company he is to have at his table.'

'I beg your pardon, Sir, for wishing to prevent you from meeting people whom you might not like. Perhaps he may have some of what he calls his patriotic friends with him.'

'Well, Sir, and what then? Pray what care *I* for his *patriotic friends*? Poh!'

'I should not be surprised to find Jack Wilkes there.'

'And if Jack Wilkes *should* be there, what is that to *me*, Sir? My dear Sir, let us have no more of this. I am sorry to be angry with you; but really it is treating me strangely to talk to me as if I could not meet any company whatever, occasionally.'

Boswell, accordingly, called upon him half an hour before the appointed time, as was his custom when they were to dine together, to make sure that he was ready and to accompany him on his way. He found him in his library, surrounded by clouds of dust, 'buffetting his books' which, on

271

rare occasions, he took it into his mind to do, banging them together, putting them into some sort of order, wearing a huge pairs of gloves such as hedgers used. He had forgotten all about the dinner at Dilly's.

'How is this, Sir. Don't you recollect that you are to dine at Mr Dilly's?'

'Sir I did not think of going to Dilly's. It went out of my head. I have ordered dinner at home with Mrs Williams.'

'But, my dear Sir, you know you were engaged to Mr Dilly, and I told him so. He will expect you, and will be much disappointed if you don't come.'

'You must talk to Mrs Williams about this.'

So Boswell went downstairs, much afraid that if Miss Williams proved obstinate, Johnson would not stir from the house, so accustomed was he to show the old lady 'such a degree of humane attention, as frequently imposed some restraint upon him'. Miss Williams was in her, by now customary, peevish mood.

'Yes, Sir,' she said crossly to Boswell, 'Dr Johnson is to dine at home.'

'Madam, his respect for you is such, that I know he will not leave you, unless you absolutely desire it. But as you have so much of his company, I hope you will be good enough to forego it for a day, as Mr Dilly is a very worthy man, has frequently had agreeable parties at his house for Dr Johnson, and will be vexed if the Doctor neglects him to-day. And then, Madam, be pleased to consider my situation. . . .'

Miss Williams at length relented and Boswell flew upstairs to tell Johnson so. Johnson was still buffeting his books, pretending, apparently, to be indifferent as to whether he went out or stayed at home; but when he heard that Miss Williams had consented to dine alone, he immediately and enthusiastically roared out, 'Frank, a clean shirt!'

When at last Johnson was safely in a hackney-coach on his way to the party, Boswell disarmingly confessed that he felt as excited as if he had been a fortune-hunter who had got an heiress into a post-chaise with him on his way to Gretna Green.

On their arrival at Dilly's, Boswell kept himself 'snug and silent', standing back from the stage, as it were, to observe the scene unfold. The room was full of strangers. Johnson asked Dilly in a hoarse whisper who they were, and was told that the first of those he indicated was Arthur Lee. 'Tooh! Tooh! Tooh!' Johnson muttered under his breath, for Arthur Lee was not merely a patriot, but an American as well. And who was the gentleman in lace, Johnson next enquired. That was Mr Wilkes. On receipt of this unwelcome intelligence, Johnson, stifling a protest, turned to the bookshelves, selected a volume and settled down in a window seat to read—or at least to look at the pages—until the announcement, 'Dinner is upon the table', called him away to eat.

Wilkes placed himself next to Johnson and immediately set about doing all he could to please him. 'Pray give me leave, Sir,' he said, carving a slice of fine veal for him. 'It is better here—a little of the brown—some fat, Sir—a little of the stuffing—some gravy—let me have the pleasure of giving you some butter—allow me to recommend a squeeze of this orange, or the lemon, perhaps, may have more zest . . .'

At first Johnson accepted these ministrations with a surly inclination of the head, and a 'Sir, Sir, I am obliged to you, Sir.' But gradually he began to soften to Wilkes's flattering attentions and then, having satisfied his appetite, he listened for an opportunity to enter the conversation.

Samuel Foote's name was mentioned, and he was always ready to talk about Foote. He had a very low opinion of his veracity. 'Foote,' he had said on a previous occasion—adapting a remark he had previously made about the Irish: 'a fair people; they never speak well of one another'— 'Foote is quite impartial, for he tells lies of everybody.' Nor did Johnson have a good opinion of Foote's intellectual honesty. If he was an infidel, as he was alleged to be, he was an infidel as a dog is an infidel, that was to say, he had never thought upon the subject. But Johnson could not deny that Foote was very witty and 'one species of wit he [had] in eminent degree, that of escape. You drive him into a corner with both hands; but he's gone, Sir, when you think you have got him—like an animal that jumps over your head.' Moreover, though he was not as good a mimic as people gave him credit for, he could keep the company at a dinner table roaring with laughter for minutes on end.

'The first time I was in company with Foote,' Johnson now told the guests at Dilly's, 'was at Fitzherbert's. Having no good opinion of the fellow, I was resolved not to be pleased, and it is very difficult to please a man against his will. I went on eating my dinner pretty sullenly, affecting not to mind him. But the dog was so very comical, that I was obliged to lay down my knife and fork, throw myself back upon my chair, and fairly laugh it out. No, Sir, he was irresistible.'

The conversation then turned to Garrick, and Wilkes said something about his meanness, upon which Boswell, seeing his opportunity, cried out loudly, 'I have heard Garrick is liberal.'

Johnson enjoyed talking about Garrick even more than about Foote. Frequently he abused him. He affected not to regard his acting highly. He had a great range, admittedly; he could 'represent all modes of life, but that of an easy fine-bred gentleman'; yet there was, perhaps, 'not any one character which has not been as well acted by somebody else'. As for the contention that he had brought Shakespeare into notice by his productions and performances, why, 'Sir, to allow that, would be to lampoon the age.' Furthermore, many of Garrick's more famous performances were too highly charged. Johnson had, in any case, a contempt for tragic acting, and totally disagreed with Fielding, who made Partridge say of Garrick, 'Why I could act as well as he myself. I am sure, if I had seen a ghost, I should have looked in the very same manner, and done just as he did.' When asked if he did not really think he would start just in the way that Garrick did if he saw a ghost himself, Johnson had immediately replied, 'I hope not. If I did, I should frighten the ghost.'

Johnson professed an even lower opinion of Garrick as a writer. It being once mentioned that Garrick assisted Dr Brown, the author of *The Estimate*, in writing some play, Johnson hotly denied the possibility. 'No, Sir, Brown would no more suffer Garrick to write a line in his play, than he would suffer him to mount his pulpit.' And when Mrs Thrale had praised Garrick's talent for light verse, citing as an example his song in *Florizel and Perdita* and repeating the line, 'I'd smile with the simple, and feed with the poor', Johnson had broken out, 'Nay, my dear lady, this will never do. Poor David. Smile with the simple! What folly—that? And who would feed with the poor that can help it? No, no. Let me smile with the wise, and feed with the rich.'

George Steevens was 'convinced that Johnson and Garrick had no reciprocal affection'. Johnson admitted that Garrick was a 'pleasant companion', 'the cheerfullest man of his age'; 'but the mere power of exciting laughter is an unsubstantial talent; and who rises up contented from a table on which whipt syllabub was the principal dish?'

Yet whenever someone else criticized Garrick—whom he seemed to regard as his own property, so Reynolds said—Johnson flew to his defence, as Mrs Thrale had so often noticed. He would not, for instance, allow that Garrick was vain, or, if he did allow that he was vain, he insisted that he had every reason to be so. 'No wonder Sir that he is vain, a man who is perpetually flattered in every mode that can be conceived,' he had cried across the table to a fellow guest at the Thrales'. 'So many billows have blown the fire, that one wonders he is not by this time become a cinder.... When he whom every body else flatters, flatters me, I then am truly happy.'

'Sir, it is wonderful how *little* Garrick assumes,' he had elsewhere protested upon it being suggested that Garrick assumed too much. 'Sir

Garrick did not *find* but *made* his way to the tables, the levees, and almost the bed-chambers of the great. . . . Here is a man who has advanced the dignity of his profession. Garrick has made a player a higher character. . . . If all this had happened to me, I should have had a couple of fellows with long poles walking before me, to knock down everybody that stood in the way. Consider, if all this had happened to Cibber or Quin, they'd have jumped over the moon. Yet Garrick,' he added smiling, 'Garrick speaks to *us*.'

Nor would Johnson let anyone say that Garrick was mean. Certainly, he had once been a trifle careful with his money. Johnson remembered having called upon him when he was living with Peg Woffington and having been disgusted by Garrick's anger with his mistress for making the tea too strong. But he would not let Wilkes say that he was mean. No, Garrick had given away more money than any other man he knew, and that not from ostentation. 'Garrick was very poor when he began life; so when he came to have money, he probably was very unskilful in giving away, and saved when he should not. But Garrick began to be liberal as soon as he could.'

When the conversation turned to Scotland, however, Johnson and Wilkes were at one, delighting each other and the company in their sallies, or, as Boswell put it, 'persevering in the old jokes'. Wilkes asked Boswell what the annual income was of an advocate at the Scotch bar. Boswell replied that he believed it was two thousand pounds.

'How can it be possible,' Wilkes asked, 'to spend that money in Scotland?'

'Why, Sir, the money may be spent in England,' Johnson said. 'But there is a harder question. If one man in Scotland gets possession of two thousand pounds, what remains for all the rest of the nation?'

Upon Arthur Lee's mentioning some Scotch people who had settled in a particularly barren part of America and expressing wonder why they had chosen it, Johnson said, 'Why, Sir, all barrenness is comparative. The *Scotch* would not know it to be barren.'

'Come, come,' protested Boswell, 'you have been in Scotland, Sir, and say if you did not see meat and drink enough there.'

'Why, yes, Sir. Meat and drink enough to give the inhabitants sufficient strength to run away from home. . . . You must know, Sir,' he continued, turning to Wilkes, 'I lately took my friend Boswell, and showed him genuine civilized life in an English provincial town. I turned him loose at Lichfield, my native city, that he might see for once real civility. For, you know, he lives among savages in Scotland, and among rakes in London.'

'Except,' said Wilkes, 'when he is with grave, sober, decent people, like you and me.'

'And we ashamed of him.'

After dinner Mrs Mary Knowles, the Quaker lady, and William Lee, a merchant, joined the company and Lee, despairing of the country's future, regretted that 'poor old England' was lost. Here was another irresistible opportunity for Johnson. 'Sir,' he observed, 'it is not so much to be lamented that old England is lost as that the Scotch have found it.'

He was obviously enjoying himself greatly, and noted with profound satisfaction that Wilkes was an agreeable fellow after all. He was also, so Wilkes insisted, much taken with the physical charm of Mrs Knowles. He paid little attention as Wilkes, holding up a candle to the print of a beautiful female figure on the wall, pointed out the elegant contour of the bosom with the finger of an arch connoisseur. Yet all the time, so Wilkes assured Boswell waggishly, he was showing 'visible signs of a fervent admiration of the corresponding charms of the fair Quaker'.

Even when there were no dinner parties to attend, there were always his friends and acquaintances to distract him from his work, both old friends like Boswell and Reynolds, and those new acquaintances he remained anxious to make up to the very end of his life, acquaintances of every kind, clever men like those who sought election to the Club and simple men like Oliver Edwards.

Johnson met Edwards, 'a decent-looking elderly man in grey clothes, and a wig of many curls', one day on returning from church. He did not at first recognise him; but after they had been walking along together for a while he remembered that they had been at Pembroke College together, and he later exclaimed suddenly, 'Oh! Mr Edwards! I'll convince you that I recollect you. Do you remember our drinking together at an alehouse near Pembroke Gate? At that time you told me of the Eton boy, who, when verses on our saviour's turning water into wine was prescribed as an exercise, brought up a single line which was highly admired:

Vidit et erubuit lympha pudica Deum.

And I told you of another fine line in Camden's *Remains*, an eulogy upon one of our kings, who was succeeded by his son, a prince of equal merit:

Mira cano, Sol occubuit, nox nulla secuta est.'

'You are a philosopher, Dr Johnson. I have tried too in my time to be a philosopher; but I don't know how, cheerfulness was always breaking in.'

Edwards certainly seemed a contented man. He had practised for many years as a lawyer, but had now retired as a widower to a small farm in Hertfordshire from which he came up about twice a week to chambers in Barnard's Inn.

Johnson asked him directly, 'From your having practised the law long, Sir, I presume you must be rich.'

'No, Sir. I got a good deal of money; but I had a number of poor relations to whom I gave a great part of it.'

'Sir, you have been rich in the most valuable sense of the word.'

'But I shall not die rich.'

'Nay, sure, Sir, it is better to *live* rich than to *die* rich.'

'I wish I had continued at College.'

'Why do you wish that, Sir?'

'Because I think I should have had a much easier life than mine has been. I should have been a parson, and had a good living . . . and lived comfortably.'

'Sir, the life of a parson, of a conscientious clergyman, is not easy, I have always considered a clergyman as the father of a larger family than he is able to maintain. I would rather have Chancery suits upon my hands than the cure of souls. . . . I ought to have been a lawyer[1]. . . . No, Sir, I do not envy a clergyman's life as an easy life, nor do I envy the clergyman who makes it an easy life . . .'

'How do you live, Sir? For my part, I must have my regular meals, and a glass of good wine. I find I require it.'

'I now drink no wine, Sir. Early in life I drank wine: for many years I drank none. I then for some years drank a great deal.'

'Some hogsheads, I warrant you.'

'As to regular meals, I have fasted from the Sunday's dinner to the Tuesday's dinner without any inconvenience. I believe it is best to eat just as one is hungry: but a man who is in business, or a man who has a family, must have stated meals. I am a straggler. I may leave this town and go to Grand Cairo, without being missed here, or observed there.'

'Don't you eat supper, Sir?'

'No, Sir.'

'For my part, now, I consider supper as a turn-pike through which one must pass, in order to get to bed.'

'You are a lawyer, Mr Edwards. Lawyers know life practically. A bookish man should always have them to converse with. They have what he wants.'

'I am grown old: I am sixty-five.'

'I shall be sixty-eight next birthday. Come, Sir, drink water, and put in for a hundred.'

Although he had clearly enjoyed this unexpected renewal of acquaintance and recorded in his journal that he 'purposed to continue it', he did not, in fact, take much trouble to continue it. Edwards's mind was evidently one soon travelled over.

They met, however, regularly at church. 'I think Sir, you and Johnson meet only at church,' Boswell said to Edwards one Sunday; and Johnson replied for him, 'Sir, it is the best place we can meet in, except heaven, and I hope we shall meet there too.' They also met once by chance in the street, when Edwards said to him, 'I am told you have written a very pretty book called " *The Rambler*".' So Johnson sent him a set of *Ramblers*, unwilling, as he confided with a smile to Boswell, that Edwards should 'leave the world in total darkness'.

Presumably Mr Edwards did not know that his old Oxford friend had just completed, in his 'usual way', as Johnson put it himself, 'dilatorily and hastily, unwilling to work, and working with vigour and haste', another 'very pretty book' which was to find more admirers than even *The Rambler* had had. This was the long-awaited—and long since commissioned—*Lives of the Poets*.

Johnson had found it as difficult to begin work on the *Poets* as on his *Shakespeare*. Indeed, since he was nearly seventy when the work was commissioned, he might justly have considered himself under no obligation to write another word, and he reacted very strongly to any suggestion that he had a duty to perform. When at last the *Lives of the Poets* was finished and some well-meaning person proposed that he should now set about a companion work on the prose writers of the country he cried out in ringing tones, '*Sit down, Sir!*'

He was still prepared to help his friends, and those whom he felt to be in deserving need of his peculiar talents. Since the completion of his *Journey to the Western Isles of Scotland*, which was published in 1775, he had composed some political pamphlets, notably *Taxation No Tyranny*, which supported the actions of the British Government against the Americans.[2] He had also written sermons for Taylor, election addresses for Thrale, who was Member of Parliament for Southwark, proposals for an edition of the works of his friend, Charlotte Lennox, a preface to Baretti's *Easy Phraseology for ... Young Ladies*, and various sermons, letters and declarations for the unfortunate Rev William Dodd whose expensive habits of living had led him to forge a bond in the name of the Earl of Chesterfield, a crime for which he was executed but which Johnson assured him, 'morally or religiously considered', had 'no very deep dye of turpitude, corrupting no man's principles, attacking no man's life, and involving only a temporary and reparable injury'.[3]

The main reason for Johnson's failure to complete the *Lives of the Poets* as early as the booksellers had hoped, was his increasing ill health and 'very unquiet' nights. For much of 1777, the year in which he attempted to save the life of William Dodd, his mind was 'unsettled and perplexed', and he was in the depths of gloom, beset by melancholy forebodings, 'very near to madness'.

Slowly and spasmodically, however, between 1778 and 1781 the work on the *Poets* went on, interrupted by his 'rambles' and by such disturbing events as the anti-popery Gordon Riots of 1780 during which Miss Williams fled to the country, but he walked about watching the activities of the rioters and inspecting the smouldering ruins with so little concern for his safety that William Strahan—who 'got a garrison into his house, maintained them a fortnight', and was 'so frightened that he removed part of his goods'—felt obliged to warn Johnson to take more care of himself.

Eventually, with the help of Mrs Thrale who acted as amanuensis and in whose houses at Southwark and Streatham most of the writing was done, the last of the *Lives* was finished and the final six volumes published in 1781. Johnson had not been responsible for choosing the poets to be commemorated, though some were added to the original list upon his recommendation and one, so Mrs Thrale said—Churchill—was excluded upon his insistence. Nor had he been to undue trouble to collect new biographical material about the poets on the final list. He showed a strong disinclination even to talk to Pope's friend, Lord Marchmont, when Boswell advised him to do so.

'I shall not be in town to-morrow,' he replied huffily to Boswell's suggestion. 'I don't care to know about Pope.' And when further pestered by Mrs Thrale, who said that he must surely wish to know about Pope if he were going to write about him, he exclaimed irritably, '*Wish!* Why, yes. If it rained knowledge I'd hold out my hand; but I would not give myself the trouble to go in quest of it.'

Although he did, of course, do a certain amount of research, he relied principally upon his astonishing memory, feeling so indifferent to minor mistakes that when two were pointed out to him he did not even trouble to alter them.[4] When handing in his work on Rowe he conceded, according to Nichols, the printer, that the criticism was 'tolerably well done considering that he had not read one of Rowe's plays for thirty years'.

For all his apparent indifference, however, Johnson took the work seriously and wrote it with as much pleasure as he ever wrote anything— writing, in fact, far more than he had originally contracted to do. That he only received, after the appearance of a new edition, four hundred guineas in all for work for which, Malone thought, he could have asked and got fifteen hundred, disturbed Johnson not at all. The booksellers, he still believed, were an honourable and generous set of men; he had no reason to complain. 'The fact is,' he said, 'not that they have paid me too little, but that I have written too much.'

He expected that the work would be attacked, particularly for his strictures on the character and beliefs, both political and religious, of Milton, and for his treatment of Gray and of Lord Lyttelton. Yet the prospect of this did not, he claimed, much daunt him. 'I would rather be attacked than unnoticed,' he said. 'For the worst thing you can do to an author is to be silent as to his works. An assault upon a town is a bad thing, but starving it is still worse; an assault may be unsuccessful; you may have more men killed than you kill; but if you starve the town you are sure of victory.'

It was a familiar theme. 'Surely it was better,' he used to say, that a man should be abused than forgotten. When mention was made of the attacks on *Taxation No Tyranny*, he complacently observed, 'I think I have not been attacked enough for it. Attack is the re-action. I never think to have hit hard unless it rebounds.' While in Scotland he assured Boswell, 'A man who tells me my play is very bad, is less my enemy than he who lets it die in silence. A man, whose business it is to be talked of, is much helped by being attacked. . . . Every attack produces a defence; and so attention is engaged. There is no sport in mere praise; when people are all of a mind.' 'It is advantageous to an author, that his book should be attacked as well as praised,' he insisted on yet another occasion. 'Fame is a shuttlecock. If it be struck only at one end of the room, it will soon fall to the ground. To keep it up, it must be struck at both ends.' According to George Steevens he was not, however, as unconcerned by the attacks of critics as he affected to be. One evening when 'much pleasantry was passing on the subject of commentatorship', all of a sudden he looked at his watch and cried out, 'This is sport to you, gentlemen; but you do not consider that there are at most only four hours between me and criticism.'

As it happened *The Lives of the English Poets* was harshly attacked by several critics, notably by Mrs Montagu who so strongly objected to

Johnson's remarks about her hero, Lord Lyttelton, that she never invited their author to her house again.[5] 'The world in general,' Boswell said, 'was filled with admiration for Johnson's 'ample, rich, and most entertaining work'. But as a later critic, Patrick Cruttwell, has observed, 'the general reception of the *Lives* was far from universally favourable . . . the fact is that the taste which they represent was already, by 1780, old-fashioned: in this again Johnson had become alienated from his age. He was upholding the Augustan standards; the age was groping its way, half-consciously, to romanticism.' Yet the whole work 'has an air of ease; its prose is relaxed and colloquial, the paragraphs and sentences simple and short. It reflects the Indian summer of Johnson's life, the few years of fame, comfort and tranquillity, before the physical collapse and emotional misery of the last year or two. Amid the rest, the *Life of Savage*, inserted unchanged as it had been written thirty-five years before, stands out enormously different, "young Sam Johnson", enclosed but far from killed, within the venerable sage he had become.'

15
'Formidable and Dangerous Distempers'

'Alas! See how very ill he looks; he can live but a very short time. Would you refuse any slight gratifications to a man under sentence of death.'   General Pasquale Paoli

The satisfaction that Johnson may have derived from having finished his last important work and having done it well, was overshadowed in April 1781 by the death of Henry Thrale.

Thrale had been in indifferent health and melancholy spirits for a long time. While Johnson and Boswell were in Lichfield together in 1776 he had lost his only son, a loss which Johnson, with that kind of exaggerated emphasis he so strongly condemned in others, had announced in agitated tones to Boswell with the introductory warning, 'One of the most dreadful things that has happened in my time'. Boswell who thought that at least the King had been assassinated and the Houses of Parliament blown up in a new gunpowder plot, was both disconcerted and relieved to find that the 'dreadful thing' was not a national catastrophe. Johnson, however, continued to talk of it in such terms. 'This is a total extinction to their family,' he said, 'as much as if they were sold into captivity.'

Thrale himself appeared to suffer the loss with less concern, with what Boswell, when he next saw him, described as 'manly composure'. Soon afterwards, however, he was struck with apoplexy in his sister's house on learning that her husband, to whom he was bound for a large sum of money, had died insolvent. From that day onwards, Mrs Thrale said, 'tho' he lived near two years . . . he never looked up more'. He sought relief from his depression in trips to Brighton, in moving from Southwark to a more fashionable house in Grosvenor Square, in lamenting his sorrows to the lovely Sophy Streatfeild, while pressing her hand to his heart, above all in eating mountainous meals and in drinking gallons of his beer. It was suicide to eat so much, Johnson warned him; and Thrale responded by asking when the lamprey season was due to come in. His doctor was of the opinion that there must either be 'legal restraint or certain death'. But this merely drove Thrale to even greater excess.

On his last day he ate so 'enormously', his wife said, 'with strong Beer in *such* quantities, the very servants were frightened'. After the meal he went to his bedroom where Queeney found him, twenty minutes later, lying on the floor. What was he doing? she asked him, frightened to see him there. 'I choose it,' he said. 'I lie so o'purpose.' He fell into a violent fit of apoplexy that night, and the following morning he was dead.

Johnson was with him when he died. 'I almost felt the last flutter of his pulse,' he wrote in his journal, 'and looked for the last time upon the face that for fifteen years had never been turned upon me but with respect and benignity.'

He was profoundly upset by Thrale's death; and on being served with an omelette soon after the funeral cried out—'quite in an agony', as the widow said—'Ah, my poor dear friend! I shall never eat omelette with thee again.' ' "Poor, dear Mr Thrale," ' William Bowles confirmed, 'were words often in his mouth.'

Yet, although he could grieve so sorrowfully for Thrale, could weep when reminded of Bathurst's death, and even when told a melancholy tale about the death of an only child of a widow he did not know, if others lamented a bereavement thus, he would strongly condemn their 'sentimental sorrow'. 'We must either outlive our friends,' he said sternly, 'or our friends must outlive us; and I see no man that would hesitate about the choice.' Lady Tavistock, who was said to have grieved herself to death for the loss of her husband, would have survived without question if she had been given a small chandler's shop to look after and a nurse-child to tend. In the same way, a man who suffered grievously at the loss of a beloved friend would have soon recovered if he had been made prime minister. Mrs Thrale herself, who lamented the loss of a favourite cousin killed in America, received the rebuke, 'Prithee, my dear, have done with canting. How would the world be worse for it, I may ask, if all your relations were at once spitted like larks, and roasted for [your dog] Presto's supper?'

It was just as much cant, in Johnson's opinion, to protest great distress about the misfortunes of others. If a madman came into the room wielding a stick, 'no doubt we should pity the state of his mind; but our primary consideration would be to take care of ourselves. We should knock him down first, and pity him afterwards.'

'Pity is not natural to man,' he thought. 'Children are always cruel. Savages are always cruel. Pity is acquired and improved by the cultivation of reason. We may have uneasy sensations from seeing a creature in distress, without pity; for we have not pity unless we wish to relieve them. When I am on my way to dine with a friend, and finding it late, have bid the watchman make haste, if I happen to attend when he whips his horses, I may feel unpleasantly that the animals are put to pain, but I do not wish him to desist. No, Sir, I wish him to drive on.' When Baretti was on trial for his life at the Old Bailey after having, in self defence, stabbed a whore's bully to death in the Haymarket, his friends—including Johnson himself—rose up to speak in his defence on every side. They expressed deep concern about him, but none of them ate 'a slice of pudding the less' on the eve of the trial.

Johnson found it equally exasperating when people talked cant about their being distressed concerning public affairs. When Boswell mentioned his desire to enter parliament, but said that he would be vexed if things went wrong, this conversation ensued:

JOHNSON 'That's cant, Sir. It would not vex you more in the house than in the gallery: publick affairs vex no man.'
BOSWELL 'Have not they vexed yourself a little, Sir? Have you not been vexed by all the turbulence of this reign, and by that absurd vote of the House of Commons, "That the influence of the Crown has increased, is increasing, and ought to be diminished?"'
JOHNSON 'Sir, I have never slept an hour less, nor eat an ounce less meat. I would have knocked the factious dogs on the head, to be sure; but I was not *vexed*.'
BOSWELL I declare, Sir, upon my honour, I did imagine I was vexed, and took a pride in it; but it *was*, perhaps, cant; for I own I neither eat less, nor slept less.'
JOHNSON 'My dear friend, clear your *mind* of cant. You may *talk* as other people do: you may say to a man, "Sir, I am your most humble servant." You are *not* his most humble servant. You may say, "These are bad times; it is a melancholy thing to be reserved to such times." You don't mind the times. You tell a man, "I am sorry you had such bad weather the last day of your journey, and were so much wet." You don't care six-pence whether he is wet or dry. You may *talk* in this manner; it is a mode of talking in Society: but don't *think* foolishly.'

Within three weeks of Thrale's death, William Strahan, the eldest son of his old friend, the printer, also died, and in a sad letter to the bereaved mother Johnson lamented that he had had 'a friend, another friend', taken from him.

Already he had lost both Beauclerk—'a loss that perhaps the whole nation could not repair . . . such another will not often be found among mankind'—and Garrick, whose death had 'eclipsed the gaiety of nations'. 'Ah, Sir,' he lamented, 'they were two such friends as cannot be supplied.' Then, within a few months of the deaths of Thrale and Strahan, he lost Levett, too, 'a very useful and very blameless man', and 'an old and faithful friend'.

Levett was seventy-eight at the time of his death; but he had continued working up to the end and in verses written to commemorate his worth, Johnson—who had valued him highly in his lifetime but wished now that he 'had valued him more'—praised his constant readiness to help the unfortunate:

> His virtues walk'd their narrow round,
> Nor made a pause nor left a void;
> And sure th' Eternal Master found
> The single talent well employ'd.

Johnson felt himself sadly afflicted; a week or so before he had been in Staffordshire, but it had not been pleasant, 'for what enjoyment has a sick man visiting the sick'. His own health, indeed, was once more 'tottering'; could he ever hope to have, he asked Boswell pathetically, 'another frolick like our journey to the Hebrides?'

'This little habitation is now but a melancholy place, clouded with the gloom of disease and death,' he told Mrs Strahan soon after his return to Bolt Court. 'Of the four inmates, one has been suddenly snatched away; two are oppressed by very afflictive and dangerous illnesses; and I tried yesterday to gain some relief by a third bleeding from a disorder which has for some time distressed me.' Writing to Lucy Porter a few weeks later, he was more explicit: 'Both Williams and Desmoulins, and myself, are very sickly. Frank is not well; and poor Levett died in his bed the other day, by a sudden stroke. . . . I have had a troublesome time with my breath; for some weeks I have been disordered by a cold, of which I could not get the violence abated, till I had been let blood three times.'

In the early summer he developed a catarrhal cough and went to Oxford 'to seek relief by change of air'. From there he went to Brighton where he arrived 'in a state of so much weakness', that he had to rest four times in walking between the inn where he dined and his lodgings.

At Brighton, 'by physick and abstinence', he grew a little better; but in the spring of the following year he was still, as he said, 'very ill'. He tired easily and often found the effort even to talk too much for him. He was also given to outbursts of peevish querulousness. 'Am I to be *hunted* in this manner,' he burst out vehemently when told that General Oglethorpe, of whom he was very fond, was planning to visit him. 'Don't talk so childishly,' he snapped in answer to another visitor, who asked him if he had been out of the house that day. 'You may as well ask if I hanged myself to-day.' And when Mrs Desmoulins and Boswell regretted, in his presence at tea one day, that he had attained neither great office nor great wealth, he flew into a violent passion and told them to be quiet. 'Nobody, has a right to talk in this manner,' he said, 'to bring before a man his own character, and the events of his life, when he does not choose it should be done. I never have sought the world; the world was not to seek me. It is rather wonderful that so much has been done for me. All the complaints which are made of the world are unjust. I never knew a man of merit neglected: it was generally by his own fault that he failed of success. A man may hide his head in a hole; he may go into the country; and publish a book now and then, which nobody reads, and then complain he is neglected. There is no reason why any person should exert himself for a man who has written a good book; he has not written it for any individual. I may as well make a present to the postman who brings me a letter.'

As the weeks passed he became even more cantankerous and more vehement in his opinions. 'Sir,' he cried irritably when some new publication appeared, 'If you should search all the madhouses in England, you would not find ten men who would write so, and think it sense.' 'No, Sir,' he objected categorically to a man who said that the abolition of public hangings at Tyburn was an improvement, 'it is *not* an improvement; they object that the old method drew together a number of spectators. Sir, executions are intended to draw spectators. If they do not draw spectators, they don't answer their purpose. The old method was most satisfactory to all parties; the publick was gratified by a procession; the criminal was supported by it. Why is all this to be swept away?'[1]

The age was 'running mad after innovation'. The hand of the cursed

Whigs could be seen in this, they were all *'bottomless* now'. In his agitation and in the 'irritability of his blood', he pared his nails to the quick and scraped the joints of his fingers with a penknife until they seemed quite red and raw.

Then, as though this turbulence had been building up to a crisis, during the night of 16 June 1783, he suffered a sudden stroke. For some time past, as he told Robert Chambers, his thoughts had been disturbed, his nights 'insufferably restless'. The spasms in his breast which condemned him to 'the torture of sleepyness without the power to sleep', had, after more than twenty years, been relieved 'by three powerful remedies, abstinence, opium and mercury', only to give way to a 'sensation like flatulence or intumescence' which he could not describe.

On this morning of 16 June he had sat for his portrait, and afterwards walked a considerable way. In the afternoon and evening he had felt himself 'light and easy', and had begun to 'plan schemes of life'. Soon after going to bed he woke up, and then sat up, as had long been his custom. Suddenly he felt 'a confusion and indistinctness' in his head which lasted for about half a minute. 'I was alarmed,' he told Mrs Thrale, 'and prayed God, that however he might afflict my body he would spare my understanding. This prayer, that I might try the integrity of my faculties I made in Latin verse. The lines were not very good, but I knew them not to be very good. . . . Soon after I perceived that I had suffered a paralytick stroke, and that my speech was taken from me.'

He had no pain, and felt apathetic rather than afraid; but he got out of bed, put himself 'in violent motion' and drank two glasses of wine so as to bring his voice back. But all was in vain. He went to bed, and 'strange as it may seem', slept. At daylight he wrote a note for Frank who came into the room talking and could not at first comprehend what had happened or why he should have to read the paper that his master pressed into his hands. He then wrote to his friend and landlord, Edmund Allen, the printer, who lived next door, making several mistakes in the arrangement of the letters. He also wrote to John Taylor, who was staying in London, asking him to bring over Dr Heberden who had succeeded Dr Lawrence as his physician, and he sent as well for Dr Brocklesby who lived nearby.

The physicians were kind and helpful, advising a blister for his back and one on each side of his throat; they also prescribed salt of hartshorn. But he had never been an easy patient and was not so now. He quarrelled with the apothecary about the salve to be used on the blisters, insisting that it should be made 'according to the Edinburgh dispensatory'; and he took the salt of hartshorn reluctantly, 'with no great confidence' in its efficacy.

His recovery was slow. He was soon able to speak again, but he was still very weak at the beginning of July and could not keep up a conversation for long, although he assured Boswell that most of his friends were being 'very attentive', that he had 'many kind invitations', and that he was strong enough to go to church and even to attend meetings of the Club. Even so, two days later he lamented to Lucy Porter, 'I live now in a melancholy way. Mrs Desmoulins is gone away; and Mrs Williams is so much decayed that she can add little to another's gratifications. The world passes away, and we are passing with it; but there is, doubtless another world, which will endure for ever. Let us fit ourselves for it.'

By the middle of August he was still complaining to Mrs Thrale that he was 'broken with disease', that he was 'without the alleviation of familiar friendship, or domestick society. . . . Levett is dead and Williams is making haste to die. . . . I am now quite alone.'

Not only was he suffering from the after effects of the stroke; but he was also 'much harassed with the gout', and with a malignant growth of tissue in his left testicle which had been increasing in bulk ever since the end of 1781, until by the summer of 1783, it was extremely painful and so distended that his breeches could not conceal the bulge. He believed that the only cure would be to cut it out and he wrote to a distinguished surgeon he knew at Plymouth to ask if he thought this would be a dangerous operation. Painful, he knew it would be, and he hoped to be able to endure the pain 'with decency', but he was loth 'to put life into much hazard'. The surgeon advised immediate amputation, but this proved to be unnecessary, for the swelling eventually subsided of its own accord.

After visits to Bennet Langton at Rochester and to William Bowles at Heale near Salisbury—where he learned that Miss Williams had died in her room at Bolt Court on 6 September—his health and spirits were gradually restored.

On occasions, indeed, that autumn, he seemed almost mellow. 'As I know more of mankind,' he said, 'I expect less of them, and am ready now to call a man a *good man* upon easier terms than I was formerly.'

When the aged actress Mrs Siddons came to see him in October, he behaved towards her with all his old gallantry, apologising for the fact that there happened to be no chair ready for her with, 'Madam, you who so often occasion a want of seats to other people, will the more easily excuse the want of one yourself.' And, upon agreeing with her that of all Shakespeare's female characters, Queen Catherine in Henry VIII was the most natural, he added, in a sprightly way, 'whenever you perform it, I will once more hobble out to the theatre myself'.

Two months after his visit from Mrs Siddons, at eleven o'clock at night on 1 January 1784, Johnson inscribed in his diary his prayer for the New Year. He entreated God that the rest of his time on earth might be spent in His fear and to His glory, that he might be granted such 'ease of body' as would enable him to be useful, and that he might be relieved from 'all such scruples and perplexities as encumbered and obstructed' his mind. Still suffering from gout and asthma, obliged to sit up all night in cold weather so constricted was his chest, getting to sleep only after liberal doses of laudanum and syrup of poppies, he was now again in a pitiable state of health. 'I know not when I shall be able to go even to church,' he wrote to Boswell at the beginning of February. 'A Dropsy gains ground upon me; my legs and thighs are very much swollen with water. . . . My nights are very sleepless and very tedious. And yet I am extremely afraid of dying . . . I should be glad to try a warmer climate; though how to travel with a diseased body, without a companion to conduct me, and with very little money, I do not well see. Ramsay has recovered his limbs in Italy; and Fielding was sent to Lisbon where, indeed, he died; but he was, I believe, past hope when he went. Think for me what I can do. . . . Ask your physicians about my case.'

Thoughts of death were still uppermost in his mind towards the end of the month when he told Lucy Porter, 'Death, my dear, is very dreadful; let us think nothing worth our care but how to prepare for it.' But his health by then was a little improved; he had had 'sudden and unexpected relief by the discharge of twenty pints of water'; and when the warmer weather came at the end of March he was able to inform Bennet Langton that he grew better with respect to all his 'formidable and dangerous distempers'. He had to admit that he had contracted 'a very troublesome cough' by standing carelessly at an open window and had had to resort to opium in larger quantities than he liked to risk; also his asthma was still with him spasmodically, but that was 'constitutional and incurable', and, after all, Sir John Floyer who suffered from it, 'panted on to ninety'. Yet the prospect of death still harrowed him. 'O! My friend, the approach of death is very dreadful,' he wrote to John Taylor on 12 April. 'I am afraid to think on that which I know I cannot avoid. It is vain to look round and round for that help which cannot be had.'

He was feeling very lonely and sorry for himself that day. Of his household only Frank now remained, for Mrs Desmoulins, driven from the house by Miss Williams in 1783, had not yet returned. 'I want every comfort,' he told Taylor. 'My life is very solitary and very cheerless. . . . I am yet very weak and have not passed the door since the 13th of December. . . . I could not have the consent of my physicians to go to church yesterday; I therefore received the holy sacrament at home, in the room where I communicated with dear Mrs Williams, a little before her death. . . . What can be the reason that I hear nothing from you. . . . Do not omit giving me the comfort of knowing, that after all my losses I have yet a friend left. . . . I have no friend now living but you and Mr Hector that was the friend of my youth. . . .'

A few days later, however, on 21 April, he was so far improved as to go to church to return thanks for a recovery such as neither himself 'nor the physicians at all expected'. 'Very few examples have been known of the like,' he assured Lucy Porter. 'Join with me, my dear love, in returning thanks to God.'

Soon he was out and about again, lumbering about the town with much of his former restless and erratic gusto. He went to big dinner parties at Dr Brocklesby's house, at Dr Paradise's, at Mr Jodrell's, at Hoole's and Dilly's; he attended once more the meetings of the Club. He appeared almost his old self again, as eager for society, conversation and dispute as ever, as ready to knock a man down with the butt end of his pistol when the shot misfired as he had been in the days of his earlier triumphs. At Brocklesby's someone mentioned a man who claimed that in fifty-one years in this world he had not ten minutes of uneasiness. This was a notion that Johnson had long ridiculed. It was cant, just as it was 'all *cant*' when anyone said he was happy or that someone else was so. It was enough to make a man hang himself to hear a creature like Mrs Thrale's sister-in-law, 'ugly, sickly, foolish and poor', say that she was happy. Now, at Brocklesby's, he grew quite as angry about the unnamed man who had not known ten minutes of uneasiness in a lifetime. 'The man who says so lies; he attempts to impose on human credulity.'

A fellow guest contended that it was not necessarily a lie, for all men were different; and he quoted something from Johnson's own writings in support of his contention. Johnson who violently objected to having his own works quoted against him, turned in fury upon the offender whom he did not, surely, recognise as the Bishop of Exeter. 'Sir,' he roared at him, 'there is one passion I would advise you to command: when you have drunk out that glass, don't drink another.'

Boswell found Johnson in as equally characteristic a mood that same evening at the Essex Head, where he had instituted a new club the year before. He was 'in fine spirits' after his altercation with the Bishop of Exeter, and said enthusiastically, 'I dined yesterday at Mrs Garrick's with Mrs [Elizabeth] Carter, Miss Hannah More, and Miss Fanny Burney. Three such women are not to be found: I know not where I could find a fourth, except Mrs [Charlotte] Lennox who is superiour to them all.'

'What! Had you them all to yourself, Sir?' asked Boswell.

'I had them all, as much as they were had; but it might have been better had there been more company there.'

'Might not Mrs Montagu have been a fourth?'

'Sir, Mrs Montagu does not make a trade of her wit; but Mrs Montagu is a very extraordinary woman: she has a constant stream of conversation, and it is always impregnated; it has always meaning.'

'Mr Burke has a constant stream of conversation.'

'Yes, Sir. If a man were to go with Burke under a shed to shun a shower, he would say, "This is an extraordinary man." If Burke should go into a stable to see his horse drest, the ostler would say, "We have had an extraordinary man here."'

'Foote was a man who never failed in conversation. If he had gone into a stable—'

'Sir, if he had gone into the stable, the ostler would have said, "Here has been a comical fellow." But he would not have respected him.'

Having settled the matter of Samuel Foote, Johnson suddenly called out in exultation, 'O! Gentlemen. I must tell you a very great thing. The Empress of Russia has ordered *The Rambler* to be translated into the Russian language: so I shall be read on the banks of the Wolga. Horace boasts that his fame would extend as far as the banks of the Rhone; now the Wolga is farther from me than the Rhone was from Horace.'

'You must certainly be pleased with this, Sir.'

'I am pleased, Sir, to be sure. A man is pleased to find he has succeeded in that which he has endeavoured to do.'

Johnson was still in good spirits when, at the beginning of June, he and Boswell set off on a visit to Oxford. In the post-coach were two American ladies on their way to Worcestershire, a Mrs Beresford and her daughter. Mrs Beresford, who had read Johnson's name on the way-bill, whispered to Boswell, 'Is this the great Dr Johnson?' And upon learning that it was indeed the great Dr Johnson, she settled back to listen to him talk. She was not disappointed, for Johnson talked a great deal. 'How he does talk!' she murmured to Boswell. 'Every sentence is an essay.' In a moment of silence, Mrs Beresford mentioned to Boswell in a low voice that her husband had been a member of the American Congress; and Boswell immediately and anxiously cautioned her to beware of introducing that subject, as she must know how very violent Johnson was against the people of that country. As it was, Mrs Beresford managed to offend him by knitting.

'Next to mere idleness,' he observed, 'I think knotting is to be reckoned in the scale of insignificance; though I once attempted to learn knotting. Dempster's sister,' he added, looking at Boswell, 'endeavoured to teach me it; but I made no progress.'

He talked unreservedly of his financial affairs, calculating—with little accuracy for, despite the advice he was only too willing to give to others, he had scant grasp of his own economy—how much money he had and how much he would leave to Frank who was following in the heavy coach. He seemed quite unperturbed by the discomforts of the journey, though the two American ladies were rather disconcerted to hear him angrily scold the waiter at the inn where they stopped on the way for serving mutton which was 'as bad as bad can be, ill-fed, ill-killed, ill-kept, and ill-drest'.

At Oxford they stayed at Pembroke College with Dr Adams, who greeted Johnson with enquiries about his illnesses and recovery; but he was in no mood to discuss them. He despatched the questions with 'a short and distinct narrative'; and then assuming a gay air, repeated from Swift,

> Nor think on our approaching ills,
> And talk of spectacles and pills.

He wanted to talk of other things and soon showed that he had lost none of his powers.

Upon mention being made of Dr Thomas Newton, who had criticised the *Lives of the Poets* for being more concerned with 'exposing blemishes than with commending beauties', Johnson exclaimed, 'Tom knew he should be dead before what he has said of me would appear. He durst not have printed it while he was alive.'

'I believe his *Dissertations on the Prophecies* is his great work,' commented Adams.

'Why, Sir, it is *Tom's* great work; but how far it is great, or how much of it is Tom's, are other questions.'

He talked well at dinner and well at breakfast; he was delighted by the charm and intelligence of Adams's daughter and by her constant attentions to him. When she told him that a little coffee pot in which she made him coffee was the only thing she could call her own, he gallantly replied, 'Don't say so, my dear. I hope you don't reckon my heart as nothing.'

One morning at breakfast Mrs Kennicott, widow of the Biblical scholar, who was also staying in the Master's Lodge, recalled his reply to Hannah More's expressed surprise that the author of *Paradise Lost* should have written such poor sonnets. 'Milton, Madam, was a genius who could cut a Colossus from a rock, but could not carve heads upon cherrystones.' No one at Oxford could doubt that he was still capable of such marvellous flights of fancy.

But it could also not be doubted that thoughts of death were constantly disturbing his mind, as they had done so often in the past. 'Speak for yourself, Sir,' he had cried out one day at Salisbury when someone had suggested that no one in the room in which they sat was afraid of death. 'For indeed I am.'

'I did not say of dying, but of death, meaning its consequences.'

'And so I mean. I am very seriously afraid of the consequences.' In this respect—and not only in this respect—his religion gave him scant comfort. 'There are many good men whose fear of God predominates over their love,' Johnson insisted, in protest against Hugh Blair's belief that a man who did not feel joy in religion was 'far from the kingdom of heaven'.

Often he had revealed to Boswell his dread of death, admitting that he had 'never had a moment' in which it was not terrible to him. No rational man could die 'without uneasy apprehension'. 'The whole of life,' he said, 'is but keeping away the thoughts of death.' And when Boswell had persisted in talking about it one evening, he had grown extremely agitated and for once in his life had urged a visitor to leave him and go home. As Boswell left he had called out to him sternly, 'Don't let us meet to-morrow.'

He had a profound horror of dead men's bones—with a corresponding predilection for very old people who survived with their faculties unimpaired—and a scarcely less intense terror of urns. 'Sir,' he said, 'I hate urns,' when a particularly graceful one was pointed out to him in Mr Wickins's garden at Lichfield. 'They *are* nothing, they *mean* nothing, convey no ideas but ideas of horror—would they were beaten to pieces to pave our streets.'

Now at Oxford on this visit in June 1784, he acknowledged one evening at supper to John Henderson, a remarkably clever undergraduate at

Pembroke, that he was 'much oppressed by the fear of death'. He was afraid, he added to Dr Adams who tried to comfort him with the observation that God was infinitely good, that he had not fulfilled the conditions upon which salvation is granted, that he might be 'one of those who shall be damned'.

'What do you mean by damned?' Adams asked him.

'Sent to Hell, Sir,' exclaimed Johnson loudly and passionately, in turbulent agitation. 'Sent to Hell, Sir, and punished everlastingly.'

This disturbing conversation continued for a time, Johnson vehemently refusing to be reconciled by Mrs Adams's gentle reminder of the merits of his Redeemer.

'Madam, I do not forget the merits of my Redeemer,' he assured her. 'But my Redeemer has said that he will set some on his right and some on his left.' Then he suddenly stopped himself, as though unwilling to think where *he* might be set: 'I'll have no more on't.'

There *was* more talk about it though; and when it was remarked how strange it was that a man who could so often delight his company by his lively and brilliant conversation should say he was miserable, he gloomily commented, 'Alas! It is all outside. I may be cracking my joke and cursing the sun. *Sun, how I hate thy beams.*'

One day at breakfast, a few days before he left to return to London, Adams asked him to compose some family prayers. This, he said, he would not do, but he had thought of compiling an anthology of prayers, adding one or two of his own and writing an introduction. At this Adams, Boswell, and the others crowded round his chair and urged him to execute the plan. Exasperated by being pressed to write again, and horrified by the thought that he might not live to finish the task, he called out in great agitation, 'Do not talk thus of what is so awful. I know not what time God will allow me in this world. There are many things that I wish to do.'

Yet Boswell persisted in his efforts to extract a promise from him that he would undertake the work, while Adams said, 'I never was more serious about anything in my life.'

'Let me alone,' Johnson pleaded. 'Let me alone. I am overpowered.' He put his hands in front of his face, and 'reclined for some time upon the table'.

On Wednesday 19 June he and Boswell returned to London. In contrast with his volubility on the northward journey, Johnson was silent and preoccupied, reading Euripides for much of the way, and rebuking Boswell for not taking more notice of what was to be seen upon the road: 'If I had your eyes, Sir, I should count the passengers.'

The following Saturday he attended a dinner at the Club; but he looked tired and ill; the other members showed 'evident marks of kind concern about him with which he was much pleased, and he exerted himself to be as entertaining as his disposition allowed him'. But it obviously *was* an exertion, and Boswell records nothing of his talk. On 25 June he dined at General Paoli's and looked more ill than ever. 'Alas! see how ill he looks,' whispered his host to Boswell who, concerned by the amount Johnson was eating of his favourite dishes that covered the table, had begged the General not to press him to eat any more. 'He can live but a very short time,' Paoli said. 'Would you refuse any slight gratifications to a man under sentence of death? There is a humane custom in Italy, by which persons in that melancholy situation are indulged with having whatever they like best to eat and drink, even with expensive delicacies.'

It was at General Paoli's that Boswell and some of Johnson's other friends decided to try to arrange for money to be raised so that Johnson could visit Italy himself. After consulation with Reynolds, Boswell wrote to the Lord Chancellor, Lord Thurlow, to ask him to use his influence, which Thurlow agreed to do.

When Johnson learned what was being done on his behalf, he listened with deep attention, then declared, 'This is taking prodigious pains about a man.'

'O, Sir,' said Boswell, 'your friends would do everything for you.'

Johnson was about to reply to this, then hesitated as tears started to his pale grey eyes. At length he exclaimed with fervent emotion, 'God bless you all.'

Overcome with emotion himself, Boswell then burst into tears; and Johnson said again, 'God bless you all, for Jesus Christ's sake.'

They then sat in silence for a time, unable to speak, until, as though afraid he might break down again, Johnson abruptly stood up and left the room.

The next day Johnson, Boswell and Reynolds met at Reynolds's house to discuss the details of the proposed Italian journey. Full of confidence that the application to the Government would be favourably considered, Johnson's two friends expatiated on the liberal provision which they felt sure would be made to him. Johnson caught their enthusiasm and declared that he would rather have his pension doubled than a grant of a thousand pounds. 'For,' he said, 'though probably I may not live to receive as much as a thousand pounds, a man would have the consciousness that he should pass the remainder of his life in splendour, howsoever it might be.' He added, in a faltering tone, as an instance of the extraordinary liberality of his friends, that Dr Brocklesby had offered him a hundred a year for life, which he had, of course, refused.

To cheer him up, Reynolds and Boswell assured him how lovely Italy was and how happy he would be there; but this was going rather too far for him to accept. 'Nay,' he said, 'I must not expect much of that. When a man goes to Italy merely to feel how he breathes the air, he can enjoy very little.' However, it would certainly be better than living in the country in England which would be to him a kind of mental imprisonment.

'Yet, Sir,' said Boswell, 'there are many people who are content to live in the country.'

'Sir, it is in the intellectual world as in the physical world: we are told by natural philosophers that a body is at rest in the place that is fit for it. They who are content to live in the country, are fit for the country.'

On leaving Reynolds's house Boswell accompanied him in their host's coach to the entry to Bolt Court. Johnson asked him to come into the house; but Boswell, who had to return to Scotland in two days, refused, 'from an apprehension,' so he wrote, 'that my spirits would sink. We bade adieu to each other affectionately in the carriage. When he had got down upon the foot-pavement, he called out, "Fare you well!"; and without looking back, sprung away with a kind of pathetic briskness.' Boswell was never to see him again.

16

The Race with Death

'He bade me draw near him, and said he wanted to enter into a serious conversation with me; and, upon my expressing a willingness to join in it, he, with a look that cut me to the heart, told me that he had the prospect of death before him and that he dreaded to meet his Saviour.' John Hawkins

Soon after Boswell's return to Scotland, it was learned that the application to the Government had been unsuccessful. Thurlow offered to help personally, but Johnson gratefully declined on the improbable grounds that it had pleased God to restore him to so great a measure of health that to go to Italy now would be to go under false pretences. Since he had not 'rioted in imaginary opulence', the Government's cold reception of his friends' request had been 'scarce a disappointment'.

Far worse than a disappointment, however, far more cruel than any slight of a disobliging Government, was the savage wound that was dealt to him this summer by Mrs Thrale.

For some time after the death of Henry Thrale, the relationship between Johnson and his widow had little changed. Thrale, as well as leaving him the meagre sum of £200, had appointed Johnson one of his four executors; and Johnson, who had always fancied himself as something of an expert in business affairs and loved dabbling in other people's, entered upon his duties with high enthusiasm, talking in a deeply consequential manner of his new office and the responsibilities that had been thrust upon his shoulders, writing in an important tone to Lucy Porter that he did not know whether or not he would be able to get up to Lichfield that year as he might not be spared from his duties. Mrs Thrale wrote of the delight he took in 'seeing his Name in a new Character flaming away at the bottom of Bonds and Leases'; and Lord Lucan told the story that when the sale of the brewery was going forward, 'Johnson appeared bustling about, with an ink-horn and pen in his button-hole, like an excise-man; and on being asked what he really considered to be the value of the property which was to be disposed of, answered, "We are not here to sell a parcel of boilers and vats, but the potentiality of growing rich beyond the dreams of avarice."'

The brewery was, in fact, sold to David Barclay and John Perkins for £135,000 and Mrs Thrale—thankful to have lost the 'Golden Millstone' from her neck, to have washed her hands of vulgar trade, and to be able to face the world in her 'restored Character of a Gentlewoman'—was, at the age of forty, a rich and still lively and attractive woman.

She had been fond enough of her husband but she had never loved him, and she naturally welcomed the opportunity presented by his death to find a new life for herself. She took a house in Harley Street, gave a large assembly there before the traditional year of mourning for her husband was over, declined three offers of marriage from men considerably older than herself, and in October 1782 let the house at Streatham for three years to Lord Shelburne. To Johnson the letting of what he had come to consider as his country home was a hard and bitter blow.

Up till then he had used Streatham with the same sort of freedom as he had done when its master was alive. Not feeling well, so he had told Edmond Malone, he had gone there in February, as at Streatham he could still use 'all the freedom that sickness requires'. He liked to think that he could still rely on its comforts when in need and upon the ministrations of its mistress; and she, for her part, as she implied in a letter to a friend, was still prepared to indulge him, to look after him, to maintain responsibility for him. 'Dr Johnson has been ill,' she wrote, 'and is sadly broken; was he either to die or recover a firm state of health, I think I should try Continental Air for myself.' But so long as he was ill, she felt unable to leave him, though he was often an exhausting burden to her. During one bout of sickness Sir Richard Jebb, the distinguished physician to the Prince of Wales, was 'perpetually on the road to Streatham', yet Johnson seemed to think himself neglected. 'I made him a steady, but as I thought a very gentle harangue, in which I confirmed all that the Doctor had been saying, how no present danger could be expected; but that his age and continued ill health must naturally accelerate the arrival of that hour which can be escaped by none: "And this (says Johnson, rising in great anger) is the voice of female friendship I suppose, when the hand of the hangman would be softer."

'Another day, when he was ill, and exceedingly low-spirited, and persuaded that death was not far distant, I appeared before him in a dark-coloured gown, which his bad sight, and worse apprehensions, made him mistake for an iron-grey. "Why do you delight (said he) thus to thicken the gloom of misery that surrounds me? Is not here sufficient accumulation of horror without anticipated mourning?"'

Tiresome as he could be, however, Mrs Thrale remained for the moment devoted to him. 'If I lose *him* I am more than undone,' she recorded in her journal. 'Friend, Father, Guardian, Confidant! God give me health and patience—what shall I do?'

Now that Streatham was to be let, Johnson prayed to God that he would be able to resign its 'comforts and conveniences' with 'holy submission'. This he found it impossible to do. He wrote in his journal, in the middle of a note recording his last visit to Streatham church, of his last meal in the house, 'roast lamb, stuffed with raisins, a sirloin of beef, turkey, figs, grapes and peaches'. The grapes, admittedly, were not very ripe and the 'peaches hard!' Yet where else in the world could he so freely indulge himself?

He accompanied Mrs Thrale to Brighton, which he had never very much liked; and Fanny Burney, who was there at the same time, noted how very grumpy he was. 'He has been in a terrible severe humour of late,' she wrote, 'and has really frightened all the people, till they almost ran from him. I am quite sorry to see how unmercifully he attacks & riots the people. He has raised such a general alarm, that he is now omitted in all cards of invitation sent to the rest of us. What a pity he will never curb himself! nor restrain his tongue. . . . To me only I think he is now kind, for Mrs Thrale fares worse than anybody.'

Even more disagreeable to Johnson than the loss of Streatham was a change he now detected in Mrs Thrale's attitude towards him. She seemed to him to be becoming increasingly indifferent to his welfare, more and more concerned with other people whom he did not know and did not care to know. Already in April he had felt injured enough to write to her, 'Madam, I have been very much out of order . . . but why should I tell you, who do not care nor desire to know?' Later, in recounting to her the history of his stroke, he told her pathetically and self-pityingly in a letter addressed to Bath, 'I am sitting down in no cheerful solitude to write a narrative which would once have affected you with tenderness and sorrow, but which you will perhaps pass over now with the careless glance of frigid indifference. . . . I have honoured You with sincere Esteem. Let not all our endearment be forgotten, but let me have in this great distress your pity and your prayers. You see I yet turn to You and my complaints as a settled and unalienable friend, do not, do not drive me from You, for I have not deserved either neglect or hatred.'

On receipt of the news of his stroke, Mrs Thrale wrote in her journal of the 'dreadful Event' that had happened to the 'poor Fellow'. But she made no attempt to go to London to see him, and had 'no Desire that he should come to Bath'. For by now there was only one person in the world to whom she wished 'to be near'.

She had met this man for the first time while her husband was still alive. It was at a party at Dr Burney's where Johnson was also present together with Fulke Greville to whom Burney had been anxious to introduce him. It had been a disastrous evening. Johnson had been at his most silent and disgruntled; Greville, at his most haughty and aloof. Suffering from fearful toothache, Greville had 'planted himself', so his host's daughter said, 'immovable as a noble statue, upon the hearth, as if a stranger to the whole set', until Johnson—already exasperated by the repeated performances of a protégé of Burney's, an Italian singer—had burst out, 'If it were not for depriving the ladies of the fire, I should like to stand upon the hearth myself.' Greville had hesitated for a moment, uncertain whether to smile and hold his place, or sit down. He had chosen to sit down, forcefully ringing the bell for his carriage on his way to the chair.

To add to Burney's discomfiture, Mrs Thrale, in an effort to enliven the party, had stood behind the singer, extravagantly imitating his every action, squaring her shoulders in time with his own, raising her eyebrows, lowering her head, until Burney persuaded her to abandon the antics which no one had found amusing.

It was not until over two years later that Mrs Thrale again met the singer, Gabriel Piozzi, as she was coming out of a bookshop in Brighton. She spoke to him in Italian, asking him if he could find time to give her daughter, Hester, music lessons. Piozzi, who had made something of a name for himself since their earlier meeting, had rather coldly refused the importunate request of the English lady whom he did not recognise. When he had discovered who she was, however, he agreed to become her daughter's music master; and in recording his acceptance in her journal his employer added the comment, 'He is amazingly like my Father.'

He was a year older than she was, a kind, amiable, handsome man, charming in a quiet unobtrusive way; and Mrs Thrale had soon grown very fond of him. Within a few weeks of the beginning of his employment he had become 'a prodigious Favourite' with her. 'He is so intelligent a Creature,' she confided to her journal, 'so discerning, one can't help wishing for his good Opinion: his singing surpasses everybody's for Taste, Tenderness, and True Elegance; his Hand on the Forte Piano too is so soft, so sweet, so delicate . . .'

Yet for a long time she had refused to admit, even to herself, that she was falling in love with him, or that he was falling in love with her. When a friend had remarked to her, a few hours before her husband's death, 'You know, I suppose, that that man is in love with you?' she had replied, 'I am too irritated to care who is in love with me.'

After several months of widowhood she had continued to declare that her heart was still her own, that it vexed her when people assumed that she would marry again. But by the autumn of 1782, shortly before she let Streatham, she had begun to change her mind. 'Now! that little dear discerning creature Fanny Burney says I'm in love with Piozzi—very likely!' she wrote. 'He is so amiable, so honourable, so much above his Situation by his Abilities.' She was obliged to face the unpalatable fact that her friends and elder daughters, particularly the snobbish Queeney, would raise against him the disadvantages that he was socially inferior, a foreigner and a Roman Catholic, whereas she, in her own description, was 'of passable Person, ancient Family, respectable Character, uncommon talents, and Three Thousand a year'.

She had, therefore, continued to try to conceal from her friends—even after she had admitted the fact to herself—that she loved Piozzi; and it was not until November that she had brought herself to break to Queeney the news of what she described as 'the Strength of [her] Passion' for him, 'the Impracticability of [her] living without him'.

Queeney had taken the news as badly as her mother had feared she would. At first she had seemed content to believe that her mother would at least wait for a time before doing anything so disgraceful as marrying an Italian music-master; then, when it seemed that her mother could not bear to wait, there was a painful and tearful scene—the mother lying on her bed and sobbing in misery, the daughter looking down pitilessly and declaring heartlessly that if she must abandon her children, then she must, but that her father had not deserved such treatment, that she would be punished before long by Piozzi, who, far from loving her, in fact hated her.

In the end it had been decided that Piozzi would have to go abroad for a while; and Mrs Thrale would have to go to Bath. Languishing at Bath, however, declining to go out into society, failing in health, Mrs Thrale had seemed so close to the verge of collapse that her physicians had become seriously alarmed. Queeney had eventually been persuaded to agree that Signor Piozzi must be asked to return.

Of all this Mrs Thrale took care to keep Johnson in the dark. Already she had done her best to persuade herself that he did not really need her anymore. Before the thought of marriage had firmly settled in her mind she had proposed a visit to Italy, and when Johnson had readily agreed that she should go she had used his easy permission to prove to herself how little he truly cared for her: 'I fancied Mr Johnson could not have existed without me forsooth, as we have now lived together above 18 years, and I have so fondled and waited on him in Sickness and in Health—Not a bit on't! he feels nothing in parting with me, nothing in the least; but thinks it a prudent Scheme and goes to his Book as usual. . . . I begin to see (now everything shews it) that Johnson's connection with me is merely an interested one—he *loved* Mr Thrale I believe, but only wish'd to find in me a careful Nurse and humble Friend for his sick and his lounging hours: yet I really thought he could not have existed without *my conversation* forsooth—He cares more for my roast Beef and plum Pudden which he now devours too dirtily for endurance; and since he is glad to get rid of me, I'm sure I have good Cause to desire the getting Rid of *him*.'

In her *Anecdotes of Dr Johnson* which were published during her lifetime, she explained herself less heatedly: she had gone on so long with Johnson out of deference to her husband's wishes, and veneration for Johnson's 'virtue, reverence for his talents, and delight in his conversation', but the 'perpetual confinement I will own to have been terrifying in the first years of our friendship and irksome in the last; nor could I pretend to support it without help when my coadjutor was no more'.

She might more honestly have said that her husband's death left her free to start a new life. She might reasonably have asked how could she be expected to sink into retirement as a widow for the sake of a demanding old man who, without much thought for her age or situation, seemed to consider that he had a pre-emptive right to her continued attentions? For all her protestations of 'perpetual confinement' and the 'yoke' that her husband put upon her, she had once been deeply attached to Johnson. As late as the summer of 1780 she had recorded, 'Johnson and I have been uncomfortably parted this year, we never lived asunder so long since our first Connection I think, yet our mutual Regard does not decay that's certain—how should it? founded on the truest principles, Religion, Virtue and Community of Ideas—saucy Soul! Community of Ideas with Dr

Johnson: but why not? he has fastened so many of his own Notions so on my Mind before this Time, that I am not certain whether they grew there originally or no: of this I am sure, that they are the best and wisest Notions I possess; that I love the Author of them with a firm Affection: such is my tenderness for Johnson, when he is out of my sight I always keep his Books about me, which I never think of reading at any other Time: but they remind me of *him* and please me more than even his letters.'

But that was all over now; there could in the future be room for only one man in her life. Gabriel Piozzi came home to her at Bath on 1 July 1784. It was, she thought, the happiest day of her whole life—'Yes, *quite* the happiest'.

When it was announced that Mrs Thrale was indeed to marry the Italian and that her daughters were not to remain with her, the public outcry against her was vituperative. In addition to Queeney, there were three surviving daughters, Susannah, aged fourteen, Sophia, thirteen and Cecilia, ten. They all appear to have been under Queeney's dominance, and none of them seems to have objected when it was decided that they could not possibly live with their mother after her second marriage. Nor does their mother appear to have opposed the separation; she had never been a particularly affectionate parent and must have realised that opposition in the face of the adamant Queeney and the executors of her husband's will would not have served to keep her children but to lose her Piozzi. Her decision, in the opinion of London society, was unforgivable; her former friends condemned her harshly. Mrs Thrale was 'fallen below pity', said Mrs Montagu who also expressed the view that the 'poor woman' must be mad. Fanny Burney referred to her, in letters to the children, as their 'poor fallen mother'. Giuseppe Baretti wrote of that 'frontless female, who goes now by the mean appellation of Piozzi'. But of all her critics Johnson was by far the most savage, and the most unforgiving.

Although he had heard rumours for some time, and, according to Fanny Burney, knew something of the 'horrible affair' as early as the November of the previous year, he had chosen to close his mind to the idea that Mrs Thrale was lost to him. But at the beginning of July he had received a letter confirming his worst fears. She begged pardon, she wrote, 'for concealing from you a Connection which you must have heard of by many, but I suppose never believed. . . . Indeed, my dear Sir, it was concealed only to save needless pain; I could not have borne to reject that Council it would have killed me to take; and I only tell it you now, because it is all *irrevocably settled*, and out of your power to prevent.'

Johnson's reaction was ferocious. In a cruel letter, he replied,

If I interpret your letter right, you are ignominiously married, if it is yet undone, let us once [more] talk together. If you have abandoned your children and your religion, God forgive your wickedness; if you have forfeited your Fame and your country, may your folly do no further mischief. If the last act is yet to do, I who have loved you, esteemed you, reverenced you, and served you, I who long thought you the first of human kind entreat that before your fate is irrevocable, I may once more see you. I was, I once was, Madam, most truly yours, Sam: Johnson.

To this letter, Mrs Thrale replied in an injured but dignified tone:

I have this morning received from you so rough a letter in reply to one which was both tenderly and respectfully written, that I am forced to desire the conclusion of a correspondence which I can bear to continue no longer. The birth of my second husband is not meaner than that of my first; his sentiments are not meaner; his profession is not meaner. . . . It is want of fortune then that is ignominious; the character of the man I have chosen has no other claim to such an epithet. The religion to which he has always been a zealous adherent will, I hope, teach him to forgive insults he has not deserved; mine will, I hope, enable me to bear them at once with dignity and patience. To hear that I have forfeited my fame is indeed the greatest insult I ever yet received. My fame is as unsullied as snow, or I should think it unworthy of him who must henceforward protect it.

I write by the coach the more speedily and effectually to prevent your coming hither. Perhaps by my fame (and I hope it is so) you mean only that celebrity which is a consideration of a much lower kind. I care for that only as it may give pleasure to my husband and his friends.

Farewell, dear Sir, and accept my best wishes. You have always commanded my esteem, and long enjoyed the fruits of a friendship never infringed by one harsh expression on my part during twenty years of familiar talk. Never did I oppose your will, or control your wish; nor can your unmerited severity itself lessen my regard; but till you have changed your opinion of Mr Piozzi let us converse no more. God bless you.'

Johnson's reply was more temperate than his first outburst. He lamented her conduct, but hoped that God would grant her every blessing; he advised her to settle in England where she might live with more security and dignity than in Italy; and he reminded her of the attempt by the Archbishop of St Andrews to dissuade Mary Queen of Scots from seeking shelter in England: 'The Queen went forward . . . If the parallel reaches thus far, may it go no further. . . . The tears stand in my eyes.'

A week before her marriage, Mrs Thrale wrote to Johnson again to thank him most sincerely for this last 'sweetly kind' letter, and to assure him that Mr Piozzi, 'a religious Man, a sober Man and a thinking Man' would never injure her. 'Let nobody injure him in your good opinion, which he is most solicitous to obtain and to preserve,' she concluded, 'and the harsh Letter you wrote me at first grieved him to the very heart. Accept his Esteem my dear Sir, do; and his Promise to treat with long continued Respect and Tenderness the Friend with whom you once honoured with your Regard and who will never cease to be my dear Sir your truly affectionate and faithful servant.'

Johnson rejected the opportunity of reconciliation; he did not answer the letter, nor ever wrote to her again. For the rest of his life when he spoke of her at all, he did so with a kind of contemptuous hatred. How could this woman, whom he had known so intimately for so many years, have behaved to him in such a way, how could she have rejected him? He had confided to her his most terrible fears, entrusted her with his most shameful secrets; he had abjected himself before her and had loved her. And now she was abandoning him; his 'Mistress' had forsaken him.

He did not like to hear her name mentioned. When John Hawkins's daughter mentioned it and supposed that he would be seeing her again shortly, he roared out, 'I know nothing of Mrs Thrale. . . . Why should you suppose so? Good evening to you.' And he stormed out of the house. When Fanny Burney indelicately asked if he ever heard from her, he cried out in anguish. 'No, nor write to her. I drive her quite from my mind. If I meet with one of her letters, I burn it instantly. I have burnt all I can find. I never speak of her, and I desire never to hear of her more. I drive her, as I said, wholly from my mind.' Fanny always remembered how his great body had turned convulsively, how his eyes had rolled and his chest had heaved as he struggled to find words to express his anger; and how, in the end, he had been able to utter no more than the single, explosive word, '*Piozzi!*'

Mrs Piozzi had become 'a subject for her enemies to exult over,' Johnson told Hawkins, 'and for her friends, if she has any left, to forget, or pity. . . . Poor Thrale! I thought that either her virtue or her vice would have restrained her from such a marriage.'[1]

Two days before he wrote his last letter to Mrs Thrale, Johnson had begun what he called his 'Sick Man's Journal'. Since his stroke in 1783 he had recorded the vagaries of his state of health in letters to his 'Mistress'; but now that this was no longer possible, he kept a private record in Latin, the proper language for medical treatises, so Dr Lawrence had once told him. It was a meticulous journal in which he recorded his symptoms and cures, the medicaments and sleeping potions he took, the state of his bowels and the amount of his urine which he carefully measured against the liquids which he drank. His ailments were now numerous and chronic; he suffered from asthma, insomnia and indigestion, from convulsions of the chest, breathlessness, panting and unnatural sweating, and from dropsy which made his legs swollen and shiny. In vain attempts to get a good, painless night's sleep, and sometimes to combat bouts of depression, he took grain after grain of opium—once writing 'caveatur', as though afraid of becoming addicted after a particularly heavy dose—but opium made him constipated and drove him to violent purges and enemas. He also took syrup of wild lettuce for his asthma, rum to quieten his chest, tincture of cantharides—occasionally as many as eighty drops—to reduce the swelling in his legs, gooseberry wine to settle his stomach, numerous doses of vinegar of squills and of diacodium, regular purges of jalap and calomel, senna and, on Dr Brocklesby's recommendation, castor oil. He applied electricity to his legs and loins; he consulted his doctors regularly, writing to them long letters with detailed accounts of his progress; and he read what medical authorities he could lay his hands on. But he obtained only temporary relief; painless, undisturbed nights were very rare.

Frequently in the morning he could be found sitting in a chair by his bed, so restless and suffocated did he feel lying down. Part of his problem was his undiminished appetite. Occasionally he records a milk breakfast without solids or a dinner without meat; but more often he had a good meal which he afterwards had reason to regret.

In July he went to stay with Taylor at Ashbourne and there the temptation of the rich parson's excellent table was too much for him. One night there was an enticing spread of venison, fowl, pork, goose and dessert for dinner; another day there was some splendid fish with peas and Johnson ate too much of them. He also habitually ate too much fruit, particularly plums and pears and gooseberries; for he still had, as he confessed to Brocklesby, 'a voracious delight in raw summer fruit'. After an unusually comfortable night and a refreshing drive in the country, his appetite would be sharpened, and he would—as he did on 11 September— help himself to plums and pears, 'perhaps too many' before a heavy dinner of baked veal. One day, Taylor told Boswell—who discreetly omitted the anecdote from his *Life*—there was 'a glorious haunch of venison' for dinner. Johnson ate an enormous quantity of it. A fellow-guest, John Alsop, a local squire who did not like Johnson, 'wickedly prest him to eat more—which he did. He grew so ill that it was feared he would have died of downright eating, and had not a Surgeon been got to administer to him without delay a glister he must have died. After this he took to a milk diet, and improved so much in his health that he became quite a new man and beat them all in walking home from Church.'

Johnson's indulgences would make him low-spirited, so he would dose himself with diacodium. He tried to persuade himself that he did not eat more than he should. 'My appetite is, I think, less keen than it was,' he assured Heberden; but he had to admit that it was 'not so abated as that its decline can be observed by anyone but myself'.

He was often low-spirited. He was still troubled with religious doubts and 'shameful thoughts', still concerned about his idleness, still worried that, despite all his resolutions, he had not studied his Bible as thoroughly as he had intended. To make matters worse, he was frequently left by himself in the big house in Ashbourne while Taylor went about the business of his estate.

'In this place I have everything but company,' he lamented to Lucy Porter, 'and of company I am in great want. Dr Taylor is at his farm and I sit at home.' To Boswell he wrote, 'I have no company; the Doctor is busy in his fields, and goes to bed at nine, and his whole system is so different from mine, that we seem formed for different elements; I have, therefore, all my amusements to seek within myself.'

He was even reduced to thinking about the weather and to commenting on it in his letters. Conscious of how in the past he had derided those who remarked that it was hot or cold—rebuking them with a 'Poo! Poo! You are telling us that of which none but men in a mine or a dungeon can be ignorant'—he sadly recorded, 'Pride must have a fall.'

'Abandoned to the contemplation of my own miseries,' he further complained to Dr Brocklesby, 'I am something gloomy and depressed; this too I resist as I can, and find opium, I think useful; but I seldom take more than one grain. . . . I have no company here and shall naturally come home hungry for conversation: To wish you, dear Sir, more leisure, would not be kind; but what leisure you have you must bestow upon me.'

He left Ashbourne for Lichfield at the end of September, and found more company there; but he was rarely able to enjoy it. The first four nights of October were '*noctes miserae*'; his asthma was very troublesome, and the opium he took made him very drowsy and constipated. When he walked to Stowe, although it was downhill all the way, he had to rest frequently because he was so breathless. 'My legs would not carry me far if my breath would last,' he wrote with wry humour to his friend, Sir William Scott, the lawyer, 'and my breath would not last if my legs would carry me.' At the beginning of November he told Hawkins, 'I am relapsing into the dropsy very fast.'

Yet he still had hopes to 'find new topicks of merriment or new incitements to curiosity' when he was back in London talking to William Gerard Hamilton. 'The town is my element,' he reminded Brocklesby, 'there are my friends, there are my books to which I have not yet bidden farewell, and there are my amusements.' Even at this time, so he said, he looked upon every day to be lost upon which he did not make a new acquaintance. Referring to his illnesses, he exclaimed doggedly, 'I will be conquered; I will not capitulate.'

He returned to London, after paying his last visits to Edmund Hector in Birmingham and to Dr Adams in Oxford, on 16 November. The following day he wrote to Hector, 'This world must soon pass away. Let us think seriously on our duty. . . . We have all lived long and must soon part. God have mercy upon us, for the sake of our Lord Jesus Christ. Amen.'

While in Ashbourne he had told Dr Burney, 'I struggle hard for life. I take physick, and take air; my friend's chariot is always ready. We have run this morning twenty-four miles. . . . *But who can run the race with death?*' He recognised now that he was soon to die.

In the past, when he was ill, he had been only too eager to hear his friends tell him that he looked well; and one of them remembered an occasion when he conversationally assured Johnson that he was looking very much better than of late. Johnson seized him by the hand and vehemently declared, 'Sir, you are one of the kindest friends I ever had.'[2]

But now there could be no further pretence. When Dr Richard Warren, a member of the Club who with Dr William Heberden now helped Brocklesby look after him, said that he seemed a little improved, he answered, 'No, Sir. You cannot conceive with what acceleration I advance towards death.'

He arranged for a memorial to his parents and brother to be placed in St Michael's church at Lichfield, and for a memorial to Tetty—misremembering the date of her death—to be inserted in stone over her grave at Bromley; and after a good deal of urging from Sir John Hawkins—whom with Reynolds and William Scott he appointed his executor—he made his will. He had little to leave, and most of what he had went to Frank Barber. He had asked Brocklesby what would be a proper sum to leave by way of annuity to a favourite servant; the doctor had replied that that would depend upon the circumstances of the matter; in the case of a nobleman fifty pounds a year would be considered a just reward for many years faithful service. 'Then,' Johnson had said, 'shall I be *nobilissimus*, for I mean to leave Frank seventy pounds a year, and I desire you to tell him so.'

Having made his will, he burned huge piles of private papers, including, Boswell felt certain, 'two quarto volumes, containing a full, fair and most particular account of his own life, from his earliest recollection'. Boswell admitted that he had once 'accidentally seen' these volumes and had 'read a great deal in them'. He confessed as much to Johnson, apologised for the liberty, and asked if Johnson thought that he could help it. Johnson, so Boswell said, 'placidly answered, "Why, Sir, I do not think you could have helped it"', with the emphasis, perhaps, upon the 'you'. Boswell further confessed that it had even come into his mind to steal the books and never see their author again. How would that have affected him? he asked. 'Sir,' said Johnson, 'I believe I should have gone mad.'

He certainly did become exceedingly distressed when he learned that Hawkins, without saying anything to him, had slipped one of the volumes into his pocket. Hawkins excused himself on the grounds that he meant to keep it out of the hands of George Steevens who, he suspected, might find it and 'make an ill use of' it. 'You should not have laid hands on the book,' Johnson angrily told him when he discovered what Hawkins had done; 'for had I missed it, and not known you had it I should have roared for my book, as Othello did for his handkerchief, and probably have run mad.'

Hawkins thought it advisable to leave the house to give Johnson time 'to compose himself' before writing a letter of explanation. Johnson accepted the apology when he received it; but the next day, when Hawkins again visited him, he found the patient far from composed. Dr Brocklesby was with him and took up his wrist to feel his pulse, whereupon Johnson 'gave him a look of great contempt, and ridiculed the judging of his disorder [by this method]'. He complained that the sarocele in his testicle had again made its appearance and suggested that it ought to be punctured. Brocklesby agreed that a puncture might be a good idea, but insisted that Johnson's surgeon was the best judge. At this the difficult patient burst out, 'How many men in a year die through the timidity of those whom they consult for health! I want length of life, and you fear giving me pain, which I care not for.' When the surgeon, William Cumberland Cruickshank, scarified his leg he reproached him also with timidity. 'Deeper, deeper,' he cried out at him, 'I will abide the consequence: You are afraid of your reputation, but that is nothing to me.' Turning to the others in the room, he exclaimed, 'You all pretend to love me, but you do not love me so well as I myself do.'

Rarely, indeed, did either Cruickshank or Brocklesby come to visit him without there being some altercation. Once Johnson became heated, not over a difference about how he should be treated, but over a mistake Brocklesby made when repeating a line from Juvenal. 'Johnson's critical ear instantly took offence, and discoursing vehemently on the unmetrical effect of such a lapse, he shewed himself as full as ever of the spirit of the grammarian.'

Another day he told Brocklesby, 'Now, will you ascribe my death to my having taken eight grains of squills, when you recommended only three; Dr Heberden, to my having opened my left foot, when nature was pointing out the discharge in the right.'

Just as he complained about the doctors, so he complained of the incompetence of the male nurse whom Hawkins employed to sit by his bed at night. 'The fellow's an idiot,' he decided, 'as awkward as a turnspit just put into the wheel, and as sleepy as a dormouse.' It was intolerable to have such a fellow by his bed when he could not sleep at night, for he was now quite unable to read during his hours of restlessness. This was very hard for him, he lamented. 'I used formerly when sleepless in bed *to read like a Turk.*'

He wanted desperately to live. 'I would give one of these legs for a year of life,' he said. 'I mean of comfortable life, not such as that which I now suffer.' Yet in his heart he knew that he could never lead a comfortable life again. He asked Dr Brocklesby to tell him plainly whether or not he would recover. 'Give me,' he urged, 'a direct answer.' Brocklesby asked him if he could bear the whole truth. Johnson assured him that he could; and when he was told that nothing but a miracle could save him, he accepted the verdict as though he had expected it.

When his friends called to see him—Hawkins, Langton, Burke, Reynolds, Burney, Taylor, John Hoole, William Windham, and William

Strahan's second son, the Rev George Strahan, all seem to have been regular visitors—he urged them with an almost violent intensity to let his 'present situation' have a 'due effect' upon them. 'Let me exhort you,' he said to the young Italian translator, Francesco Sastres, 'always to think of my situation, which must one day be yours; always remember that life is short and eternity never ends. I say nothing of your religion; for if you conscientiously keep to it, I have little doubt but you may be saved. If you read the controversy, I think we have the right on our side; but if you do not read it, be not persuaded, from any worldly consideration, to alter the religion in which you were educated. Change not but from conviction and reason.'

He talked to his visitors at length about the Christian religion, lamenting how he himself had neglected it for so long and had not read the Bible as diligently as he should have done; he earnestly advised them to set apart every seventh day for the care of their souls. When Joshua Reynolds came he asked him to promise him, as a dying friend, to read the Bible regularly, never omitting Sunday, and never to paint on a Sunday; Reynolds hesitated but finally agreed. When William Windham came he urged him, too, to keep Sunday as a day apart: 'Such a portion of time was surely little enough for the meditation of eternity.' When John Hoole visited him he conjured him vehemently to read and meditate upon the Bible and talked with 'a fervour of religious zeal and personal affection', begging him to write down all that passed between them. 'Promise me,' he pleaded, 'that you will do it.'[3]

He begged Sastres and Brocklesby, too, to write down what he said. 'Doctor, you are a worthy man and my friend,' he told Brocklesby, 'but I am afraid you are not a Christian! What can I better do for you than to offer up, in your presence, a prayer to the great God, that you may become a Christian in my sense of the word?'

He instantly fell on his knees, and put up a fervent prayer. When he got up he caught hold of the doctor's hand with great eagerness, and cried, 'Doctor! You do not say Amen!'

The doctor looked embarrassed, but after a pause murmured, 'Amen!'

'My dear Doctor,' Johnson said, 'believe a dying man, there is no salvation but in the sacrifice of the lamb of God. Go home, write down my prayer, and every word I have said, and bring it for me tomorrow.'

Before they left he always asked his visitors to say a prayer with him, and every night before he went to bed and tried to sleep he knelt to pray

with Frank. He asked William Windham to allow him to tell Frank
that he could look up to him as his friend, adviser and protector; Windham
said he would look after him, so Johnson called Frank in and asked them
to hold hands while Windham repeated his promise.[4]

On Sunday 5 December, before receiving the Sacrament, Johnson composed his last prayer:

> Almighty and most merciful Father, I am now, as to human eyes it
> seems, about to commemorate for the last time, the death of thy son
> Jesus Christ, our Saviour and Redeemer. Grant, O Lord, that my
> whole hope and confidence may be in his merits and thy mercy: forgive
> and accept my late conversion, enforce and accept my imperfect repen
> tance. . . . Have mercy upon me and pardon the multitude of my
> offences. Bless my friends, have mercy upon all men. Support me by
> the grace of the Holy Spirit in the days of weakness, and at the hour
> of death, and receive me, at my death, to everlasting happiness, for
> the sake of Jesus Christ.   Amen.

At last, after years of 'vain scruples'—which 'made many men miserable, but few men good'—he seems to have resolved his religious doubts
and was ready to meet death. Yet he still could not meet it with complacent confidence: he was rather despondent the day he composed his
last prayer, John Hoole thought. He said anxiously to John Ryland, the
West Indian merchant, his friend since the days of the Ivy Lane Club,
'I hope I shall arrive safe at the end of the journey, and be accepted at
last'; and when Ryland tried to comfort him with the observation that
we had great hopes given to us, he exclaimed, 'Yes, we have hopes given
us; but they are conditional, and I know not how far I have fulfilled these
conditions.' Some time later, however, he added, more hopefully, 'I
think that I have now corrected all bad and vicious habits.'

Only a week before he had confessed that the thought of death was
still very terrible to him; but now he was more or less reconciled. 'All his
fears were calmed and absorbed by the prevalence of his faith,' Brocklesby
thought. 'His doubts were overcome; his trust confirmed in the merits
and *propitiation* of Jesus Christ.'

On Monday, 7 December—though he admitted to John Hoole that he
had been 'quarrelling with all his physicians'—he seemed 'in tolerable
spirits'. The next day he was further improved, and he ate 'a very good
dinner'. But on 8 December he was 'very poorly and low after a very bad

night'; and by 9 December he was unable to kneel down, so weak had he become. This distressed him deeply since he had to pray sitting up against the pillows or lying down, and he could not hear the prayers so well. 'Louder, my dear Sir, louder, I entreat you,' he implored John Hoole's son, the Rev Samuel Hoole, who was repeating a prayer too softly, 'louder, I entreat you, or you pray in vain.' When the prayers were over 'he uttered extempore,' so Hawkins said, 'a few pious ejaculations'.

He had given up taking opium now for fear lest he might be called to meet God with his mind clouded; he had also decided to drink no more wine for the same reason. He seemed restless, but not frightened, and occasionally almost playful. On 11 December in reply to a note of Hoole's recommending an 'irregular' physician for his dropsy, he said to him when he called that it was too late now for doctors, *'regular* or *irregular'*. He was even 'cheerful' with Cruickshank, calling to him, 'Come give me your hand'; and, shaking it warmly, he told him, 'You shall make no further use of it now.' Cruickshank protested mildly, saying that he really ought to examine his legs; but Johnson refused to let him, and Cruickshank did not persist.

That day several of his old friends called to see him for the last time. One of them was Charles Burney, who recorded that Johnson, although 'extremely feeble', insisted on getting up, 'wrapt in a Night gown', and 'desired that his friends sh^d be called into the next room one at a time'. 'At length it came to my turn,' Burney went on, '& I approached him with reverential awe & heart-felt affliction—Johnson, sitting propt up in a great Chair, took hold of my hand & asked after the whole Family . . . after wch still holding my hands he made one of the most fervent & Eloquent prayers that was ever uttered in the last moments of a saint.'

The next day Johnson remained in bed all day, for the first time since this last illness had begun, refusing not only wine and opium but food as well. Windham, on Cruickshank's advice, pressed him to eat something on the grounds that such total abstinence might defeat its purpose and render his mind not clear but muddled. ''Tis all very childish,' Johnson replied. 'Let us hear no more of it.' Windham urged him to drink at least a little milk which he had taken to now instead of tea—dismissed at last with 'all similar potations' as being 'adscititious'—but Johnson broke out in irritation, begging that 'there might be an end of it'. Then, as though regretting his impatience, he said fervently, 'God bless you, my dear Windham, through Jesus Christ.'

That night when the visitors had gone and Frank and Mrs Desmoulins's son, John, were sitting with him, he asked them to bring him a case from which he took a tray of lancets and, selecting one, he conveyed it beneath the bedclothes, determined to take his treatment into his own hands and relieve the swelling in his legs. Frank and Desmoulins begged him not to injure himself, and there seems to have been a struggle in which, according to William Windham's account, Johnson grew 'very outrageous, so as to call Frank scoundrel and threaten Desmoulins that he would stab him'. Eventually they managed to get him to agree that he would not do anything rash. 'But under the bedclothes,' John Hawkins recorded, having interviewed Frank about it, 'they saw his hand move. Upon this they turned down the clothes, and saw a great effusion of blood, which soon stopped. . . . Soon after he got at a pair of scissors that lay in a drawer by him, and plunged them deep in the calf of each leg. . . . Immediately they sent for Mr Cruickshank, and the apothecary, and they, or one of them, dressed his wounds.'

The next morning he was calm again, though his legs were in great pain. Frank and a servant of William Windham's who had come in to help him, assisted him to sit up at intervals which he found some sort of relief. 'Regularly,' Windham's servant said, 'he addressed himself to fervent prayer; and though, sometimes, his voice failed him, his sense never did, during that time. The only sustenance he received was cyder and water.' At six o'clock he asked the time, and, on being told, said that he felt he had but a few hours left to live.

Soon afterwards the daughter of a friend of his came to the house and begged Frank to 'be permitted to see the Doctor that she might earnestly request him to give her his blessing'. The girl followed Frank into the room as he delivered her message and Johnson turned to her and said, 'God bless you, my dear!'

They were the last coherent words he spoke. He lived on throughout the day in a kind of doze, speaking to nobody, though Francesco Sastres thought he caught the words 'I am about to die', muttered in Latin. He took a little warm milk in a cup and murmured something about it not being put into his hand properly.

In the afternoon his breathing became heavier, and towards seven o'clock it stopped. Frank and Mrs Desmoulins who were sitting in his room went over to the bed, and, looking down upon him, saw that he was dead.

A few days earlier he had asked John Hawkins where he would be buried. Hawkins had replied that it would doubtless be in Westminster Abbey; and Johnson had seemed pleased by this. On Monday 20

December 1784 he was buried there in the fourth transept near the foot of Shakespeare's monument. In accordance with his request a stone of black marble was placed over the grave to protect his body from injury; and on it were inscribed these few and simple words:

SAMUEL JOHNSON, LL.D.,
OBIIT XIII DIE DECEMBRIS,
ANNO DOMINI
MDCCLXXXIV
AETATIS SUAE LXXV

Notes

Chapter 1 (Pages 3–30)

1 Aleyn Lyell Reade suggested that Michael Johnson's finances never recovered from his purchase, shortly before his elder son was born, of the Knowsley library from the heir to the ninth Earl of Derby—a collection of nearly 3,000 volumes described as 'great and noble'.

2 Johnson told Boswell that he would rather 'have the rod to be the general terror to all, to make them learn, than tell a child, if you do thus, you will be more esteemed than your brothers and sisters. The rod produces an effect which terminates in itself. A child is afraid of being whipped, and gets his task, and there's an end on't; whereas, by exciting emulation and comparisons of superiority, you lay the foundation of lasting mischief; you make brothers and sisters hate each other.' When Bennet Langton asked him how he had acquired such a mastery of Latin, Johnson replied, 'My master whipped me very well. Without that, Sir, I should have done nothing.'
   'No attention can be obtained from children without the infliction of pain,' he assured Mrs Thrale, but then he added, 'and pain is never remembered without resentment.'
   He was not, however, in favour of sending timid children to public schools so that they might acquire confidence. This was 'a preposterous expedient'; it was like 'forcing an owl upon day'.

3 Throughout his life Johnson persisted in this 'cursory mode of reading', as Boswell described it. Sometimes he did not even trouble to cut the leaves of a new book, content to read in it where the pages were open. But as Mrs Mary Knowles said, Johnson knew how to read 'better than anyone'; he got at the substance of a book directly; he tore out the heart of it.
   He derided the belief that one ought to read to the end of any book that one had once begun—that was 'strange advice; you may as well resolve that whatever men you happen to get acquainted with, you are to keep to them for life'. He also said, 'If a man begin to read in the middle of a book, and feels an inclination to go on, let him not quit it to go to the beginning. He may perhaps not feel again the inclination.'
   'I have read few books, though,' he confessed to William Bowles, 'they are generally so repulsive that I cannot.'

4 The phrase appears as 'mad and violent' in Boswell's *Life*. Boswell, so it

appears from the Yale Edition of the *Private Papers*, misread his own hand-writing when working from his original notes.

5 The Rev Richard Warner described how, on his last visit to Lichfield, Johnson was missed one morning at the breakfast-table. The servants said he had left the house at an early hour without saying where he was going. The day passed and the party became uneasy at his absence. Just before supper he reappeared. He apologised to his hostess: 'Madam I beg your pardon for the abruptness of my departure from your house this morning, but I was constrained to it by my conscience. Fifty years ago, Madam, on this day, I committed a breach of filial piety, which has ever since lain heavy on my mind, and has not till this day been expatiated. My father, you recollect, was a book-seller, and had long been in the habit of attending Uttoxeter market, and opening a stall for the sale of his books during that day. Confined to his bed by indisposition, he requested me, this time fifty years ago, to visit the market, and attend the stall in his place. But, Madam, my pride prevented me from doing my duty, and I gave my father a refusal. To do away the sin of this disobedience, I this day went in a postchaise to Uttoxeter, and going into the market at the time of high business, uncovered my head, and stood with it bare an hour before the stall which my father had formerly used, exposed to the sneers of the standers-by and in the inclemency of the weather; a penance by which I trust I have propitiated heaven for this only instance, I believe, of contumacy towards my father.'

6 In later life Johnson was rather ashamed of this translation of Lobo's *Travels*. When Boswell showed him a copy 'as a curiosity', he said, '"Take no notice of it", or "Don't talk of it." He seemed to think it beneath him, though done at six-and-twenty.' Boswell said, 'Your style, Sir, is much improved since you translated this.' Johnson answered, 'with a sort of triumphant smile, "Sir, I hope it is."'

7 The first of these descriptions of Tetty is that of Anna Seward, an unreliable witness, who added, so Boswell recorded, in his *Private Papers*, 'She had a very red face, and very indifferent features. . . . The rustic prettiness, and artless manners of her daughter [Lucy Porter] had won Johnson's heart, when she was upon a visit to my grandfather's [John Hunter's] in Johnson's school days. Disgusted by his unsightly form, she had a personal aversion to him . . .'. The second description is David Garrick's.

8 Johnson's reply to his mother was reported by Anna Seward. Attempts to discover an uncle of Johnson's who had been hanged have proved fruitless. Mrs Mary Cobb, the widow of a Lichfield mercer, who knew the family well, told Boswell, 'I have enquired *Again* and *Again* of the oldest Inhabitants of this Place but cannot learn the smallest circumstance of it—*had* it been so, it wou'd *certainly* have been remember'd. . . . I am Inclined to think it might be Said jestingly.' Aleyn Lyell Reade also investigated the problem without success. All Anna Seward's stories must be treated with caution.

Chapter 2 (Pages 31–61)

1 Johnson thought that a trade would be even easier to master than the profession of law. 'Trade could not be managed by those who manage it, if it had much difficulty,' he told Mrs Thrale after the death of her husband had left the brewery in her possession. 'Their great books are soon understood, and their language . . . is understood with no very laborious application.'

Chapter 3 (Pages 62–78)

1 Boswell also noted these remarks though they do not, of course, appear in the *Life*. This is not to say that Johnson actually used the words set down. It must be said that Murphy is a bad witness and that Garrick was much given to exaggeration.

2 'He wrote his prose for the public, as most people do,' commented David Nichol Smith, '. . . much of his verse he wrote for himself or for his closest friends. His minor pieces which he never hoped to see printed, have more to tell us about himself than we might have expected. But in order to get this picture at its truest, we have to read his Latin verse as well as his English. Latin was a living language to Johnson, and it was the language which he preferred for the expression of certain moods and feelings. . . . Poems about himself and his feelings he did not write in English.'

3 The first edition of the poem has 'garret' not 'patron'. The alteration was prompted by Johnson's quarrel with Lord Chesterfield over the patronage of the dictionary. 'Tardy busts' of poets in Westminster Abbey included that of Shakespeare placed there 125 years after his death. Johnson's own bust, in St Paul's, was put up within twelve years.

4 It seems to have been true that in his youth Garrick could 'put off tragedy and put on comedy like a garment', which makes Johnson's comment more excusable. Also, Johnson was very concerned with the moral implications of the actor's *pretences*, especially to wickedness in a dramatic character. But Johnson was certainly a tiresome man to have in an audience. Mrs Thrale said he was 'an exceedingly bad playhouse companion, as his person drew people's eyes upon the box, and the loudness of his voice made it difficult for me to hear anybody but himself'.

5 'The late Mr Topham Beauclerk, who had a great deal of that humour which

pleases the more for seeming undesigned,' recalled Arthur Murphy, 'used to give a pleasant description of this green-room finery, as related by the author himself. "But," said Johnson, with great gravity, "I soon laid aside my gold-laced hat, lest it should make me proud."'

6 The fifth act of *Irene* was hissed again on the second night. The offence of strangling Mrs Pritchard—not Johnson's idea, it seems, but Garrick's—was then removed from the text and she went off the stage to die.

7 Charles XII does, however, appear in *The Vanity of Human Wishes* where his tragic fate is lamented in fine lines which include these:

> His fall was destin'd to a barren strand,
> A petty fortress, and a dubious hand;
> He left the name, at which the world grew pale,
> To point a moral, or adorn a tale.

'If these lines are not poetry,' commented T. S. Eliot, 'I do not know what it is.'

8 'A conspicuous ingredient of Johnson's ample style,' R. T. Davies has written, 'is his polysyllabism. He used big words deliberately and typically, and it is something in which his style shows itself to be the man. One may sometimes suspect that he was partly laughing at himself as he played this role of the orotund man of learning or magniloquent moralist. In the final *Rambler* essay, however, he justified his use of big words by explaining that he had "familiarized the terms of philosophy" where "common" words would be "less pleasing to the ear or less distinct in their signification".'

9 Johnson makes a similar criticism of Lyttelton whose *Dialogues* he deemed 'a nugatory performance. "That man, (said he) sat down to write a book, to tell the world what the world had all his life been telling him."'

Chapter 4 (Pages 79–96)

1 Purely on the strength of his friendship with Johnson, Levett earned a place in the *Dictionary of National Biography*. Topham Beauclerk and Bennet Langton are also included for no other reason; and it is presumably because of her friendship with Johnson, rather than because of her poetry, that Anna Williams can also be found there.

2 Probably Bromley was chosen as a suitable place for Tetty to be buried because Johnson's friend, Hawkesworth, lived there. It is said that John Taylor

declined to preach the funeral sermon that Johnson wrote for Tetty on the grounds that the praise of her virtues was too fulsome—grounds which would not have met with Johnson's approval even had he agreed that the eulogy was overdone. 'The writer of an epitaph should not be considered as saying nothing but what is strictly true,' he told Alexander Maclean. 'Allowance must be made for some degree of exaggerated praise. In lapidary inscriptions a man is not upon oath.'

3 According to William Cooke, whose anonymous *Life of Johnson* appeared in 1785, the year after its subject's death, it was Johnson, not Bathurst, who sent Barber to school in Yorkshire, intending to train him as a missionary. Barber's 'parts, however, not admitting this cultivation, Johnson took him into his service'.

4 The second of the two definitions was added in the fourth edition. It is largely, though not wholly, in this sense that Johnson used the word when on 7 April 1775 he uttered 'in a strong determined tone, "Patriotism is the last refuge of a scoundrel."'

5 Johnson received the degree of LL.D. from Dublin in 1756 and from Oxford in 1775.

Chapter 5 *(Pages 99–119)*

1 Against Peter Garrick's story of Johnson having seduced the 'very fine woman', Boswell noted in his journal, 'not very probable'; but he did not discount the possibility that he had indulged his 'strong amorous passions' as a young man. It seems that Boswell, who had looked into the diary that Johnson destroyed, met Hawkins at Bennet Langton's house to discuss the 'delicate matter' of using it as a source in their biographies. Perhaps they agreed not to cite it as a source, but to mention guardedly the sexual adventures which— so they evidently believed—Johnson had enjoyed as a young man and which afterwards so troubled his conscience. As Professor Pottle has observed they presented this 'delicate matter' at exactly the same spots in their respective narratives. Hawkins made use of a lawyer's ploy for getting in excluded testimony by writing 'though I am not warranted to say . . .'. Boswell, leading into his final statement, said, 'On that account, therefore, as well as from the regard to truth which he inculcated, I am to mention, (with all possible respect and delicacy however) . . .'. That *I am to mention*, Professor Pottle says, has no parallel anywhere else in Boswell's *Life*.

2 The woman was Topham Beauclerk's wife, Lady Diana, daughter of the

second Duke of Marlborough. She had been unfaithful to her first husband, Frederick St John, nephew of Lord Bolingbroke.

3 According to Joseph Nollekens's pupil, John Thomas Smith, Johnson at one time had thoughts of marrying Saunders Welch's daughter, Mary, who married Nollekens in 1772. 'I have heard Mr Nollekens say,' wrote Smith, 'that the Doctor, when joked about her, observed: "Yes, I think Mary would have been mine if little Joe had not stepped in."'

4 Johnson took great pride in this evident facility; but, of course, he did not sit down to write until he had it clear in his mind what he wanted to say. 'What is written without effort,' he said, 'is in general read without pleasure.'

5 George Irwin has suggested that Johnson to the end remained subconsciously afraid of the 'tyrant of his childhood': if, instead of writing in *The Idler*, 'the life which made my own life pleasant is at an end', he had written '"the life that made my own life Hell is at an end", he would have been much nearer the truth'.

6 A more recent critic, Frederick W. Hilles, has written, 'In *Rasselas* Johnson tells us nothing that is new, but he tells us what is true, and tells it so effectively that people in all parts of the globe and from all walks of life have come under its spell. . . . We do not read *Rasselas* for the story. We read it for a view of life that is presented majestically in long sweeping phrases.'

Rasselas, following upon his translation of Lobo's *Travels*, gained for Johnson an undeserved reputation as an authority on Ethiopia. His expressed doubt that the explorer, James Bruce, had ever even entered the country contributed much, therefore, to Bruce's early failure to gain credence for his exploits.

7 From Boswell's *Private Papers* it appears that William Julius Mickle, the Scottish poet, said that at a dinner party at John Hoole's, Johnson once spent 'more than a quarter of an hour in execrating the sea life; he once slept on board a man of war in the river and thought he was in Hell. He said it was corrupting the morals of boys to send them on board a man of war. M. "The destitute pickpocket wicked boys of the streets of London?" JOHNSON. "Yes, even them, Sir. A man of war will make them ten times worse."'

Nevertheless, Johnson said that, 'every man thinks meanly of himself for not having been a soldier, or not having been at sea'.

8 Although his own experiences as an undergraduate had been far from happy, Johnson always did enjoy himself at Oxford, and took great pleasure in extolling the virtues of the university, comparing it favourably with Cambridge. 'He delighted in his own partiality for Oxford,' Mrs Thrale said; 'and one day, at my house, entertained five members of the other university with various instances of the superiority of Oxford, enumerating the gigantic names of many men whom it had produced, with apparent triumph. At last I said to him, "Why there happens to be no less than five Cambridge men in the room

now." "I did not (said he) think of that till you told me; but the wolf don't count the sheep."'

9 Johnson sometimes grew almost violent in his condemnation of *Tom Jones*, and was driven by his anger to bestow the most fulsome praises upon Samuel Richardson. 'I am shocked to hear you quote from so vicious a book,' he once scolded Hannah More, who said that this was 'the only occasion of Johnson's being really angry with her'. 'I am sorry to hear you have read it: a confession which no modest lady should ever make. I scarcely know a more corrupt work.' 'His displeasure did him so much honour I loved him the better for it,' Hannah More commented. 'I thanked him, reassured him of my better judgment and stated my dislike of another work of Fielding. Johnson denied Fielding's talents, comparing him with Richardson who he affirmed to be the greatest genius that had shed his lustre on this path of literature.'

10 Samuel Richardson, in fact, well bore out Johnson's contention that 'the best part of every author is in general to be found in his book'.

Chapter 6 (*Pages 120–139*)

1 No saint, Boswell said, was 'more sensible of the unhappy failure of pious resolves than Johnson. He said, one day, talking to an acquaintance on this subject, "Sir, Hell is paved with good intentions."' He vehemently advised Boswell never to make a vow to bind himself to his moral duty: 'He gave me some salutary counsel, and recommended vigorous resolution against any deviation from moral duty. BOSWELL. "But you would not have me to bind myself by a solemn obligation?" JOHNSON (much agitated). "What! a vow—O, no, Sir, a vow is a horrible thing, it is a snare for sin. The man who cannot go to heaven without a vow—may go——" Here, standing erect, in the middle of his library, and rolling grand, his pause was truly a curious compound of the solemn and the ludicrous; he half-whistled in his usual way, when pleasant, and he paused, as if checked by religious awe. —Methought he would have added—to Hell—but was restrained.'

2 'It is curious,' Macaulay wrote, 'to observe . . . the contrast between the disdainful manner in which he rejects unauthenticated anecdotes, even when they are consistent with the general laws of nature, and the respectful manner in which he mentions the wildest stories relating to the invisible world.' On this Bertrand H. Bronson has commented, 'But the paradox is not a paradox when we understand that it was the sceptical habit of mind, requiring rational demonstration of what he *had* to believe, that drove him to personal investigation of all reports of the supernatural. Not superstition but the opposite. To the

question, were not the evidences of Christianity sufficient? he replied, "Yes, but I would have more."'

3 'Why, Sir, I never was near enough to great men to court them,' Johnson told Boswell on another occasion. 'But if you can get a shilling's worth of good for sixpence worth of court, you are a fool if you do not pay court.'

4 Johnson's Jacobite feelings seem never to have been very intense. He confessed that if 'holding up his right hand would have secured victory at Culloden to Prince Charles's army, he was not sure he would have held it up'; and by 1773 he had decided that the House of Hanover had by then established as good a right to the throne as the former family, 'by the long consent of the people'. On attending an assembly in 1780, Hannah More, 'gorgeous in scarlet', found everyone else in blackest mourning for some German relations of the royal family. 'Even Jacobite Johnson was in deep mourning.'

5 These remarks were addressed to Mrs Thrale, whom he liked to tease about the quality of cooking in her house, excellent though it was. One day having supped the evening before with some fashionable people at Mrs Frances Abington's—and seeming much pleased with having been a member of so elegant a circle—he said to Mrs Thrale with a smile, 'Mrs Abington's jelly, my dear lady, was better than yours.'

6 Johnson also prided himself on his mastery of household economy. He condemned all forms of petty saving. On hearing that a certain lady, whose husband was alleged to be living beyond his income, had objected to the cutting in half of a two-shilling mango, he had exclaimed, 'Sir, that is the blundering economy of a narrow understanding. It is stopping one hole in a sieve.' Nor did Johnson consider it worthwhile keeping accounts if one had no one to account to: 'You won't eat less beef to-day, because you have written down what it cost yesterday.'

7 Johnson sometimes went up to this garret to read a book amidst the spirit lamps and bottles without telling Frank where he was going, for he would not allow his servant to say that he was not at home when he really was. 'A servant's strict regard for truth,' he explained, 'must be weakened by such a practice. A philosopher may know that it is merely a form of denial; but few servants are such nice distinguishers. If I accustom a servant to tell a lie for *me*, have I not reason to apprehend that he will tell many lies for *himself*.'

8 Johnson thought it was equally unbecoming of Lord Camden to associate on familiar terms with Garrick. Boswell told Johnson that one morning he had called upon Garrick, 'who was very vain of his intimacy with Lord Camden', and had been accosted thus: '"Pray now, did you—did you meet a little lawyer turning the corner, eh?"—"No, Sir, (said I). Pray what do you mean by the question?"—"Why, (replied Garrick, with an affected indifference, yet as if standing on tip-toe,) Lord Camden has this moment left me. We have

had a long walk together." JOHNSON. "Well, Sir, Garrick talked very properly. Lord Camden was a little lawyer to be associating so familiarly with a player."'

9 Another effective reply by Goldsmith to a rude remark by Johnson was recorded by Benjamin Rush, an American doctor, who met them at the house of Sir Joshua Reynolds. 'Dr Goldsmith,' Rush wrote, 'asked me several questions relative to the manners and customs of the North American Indians. Dr Johnson, who heard one of them, suddenly interrupted him and said, 'There is not an Indian in North America who would have asked such a foolish question." "I am sure," said Goldsmith, "there is not a savage in America that would have made so rude a speech to a gentleman."'

10 Charles Burney gave a similar judgment. Johnson was 'as good-natured as a family mastiff, whom you may safely pat and stroke at the fireside without the least fear of his biting you. The utmost he will do if you are a little rough with him is to growl.'

Chapter 7 (Pages 140–155)

1 Johnson himself always took good care to ensure that his own mind had constant occupation, even though it might be of the most trivial nature. One day when Edmond Malone called upon him he found him reading the *History of Birmingham* in an armchair by the fireside before which a few apples were laid. Malone supposed he was preparing the apples for some medicine. 'Why, no, Sir,' Johnson replied, 'I believe they are only there because I want something to do.'

2 When Johnson and Boswell did meet again, Boswell recorded in his journal, 'You kneel'd, and ask'd his blessing . . . he hug'd you to him like a sack, and grumbl'd, "I hope we shall pass many years of regard together."'

3 'When Johnson kicked the stone he was not refuting Berkeley, in spite of what he said at the moment,' Herman Liebert comments. 'He was rather attacking the fact which he always greeted with impatience: that in a world, in his own phrase, "bursting with sin and sorrow", men should wander in the endless labyrinths of metaphysics when they might be improving the lot of others in this world or their own in the next. As a philosophical answer to Berkeley his gesture is meaningless; as an emphatic assertion of the imperative reality of a world in which men live and suffer, it is the essential statement of Johnson's doctrine.'

4 Although he claimed never to have paid court to the great, Johnson was always insistent that a man should be respected for his rank, and always prided

himself upon the fact that he was zealous for subordination. 'I have great merit for being zealous for subordination and the honours of birth,' he said, 'for I can hardly tell who was my grandfather.' When the Rev William Maxwell stepped aside to let him walk out of a room ahead of him, Johnson firmly declined to do so, saying that he hoped he knew his rank better than to take precedence over a Doctor of Divinity.

'Were I a man of rank,' he used to say, 'I would not let a daughter starve who had made a mean marriage; but having voluntarily degraded herself from the station which she was originally entitled to hold, I would support her only in that which she herself had chosen, and would not put her on a level with my other daughters. You are to consider that it is our duty to maintain the subordination of civilised society; and when there is a gross and shameful deviation from rank, it should be punished so as to deter others from the same perversion. . . . It is better that some should be unhappy, than that none should be happy, which would be the case in a general state of equality. . . . I believe we hardly wish that the mob should have liberty to govern us. When that was the case some time ago, no man was at liberty not to have candles in his windows.'

'The superiority of a country gentleman over the people upon his estate is very agreeable', he thought, and he contended that if he were a gentleman of landed property, he would turn out all his tenants who did not vote for the candidate whom he supported. 'High people, Sir, are the best; take a hundred ladies of quality, you'll find them better wives, better mothers, more willing to sacrifice their own pleasure to their children, than a hundred other women. Tradeswomen (I mean the wives of tradesmen) in the city, who are worth from ten to fifteen thousand pounds, are the worst creatures upon the earth, grossly ignorant, and thinking viciousness fashionable. Farmers, I think, are often worthless fellows. Few lords will cheat; and, if they do, they'll be ashamed of it: farmers cheat and are not ashamed of it. . . . There is generally a *scoundrellism* about a low man. . . . A poor man has no honour.'

Boswell said that he preferred to be known as Mr Johnson and addressed as Samuel Johnson, Esquire, rather than as Dr Johnson; and that once when Boswell objected to the designation of *Esquire* on a letter addressed to Johnson as being inferior to that of Doctor, Johnson disagreed and 'seemed pleased with it because . . . he liked sometimes to be taken out of the class of literary men, and to be merely *genteel*'.

When in the company of booksellers, however, he was at pains to establish his superiority over them; and he told Joshua Reynolds that rather than give up his place at the head of a dinner-table at which sat a numerous company of booksellers, he suffered the discomfort of having his back toasted at a hot fire.

Chapter 8 (Pages 156–175)

1 He composed his own material and superintended the baking of it. But the overseer said that he never really understood the nature of the operation, imagining that a single substance was sufficient in the composition of the clay, whereas he, an experienced practitioner, always used sixteen.

2 Johnson never tired of making such remarks about Whigs:
'BOSWELL. "I drank chocolate, Sir, this morning with Mr Eld; and, to my not small surprise, found him to be a *Staffordshire Whig*, a being which I did not believe had existed." JOHNSON. "Sir there are rascals in all counties."'

3 However, Johnson claimed that he 'would not give half a guinea to live under one form of government rather than another. It is of no moment to the happiness of an individual. Sir, the danger of the abuse of power is nothing to a private man.' He propounded similar views on the liberty of the press: 'Now, Sir, there is the liberty of the press, which you know is a constant topick. Suppose you and I and two hundred more were restrained from printing our thoughts: What then? What proportion would that restraint upon us bear to the private happiness of the nation?'

4 Boswell made a very pertinent observation in his journal about Johnson's savage tongue: 'Dr Johnson's harsh attacks on his friends arise from uneasiness within. There is an insurrection abroad. His loud explosions are guns of distress.'

5 In the *Life*, Boswell did not care to reveal that the object of this rebuke was himself.

6 Benjamin Rush who met Johnson in 1769, said that upon being asked what was his opinion of Mr Boswell, Johnson replied, 'He is much given to asking questions and they are not always of the most interesting nature. For instance, he will sometimes ask. "Pray, Doctor, why is an apple round, and why is not a pear so?"'

7 Presumably the bits of dried orange peel were used as a 'remedy for indigestion and lubricity of the bowels' as recommended to Hill Boothby in Johnson's letter of 31 December 1755.

8 Sometimes Johnson seemed only to be aware of his own rudeness when an offensive remark brought all conversation around him to a halt. Samuel Rogers was given an example of this by a friend: 'During dinner while [Dr Samuel] Musgrave was holding forth very agreeably on some subject, Johnson suddenly interrupted him with, "Sir, you talk like a fool." A dead silence ensued; and Johnson, perceiving that his rude speech had occasioned it, turned to Musgrave and said, "Sir, I have hurt your feelings." "Dr Johnson," replied Musgrave, "I feel only for you."'

9 Some observers thought Boswell's imitation of Johnson's manner better than Garrick's. Fanny Burney said that Boswell's 'imitations, though comic to excess, were so far from caricature that he omitted a thousand gesticulations which I distinctly remember'. Hannah More considered that although Garrick imitated Johnson's manner in reciting poetry better than Boswell did, Boswell was the more accurate in mimicking Johnson's style in ordinary conversation.

10 The culprit was identified in T. Green's *Diary of a Lover of Literature* as Dr Bernard, President of Jesus; but as Dr Hill pointed out no Principal (not President) of Jesus has ever borne the name Bernard.

11 Frank Barber was reported in a 1793 issue of the *Gentleman's Magazine* as saying that he never heard his master swear. 'The worst word he ever uttered when in a passion was, *you dunghill* dog.'

A rare record of Johnson swearing in Boswell's presence is given in the *Tour to the Hebrides*. On Coll they were disputing 'whether sand-hills could be fixed down by art'. Dr Johnson said, "How *the devil* can you do it?" but, instantly corrected himself, "How can you do it?"' Boswell had never before 'heard him use a phrase of that nature'. But Johnson admitted that 'at an early part' of his life he 'drank enough and swore enough, to be sure'.

12 'With regard to Drink his liking is for the *strongest*,' Mrs Thrale recorded, 'as it is not the Flavour but the Effect of Wine which he even professes to desire.'

Chapter 9 (*Pages 179–192*)

1 This is from *Thraliana*. The date is incorrectly given as 1764 in the *Anecdotes*. Johnson did not think much of his fellow-guest, the poetical shoemaker. 'They had better,' he said, 'furnish the man with good implements for his trade, then raise subscriptions for his poems. He may make an excellent shoemaker, but can never make a good poet. A school-boy's exercise may be a pretty thing for a school-boy; but it is no treat for a man.'

2 Johnson always entertained a warm regard for Warburton who had commended Johnson's earlier notes on *Macbeth*. 'He praised me,' Johnson said, 'at a time when praise was of value to me.' To be sure, Warburton had 'a rage for saying something when there's nothing to be said', but he was a far superior critic to Theobald, 'poor Tib'. 'Oh, Sir,' Johnson exclaimed when a comparison was made between them, Warburton would 'make two-and-fifty Theobalds, cut into slices!' As for that other Shakespearean critic, Edward

Capell, his talents were 'just sufficient, Sir, to enable him to select the black hairs from the white ones, for the use of the periwig-makers'.

3 Johnson's friend, William Strahan, the printer, who was a Member of Parliament, had earlier tried to get a seat for him in the House of Commons. He had written to one of the Secretaries of the Treasury asking him to 'take a convenient opportunity of mentioning the matter to Lord North'. Nothing came of the application; but some years later Burke said that if Johnson had entered Parliament he would certainly have been the greatest speaker that ever was there. When Reynolds told him what Burke had said, Johnson exclaimed: 'I should like to try my hand now.'

He did not have a high opinion of Members in general, however. 'He grudged that a fellow who makes no figure in company, and has a mind as narrow as the neck of a vinegar cruet, should make a figure in the House of Commons, merely by having the knowledge of a few forms, and being furnished with a little occasional information.'

4 Again Boswell chose to remain anonymous in the *Life*. The 'poor speculatist', as the journal reveals, was, in fact, himself.

Chapter 10 (Pages 193–215)

1 Although he hated being pressed to eat or drink anything, he did not usually behave so alarmingly. When at Inverness he and Boswell dined at Mrs James Keith's, she was over-attentive to him and asked him many questions about his drinking only water. He silenced her by saying to Boswell, 'You may remember that Lady Errol took no notice of this.'

2 Presumably Johnson made this apology on religious rather than on musical grounds. When Boswell confessed that music agitated his nerves painfully, producing in his mind 'alternate sensations of pathetic dejection . . . and of daring resolution', Johnson scornfully commented, 'Sir, I should never hear it, if it made me such a fool.' 'No man of talent, or whose mind was capable of better things,' he claimed on another occasion, 'ever would or could devote his time and attention to so idle and frivolous a pursuit.' Indeed, he confessed to Frances Reynolds that music had such 'a power to disgust him, particularly in Churches' that he was 'almost tempted' to walk out of the service. And Hawkins believed that 'music was positive pain' to Johnson. However, he observed to William Seward that music was the 'only sensual pleasure without vice', and he was at least once himself pleasantly 'affected by musical sounds'. This was upon going to see a Freemason's funeral procession while at Rochester

with Bennet Langton when he heard 'some solemn musick being played on French-horns'.

He went so far as to buy himself a flageolet, but he was never able to 'make out a tune'. Had he learned to fiddle, he told Boswell more than once, he would have done nothing else: 'No, Sir, a man would never undertake great things, could he be amused with small.'

Johnson's lack of appreciation of music was matched by what Mrs Thrale described as his 'utter scorn of painting'. He claimed that if he were in a room, on the walls of which were hung the works of the greatest masters with their backs outermost, he would not trouble to turn them round to look at them. 'When painting was discussed,' Frances Reynolds said, 'Johnson seemed ill at ease; conscious of the handicap of his short sight, he avoided giving any opinion of a picture but, if pressed, held it close to his eye as he did his book. Unwillingness to expose this defect caused his displeasure with Sir Joshua for drawing him in this posture and was probably the reason why the portrait remained unfinished.'

3 It was rarely, however, that he objected to flattery, particularly from young women. Miss Reynolds recalled an occasion when a lady to whom he had been rude, forgave him with the words; 'Oh! Dear, good man!' When told of this remark, '*he seem'd much delighted* and sometime after, as he was lying back in his Chair, seeming to be half asleep, but more evidently musing on this pleasing incident, he repeated in a loud whisper, "Oh! Dear, good man!" This was a common habit of his, when anything very flattering, or very extraordinary ingross'd his thoughts.'

After an evening at Mrs Montagu's, Boswell found him highly pleased with the flattery bestowed upon him; he said that he could not recollect having passed many evenings '*with fewer objections*'.

'The applause of a single human being is of great consequence,' he said towards the end of his life. And when that human being was a person of consequence, the applause was delightful to him. Boswell recorded a most amusing instance of this: 'A foreign minister of no very high talents, who had been in his company for a considerable time quite overlooked, happened luckily to mention that he had read some of his *Rambler* in Italian, and admired it much. This pleased him greatly and finding that this minister gave such a proof of his taste, he was all attention to him, and on the first remark which he made, however simple, exclaimed, "The Ambassador says well;—His Excellency observes—;" And then he expanded and enriched the little that had been said, in so strong a manner, that it appeared something of consequence. This was exceedingly entertaining to the company who were present, and many a time afterwards it furnished a pleasant topick of merriment: "The Ambassador says well," became a laughable term of applause, when no mighty matter had been expressed.'

4 Certainly Johnson employed a respectable tailor—first Harrison on Ludgate

Hill, then, after his death, Cooke, of King Street, Bloomsbury. His shoemaker was Owen of Bond's Stables, Fetter Lane; and his barber, to whom he sometimes lent money, was Collet of Plum Tree Court, Shoe Lane.

5 Queeney seems to have been as fond of Johnson as he was of her. Among the imaginary misfortunes listed by her to amuse herself in 1774, so her mother recorded in her 'Children's Book or Rather Family Book', was 'Mr Johnson shall be affronted and never come here again'.

6 Giuseppe Baretti was another devoted admirer of Queeney when she was a child. 'She resembles the angels in every way,' he told his brothers in Italy, and I am seven thousand times fonder of her than I have ever been of anyone. . . . I shall want my darling Esteruccia to kiss you all three, despite her charming little blushes and a certain timid waywardness which makes her silent with everybody and familiar and bold with no one but me.'

Chapter 11 *(Pages 216–234)*

1 Apparently Boswell should have written Glencoe not Glencro. Dr Edward Daniel Clarke, the traveller and antiquary, told the story that Lochbuy, 'according to the usual custom among the Highlanders, demanded the name of his guest; and upon being informed that it was Johnson, inquired: *"Which of the Johnstons? of Glencoe or Ardnamurchan?"* "Neither!" replied the Doctor, somewhat piqued by the question, and not a little sulky with the fatigue he had encountered during the day's journey. *"Neither!"* rejoined the Laird, with all the native roughness of a genuine Highlander, *"then you must be a bastard."*'

2 'I never knew any man who was less disposed to be querulous than Johnson', wrote Boswell. 'Whether the subject was his own situation, or the state of the publick, or the state of human nature in general, though he saw the evils, his mind was turned to resolution, and never to whining or complaint.'

3 Although Johnson condemned smoking as 'a shocking thing, blowing smoke out of our mouths into other people's mouths, eyes, and noses, and having the same thing done to us', he could not account 'why a thing which requires so little exertion, and yet preserves the mind from total vacuity, should have gone out. Every man has something by which he calms himself: beating with his feet, or so.' Hawkins said Johnson had been heard to remark that 'since the disuse of smoking among the better sort of people, suicide has been more frequent in this country than before'.

4 'I used to go pretty often to Campbell's on a Sunday evening,' he told Boswell, 'till I began to consider that the shoals of Scotchmen who flocked about him

might probably say, when any thing of mine was well done, "Ay, ay, he has learnt this of CAWMELL!"'

5 As Patrick Cruttwell has commented, Lady Macleod was right. 'Like Swift Johnson had longed to be more "respectable", more unquestionably a member of that fixed hierarchy which he venerated, though the principle of contradiction within him was always impelling him to criticize and satirize in detail what he revered in gross. . . . He was much more akin to Swift than he realized or would have liked to acknowledge. And that is why he hated Swift.' A similar point was made by a friend of Samuel Rogers, 'a very old gentleman, who had known Johnson intimately'. This gentleman assured Rogers that the bent of Johnson's mind 'was decidedly towards scepticism; that he was literally afraid to examine his own thoughts on religious matters; and that hence partly arose his hatred of Hume and other such writers'.

6 His condemnation of the Methodists was quite as severe. When Johnson spoke of the expulsion of six Methodists from Oxford University, this conversation ensued:
'Sir, that expulsion was extremely just and proper. What have they to do at an University, who are not willing to be taught, but will presume to teach? Where is religion to be learnt, but at an University? Sir, they were examined, and found to be mighty ignorant fellows.' BOSWELL. 'But, was it not hard, Sir, to expel them, for I am told they were good beings?' JOHNSON. 'I believe they might be good beings; but they were not fit to be in the University of Oxford. A cow is a very good animal in the field; but we turn her out of a garden.'

7 Johnson was well aware that Mrs Boswell had not taken to him, and in almost every letter that he afterwards wrote to her husband this dislike is mentioned with a persistence that seemed to ask for reassurance. 'Make my compliments to Mrs Boswell, though she does not love me. . . . I know that she does not love me. . . . My compliments to Mrs Boswell, who does not love me. . . . I know she does not love me. . . . Make my compliments to Mrs Boswell, though she does not love me. . . . Mention very particularly to Mrs Boswell my hope that she is reconciled to [me]. . . . I hope my irreconcilable enemy, Mrs Boswell, is well. . . . I do not suppose the lady is yet reconciled to me. . . . . I shall never persuade [her] to love me. . . .'
Towards the end of his life relations between Margaret Boswell and Johnson became more cordial; but future generations of the Boswell family at Auchinleck preferred to forget their ancestor's connection with the low-born writer. Sir Walter Scott said that Reynolds's portrait of Johnson was removed from the drawing-room to the attic, where it hung face to the wall.

8 Johnson derived as much pleasure in condemning Scotland and the Scotch after his visit as he had done in the days before it when he had cut short Adam Smith's eulogy of the beauties of Glasgow by sharply asking him, 'Pray, Sir, have you ever seen Brentford?' Upon being asked by a Scotchman what he

thought of his native country, Johnson immediately replied that it was a very vile country to be sure. 'Well, Sir,' said the mortified Scotchman, 'God made it.' Certainly he did, Johnson agreed, but it must be remembered that he made it for Scotchmen and that he made Hell, too.

'Seeing Scotland, Madam, is only seeing a worse England,' he told Mrs Thrale. 'It is seeing the flower gradually fade away to the naked stalk.' Later, when he had praised the literary merits of George Buchanan, 'a Scotchman, imagining that on this ground he should have an undoubted triumph over him, exclaimed, "Ah, Dr Johnson, what would you have said of Buchanan, had he been an Englishman?" "Why, Sir, (said Johnson, after a little pause) I should *not* have said of Buchanan, had he been an *Englishman*, what I will now say of him as a *Scotchman*,—that he was the only man of genius his country ever produced."'

Richard Cumberland did, however, manage to draw some sort of apology from Johnson when, speaking of his *Journey to the Hebrides*, Cumberland observed that some passages were 'rather too sharp upon a country and people who had entertained him so handsomely'. 'Do you think so, Cumbey,' he said. 'Then I give you leave to say, and you may quote me for it, that there are more gentlemen in Scotland than there are shoes.'

The *London Chronicle* for 29 April–2 May, however, reported: 'A Gentleman, the other day, in conversation with Dr Johnson, was very gravely expressing his amazement that the Doctor should entertain so much hatred and aversion to the Scots, who had treated him so civilly in the late tour amongst them; when he received the following short reply: "Sir, you are exceedingly misinformed with respect to this matter; I do not *hate* the Scots: Sir, I do not *hate* frogs, in the water, though I confess I do not like to have them hopping about my bedchamber."'

Chapter 12 (Page 235–247)

1 It was of the third Duke of Devonshire that Johnson made the characteristic observation, 'He was not a man of superior abilities, but he was a man strictly faithful to his word. If, for instance, he had promised you an acorn, and none had grown that year in his woods, he would not have contented himself with that excuse; he would have sent to Denmark for it.'

2 The public bathing at Bath, where men and women went into the water together, Johnson thought disgraceful. According to Ozias Humphry he deemed it 'an instance of barbarity that he believed could not be paralleled in any part of the world'.

3 In the *European Magazine* in 1798 there appeared a story about Johnson during this visit to Gwaynynog which is worth repeating. The gardener caught a hare in the potato plants; when Johnson heard it was to be taken to the cook, he asked to have it put into his arms, and then immediately dropped it out of the window, shouting after it to accelerate its speed. Reproached by Myddleton for having lost them what promised to be an excellent dinner, he replied, 'So much the better, Sir, for if your table is to be supplied at the expense of the laws of hospitality, I envy not the appetite of him who eats it. This, Sir, is not a hare *ferae naturae*, but one which had placed itself under your protection; and savage indeed must be that man who does not make his hearth an asylum for the confiding stranger.'

4 Sir Robert Cotton was Mrs Thrale's cousin. His wife, Mrs Thrale said, was 'a most amiable being, charitable, compassionate, modest, and gentle to a degree'. Johnson, however, qualified the praise. She had a sweetness of disposition, to be sure, but it was in her nature; one thanked her 'no more for being sweet than a honeycomb'.

5 Boswell condemned Mrs Thrale for not adding that when Johnson had been 'made sensible of what had doubtless a strange appearance, took occasion, when he afterwards met [Cholmondeley] to make a very courteous and kind apology'.

6 'If convents should be allowed at all,' Johnson thought, 'they should only be retreats for persons unable to serve the publick, or who have served it. It is our first duty to serve society; and, after we have done that, we may attend wholly to the salvation of our own souls. A youthful passion for abstracted devotion should not be encouraged.'

7 Madame du Boccage, a correspondent of Chesterfield, translated Milton into French. She was on friendly terms with Voltaire and Condorcet. Having tea with her was the nearest contact Johnson made with the *philosophes*.

8 When Frances Reynolds told Baretti that Johnson gave as an instance of the stupidity of the French that all the jockeys wore the same colour of coat at their horse-races, Baretti replied, 'That was like all Johnson's remarks, he could not see.' But he could enquire, Miss Reynolds protested. Yes, that was the trouble Baretti said, 'for he ask'd "what did the first jockey wear?" answer, "Green." "What the second?" "Green" "What the third?" "Green;" which was true; but then the greens were all different greens, and very easily distinguish'd. Johnson was perpetually making mistakes; so, on going to Fountainblue when we were about three-fourths of the way, he exclaimed with amazement that now we were between Paris and the King of France's Court, and yet we had not mett one carriage coming from thense, or seen one going thither! on which all the company in the coach burst out laughing, and immediately cry'd out, look, look, there is a coach gon by, there is a chariot, there is a post-chaise. I dare say we saw a hundred carriages at least, that were going to, or coming from, Fountainblue.'

Chapter *13* (*Pages 257–268*)

1 Mrs Thrale said it made her mother very cross when she discovered the tricks that had been played upon her. It was one of the causes, she said, of her mother's aversion to Johnson. They were later reconciled, however, and Mrs Thrale wrote in her 'Children's Book' at the time of her mother's death, 'I then called up Mr Johnson who when he felt her Pulse wonder'd at its Vigor but when he observed the dimness of her eyes and universal languor, he leaned on the bed, kissed her cheek and said in his emphatical way—May God bless you Dear Madam for Jesus Christ's sake. At these words she looked up and smiled with a sweet Intelligence.'

2 Mrs Thrale went so far as to record in her journal, 'of all his intimates and Friends, I think I never could find any who much loved him Boswell and Burney excepted'. Johnson returned the love, although he had at first dismissed Burney as 'a very pretty kind of man'—'pretty' in this sense being, according to the *Dictionary*, 'a kind of diminutive contempt'. He was sincere, however, in his admiration of Burney's *German Tour*, remarking more than once that he had taken it as a model for his own *Journey to the Western Isles of Scotland*. Johnson could not get through Burney's *History of Music*, though. He 'could not read about fiddles and fiddlestrings'.

3 William Bewley's excitement over the tuft of Johnson's hearth-broom was mild compared with that aroused by the arrival of Johnson's inscribed works. He despaired of ever thanking Johnson in suitable terms. 'In my distress on this account,' he told Burney, 'I have sometimes been tempted to make so gross a return, as a fat Norfolk turkey.' Three months later he had neither written a single line nor sent a turkey. Two years passed in fruitless endeavours to write a suitable letter, and he was finally driven to asking Burney to thank Johnson on his behalf.

4 Johnson always affected a deep contempt for Garrick's library, magnificent though it was. In William Cooke's biography of Samuel Foote there is a description of Johnson handling 'the elegantly-bound volumes in his usual coarse and negligent manner—opening the books too wide and flinging them on the floor with contempt'.

'Zounds!' protested Garrick. 'You'll spoil all my books!'

'No, Sir,' answered Johnson. 'I have done nothing but treat a pack of silly plays in fops' dresses just as they deserve. But I see no *books*.'

Johnson was also careful not to show too much interest in Garrick's other possessions. After showing Johnson round his splendid house and grounds at

Hampton Court, Garrick asked, 'Well, Doctor, how do you like all this?' 'Why, it is pleasant enough,' Johnson growled in reply, then added, 'but all these things, David, make death very terrible.'

5 On other occasions he was quite as attentive to Fanny's sister, Susan. 'At dinner he invited me to sit by him', Susan Burney wrote on 20 April 1780,— '*"Come here my Love*, sd he,—It shall be you and I"—and he kiss'd my hand! should I forget that?'

6 Behind the house in Bolt Court there was a garden which, so Hawkins said, 'he took delight in watering; a room on the ground floor was assigned to Mrs Williams, and the whole of the two pair of stairs floor was made a repository for his books; one of the rooms thereon being his study. Here, in the intervals of his residence at Streatham, he received the visits of his friends, and, to the most intimate of them, sometimes gave not inelegant dinners.' On occasions, he would talk to his friends in the garden, sitting on one of the stone seats by the garden door.

7 This baby and the Barber's second child both became members of Johnson's household. After her husband's death, Mrs Barber, a sensible and well-informed woman, kept a school at Lichfield with one of these children.

8 Johnson was naturally much oppressed by writers who wanted him to read their manuscripts. 'I used once to be sadly plagued with a man who wrote verses, but who literally had no other notion of a verse, but that it consisted of ten syllables. *Lay your knife and your fork across your plate*, was to him a verse:
Lay yōur knife ānd your fōrk acrōss your plāte.
As he wrote a great number of verses he sometimes by chance made good ones, though he did not know it!'

He was 'very unwilling to read the manuscripts of authors and give them [his] opinion', he confessed. If a bookseller brought him a manuscript he desired him to take it away. When he could not avoid the task, however, he did his best to read or to listen without undue impatience; and John Hoole testified to the trouble he sometimes took. He tried hard to say something to comfort anxious authors without being dishonest. 'Is that poetry, Sir?' asked the Rev William Tasker eagerly when Johnson was reading one of his poems. 'Why, Sir,' Johnson replied cautiously, 'there is a great deal here of what is called poetry.' One day Boswell interrupted him with some legal papers when he was busy preparing a fourth edition of the dictionary and, at the same time, carrying out 'some sort of chymical operation'. He was prevailed upon to read the papers which he turned over with obvious reluctance. 'I am afraid, Sir, it is troublesome,' Boswell said. 'Why, Sir,' he replied manfully, 'I do not take much delight in it; but I'll go through it.'

Sometimes, however, as he admitted to Mrs Thrale, he could not get beyond the first page, and added, 'Alas, Madam! How few books are there of which one can possibly arrive at the *last* page! Was there ever yet anything written by mere man that was wished longer by its readers, excepting *Don Quixote*, *Robinson Crusoe* and the *Pilgrim's Progress*.'

9 When Johnson was preparing the fourth edition of his dictionary, Boswell was amused by the way he contrived to send one of his assistants, V. J. Peyton, 'on an errand without seeming to degrade him, "Mr Peyton—Mr Peyton, will you be so good as to take a walk to Temple Bar? You will there see a chymist's shop, at which you will be pleased to buy for me an ounce of oil of vitriol; not spirit of vitriol, but oil of vitriol. It will cost three half-pence."'

Chapter *14* (*Pages 269–281*)

1 'Sir,' Johnson told Boswell in 1778, 'it would have been better that I had been of a profession. I ought to have been a lawyer.' He felt this very strongly. When William Scott remarked, upon the death of Lord Lichfield, Chancellor of Oxford University, 'What a pity it is, Sir, that you did not follow the profession of the law. You might have been Lord Chancellor of Great Britain, and attained to the dignity of the peerage, and now that the title of Lichfield, your native city, is extinct, you might have had it', Johnson was much agitated and burst out in an angry tone, 'Why will you vex me by suggesting this, when it is too late?'

2 *Taxation No Tyranny* seems very harsh, unreasonable and short-sighted now, a commendation of discipline and obedience almost for their own sakes. But many other intelligent and responsible men, both in England and America, shared the views expressed in it. What they principally objected to was the Americans' refusal to pay taxes, which were by no means burdensome, to a country protecting their interests.

3 When William Seward said that he did not think Dodd could have written one of these addresses (composed by Johnson but put out under Dodd's name) 'because it had a great deal more force of mind in it than anything known to be his', Johnson replied, 'Why should you think so? Depend upon it, Sir, when a man knows he is to be hanged in a fortnight, it concentrates his mind wonderfully.'

4 According to Reynolds it was not always indolence that induced him to leave mistakes uncorrected in his work: 'The drawback of his character is entertaining prejudices on very slight foundations; giving an opinion, perhaps, first at random, but from its being contradicted he thinks himself obliged always to support [it], or, if he cannot support [it], still not to acquiesce [in the opposite opinion]. Of this I remember an instance of a defect or forgetfulness in his

"Dictionary". I asked him how he came not to correct it in the second edition. "No," says he, "they made so much of it that I would not flatter them by altering it."'

5 In her diary Fanny Burney described the first meeting between Johnson and Mrs Montagu after her public declaration that she would never speak to him again. 'She turned from him very stiffly, and with a most distant air, and without even courtsying to him. . . . However, he went up to her himself, *longing* to begin! and very roughly said, "Well, Madam, what's become of your fine new House? I hear no more of it?" . . . She was obliged to answer him; and soon grew so frightened—as *everybody* does,—that she was as civil as ever!'

She did not remain so. At a subsequent dinner party he tried unsuccessfully to engage her in conversation, so General Paoli told Mrs Rose, receiving only cold and brief answers. At length he turned to the General, who sat next to him, and observed, 'You see, Sir, I am no longer the man for Mrs Montagu.' Johnson had never entertained a very high opinion of her talents as a critic. When Joshua Reynolds observed that her *Essay on Shakespeare* did her honour, Johnson replied, 'Yes, Sir, it does *her* honour, but it would do nobody else honour. I have, indeed, not read it all. But when I take up the end of a web, and find it packthread, I do not expect, by looking further, to find embroidery.'

Chapter 15 (Pages 282–296)

1 Thirty-three years before Johnson had expressed, in *The Rambler*, totally different sentiments: 'The learned, the judicious, the pious Boerhaave relates that he never saw a criminal dragged to execution without asking himself, "Who knows whether this man is not less culpable than me?" On the days when the prisons of this city are emptied into the grave, let every spectator of the dreadful procession put the same question to his own heart. Few among those who crowd in thousands to the legal massacre, and look with careless-ness, perhaps with triumph, on the utmost exacerbations of human misery, would then be able to return without horror and misery.'

Patrick Cruttwell suggests that the Johnson of these later years had become something of a split man, 'that this happened because a mind and soul which remained, to the end, sultry, volcanic, always "in opposition", had now to live in uneasy combination with a man living comfortably, a social prize whom it was a triumph to secure for one's salon, the gruff heart-of-gold roarer whom people delighted, half-trembling, to prod and tease. . . . In many areas of his mind there seems an increasing degree of self-conflict and confusion; one has often the impression of an immensely powerful but tortured mind which finds it desperately difficult to settle itself in anything. He mocks at those who denounce luxury, but is himself always deploring the spread of commerce and its values. He becomes, outwardly, a more and more bigoted High Churchman, bellowing hysterically against Methodists, Quakers, Presbyterians, non-conformists of all sorts; but his private prayers and journals show a man tortured to the end by doubts and scruples. His political opinions show a similar hardening; the quite inaccurate picture of Johnson as an absurdly reactionary "Tory" is largely derived from the utterances of his last fifteen years or so. In almost all respects, there is a basic alienation from the society of which, on the surface, he was an admired and comfortable member.'

Chapter 16 (Pages 297–315)

1 It should be added that an important factor in Johnson's reactions to Mrs Thrale's marriage was the fact that Piozzi was a Roman Catholic and so she would have to change her religion, simply in order to marry him, not from conviction.

2 Johnson even accepted Garrick's over-frolicsome behaviour without irritation when it was accompanied with congratulations upon his good health. Boswell recorded how pleased Johnson appeared to be on his arrival for a dinner-party at his lodgings in Old Bond Street when Garrick 'played round him with a fond vivacity, taking hold of the breasts of his coat, and, looking up in his face with a lovely archness, complimented him on the good health which he seemed then to enjoy'. Johnson, shaking his head, beheld Garrick 'with a gentle complacency'.

3 He seemed particularly anxious that the world should remember his devoutness and sound moral principles. In Pennington's *Memoirs of Mrs Carter* there is an account of Elizabeth Carter speaking highly of them to him. He seized her hand and said eagerly, 'You know this to be true, and testify it to the world when I am gone.'

4 Frank Barber died in poverty in 1801, having sold most of his master's possessions, including his tortoise-shell-covered watch for which Johnson had paid Mudge and Dulton seventeen guineas in 1768. A man who met him towards the end of his life described him as a sad, broken-down figure who had lost all his teeth and was marked with the smallpox. 'He spends his time in fishing and cultivating a few potatoes. . . . Mr Barber appears modest and humble, but to have associated with company superior to his rank in life.'

Bibliography

BAILEY, JOHN. *Dr Johnson and His Circle*, revised by L. F. Powell, Oxford University Press, 1944

BALDERSTON, KATHERINE. 'Johnson's Vile Melancholy', in *The Age of Johnson*, ed. Frederick W. Hilles, Yale University Press, 1949

BATE, WALTER JACKSON. *The Achievement of Samuel Johnson*, Oxford University Press, 1955

BLOOM, EDWARD A. *Samuel Johnson in Grub Street*, Brown University Press, 1957

BOSWELL, JAMES. *Boswelliana. The Commonplace Book of James Boswell with a Memoir and Annotations by the Rev. Charles Rogers*

— *Boswell's Life of Johnson together with Boswell's Journal of a Tour to the Hebrides and Johnson's Diary of a Journey into North Wales*, ed. G. Birkbeck Hill; revised and enlarged edn by L. F. Powell, Oxford, Clarendon Press, 6 vols, 1934–64

— *The Life of Samuel Johnson, Ll.D., by James Boswell, Esq., with marginal comments and markings from two copies annotated by Hester Lynch Thrale Piozzi*, ed. E. G. Fletcher, privately printed, 3 vols, 1938

— *Journal of a Tour to the Hebrides with Samuel Johnson, Ll.D.*, ed. by Frederick A. Pottle and Charles H. Bennett, Viking Press, 1936

— *The Private Papers of James Boswell, from Malahide Castle*, ed. Frederick A. Pottle and Geoffrey Scott, New York, privately printed, 19 vols, 1928–37

— *Boswell's London Journal, 1762–3*, ed. Frederick A. Pottle, Heinemann, 1950

— *Letters of James Boswell*, ed. C. B. Tinker, Oxford University Press, 2 vols, 1924

— Yale Edition of the Private Papers, Yale University Press: *Boswell for the Defence, 1769–1774*, ed. William K. Wimsatt, Jr, and Frederick A. Pottle, 1960

    Boswell: The Ominous Years, 1774–1776, ed. Charles Ryskamp and Frederick A. Pottle, 1963

    Boswell's Journal of a Tour to the Hebrides, ed. Frederick A. Pottle and Charles H. Bennett, 1963

    Boswell's Correspondence, Gen. Ed. Frederick W. Hilles. Vol. 1: *The Correspondence of James Boswell and John Johnston of Grange*, ed. Ralph

S. Walker, 1966; Vol. 2: *The Correspondence and Other Papers of James Boswell Relating to the Making of the Life of Johnson*, ed. Marshall Waingrow, 1969

BRAIN, W. RUSSELL. 'Some Reflections on Genius', *Lancet* (1948), pp. 661–5

BRONSON, BERTRAND H. *Johnson Agonistes and Other Essays*, University of California Press, 1965

BROWN, JOSEPH E., ed. *The Critical Opinions of Samuel Johnson*, Princeton University Press, 1926; reprinted New York, Russell, 1960

BURNEY, FANNY, *see* D'ARBLAY, FRANCES

CLIFFORD, JAMES L. *Dr Campbell's Diary of a Visit to England in 1775*, Cambridge University Press, 1947

— *Young Samuel Johnson*, Heinemann, 1955

— *Hester Lynch Piozzi (Mrs Thrale)*, Oxford, Clarendon Press, 1915; rev. edn 1952

— *Samuel Johnson: A Survey of Critical . . . Studies* (with Donald J. Greene, Minnesota University Press, 1971

COURTNEY, W. P. and SMITH, D. NICHOL. *A Bibliography of Samuel Johnson*, Oxford, 1915

D'ARBLAY, FRANCES (Fanny Burney). *Diary and Letters of Madame D'Arblay, 1778–1840*, ed. Charlotte Barrett, with notes by Austin Dobson, 1904

DAVIES, THOMAS. *Memoirs of the Life of David Garrick*, 1781

DAVIS, BERTRAM. *Johnson before Boswell*, Yale University Press, 1960

GRANGE, KATHLEEN M. 'Dr Samuel Johnson's Account of a Schizophrenic Illness in *Rasselas*', *Medical History*, vi (1962), 162–8

GREENE, DONALD J., ed. *The Politics of Samuel Johnson*, Yale University Press, 1957

— *Samuel Johnson: A Collection of Critical Essays*, Prentice-Hall, 1965

HAGSTRUM, JEAN H. *Samuel Johnson's Literary Criticism*, 2nd edn, University of Chicago Press, 1967

HAWKINS, SIR JOHN. *The Life of Samuel Johnson, Ll.D. (1787–89)*, ed. Bertram Davis, Cape, 1962

HAWKINS, LAETITIA MATILDA. *Memoirs*, 1824

HILL, GEORGE BIRKBECK, ed., *see* JOHNSON, SAMUEL *and* BOSWELL, JAMES

HILLES, FREDERICK W., ed. *The Age of Johnson: Essays presented to Chauncey Brewster Tinker*, Yale University Press, 1949

— *New Light on Dr Johnson: Essays on the occasion of his 250th birthday*, Yale University Press, 1959; Archon Books, 1967

HITSCHMANN, EDWARD. 'Samuel Johnson's Character: A psychoanalytic interpretation', *Psychoanalytic Review*, xxxii (April 1945), 207–18

HODGART, J. C. *Dr Johnson*, Batsford, 1962

HOOVER, BENJAMIN B. *Samuel Johnson's Parliamentary Reporting*, University of California Press, 1953

JOHNSON, SAMUEL. *An Account of the Life of Dr Samuel Johnson, from his Birth to His Eleventh Year, Written by Himself*, ed. Richard Wright, London, 1805

— *The Poems of Samuel Johnson*, ed. David Nichol Smith with Edward L. McAdam, Jr, Oxford University Press, 1941

— *Johnson's Journey to the Western Islands of Scotland and Boswell's Journal of a Tour to the Hebrides*, ed. R. W. Chapman, Oxford University Press, 1924; O.S.A., 1930

— *The Lives of the English Poets*, ed. G. Birkbeck Hill, Oxford University Press, 3 vols, 1905

— *Johnson's Lives of the English Poets*, ed. Robert Montagu, Folio Society, 1965

— *Johnsonian Miscellanies*, ed. G. Birkbeck Hill, Oxford University Press, 2 vols, 1897

— *A History of Rasselas*, ed. Geoffrey Tillotson and Brian Jenkins, Oxford University Press, 1971

— *Samuel Johnson: Selected Writing*, ed. R. T. Davies, Faber, 1965

— *Samuel Johnson: Selected Writings*, ed. Patrick Cruttwell, Penguin English Library, 1968

— *The Letters of Samuel Johnson, with Mrs Thrale's Genuine Letters to Him*, ed. R. W. Chapman, Oxford, Clarendon Press, 1952. See also LANSDOWNE, MARQUESS OF, ed. *The Queeney Letters*

— *The Political Writings of Samuel Johnson*, ed. J. P. Hardy, Routledge & Kegan Paul, 1968

— Yale Edition of the Works, Yale University Press, 1958: Vol. 1, *Diaries, Prayers and Annals*, ed. E. L. McAdam, Jr, with Donald and Mary Hyde, 1958

Vol. 2, *The Idler and the Adventurer*, ed. W. J. Bate, J. M. Bullitt and L. F. Powell, 1963

Vols 3, 4 and 5, *The Rambler*, ed. W. J. Bate and Albrecht Strauss, 1970

Vol 6, *The Poems*, ed. E. L. McAdam, Jr, and George Milne, 1966

Vols 7 and 8, *Johnson on Shakespeare*, ed. Arthur Sherbo, 1969

Johnson, Boswell and Their Circle: Essays presented to Lawrence Fitzroy Powell, Oxford, Clarendon Press, 1965

KINGSMILL, HUGH, *Samuel Johnson*, 1935

— ed. *Johnson Without Boswell*, 1940

KRUTCH, JOSEPH WOOD, *Samuel Johnson*, Harbinger Books edn 1963; Harcourt, Brace, 1944

LADELL, R. M. 'The Neurosis of Dr Samuel Johnson', *British Journal of Medical Psychology*, ix (1929), 314–23

LANSDOWNE, MARQUESS OF, ed. *The Queeney Letters: Being Letters addressed to Hester Maria Thrale by Dr Johnson, Fanny Burney, and Mrs Thrale-Piozzi*, Cassell, 1934

LEAVIS, F. R. *The Common Pursuit*, Chatto & Windus, 1952: 'Johnson and Augustanism' and 'Johnson as Poet'

LEWIS, D. B. WYNDHAM. *The Hooded Hawk*, Eyre & Spottiswoode, 1946

LITTLEJOHN, DAVID, ed. *Dr Johnson: His life in letters*, Prentice-Hall, 1965

MCADAM, E. L., JR. *Dr Johnson and the English Law*, Syracuse University Press, New York, 1951

MURPHY, ARTHUR. *An Essay on the Life and Genius of Samuel Johnson, Ll.D.*, 1792

NICHOLS, JOHN. *Literary Anecdotes of the Eighteenth Century*, 9 vols, 1812–15

PIOZZI, HESTER LYNCH. *Anecdotes of the Late Samuel Johnson, Ll.D.*, 1786
'The Children's Book or rather Family Book begun 17: Sept 1766', MS in the collection of Donald and Mary Hyde

— *Thraliana: The Diary of Mrs Hester Lynch Thrale (later Mrs Piozzi), 1776–1809*, ed. Katherine C. Balderston, Oxford, Clarendon Press, 2 vols, 1942

POTTLE, FREDERICK A. *James Boswell: The Earlier Years*, Heinemann, 1966 ed., see BOSWELL, JAMES

POWELL, L. F. *see* BAILEY, JOHN *and* BOSWELL, JAMES

QUENNELL, PETER. *Four Portraits: Studies of the Eighteenth Century*, Collins, 1945

QUINLAN, MAURICE. *Samuel Johnson: A layman's religion*, University of Wisconsin Press, 1963

RALEIGH, WALTER. *Six Essays on Johnson*, 1910

READE, ALEYN LYELL. *Johnsonian Gleanings*, privately printed, 11 vols, 1909–52

ROBERTS, S. C. *Dr Johnson*, Duckworth, 1935

ROBERTS, WILLIAM. *Memoirs of the Life and Correspondence of Mrs Hannah More*, 4 vols, 1834

ROGERS, SAMUEL. *The Table Talk of Samuel Rogers*, ed. Morchard Bishop, Richards Press, 1952

SHAW, WILLIAM. *Memoirs of the Life and Writings of the Late Dr Samuel Johnson*, London, 1785

SLEDD, JAMES H. with KOLB, G. J. *Dr Johnson's Dictionary: Essays in the Biography of a Book*, University of Chicago Press, 1955

SMITH, J. T. *Nollekens and His Times*, 1828; reprinted Turnstile Press, 1949

THRALE, HESTER LYNCH, *see* PIOZZI, HESTER LYNCH

TINKER, C. B. *Dr Johnson and Fanny Burney*, New York, 1911

TURBERVILLE, A. S. *Johnson's England*, Oxford, Clarendon Press, 1933; new edition, 1967

TYERS, THOMAS. 'A Biographical Sketch of Dr Samuel Johnson', *Gentleman's Magazine*, Dec. 1784, reprinted by Augustan Reprint Society, 1952

VOITLE, ROBERT, *Samuel Johnson the Moralist*, Harvard University Press, 1961

WATKINS, W. B. C. *Perilous Balance*, Princeton University Press, 1939

WIMSATT, W. K., JR. *The Prose Style of Samuel Johnson*, Yale University Press, 1941

WINDHAM, WILLIAM. *Diary of the Rt Hon William Windham*, 1866

Index

Index

Johnson, Samuel—*cont.*

impression of idiocy, 12, 89–90; poetic compositions, 12–13, 14, 24, 51, 72, 252, 253, 285; and religion, 13, 14, 18, 293, 311, 331; and the family business, 14–15, 16, 21, 47; attitude to women, 15, 25, 100, 193, 197–200; politics, 16, 39, 81, 231, 286–7; university ambitions, 16; up at Oxford, 17–20; money problems, 19–20, 31, 40–1, 44, 46, 51, 58, 75, 105, 109, 123; the Uttoxeter penance, 21, 317; teacher, 21–2, 27–30, 46–7; his dislike of solitude, 23, 70, 109, 119, 120, 133, 185, 251; eccentric behaviour, 23, 196, 200–3, 211; marries, 26–7; goes to London, 30, 31; attitude to London, 32, 233; attitude to cruelty, 32; pronunciation, 33; reports on proceedings in Parliament, 39–40; prays, 40, 85, 86, 100, 107, 121–2, 174, 175, 185, 192, 196, 289, 299, 311–12, 313, 314; and prostitutes, 41, 100, 149, 260–1; Lichfield house mortgaged, 50; frequents coffee-houses, 51, 55–6; and alcohol, 51, 68–9, 113, 115, 148, 171–3, 174, 225, 277, 313; and James's *Medicinal Dictionary*, 56, 103; catalogues Harleian library, 56–7; generous with his help, 58, 71, 85, 122–3, 186, 278; attitude to sex, 68–9, 100–2; a moralist, 69, 76; and the acting profession, 72–3; at the tavern, 79; reputation as a talker, 79–80, 152, 158; Ivy Lane Club, 80–2; attitude to church dignitaries, 81–2; his hospitality, 84, 131, 182; and Tetty's death, 85–8; a late riser, 90–1, 189; makes resolutions, 91, 121–2; attitude to Scotchmen, 95, 123, 143, 144, 217–18, 223, 224, 230–2, 275–6, 331–2; considers marrying again, 99–100; his knowledge of medicine, 103; journalism, 105–6, 122; his passion for tea, 106, 120, 131–2, 191, 209, 217, 229, 231; attitude to death, 109, 251, 289, 293–4, 308, 312; moves house, 111; visits Oxford, 112–14, 209, 291–4; fear of madness, 121, 174, 212–3, 214; visits Lichfield, 122, 190–1, 209, 236–7, 270; investigates Cock Lane ghost, 124–6; his pension, 126–9, 143; his kindliness, 131, 134, 174, 263–8; his eating habits, 131, 196–7; and food, 132–3, 210, 245, 254; his visitors, 133, 209–10, 310; scientific experiments, 134, 194; dines out, 134; breadth of his knowledge, 158–9; the conversationalist, 159–60, 167, 168; his rudeness, 160–2, 170, 232, 241–2, 255, 324, 326; his opinion of himself, 161; irritated by questioning, 162–3; makes amends for rudeness, 164–5, 166–7; cannot be laughed at, 169, 170, 223; disapproval of swearing, 170–1, 327; his untidiness, 173–4; takes opium, 174, 191, 287, 289, 306, 307, 308; at Johnson's Court, 182, 189, 191; miscellaneous writings, 186; in danger of mental collapse, 190; attitude to flattery, 198, 329; performs physical feats, 203–5; attitude to children, 206–8; his enjoyment of travelling, 208–9; loves fireworks, 210; fetters and padlock, 213; in Scotland, 216–34; takes lemonade, 217, 219; his fortitude, 221, 225; his grumpiness, 221–3, 238, 286, 299, 300; attitude to danger, 225, 226, 279; and the old woman by Loch Ness, 226–7; the Welsh holiday with the Thrales, 236–42; to France with the Thrales, 243, 244; attitude to foreigners, 243, 292; explores Paris, 245; in

357

Index